THE ILLUSTRATED HISTORY OF ORGANIZED CRIME

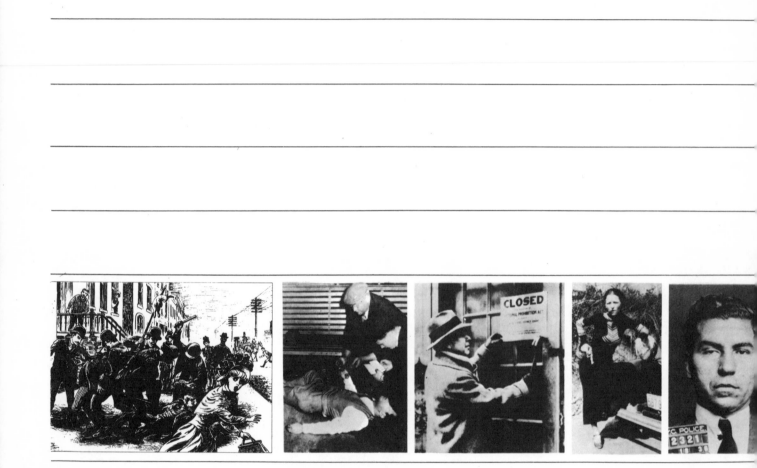

THE ILLUSTRATED HISTORY OF ORGANIZED CRIME

    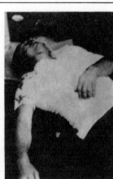

Richard Hammer

COURAGE BOOKS

an imprint of
Running Press
Book Publishers
Philadelphia, Pennsylvania

Originally appeared in the monthly issues of *Playboy* magazine, August 1973 through July 1974.

Canadian representatives: General Publishing Co., Ltd., 30 Lesmill Road, Don Mills, Ontario M3B 2T6.

International representatives: Worldwide Media Services, Inc., 115 East Twenty-third Street, New York, New York 10010.

9 8 7 6 5 4 3 2 1

Digit on the right indicates the number of this printing.

Library of Congress Cataloging-in-Publication Number 89-42976

ISBN 0-89471-772-3

Designed by Bob Antler.

CONTENTS

THE ILLUSTRATED HISTORY OF ORGANIZED CRIME

CHAPTER I THE AMERICAN DREAM

IN THE BEGINNING WAS DISORGANIZATION. The world of crime—chaotic, violent, often purposeless, sometimes internecine—mirrored the society in which it grew and flourished, and in the 19th Century, American society—pushing outward in every direction with often uncontrolled energy—was chaotic, violent, sometimes purposeless and at war with itself and its nobler aspirations and philosophies.

The tone of a society is inevitably set by those at the top. And the period between the end of the Civil War and the beginning of World War I was the age of the robber barons, an age when the only goal seemed the accumulation of vast wealth and power. In that untrammeled quest, conscience played no part. Members of presidential cabinets—and there were rumors even about presidents themselves—and of Congress, politicians on every level, from the local precincts to the national government, became rich selling inside information, trading favors, using secrets entrusted to them for their own ends. Some became the servants of their corrupters and kept themselves in power and in office by corrupting those they were supposed to represent: by buying votes, by employing gangs of hoodlums to make sure the votes were cast the right way, by wheeling and dealing with absolute scorn for the public good. The man with enough dollars could buy anything: from a senator to a railroad right of way to respectability

3

and honor. Jay Gould and Jim Fisk went too far and eventually tumbled. But not before they had amassed millions and accumulated inordinate power, which was, of course, their goal. The Vanderbilts and Harrimans, the Carnegies and Rockefellers and the rest, though, bought and sold politicians, officeholders, ordinary people as though they were stacks of wheat, railroad ties or barrels of oil. And they bought honored places in society as well. Boss Tweed ran New York, and his counterparts around the country ran their cities, not for the people who lived there but as personal fiefdoms. Only when their arrogance and greed, which were never secret, became so overweening that the cloak of caution fell away was there any retribution—and it was always mild.

But these decades were not just the age of the robber barons. This was the age, too, of the poor, when the gap between those at the top and those at the bottom was growing ever wider, turning into an unbridgeable chasm. It was the age when the myth of the American dream was spread, nourished and magnified in every city and village of Europe. Across the ocean was the biblical land of milk and honey, where the streets were paved with gold, where opportunities were limitless, where even the powerless had power. To escape the noose of poverty, ignorance, tradition and caste of the old world, it was necessary only to board a ship and endure a few weeks in the misery of overcrowded steerage. At the end, there would be riches and power and respectability for all. And there were no bars; everyone was welcome:

> Give me your tired, your poor,
> Your huddled masses yearning to breathe free,
> The wretched refuse of your teeming shore,
> Send these, the homeless, tempest-tossed, to me:
> I lift my lamp beside the golden door.

They came by the thousands through Ellis Island, eager to start a new life.

The dream that it was possible to exchange the privations and persecutions of the old world for the riches and freedom of the new brought, in the decades after the Civil War (until restrictive legislation was finally passed), more than 25,000,000 immigrants to the United States. They came in successive and mounting waves, led by 3,000,000 Irish and millions more from western and northern Europe, followed by 4,000,000 Italians, a similar number of Jews from central and eastern Europe and millions more from eastern and southern Europe.

But in America, the dream became little more than a nightmare for many of the new arrivals. They quickly perceived, for it was impossible not to, the gap between the philosophy of the American dream and its reality. Crammed into teeming urban ghettos along the coast, or into new ghettos arising in the interior, piled into buildings that seemed to deteriorate

But the new life often started in crowded ghettos (top left). Their hopes and the dreams of arrival (top right) often ended in a short walk across the Bridge of Sighs in the old Tombs prison (bottom right).

into uninhabitable slums even before they were completed, bewildered by the multiplicity of strange customs and languages that beat upon them in a never-ending din, the poor of Europe became only the poor of America. Their opportunities were narrowly restricted in this strange new land by their ignorance of its customs, mores and language. And by the contempt in which they were held by those who had preceded them.

There were no golden streets. But America, they were still told, was the land of opportunity. If they lived according to the philosophy by which the nation theoretically lived, the Puritan ethic—shunning gambling, liquor, loose women and all the other base and sensual pleasures, working long and hard and honestly, and saving their money—success would surely come, the dream would surely be realized. But for many who settled in the cities, the only opportunities were in the sweatshops and the only rewards were fatigue, uncertain employment, deeper poverty, disease and early death—the end of hope.

Even worse was the discovery that no one but the poor newcomer was expected to give more than a perfunctory nod to the Puritan ethic, to morality, to conscience. Certainly not those who had made it or were making it. And there was no one to protect the interests of the poor. The politicians and the police wallowed in

The Dead Rabbits Gang attacked New York citizens in broad daylight.

corruption and barely bothered to hide it. They bought and sold favors, votes and protection to those with the money, and for those without money, there was nothing. It was an experience from which many never recovered. Alienated from the countries of their birth, from their new country, and from their children, who adapted easily and quickly to the new ways and the new environment, many of the immigrants froze into an almost psychotic isolation and despair.

However, there were some, especially the young, who looked at the new land, recognized instinctively its hypocrisy and emulated those in society's upper strata. If violence permeated society and those at the top employed it to further their own ends, then those at the bottom would unleash their own violence—often just for its own sake, with a kind of uncontrolled exuberance and sometimes in the employ of those above them who needed violent men. If those at the top were not bound by laws and codes of moral conduct, then neither would be those at the bottom.

Across the nation, every urban ghetto—in New York, Boston, Philadelphia, Cleveland, Detroit, New Orleans, Chicago, San Francisco and the rest, as they turned from frontier settlements into metropolitan centers—swarmed with gangs, collections of young toughs made tougher, more belligerent and violent, given more strength through unity and numbers. They were the children of immigrants or immigrants themselves forging their own paths to a share of

riches and power they were certain they could get no other way. Frightened, and so enraged, the young reacted by joining gangs and giving themselves guises and names that would create around them an aura of fear. Some shaved their heads and others let their hair grow long; some wore iron-lined derbies both as a trademark and as a weapon, while others wore distinctive caps; some dressed in little more than rags and others wore nearly formal clothes; some sported distinctive scarves or sashes; some wore hard-toed, hobnailed boots—the better to stomp their victims into submission; all carried knives, truncheons, guns or weapons of some kind. They called themselves by a thousand different names, reflecting neighborhood, origin, purpose: They were the Whyos, the Bowery Boys, the Dead Rabbits (rampaging with a rabbit impaled on a stake), the Gophers, the Short Boys, the Whitehall Boatmen (looting the waterfront from small skiffs), the Tenth Avenue Gang, the Street Cleaners, the Four Gun Battery Brigade, the Moonshiners, the Village Gang, the Rag Gang, the West Side Gang, the Wellington Association, the Gas House Gang, the Midnight Terrors, the Growler Gang, the Five Points Gang, the Eastmans, the Madison Street Marauders, the Grant Street Gang—the list is endless.

Almost without exception, they were jingoistically ethnic, restricting membership to those of similar origin and from the same small neighborhood enclave (in an age when the telephone and other devices were a restricted novelty, intercity or even interneighborhood communication, and so association, would have been almost impossible). If the Irish formed a gang, then nobody but another Irishman, and a neighborhood Irishman, at that, could join; and the same rule applied for gangs of Neapolitans, Sicilians, Jews and all the rest as they arrived in America and settled into the cities. There was no overlapping, for strangers were both feared and despised.

If some of the gangs were formed initially as a means of self-protection, to provide safety in a group of friends where such safety would be absent for the individual, that purpose did not long remain primary. In the jungle of the slum neighborhoods where they operated, the gangs became a kind of untamed beast that roved and rampaged with few restrictions. As long as they limited their activities to their own domain and did not encroach on the world outside, on the rich and the growing middle class, nobody seemed to pay any real attention or care very much. It was a social attitude that persisted. As long as *they* stole only from each other and maimed and killed only their own kind, why should anyone give a damn or try to do anything to stop them? The aim of the police and civic authorities often seemed to be to keep the gangs bottled up within their own territory but to permit them free license there. The victims were, after all, only the poor and the alien, whose traditions had taught them to fear and so expect the worst from authorities; they rarely complained, because they were certain complaints were useless. Besides, they had little political clout or influence to persuade or force those in power to come to their assistance.

So, in the poor neighborhoods of the cities, hardly a store was safe, hardly a home or business not a potential target, hardly a lonely pedestrian not a likely victim. The gangs robbed and pillaged, terrorized and brutalized with impunity. They made no pretense of being anything but what they were. Violence came easily, almost naturally. The Whyos, for instance, would not even enlist a new member unless he had already committed at least one murder, and this requirement was well publicized.

At first, much of the violence was indiscriminate and purposeless—or to minor purpose. The targets and the victims were chosen by whim; they could be anything or anybody that was there; and, as a result, the rewards of crime were just as uncertain. A young waiter named August Hoffman could take a rest during a work break on 11th Avenue at 28th Street in New York in 1875 and suddenly be attacked, beaten and robbed of the few cents he had in his pockets by members of the Tenth Avenue Gang who just happened to be passing by and spotted him. Twenty years later, a gentleman strolling on Fifth Avenue on the border of the poor areas could suddenly meet members of the Wellington Association on their way home from a chowder party; his eyes would be blackened and his wallet stolen. And about the same time, the Midnight Terrors could decide to form a baseball team, realize they didn't have the money for uniforms, gloves, balls and other equipment and so maraud through New York's First Ward, beating and robbing anyone they came across in hopes of getting the money. "We eat most everything," said one of the Terrors, "and what we couldn't eat, we sold; dat's de way we was to get de uniforms for de ball club."

While most gangs were narrowly local, the province of the young and concerned with small, indiscriminate depredations, some, though retaining the ethnic balance, broke the pattern. They were not native to America at all but were brought over by immigrants who had come of age at home and had received their training there. They adapted their groups to the new environment and, in some cases, even spread across the country, though until the development of fast and widespread communications, their links with one another tended to be rather hit or miss. Among them were the Mafia, the Camorra and similar secret terrorist societies brought to the States from Sicily, Naples, Calabria and elsewhere in Italy, and the Chinese tongs.

It was inevitable that in the massive wave of Italian and Sicilian immigrations in the last decades of the 19th Century, as with other waves from other areas, some of those who arrived would have been bandits at home. They carried their calling with them, setting up shop in the

The Black Hand was an early symbol of extortion and terror.

narrow enclaves where their countrymen settled. Almost as soon as a substantial Italian settlement was established anywhere in the United States—in New York, Chicago, Kansas City, in the shrimp and fishing areas around New Orleans and the Gulf Coast—those who had preyed on Italians at home would be preying on them here. From bitter experience in their own land, the immigrants had learned neither to trust nor rely on official authority for protection or help, and nothing in the initial American experience persuaded them that any could be expected here. Thus, the immigrants were open to threats, extortion and blackmail, and they felt they had no choice but to pay for safety.

The technique was simple and every Italian in the United States was a potential mark. A letter would arrive bearing the imprint of a black hand—giving rise to the theory that a secret society called the Black Hand was behind it, when, in reality, it was just another operation of the Mafia brought over and adapted. In the old country, such extortion demands were common and the letters were often marked with a drawing of a dagger or a pistol or some other threatening design. The letter would demand money in exchange for protection. If the money was paid, there would be no trouble—until the next demand. If it was not paid, then the store or business of the recipient would be wrecked, a member of his family would be abducted or beaten, he himself assaulted or even killed. "My father," explained one Sicilian immigrant to writer Frederic Sondern, Jr., of those days around the turn of the century, "would pay. He would say, 'Giuseppe, you see, it is the same as at home. The Mafia is always with us.' Then I would plead with him to go to the police. After all, we were in America. 'No, Mother of God, no,' he would shout. 'The police here cannot do even as much as the police at home. They do not know the Mafia. We get put out of business or killed and no one will know why. They do not understand the *mafiosi* and they never will.'"

The price of resistance was well known, for there were numerous examples. In 1905, a wealthy Brooklyn butcher named Gaetano Costa re-

Caruso himself became a victim of extortionists.

ceived a Black Hand letter informing him, "You have more money than we have. We know of your wealth and that you are alone in this country. We want $1000, which you are to put in a loaf of bread and hand to a man who comes in to buy meat and pulls out a red handkerchief." Unlike most of his neighbors, Costa refused to follow instructions. He was shot one morning while working behind the counter in his store. His killers were never found, for the witnesses wouldn't cooperate with the police.

"They were panic-stricken," said one detective working on the case, "and said it would be worth their lives if they said a word."

So the victims, great and small, usually just paid. It became part of their lives. No one but a *mafioso* was immune. Even such as Big Jim Colosimo, boss of prostitution and vice in Chicago's Levee—the notorious First Ward—during the first two decades of the 20th Century, was not immune and, for a time, even the police on his payroll could not protect him. So he paid. The great Italian tenor Enrico Caruso was another victim. During an engagement at the Metropolitan Opera, shortly before World War I, Caruso received a Black Hand letter demanding $2000. He came across without a murmur. It was only when a second demand was made, this one for $15,000, that Caruso balked. He went to the police, who set a trap and captured two prominent Italian businessmen picking up the money where Caruso had been instructed to leave it, beneath the steps of a factory. The two were convicted of extortion and sent to prison in one of the few successful forays against the racket. But Caruso, despite his fame, was considered in grave danger and for some time required protection from police and private detectives.

Though extortion would always remain a major element in the underworld's operations—particularly in its moves into legitimate business in later decades—the Black Hand technique of looting a whole community of the poor and not-so-poor was a passing phenomenon, even among a tightly knit and easily cowed group, for it only took and in return gave nothing but protection against itself. It lasted about 20 years, from the turn of the century to the dawn of Prohibition, and roughly coincided with the rule over the American Mafia, and particularly over the organization in New York, of its major advocate, the brutal and vicious Ignazio Saietta, known as Lupo the Wolf. A *mafioso* in his native Sicily, he had arrived in the United States a grown man in 1899 and, almost immediately, the Black Hand terror erupted. It lasted until 1920, when federal authorities caught up with him, not for extortion but for counterfeiting, and sent him to prison for 30 years.

Though Lupo the Wolf perfected and fostered the Black Hand extortion technique in America, the Mafia had taken root long before he arrived. It existed and ruled in most Italian communities, though known only to the residents, who would not talk about it. It established its domain among them and rarely moved outside. Within its own sphere, though, the Mafia was alternately giver and taker, protector and violator, hero and villain. *Mafiosi* like Giuseppe "Joe the Boss" Masseria, Ciro Terranova, Francesco "Frankie Yale" Uale, Salvatore Maranzano and others captured a monopoly on artichokes, olive oil, wine grapes and other necessities of Italian life and extracted a price for permitting their distribution. They ran Italian lotteries and other gambling games, the houses of prostitution, almost everything on which the immigrant community sustained its life. They were the bankers and moneylenders to the poor, who could

The assassination of New Orleans Police Chief Hennessey triggered such public anger that the suspects were pulled out of jail and lynched.

borrow nowhere else, and they charged interest rates to keep the borrower forever in debt. They made arrangements for relatives to come to the United States, legally and illegally, but at such a cost that both the new arrival and those who had sent for him would be forever at the bidding of the "honored society." They had been evil men, parasites, in Italy and Sicily, and they were evil men, parasites, in America, but there were few who would challenge them.

For the most part, the Mafia succeeded during these years in keeping its very existence a secret. But this was not always possible. The Mafia surfaced first in America in New Orleans in 1890. Antonio and Carlo

Matranga, two members of the honored society in their native Palermo, arrived in New Orleans and promptly moved in on the Mississippi River docks, seizing control and extracting tribute before a freighter could be unloaded. But the Matranga dominance was soon challenged by the Provenzano brothers, also from Sicily and leaders of a rival Mafia faction. War broke out and murder along the docks became a daily occurrence. When regular police investigation got nowhere, New Orleans Police Chief David Hennessey got into it himself and quickly discovered blocks wherever he turned. His own police force, heavily Italian, had no leads and could not develop any; the entire Italian community shrugged and played dumb. Then warnings were sent to Hennessey ordering him to lay off. When that didn't work, he was offered bribes, which he rejected. Months of hard and searching labor finally paid off and Hennessey drew a picture of a Mafia war for control of the New Orleans waterfront. He requested a grand-jury investigation, but before he could testify, he was ambushed and killed by a shotgun blast.

Hennessey's murder enraged New Orleans's good citizens, and the grand jury went to work. On the basis of the evidence that the police chief had gathered about the Matranga-Provenzano War, the grand jury found that "the existence of a secret organization known as the Mafia has been established beyond doubt." And 19 Sicilians identified as members of the Mafia were indicted as principals and conspirators in the Hennessey murder. But the trial was a farce. Many of the 60 potential witnesses were intimidated and threatened by the honored society and the jury was bribed. Despite what observers at the time called overwhelming evidence, the jury acquitted all but three of the defendants and hung on those three cases.

There was a cry of public outrage and a mass meeting was held two days later. The protesters turned into a mob, several thousand strong, and marched on the jail where the defendants were awaiting release. The doors were battered in; two of the *mafiosi* were pulled out and hanged from lampposts; nine more were lined up against the prison wall and shot down with rifles, pistols and shotguns. In New Orleans, for a few years thereafter, the Mafia went underground, limiting its activities to its own community. When tempers had calmed and the events of 1890 had been forgotten, it emerged once again.

T HOUGH NICOLA GENTILE, a member of the society in his native Sicily, would find branches wherever he traveled in the United States after his arrival in 1903, few on the outside were aware of its existence. One who became suspicious, however, was New York City detective, Lieutenant Joseph Petrosino, himself a native of Italy. Assigned to the department's Italian Squad to in-

Detective Joe Petrosino, who was murdered, fought the Black Hand grip on fellow Italians.

vestigate rumors of the Black Hand terror, Petrosino became convinced that the organization had its roots in Italy and Sicily and that many of its members were actually criminals in their native land, liable for deportation if caught. Early in 1909, he persuaded his superiors to send him to Italy to investigate and to seek the cooperation of local authorities. Petrosino sent back some early reports that he was making progress. Then on March 13, while on his way to the *questura*—the police headquarters—in Palermo, two men came up behind him, drew revolvers and fired four bullets into his head and back. The street at the time was crowded, but the assassins escaped.

However, Don Vito Cascio Ferro, the Mafia's ruler on its home ground, was charged with the murder. But the charges against him were quickly dropped. A Sicilian political leader gave him an alibi and upright Sicilians came to his defense. The Petrosino murder remains unsolved.

J UST AS THE MAFIA LIVED OFF the Italian immigrants, so, too, did the Chinese tongs live off the Oriental communities in New York and San Francisco—though there was less secrecy about their existence and power. The tongs catered to every illicit appetite among the severely restricted and persecuted Orientals. Opium was freely available and there was hardly a block in any Chinatown that did not have several opium dens. (In white society, too, narcotics addiction was widespread at the time, though legal, with millions gulping opium-laced patent medicines. It was only with the passage of the Pure Food and Drug Act in 1906 and the Harrison Act eight years later that sale and use of narcotics were restricted and the underworld began, slowly at first, to move in.) Policy, pie-gow and other gambling games were rampant; protection was sold to Chinese businessmen and individuals. The rackets in the districts were all under the control of the tongs and the police rarely interfered, indifferent to what happened among the Chinese as long as it remained an internal affair not endangering out-

side society, and as long as they got their payoffs.

But in 1905 and on into 1906, a struggle for supremacy over the Chinatown rackets broke out between the rival On Leong and Hip Sing tongs in New York. In the great tong war, as it was called, bullets flew and more than 50 rival tongmen were killed and several times that many wounded. The struggle became so ferocious that the white middle class, which had often journeyed to Chinatown in search of exotic bargains and food and to marvel at the quaintness of the people, found it suddenly expedient to seek amusement elsewhere and to complain to the authorities that Chinatown had become a dangerous war zone.

Such complaints forced the authorities to take action. The New York criminal court was assigned the task of bringing peace, not by sending tongmen to jail but by arranging a treaty. Tom Lee, the unofficial mayor of Chinatown and leader of the On Leong Tong, and Mock Duck, boss of the Hip Sing Tong, were summoned with some of their followers to the court to listen to the peace terms. From that time on, the court ordered, no Chinese would carry weapons, the payoffs for protections and other favors would come to an end and neither tong would interfere with the enterprises of the other. To ensure peace, Lee and Duck each posted a $1000 bond.

Recognizing that the war was eating up all the profits, and being good businessmen, Lee and Duck did

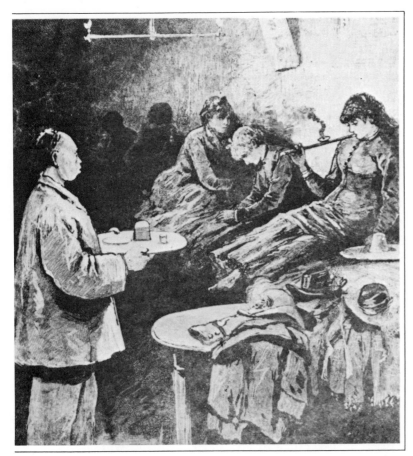

Opium dens (left) were an important source of revenue to immigrant Chinese gang leaders like Mock Duck (right).

more than agree to keep the peace. By the middle of 1906, they had arranged a merger of their tongs. Both would keep their names and would share all income from all activities, but the real power would be vested in a new supergroup called the Kown Yick Tong, with Lee and Duck as joint rulers. "All of which," *The New York Times* commented at the time, "goes to show that mergers are convenient and harmful competition much to be deplored, even among Chinamen." It was a lesson that would take decades for the rest of the underworld to understand and appreciate.

EVEN AS THE MAFIA, THE TONGS and the others flourished within their own ethnic spheres, leaving the world outside to those who inhabited it, there were some who had come to see that the power of the organizations, of the gangs, could be used for purposes with a broadened social significance. It was an idea developed, probably, by the Irish in the cities where they settled, but only because the Irish made up the first massive wave of poor immigrants and because the Irish, unhampered by a language barrier, were, perhaps, more attuned to political action than other groups. A gang meant numbers and in numbers there was power. If violence or its potential were present in those numbers, then the power could be even greater. If at least some of the energy of the gangs could be channeled into politics, their power would be multiplied.

Thus, a bargain was struck that would remain a fact of urban existence, a bargain between corrupt political leaders and the underworld. The power of the gangs would be put at the disposal of the politicians to help perpetuate them in office and enrich them in the process. Through the utilization of violence, or its threat, voters could be dragooned to the polls and forced to vote the correct line; potential challengers and reformers could be cowed into submission. As payment, the power of the politicians would be put at the disposal of the underworld, to ensure its survival and prosperity without fear of arrest or official harassment. Each would be dependent on the other. Later, the politician would become the servant, on the underworld's payroll and at its bidding, with the gangster the master. But in the early days, the politician was the master and the hoodlum his servant, on his payroll and doing his bidding.

Through the years, the leaders of New York's Tammany Hall struck a hundred such bargains that, despite scandals, revelations and occasional setbacks in the form of an election loss or a prison term, permitted the Democratic machine to rule the city almost as a fiefdom. Boss William M.

Boss William M. Tweed was the symbol of New York political corruption.

Tweed and Richard Croker were masters of the careful balance and deal. But perhaps it was best demonstrated in the arrangement struck at the end of the 19th Century between the machine's rulers, Charley Murphy and Big Tim Sullivan, and one Monk Eastman.

Born Edward Osterman in Brooklyn's emerging Jewish ghetto about 1873, where his immigrant father had set up shop as a kosher restaurateur, Eastman (in the early stages of his career, he was also known as Eddie Delaney, Bill Delaney, Joe Marvin and Joe Morris) soon proved himself adept in the violent, hectic, criminal streets of that chaotic borough. About the only gentle aspect of this squat, massive, muscular, bullet-headed, broken-nosed, cauliflower-eared thug was his love of cats and pigeons. At one time, he owned 100 cats and 500 pigeons and he usually traveled with a cat under each arm, several more tagging at his heels and a great blue pigeon that he had tamed perched on his shoulder. Once Eastman opened a pet store on Broome Street in Lower Manhattan, but more as a home for his animals than as a place to sell them, for he would rarely part with one. "I like the kits and the boids," he said often, "and I'll beat up any guy dat gets gay wit' a kit or a boid in my neck of the woods."

Leading a gang of 1200 hoodlums called the Eastmans—which even had a youth branch called the Eastman Juniors—Monk divided his time between private depredations and those done at Tammany's bidding or the bidding of a private client to whom he sold his services. The world of crime on the Lower East Side, around Chrystie and Broome streets, was Eastman's province. He and his followers engaged in every kind of mischief for profit, from simple robberies and burglaries to protection, assault, muggings and murder. Most of the houses of prostitution, gambling dens and even the free-lance streetwalkers and hoodlums paid Eastman for the right to operate on his ground.

For Tammany, and for favored private clients, Eastman was always ready and available, in exchange for continued protection and for a fee. The Eastmans, in fact, even established a price list for their strong-arm work: "Ear chawed off: $15; Leg or arm broke: $19; Shot in leg: $25; Stab: $25; Doing the big job: $100 and up." But what Eastman did best for Tammany was to make sure that in his district the voters voted early and often and only for Tammany candidates. "He was the best man they ever had at the polls," a New York detective said some years later.

Eastman's diligence and efficiency were well rewarded. Arrested often, the charges against him were always dismissed. And his followers, because of his arrangements with Tammany and the police, rarely feared or expected trouble from the authorities. When a group of Eastmans assaulted and robbed a pedestrian on Madison Street in 1903, then took refuge in one of their nearby hangouts, a neighborhood poolroom, the victim led police to the door. It was slammed in their faces. As the newspapers of the time noted, the police "were told that if they did not go about their business they would get hurt. As they started to batter down the door, they were told that they would get in trouble with 'big fellows in politics.' There was then a fierce fight between the police and the gang members. As they waited for the paddy wagon, they laughed at the sorry sight of the bedraggled police and one said, 'Youse go to entirely too much trouble. The politicians'll bail us out. They don't want no one away at registration and election time.'"

Eastman's strong point was muscle, not brains. When he and his gang came into direct conflict with Paolo Vaccarelli, who went by the name Paul Kelly, another gang leader allied to Tammany, Eastman was doomed. Even his political masters could not—and no longer wanted to—protect him. A soft-spoken, well-dressed, educated and cultured man fluent in four languages—when his criminal days ended, he would become a real-estate broker and union business agent—Kelly was boss of the notorious Italian-dominated Five Points Gang and the Paul A. Kelly Association, supposedly a political club but actually much more than that. His sphere of influence, both criminal and political, roughly adjoined Eastman's on the Lower East Side, taking in Chatham Square, the Bowery and part of Chinatown. In the first years of the new century, sporadic warfare was common between Kelly's men and Eastman's along the border of the two provinces.

General war finally broke out when Eastman himself fell victim. One summer night in 1901, while strolling through Chatham Square, Eastman met six of the Five Pointers. Recognizing him, they attacked, with guns and blackjacks. Eastman, armed only with brass knuckles that evening, fought back, knocking three of his assailants to the sidewalk. But a fourth shot him twice in the stomach. Then the Five Pointers fled. Eastman struggled to his feet, closed the wounds in his stomach with his fingers and staggered to Gouverneur Hospital. For the next several weeks he lay critically injured, but, true to

the underworld code (*omertà*, silence, is not the sole province of Italians), he refused to identify his attackers, saying only that he would take care of them himself.

Eastman was released and recovered. For the next two years, the Lower East Side was a battleground. There was hardly a night during which shots were not fired, during which some Kelly or Eastman operation, gambling game or even social affair was not broken up by attack from the opposition. The climax came in August 1903, on Rivington Street. A group of Five Pointers set out to raid a stuss game that was under Eastman's personal protection. But before they had gotten very far into Eastman territory, they were spotted by some patrolling sentries and shots were fired; one Five Pointer was killed. The others took refuge in doorways and around the pillars of the Second Avenue El, and both sides sent for reinforcements. Within a few hours, more than 100 gunmen were sniping at one another up and down Rivington Street. A couple of cops tried to intervene and were sent fleeing under a fusillade from both sides; after that, the police stayed away. The battle raged until dawn, and when the warriors faded back to their headquarters, they left behind three dead, seven seriously wounded and one slain pigeon.

For Tammany, which had always denied. both the existence of any gangs in New York and any deals with them, the battle of Rivington Street was a major embarrassment. Peace was an absolute necessity if the public wrath was not to be felt. So Tom Foley, Manhattan sheriff, Tammany district leader and major aide to Big Tim Sullivan, the East Side Tammany boss and a prime protector of Eastman, arranged a peace conference at the Palm, a dive in Eastman territory on Chrystie Street. Kelly was guaranteed safe conduct. Foley told Eastman and Kelly that unless the war was halted, the power of the Hall would descend on both and destroy them and their gangs. With no choice, the truce was agreed upon and Foley gave a ball to celebrate it; Eastman and Kelly, as a sign of new friendship, stood in the middle of the hall and shook hands.

The truce lasted—for several months. Then one of Eastman's men was badly beaten by a Five Pointer and Eastman demanded the death of the assailant. Unless the man was handed over, Eastman sent word to Kelly, "We'll wipe up de earth wit' youse guys." It looked like war once again. But again Foley and other Tammany leaders stepped in and arranged the second Palm peace conference; again Kelly and Eastman were told that war would mean their destruction, for all Tammany support would be withdrawn and the police

Gang leaders and members were treated with caution by the police; drunks from the ghetto were easier game.

New York cops were not all corrupt; most of them fought against crime but their weapons were limited.

given free rein. Kelly and Eastman decided to settle the issue by a prize fight, with the loser to become the loyal servant of the victor. The fight took place in the Bronx, lasted two hours—Eastman's massive size and strength were offset by Kelly's science and experience; he had been a bantamweight fighter in his earlier days—and ended with both men collapsed on each other.

The issue was undecided and war seemed inevitable. But Eastman settled matters all by himself. At three in the morning of February 2, 1904, he held up a richly dressed young man, reeling from too much gaiety that evening, at 42nd Street and Sixth Avenue. Unfortunately for Eastman, the young man was the

scion of wealth and his family had hired a Pinkerton detective to follow and protect him while he sowed his oats. The Pinkerton fired, Eastman fled—right into the arms of a policeman, who clubbed him into unconsciousness. When Eastman awoke, he was in a police cell, charged with felonious assault and highway robbery. Seeing this as the perfect way out of its bind, Tammany remained strictly aloof. Eastman was convicted and sent to Sing Sing for the next ten years. When he was released, all his power was gone. He became a lonely thug on the streets of New York; he enlisted in the army in World War I, fought in France, returned to pick up his old ways and, on December 26, 1920, was found dead in a back alley of his old neighborhood with five bullets in him.

The passing of Monk Eastman did not, of course, sever the links nor end the bargain between the underworld and the politicians. Eastman was a brute and while corrupt politicians had need of and could always use a brute, the day of such men as a real force was ending as society became more complex. A Paul Kelly would have more success and last longer because he had more sophistication. More powerful still, at least for a time, would be the man who gave the orders rather than took them. A man like Charles Becker, whose friends called him Cheerful Charley.

A police lieutenant, personal assistant to the incredibly inept Police Commissioner Rhinelander Waldo, who placed him in charge of the department's special crime squad, and protégé of East Side Tammany boss Tim Sullivan, to whose throne he aspired, Becker may well have been one of the most corrupt policemen in the long history of New York police corruption. It was Becker who was in charge of the payoffs to the police and politicians from gamblers, prostitutes and other illegal entrepreneurs; who used both his squads of police and specially hired underworld thugs to enforce regularity and strict accounting in those payoffs; who provided the protection to those who paid and retribution to those who did not. But Becker's ambitions went far beyond the police department and the graft he could amass there. He saw himself as the new leader of the Tammany

machine, or at least part of it. By 1911, Sullivan's powers were waning under the onslaught of advancing paresis. Becker was one potential candidate to succeed him on the East Side; the other was Tom Foley, protégé of boss Charley Murphy and himself the sponsor of another rising young Tammany district leader, James J. Hines.

For support, Becker turned to the underworld, which he knew well from his dealings and which owed him much. To ensure that the support for him would pour forth on primary and election days, he chose as his liaison man Jacob "Big Jack" Zelig. He gave Zelig strong-arm power to make certain that the graft from gambling and vice flowed in and flowed at an increasing rate. But Becker, through Zelig, made a major mistake. He put the squeeze too hard on a small-time gambler, a notoriously unsuccessful one, named Herman Rosenthal. As it happened, Rosenthal was a longtime friend of Sullivan's, and that friendship, Rosenthal felt, gave him immunity from the payoffs assessed on other gamblers. Becker thought otherwise and when Rosenthal refused to ante up, his Hesper Club was twice raided and both times he was arrested and fined.

Still Rosenthal resisted. In mid-1912, Becker's personal press agent was arrested for murdering a man during a crap game. Becker set up a defense fund and assessed every gambler in the city $500. Rosenthal refused to pay and hoodlums in Becker's employ waylaid him one night, beat him and told him the beating would be repeated unless he came up with the $500. Instead, Rosenthal began to talk about his troubles wherever he went and his tale reached *New York World* reporter Herbert Bayard Swope, who recognized a major story when he heard one, and Charles S. Whitman, the Republican district attorney of Manhattan, who saw in Rosenthal a lever to the governor's mansion in Albany (which he would later realize) and perhaps beyond.

Though Rosenthal talked to both Swope and Whitman and fed them names, dates and details of the police–underworld ties and bribes, one of the things he lacked was discretion. He repeated his story in bars around town and the word got back to Becker, who became sure that his own safety and career depended upon closing Rosenthal's mouth. Zelig was then in jail charged with assault; Becker had him sprung, gave him $2000 and told him to use it to make sure Rosenthal stopped talking permanently. Zelig did just that. He hired a quartet of mobsters—Harry "Gyp the Blood" Horowitz, Louis "Lefty Louie" Rosenberg, Francesco "Dago Frank" Cirofisi and Jacob "Whitey Lewis" Seidenshner—to murder the too verbal gambler. A couple of attempts failed. In one, the four walked in on Rosenthal in a restaurant, surrounded his table, pulled out their guns, then didn't fire, because, they said, Rosenthal's wife was at the table and they didn't want to hurt her. The attempts, though, were enough to scare

Rosenthal into silence. He sent word to Becker and Zelig that he had forgotten everything and wanted only to leave New York for safer climates. But he had gone too far and on July 16, 1912, the four killers cornered Rosenthal outside the Hotel Metropole on West 43rd Street. He had lost his final bet in a fusillade.

An investigation into the killing was ordered and, of course, Charley Becker was the man in charge. It was his final duty. Even he couldn't stop the police from rounding up the killers—whose identities were firmly established by eyewitnesses—though it took two weeks to do so. Once in custody, Horowitz, Rosenberg, Cirofisi and Seidenshner sang a long tune and Zelig was arrested; Zelig, too, decided that his only hope was to talk, and he implicated Becker, though this didn't save him—while on bail, he was gunned down as he boarded a streetcar. The killing of Zelig did not save Becker. He and his four hired killers were all convicted of the Rosenthal murder by Whitman and sent to die in the Sing Sing electric chair.

In the fall of Becker, Tammany boss Charley Murphy sensed the herald of new times. The day of the brute, as exemplified by Monk Eastman, had passed, and so, too, had the day of the official enforcer with political ambitions of his own and a power base in the underworld, as exemplified by Becker; he was just too much of a danger to the organization to which he belonged. The need for a continuing alliance with the underworld was just as great as ever and would remain so, for the gangsters could still control their districts, still bring out the votes, still provide the graft to make politicians rich. But the nation was becoming less frenetic and more business oriented in these years just before World War I. Respectable companies were doing more and more business with government at all levels and were thus becoming a new vein of graft to be mined. What Murphy realized was that in this changing society, a new type of man was needed, someone between the politician and the policeman and their allies, a man who could deal with both the underworld and the world of business but who was neither complete gangster, businessman nor ambitious politician, yet who was known, trusted and respected by all. He would have to be a man who understood money and how to get it and how to use it; who knew the value and uses of graft and the bribe; who was in all respects amoral, not shy of using muscle when needed; but who yet had a suave and polished front.

Such a man was Arnold Rothstein, nicknamed by those who knew him The Brain. The second, and prodigal, son of a middle-class Jewish family, Rothstein was born on New York's East Side in 1882. The dominant emotion of his early years was a deep hatred of his brother Harry, two years older. At three, Arnold attempted to kill Harry with a knife and, when stopped by his father, gave as his reason only, "I hate Harry." When Harry proved a brilliant student with the dream of becoming a

rabbi, and a faithful son, Arnold, potentially even brighter and something of a mathematical prodigy, took to hanging around the local pool halls and gambling dens. At 16, in 1898, he abandoned any deep religious commitment, all formal schooling and home itself to seek his fortune in the world. He had learned early, at home and in his extracurricular rounds, a lesson he would never stop preaching: Money breeds money, and the more you have, the more you can make. He was determined to make it with his talent for numbers and a seemingly golden touch at games of chance. But it didn't take him long to understand that there was even more money, and a lot safer money, in running the games and taking a percentage than in playing them (though he would never stop playing, never stop risking his own and other people's money in card games and at the tables). So he branched out and soon added loan-sharking to his enterprises, advancing money at first to those who were unlucky at his tables and then spreading it around on a wider scale. Few ever welshed on a Rothstein loan, for he employed a crew of collectors who made people glad to pay; among the collectors at times was Monk Eastman.

But Rothstein's ambitions went far beyond the world of small-time gambling and loan-sharking. He dreamed not just of wealth but of power and respectability. Money could buy some of it, and more would come from the right kind of associates and the right kind of appearance.

Carefully, he watched and listened and trained himself in speech, dress and manners to become outwardly a gentleman, soft- and well-spoken, conservatively dressed in only the best clothes from the best tailors, immaculately groomed at all times. He could have passed for a banker or a respectable sportsman. And he cultivated assiduously those in power—the politicians, the businessmen, the sportsmen, the rich—doing them favors, turning them on to sure deals. He became a familiar sight in the political clubhouses of Tammany, in the best restaurants and theaters, at the race track at Saratoga and at those social events to which he could wangle an invitation. Murphy and Sullivan, older than he, became his patrons in the world of politics, giving their protection to his gambling, bookmaking, loan-sharking and other illegal activities. Jimmy Hines, the rising star in Tammany's heaven, was a close friend. From the world of elegance, Rothstein numbered as friends and frequent companions Charles Stoneham, owner of the New York Giants baseball team (and, it later developed, Rothstein's partner in several undertakings), Herbert Bayard Swope, sportsman Harry Sinclair and many others. The world of Arnold Rothstein was a limitless one, reaching from those with power in the underworld—of all ethnic backgrounds, for he dealt with them all—to the police and politicians, whom he cultivated and paid for protection, and on to the world of business and society. He was, then, the ideal choice for Murphy as Tammany's liaison with both the under- and the upperworld, the man through whom the orders and the graft would be channeled.

The choice, however, gave Rothstein a power and a potential that neither Murphy nor anyone else could have comprehended at the time. In the nether region between the world of crime and violence and the world of politics and business, he ruled supreme in the years after Becker's fall. He was the fixer extraordinary, the man who had to be seen and to whom the money had to be paid before a business contract with the city could be made, if an arrest were to be quashed, if a gambling game or some other criminal enterprise were to be permitted to operate, if the politicians and the police were to get their fair share of the take. It all passed through Rothstein and the word from him was a necessity.

But the real world of A. R., as his business associates came to call him, was always the shadowy region of the underworld, the world of the search for the fast buck. Whenever there was a deal brewing, A. R. was the man to see—to get the OK and perhaps to cut him in for a share. And so his power and his horizons grew. He was, of course, the man F. Scott Fitzgerald called Meyer Wolfsheim in *The Great Gatsby.* "He's the man," Gatsby told Nick Carroway, "who fixed the World Series back in 1919."

It was Rothstein, they all said (including American League President Ban Johnson), who put up the money and who was the mastermind behind turning the Chicago White Sox into the Black Sox, causing the great Shoeless Joe Jackson to turn away from the boy who asked him "Say it ain't so, Joe." But, in actuality, there are some doubts as to Rothstein's direct involvement. He certainly knew about it, but he always maintained that he, like millions of other Americans, so loved the game of baseball that it would be unthinkable for him to tamper with it. The real fixers, he asserted, among those who had come to him with the deal and been turned away with sharp words, were the fighter Abe Attell and some gambling friends. He had warned them they were heading for trouble. "I don't want any part of it; it's too raw," he said he told them. "Besides, you can't get away with it. You might be able to fix a game, but the Series—you'd get lynched if it ever came out." Sure, he bet on the series, Rothstein said, but then, he was a gambler who bet on everything. And he pulled out a canceled check to show that he'd lost a $25,000 bet on one of the games. Of course, knowing what he knew, that wasn't the total of his wagers; he bet heavily and came away $350,000 in the black. But for Rothstein, that was nothing.

Compared with other opportunities that Rothstein saw and parlayed into fortunes, the World Series was only a side show. When the Black Sox scandal was going on, he was actually more heavily interested in that region in downtown New York called Wall

Arnold Rothstein allegedly fixed the World Series in 1919. Shoeless Joe Jackson was one of the players involved.

Street. During the golden age of the Twenties, he would bring to a kind of perfection the bucket shop, with its sale of worthless securities to armies of the gullible. But his initial raid coincided with the American involvement in World War I. To support the war effort, the government issued Liberty bonds, highly negotiable securities, and entrusted millions of dollars' worth to the safekeeping of Wall Street banks and brokerage houses. Over a period of about 18 months, something like $5,000,000 worth of these bonds were stolen, and the thefts all followed a remarkably simple pattern: A messenger in a bank would be handed an envelope with several thousand dollars' worth of bonds and told to take them quickly to a brokerage house (or the reverse). On his way, he would be beaten and robbed and the bonds would disappear. (Some years later, the bonds would be used to purchase whiskey in England, Bermuda and Nassau, during Prohibition and, after that, some would find their way to Cuba, France and other countries to finance the purchase of narcotics; Rothstein would be heavily involved in both.)

A break in the case came early in 1920, when a hoodlum named Joe Gluck was arrested for robbing a securities messenger. He made a deal with the authorities: in exchange for leniency, he would talk about the Liberty-bond operation, for he had been a part of it. The messengers, he said, had all been paid to take their beatings and not resist the holdups. The man behind the scheme was someone he knew as Mr. Arnold Rothstein? Not when Gluck looked at pictures. He identified Mr. Arnold as a slick confidence man named Jules W. Arndt Stein, better known as Nicky Arnstein, husband of Broadway star Fanny Brice and, as it happened, a close friend of Rothstein's. Arnstein the mastermind? Miss Brice was aghast: "Mastermind! Nicky couldn't mastermind an electric bulb into a socket."

The authorities obviously didn't agree, for an alarm went out for Arnstein and he went into hiding. Rothstein came to his rescue. He hired counsel for his friend, including the brilliant criminal lawyer William J. Fallon, known as The Great Mouthpiece, persuaded Arnstein to surrender and then put up his $100,000 bail.

Rothstein's power was never better demonstrated than at the time of Nicky's arraignment. While the court debated, Miss Brice and some friends went to a nearby speakeasy to wait, Miss Brice parking her new Cadillac just outside. When they left, the Cadillac was gone and the owner of the speak told Miss Brice to call the cops. He was then informed that she was under the personal protection of Rothstein. That changed things. He rushed to the telephone and within 15 minutes the car was back where it had been, with nothing missing and the tank filled with gasoline. Into the speak marched Eastman, a battered shell of what he had been, in the last months of his life but still practicing his old calling. He apologized for the theft. It never would have happened, he said, had he known that the car belonged to "a friend of A.R.'s."

But even Rothstein's power, in the under- and upperworld, could not save Arnstein—or, maybe, Rothstein didn't want to save him. For it was accepted that Rothstein and not Arnstein was the mastermind behind the Liberty-bond robberies and that Nicky was just marked to be his fall guy. And that's the way it worked. Arnstein was tried, convicted and sent to the federal penitentiary. And Rothstein marched into the Twenties with renewed power and new ideas. It was a new age and he was ready for it. The world was changing and the world of crime had to change to take advantage of the new times. What the underworld needed were men with brains, ideas and foresight to bring it from the old ways to the new ones, to an emerging world where victimless crime would flourish, providing goods and services that law-abiding society craved but could no longer obtain legally. In Rothstein, such a man existed.

PERHAPS ROTHSTEIN'S ONLY equal was then in Chicago. Along with him, this man would play the major role in reshaping not just the underworld but all of American society. He was Johnny Torrio, called The Fox and sometimes Terrible John. Born the same year as Rothstein, 1882, in the village of Orsara, near Naples, he had been brought to the United States at the age of two by his widowed mother and became totally adapted to the new environment, remembering and knowing nothing about the old country except what he heard. Settling on New York's Lower East Side, he showed early promise as a gangster, leading his own gang as a boy and, when a teen-ager, joining Kelly's Five Points Gang and later becoming one of Kelly's major aides during the war with Eastman and the working deals with Tammany. But the peace that followed Eastman's downfall did not appeal to young Torrio. Though, like Rothstein, whom he knew slightly in

these years and would get to know better 20 years later, he appreciated the value of appearance, and so cultivated a polished, soft-spoken, well-dressed, civilized veneer, and though he was small, sallow and outwardly flabby and nondescript—anything but a threatening or imposing figure— Torrio was basically a man who craved action, who knew the uses of violence and who was not above participating himself (though in later years he would often and publicly decry violence as a threat to the whole businesslike structure of organized crime he would have so much to do with erecting).

So, in 1908, looking for more direct action, Torrio abandoned Manhattan for Brooklyn and joined forces with Frankie Yale and his gang of stick-up men, extortionists, killers and political strong-arm experts. Soon, word of his exploits began to spread and he was emerging as the dominant underworld force in the borough. But in 1909, his career took a sharp and sudden turn. A letter arrived from a distant cousin in Chicago who had heard of his fame. Her name was Victoria Moresco and she was the madam of several whorehouses. She had married Big Jim Colosimo, who had arrived in Chicago in 1872, at the age of one, from his native Palermo, had grown up in the Levee and gotten into gambling and the rackets even before he was of age. When Victoria and Colosimo married, he had taken over the management of her houses, adding them to his own, and he had expanded the business, controlling scores of brothels and moving into gambling, the illegal sale of wine grapes and other Italian delicacies, and just about every other racket that flourished. He had become one of the major bosses in the First Ward, the city's red-light district. By 1908, Colosimo's empire was in the midst of both expansion and trouble. His political deals and payoffs gave him plenty of protection, except from Black Hand extortionists. Their demands had been growing and he had recently been accosted on the street, beaten and threatened with more dire consequences unless he upped the ante. Feeling he needed some outside help and having heard of Torrio and his prowess, he and Victoria decided to send for the young hoodlum, enclosing train ticket and expense money in their letter.

IF THE NEW YORK THAT TORRIO left was corrupt, it could still take lessons from Chicago—there were even stories that in the 1890s a group of Tammany leaders had made the trip west to sit at the feet of their Chicago counterparts and hear how it was really done. The gateway to the West, Chicago, by the time of the Great Fire in 1871, had justly won the reputation as the most corrupt city in America, and nothing in succeeding years had tarnished that image. From the 1870s to the turn of the century, under the ironfisted control of gambler–political boss Michael Cassius McDonald, every kind of vice and corruption was rampant and protected. And McDonald's successors, in both the world of politics and the world of crime—Mont Tennes, Bathhouse John Coughlin (at one time, a rubber in a massage parlor, hence the nickname), Michael "Hinky-Dink" Kenna and Jim Colosimo—carried on the good works and expanded them.

What would later become the mainstay of the national betting syndicate, the racing wire to transmit to bookies instantly track odds and results, became Tennes's province. For $300 a day, he purchased a Chicago monopoly on the service from a Cincinnati man named Payne, who had conceived it, and then demanded 50 percent of the profits of every handbook in the city. Some resisted, but a few bullets and sticks of dynamite helped change their minds. By 1910, Tennes was the undisputed wire-syndicate boss, having set up his own service, General News Bureau, and having forced Payne out. He controlled the national race wire.

And the Chicago underworld found allies in and cooperated with such supposed bastions of incorruptibility as the press. This was the era of the circulation wars, with every paper bidding to control vital street corners in an effort to get its product to the reading public. Control of street corners meant high circulation and success; loss of street corners meant lost circulation and failure. In this war, Moses Annenberg, then circulation manager of the Hearst papers in Chicago (and later to replace Tennes as overlord of the race-wire syndicate), sought out the underworld, hired goon squads to assault dealers handling other papers, to overturn trucks carrying them, to force the Hearst papers onto corner stands, and so, for a time, to win supremacy in the war.

But it was prostitution that really made the Chicago underworld rich and around which the other rackets orbited and prospered. It was the age of the Victorian morality, when sex was something nice ladies didn't talk about and practiced only reluctantly and with their husbands. So prostitution flourished. Some girls came to the trade willingly, seeking their fortunes, for in what other trade could a woman prosper in those years? Others were forced into it, for the white slaver was in his prime, luring innocent young women from the farms and the immigrant ghettos to the cities with tales of good jobs and then seducing them and forcing them to walk the streets and to ply their trade in brothels. While prostitution and white slavery existed to a greater or lesser extent in cities around the country, Chicago was the center. It was still a raw, booming, vastly expanding city with enormous appetites. And it was the city for those to the west and south to visit to seek goods and amusement, including prostitutes. So Chicago became the center of the white slaver and the training ground for those who would eventually seek their fortunes with their bodies elsewhere but wanted to learn the business first. By the end of the first decade of the 20th Century, according to a Chicago police investigation, there were 1020 brothels in the city employing 4000 whores, while another 1000 whores walked the streets. These whores participated in 27,300,000 acts of sexual intercourse each year, grossing $30,000,000, or just over a dollar a trick. Half the money went to pay off the politicians and the police. Ninety percent of the money came from the Levee.

This was the city, then, in which Johnny Torrio took up residence in 1909. He quickly proved to Colosimo—who had doubts when he first saw the unprepossessing young man—that the vice lord and his wife had made no mistake in sending for him. Torrio quickly discovered the identities of the would-be Black Hand extortionists and had them killed. And Colosimo's troubles with them ended.

If Torrio thought that his reward for such a service would be a place at Colosimo's right hand, he was mistaken. Colosimo praised him effusively—and made him manager, male madam, of the Saratoga, the bottom rung in the Colosimo vice network, a sleazy establishment where the girls charged a dollar a trick and the customers were scarce. The ever-inventive Torrio, however, saw his opportunity. With a few cans of paint and some bolts of cloth, he brightened up the place. Then he dressed his worn-out flock in childish clothes to make them look like young virgins, raised the prices and business at the

Saratoga boomed. Colosimo was impressed, enough to move Torrio up to the spot he wanted, as the chief aide and overseer.

Soon Torrio was, in fact, running the entire Colosimo empire while Big Jim dallied with some younger girlfriends. Torrio's contacts spread throughout the Levee and he attracted as allies others for whom work in the whorehouses was to be only a step to greater and wider power. Men like brothel barkeeper and financial wizard Jake "Greasy Thumb" Guzik. And in 1919, at the request of friends in New York, Torrio offered sanctuary and a job to a 19-year-old killer. He received urgent messages from his friends, Frankie Yale in Brooklyn, with whom he had worked, and one Salvatore Lucania, later to be better known as Charlie "Lucky" Luciano, whom he had known as a boy, had sponsored in various crimes and had seen on some visits back home. Both suggested that perhaps Torrio could help out their friend Alphonse Capone, whom Yale had employed as a bouncer in his Brooklyn saloon and with whom Lucania had become friends. Already suspected of at least two murders, Capone had beaten a young man during a dance-hall brawl and his victim was in the hospital with little chance given for his recovery. This killing could be pinned on Capone and it was thought it might be expeditious if he left New York for a while. Torrio agreed, sent Capone a train ticket and, when he arrived, hired him as a $35-a-week bouncer in the Four Deuces, one of the Colosimo

string of brothels. But Capone, like Torrio, was not to be satisfied with such employment.

Meanwhile, Torrio had other concerns. He had become convinced soon after his arrival in Chicago, and despite his own efforts and ingenuity in the work that Colosimo assigned him, that the day of ever-expanding vice was ending. Lurid revelations about girls trapped into a life of sin from which they were unable to escape had aroused the country and in 1910, Congress passed the White Slave Traffic Act, better known as the Mann Act, making it a crime to transport women in interstate commerce for immoral purposes. But the nation was changing anyway, becoming more settled, and while vice would remain for years as one facet and a major one in an empire of crime, its importance as the cornerstone was fading. Torrio recognized this. While still overseeing the prostitution empire—and as long as he remained in Chicago, he would never abandon it, for it earned too much money to throw away—Torrio more and more devoted himself to studying other aspects of the criminal business and other avenues of illegal enterprise: to cultivating contacts and friendships throughout both the underworld and the worlds of business and politics, to preparing himself for the new day he was certain was coming.

FOR NEARLY HALF A CENTURY, THE Anti-Saloon League, the Woman's Christian Temperance Union and

For years, Dr. Howard Russell (left) of the Anti-Saloon League, and Carrie Nation (right) fought a good fight. They finally won in 1920, to the eternal gratitude of organized crime.

other groups had been decrying the insidious and evil influence of strong drink, had been attacking with hatchets and their own persons saloons and sellers of alcohol, had been besieging Congress and the state legislatures to turn America dry. Finally, in the moral climate brought on by World War I and its exhausted emotional aftermath, they succeeded. The 18th Amendment to the Constitution, banning the manufacture, sale and transportation of all intoxicating beverages, breezed through Congress in December of 1917; by January 16, 1919, the necessary 36 of the 48 states had ratified it; one year later, on January 16, 1920, at midnight, it would become the law of the land. And then, in October of 1919, over the veto of President Woodrow Wilson, Congress

passed the Volstead Act, setting up the federal machinery to make the Prohibition Amendment work.

The nation would become dry, peaceful and prosperous with the new decade. Or so the amendment's supporters were sure. "The law," declared Congressman Andrew J. Volstead, Minnesota Republican who had written the law bearing his name, "does regulate morality, has regulated morality since the Ten Commandments." The people, he and his supporters said, would obey the law.

But in New York, Arnold Rothstein, and in Chicago, Johnny Torrio only smiled. The moment they had been awaiting had arrived.

2

CHICAGO AND THE PROHIBITION YEARS

By 1920 FRANKIE YALE HAD grown rich, powerful and almost respectable. He owned the Harvard Inn at Coney Island and the Yale Cigar Manufacturing Company (his portrait was on every box, with the cigars selling three for 50 cents, carried in every store in Brooklyn, and Frankie Yale was the generic term for a lousy smoke), had pieces of race horses, prize fighters, night clubs and assorted other enterprises, legitimate and illegitimate. He owned a fleet of fast boats and when Prohibition came, he turned them loose for quick trips out beyond the three- or 12-mile limit, to what became known as "rum row," to off-load good whiskey shipped from Europe and the Caribbean and run it through the

Coast Guard blockades to shore. He owned trucks for shipping the whiskey to speakeasies and bootleggers anywhere and everywhere. When the Mafia moved in on the Sicilian betterment and charitable organization known as the Unione Siciliana, he became its president, giving him increased power and stature as an ethnic leader. But what Yale prized most was his funeral parlor. "I'm an undertaker," he would often say. And, indeed, that was what he was, maintaining a crew of guns for hire to any paying customer.

A call came early in 1920 from his old friend and onetime Harvard Inn partner, Johnny Torrio. There was a job to be done in Chicago and the price was $10,000. Yale was not

33

only willing to oblige but said he would do the job personally, for it was one that would make Torrio the king of the rackets in the nation's second city.

The 18th Amendment gave Torrio the opportunity he and others had long been waiting for. Maybe the politicians could outlaw booze, but all the laws and all the pious pronouncements were not going to stop thirsty people from finding ways to buy and drink the stuff. And Torrio was determined to be there offering them the opportunities. There were plenty of loopholes in the Volstead Act for a persevering and farsighted man to make use of. A certain amount of liquor was still going to be made legally, kept in bonded warehouses and released upon presentation of certificates; such certificates could be bought or counterfeited. Doctors would be able to prescribe liquor for medicinal purposes, and many a doctor could be bought and millions of such liquor prescriptions accumulated. Millions more could be counterfeited. There were 18,700 miles of unguarded borders surrounding the United States across which alcohol could be smuggled with little difficulty. Every bottle of liquor, when cut and reblended, then rebottled and relabeled (with counterfeit bottles and labels indistinguishable from the real thing), could be turned into three, four or more and sold for far higher prices than before. A quart of Scotch, for instance, went for four dollars at sea, was sold by Yale and other rumrunners for $14 and was

then turned into a three-quart multiple that went for $42 or more. In a speakeasy, a shot sold for 75 cents, while in pre-Prohibition days, a shot of uncut Scotch had sold for 15 cents. Millions of gallons of liquor had been stored away for a year in anticipation of Prohibition, and they were now about to come out of hiding. In the backwoods and in the back alleys of the ghettos, there were thousands of home-grown stills. Many hard-drinking Italians, Poles and Irishmen had long made their own wine, beer and liquor. Given the right price, they would be willing to increase output and turn it over for resale. And near beer was still legal, though it was first necessary to make the real stuff, then dealcoholize it.

So the liquor was there, waiting. And it was apparent to many as early as January 17, 1920, that there were plenty of customers for it, that the Noble Experiment, as Herbert Hoover would later call it, hadn't a chance of working. (Drinking in the years ahead would become a pastime even in the White House, where President Warren G. Harding, taking office a year after Prohibition, kept a second-floor bar and maintained his own personal bootlegger, Elias Mortimer.) The law went into effect at midnight on the 16th. The first illegal drink, someone at the time noted, was sold about a minute later. And the first recorded violations of the law took place, as it happened, in Chicago before an hour had passed. Six masked gunmen drove a truck into a Chicago railroad switchyard, tied and gagged the

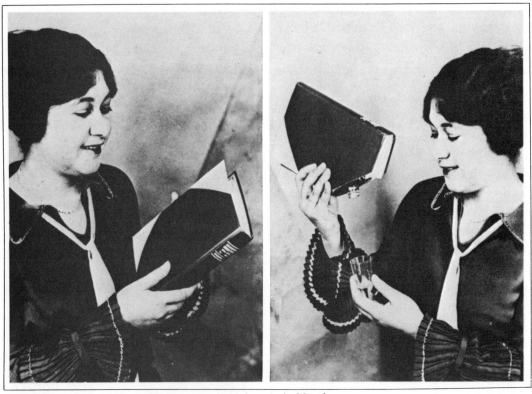

People found many innovative ways to carry their forbidden booze.

watchman, locked six engineers in a shed and then broke open two freight cars and drove away with $100,000 worth of whiskey marked FOR MEDICINAL USE ONLY. Almost simultaneously, another Chicago gang hijacked a truck loaded with medicinal whiskey and began a trend that would last through the dry years. A third group broke into a bonded warehouse and made off with four barrels of whiskey. It was just the beginning.

But Torrio realized something more than just that beer and liquor were available and that there were plenty of customers. He saw that at last the underworld could win a measure of respectability; it could move in on something that people wanted

avidly and become the sole supplier. He also realized that the law would be enforced laxly. Initially, he had not been so sure, concerned that a federal law would be enforced strenuously by federal agents. But political soundings soon persuaded him that he had nothing to fear. All those charged with enforcement would be political appointees and would be earning only about $1500 a year. And, in Chicago and its surroundings, there would be only 134 of them. If political hacks—underpaid and thinly spread ones, at that—were going to man the bureau, the feasibility of bribery was great.

The only obstacle to Torrio's major move into bootlegging was his mentor, Big Jim Colosimo. Bootlegging hardly interested him at all. More and more in the years before Prohibition, Colosimo had been turning the management of his empire over to Torrio while he devoted himself to other, more gracious pursuits. His café, Colosimo's, had become a favorite watering spot for Chicagoans; he had cultivated visiting celebrities, who would join him at his table; he had developed a passion for opera and was often seen with Caruso, Titta Ruffo, Lina Cavalieri and others when they were in town; he was adding to his already noted collection of diamonds and other gems, which gave him the sometime nickname Diamond Jim. But more than anything, there was his new love, Dale Winter, a onetime choir singer whose singing and acting lessons, even concerts, he paid for, and on whom he poured treasure. In 1920, Colosimo had become so taken with Miss Winter that he divorced his wife—Torrio's cousin, Victoria Moresco—and married the singer. "It's your funeral, Jim," Torrio said when Colosimo told him the news.

It was. Colosimo would permit Torrio to handle only enough booze to stock their whorehouses and speakeasies—to satisfy the desires of the customers. Colosimo was afraid of the feds and nothing Torrio said could persuade him that they could be bought. Blocked, Torrio made his phone call to his friend Frankie Yale in Brooklyn.

Late in the afternoon of May 11, 1920, in response to a request from Torrio, Colosimo left his bride of less

Big Jim Colosimo and his second wife, musical-comedy star Dale Winter.

than one month for a trip down to his café. There, he was to await and pay for a shipment of whiskey for the business. Yale was waiting for him and killed him with a bullet in the back of the head. (An eyewitness described Yale to the police, but must have had second thoughts on his way to New York. When confronted with Yale, he refused to identify him and was put on a train back to Chicago.)

When they broke the news to Torrio, he cried, something no one could ever remember him doing. "Big Jim and me were like brothers," he mourned. Then he arranged a fitting final tribute for three days later. It was the prototype of the Chicago gangland funeral, and all those that followed would be measured against it. Colosimo was laid to rest in a $7500 silver-and-mahogany casket; scores of cars filled with flowers followed the hearse; so, too, did 5000 mourners, including, as honorary or active pallbearers: two Congressmen, three judges, one soon-to-be federal judge, ten aldermen, a state representative and an army of other politicians and community leaders. Chicago Mayor William Hale "Big Bill" Thompson was otherwise oc-

Frankie Yale (top insert) had an obvious fondness for diamonds: he became a very bejeweled corpse.

AMONG SLAIN
GUNMAN'S EFFECTS
4 *Karat* DIAMOND RING
3 *Karat* DIAMOND RING
3 *Karat* DIAMOND STICKPIN
1 BELT BUCKLE *set with*
75 DIAMONDS

cupied, but he sent along personal representatives and his heartfelt condolences, for Colosimo had been a rock in the Republican party and had brought out huge pluralities for Thompson and his G.O.P. cohorts. Torrio, one of the most demonstrably emotional of the mourners, was taken aside for personal words with most of the famous, and on the way back from the cemetery he rode in a private limousine. Pallbearer Bathhouse John Coughlin, a First Ward alderman, marked Colosimo's passing thusly: "Jim wasn't a bad fellow. You know what he did? He fixed up an old farmhouse for broken-down prostitutes. They rested up and got back in shape and he never charged them a cent." The only sour note in the occasion was struck by Archbishop (later Cardinal) George Mundelein. Colosimo, he ruled, could not be buried in consecrated ground—because he had divorced and remarried. In lieu of clergy, Bathhouse John Coughlin led the prayers.

Jim Colosimo was laid to rest. Somehow or other, his fortune evaporated between the day of his murder

The bigger the cities became, like New York . . .

and the time, a week later, when a search of his estate was made. In addition to the millions he was rumored to have socked away, he had supposedly left home on that fatal day with $150,000 in cash in his pockets. But the search turned up only $67,500 in cash, $8894 in jewels and 15 barrels of whiskey. Nobody ever came up with a satisfactory explanation for what happened to the rest. Dale Winter, after a period of mourning, returned to New York City to pursue a stage career. She took over the lead in the hit musical *Irene* on Broadway, toured with it for some years and then, in 1924, remarried and later faded into obscurity.

So Torrio was the boss of the Colosimo empire. But his eyes were on all of Chicago. To control it, three steps had to be taken: The aid and connivance of the politicians and the police had to be assured; the source of supply of, at first, beer (for Torrio was convinced that Chicago, a workingman's town, had an insatiable thirst for beer and a lesser one for the hard stuff) and then liquor had to be gained; and unity had to be brought to the multiplicity of gangs at loose throughout the city.

Winning the police and the politicians was simple. Their cooperation had been bought in the past for prostitution, gambling and other rackets and there was no reason to suspect that more of the same could not be purchased. But now a development loomed that would have a profound effect on the future of the nation (for, almost simultaneously, parallels were

... and Chicago, the bigger the take.

occurring in New York under Arnold Rothstein and elsewhere). Until Prohibition, the gangster was generally circumscribed by the unsavoriness of his calling and limited to his own neighborhood. He was the servant of the politician, to whom he paid protection money and for whom he performed services in a variety of causes. But Prohibition cast an aura of semilegitimacy over the organized underworld, which provided a product the public desired and could get nowhere else. So the gangster moved out into the world. He was now involved in a business that had become one of the nation's largest, grossing billions of dollars annually—a government study would later claim that the public was putting $10,000,000 a day into the bootleggers' pockets. With all that money at his command, his power and influence increased geometrically. Though still dependent on the politicians and the police for protection, that dependency took a new turn. Now the gangster, with his wealth and status, was becoming the master, and the politician and the policeman his servants. "Sixty percent of my policemen are in the bootleg business," Chicago Police Chief Charles C. Fitzmorris would say later, and some would think his estimate low.

Izzy Einstein and Moe Smith (top right and also seen in disguise on page 32) were Prohibition agents who became favorites of the public. They captured stills (bottom) and headlines.

The politicians were even more dependent. Torrio and others realized that it was their money and their muscle that kept a man in office, so they acted accordingly, forcing the political bosses to come to them abjectly seeking favors. The gangster's control over the city halls and over the very life of the cities reached so far that by 1928, such an upright and impeccable public figure as Frank Loesch, president of the Chicago Crime Commission and sworn enemy of the underworld, felt it necessary to beg for an audience with Al Capone to seek his assistance to ensure an honest civic election—and Capone, with the munificence of a monarch, gave it. But toward the political hirelings, the gangster felt only contempt, paralleling, perhaps, the contempt the politician had always shown him. "There's one thing worse than a crook," Capone would say later, "and that's a crooked man in a big political job. A man who pretends he's enforcing the law and is really making dough out of somebody breaking it; a self-respecting hoodlum hasn't any use for that kind of fellow—he buys them like he'd buy any article necessary to his trade, but he hates them in his heart."

So it was no hard task to control those who governed and policed the city. And, of course, over it all in Chicago there was the figure of Mayor Thompson, whose fervent and oft-proclaimed devotion to country, city and motherhood was perhaps overshadowed only by his devotion to money. In four years under his rule, a $3,000,000 Chicago surplus was turned into a $4,500,000 deficit. As long as he was in city hall, Thompson proclaimed, Chicago would be wide open, for this was not only the way to prosperity, it was the way Chicagoans wanted it. That suited Torrio just fine.

It was just as simple to corner the supply of beer. With the advent of Prohibition, owners of breweries had few choices: They could close up or sell out and take their losses; they could go into the brewing of near beer, an expensive process; or they could enter into secret partnerships with the underworld, permitting them to continue to manufacture and sell real beer, illegally, and reap undreamed-of profits. For many, it was no choice at all. Within weeks of the Colosimo murder, Torrio had become a partner in nine breweries and several whiskey distilleries with the pre-Prohibition brewer, Joseph Stenson, heir to one of the richest and most respected Chicago families. Those interests would expand greatly and the profits would pour in: The beer cost $5 a barrel to make and was sold for $45 a barrel, sometimes $50 or more —and to special customers, at the reduced price of $35. Torrio also made other connections for liquor: with Yale and the rum-row importers in the East, and with the Purple Gang in Detroit, which had a regular ferry run from the distilleries that were springing up across the Detroit border in Canada.

Then Torrio turned to the gang wars that were erupting all over the

Bootleggers and alcohol could be found in practically any place.

city. Every section of Chicago was ruled by one gang or another. There was the O'Banion Gang on the North Side. Their activities included illegal liquor, safecracking, robberies, hijackings and protecting the political interests of the highest bidder, sometimes Democrats but more often Republicans. The gang was under the rule of a young, smiling, reckless Irishman named Dion "Deany" O'Banion, never without his guns, reputed killer of at least 25, unwilling to shake hands for fear of leaving himself vulnerable, proprietor of a profitable legitimate front, a flower shop that did a thriving business whenever a gangster went to his reward. O'Banion's chief aide was Earl Wajciechowski, better known as Hymie Weiss, to whom society and the underworld will always be in debt for inventing the "ride." In 1921, Weiss personally invited a fellow Pole, one Steve Wisniewski, who had incautiously hijacked an O'Banion beer truck, to drive with him into the country. "We took Stevie for a ride," Weiss would tell friends, "a one-way ride."

THE WEST SIDE OF CHICAGO WAS run by the O'Donnell brothers—Myles, Bernard and William Klondike—all Irish and with an abiding hatred of Italians. On the South Side, in Little Italy, reigned the Terrible Gennas, six brothers named Sam, Vincenzo, Pete, Bloody Angelo, Tony the Gentleman and Little Mike, sometimes called Il Diavolo. Good family men, ardent church- and opera-goers, suspected members of the Mafia all, these Sicilian-born brothers controlled every racket in the ghetto—from extortion to cheese, olive oil and other delicacies, to gambling, politics and booze. During Prohibition, they specialized in turning out homemade rotgut, guaranteed to kill, blind or at least sicken the drinker; but they had no trouble peddling the stuff and the demand was so constant and grew so fast that they put hundreds to work making it in kitchens, bathtubs, anywhere. It cost the Gennas between 50 and 75 cents a gallon to turn out and they sold it to speakeasies for six dollars a gallon. The speaks, in turn, diluted it, sold it by the drink and realized about $40 a gallon.

Between the Gennas and suburban Cicero was the Valley Gang, led by Terry Druggan and Frankie Lake. On the Southwest Side was the Saltis-McErlane Gang, coheaded by massive, brutal and moronic Joe Saltis and the alcoholic killer Frank McErlane, who would introduce the Thompson submachine gun to the underworld. The Ragen Colts—racists, jingoistic, bootleggers—ran the South Side around the stockyards. And on the Far South Side, the rulers were another O'Donnell Gang, unrelated to Klondike O'Donnell, led by brothers Steve, Walter, Tommy and Ed—called Spike, and the real boss. In 1920, Spike was away in Joliet Penitentiary, having been caught walking out of a bank with $12,000. His brothers, disorganized, spent their time doing errands for Torrio at his Four Deuces saloon and brothel, waiting for brother Spike to return.

The bitterness among all the gangs was intense, and blood flowed regularly. It was Torrio's conviction that unless the internecine warfare could be halted, all his plans and hopes would come to little. So he made a proposal to all the Chicago gang leaders: There would be peace, and with it cooperation and prosperity. His proposal was the essence of simplicity and good sense: In unity, there lay strength and success; in division and hostility, only weakness and failure. The main chance, he insisted, lay in making Prohibition work for all, for it would make them all millionaires. As much as possible, he argued, the old traditional activities—robberies, safecrackings, muggings and other violent crimes—should be shunned, abandoned. This was asking a lot, he realized, and total abstinence was impossible, given the nature of the personnel; but nevertheless, this was the goal they should all strive for. They should devote themselves and their energies to those things that, while they aroused society's displeasure, aroused it only mildly—things like gambling, prostitution and, particularly, booze.

But if they were to succeed and become rich, Torrio said, then they must be willing to put an end to the old enmities. He proposed that every gang have absolute control over its own territory, over the whorehouses, gambling and speakeasies, and have the right to dictate from whom the liquor and beer sold there be bought. If a gang wanted to operate its own breweries and distilleries, fine; if not, Torrio, with his vast supplies, was prepared to sell them all the beer they needed; his price, and it was increased now, following the law of supply and demand, would be $50 a barrel; he would also supply all the liquor anyone needed at competitive prices.

If an outsider tried to muscle in anywhere, all the gangs in Chicago would cooperate in meting out appropriate chastisement. And to ensure that the plan worked, Torrio proposed an all-Chicago underworld council—the forerunner of the national syndicate that would be created a decade and more later—with all the gangs represented and having equal voice, and with himself as chairman, ready to supervise all arrangements made among different gangs and to arbitrate all disputes.

Even to rival gang leaders who barely tolerated one another, Torrio's plan was so appealing that nobody resisted.

And so peace and good times, with Torrio as the boss, came to the Chicago underworld. They lasted for nearly three years and, as Torrio had prophesied, the riches poured in. So powerful did Torrio become that his influence reached Springfield and the governor's office. When Jake Guzik's brother, Harry, and Harry's wife, Alma, still plying their whorehouse trade in addition to the new Torrio rackets, enslaved a young farm girl, turning her into a prostitute, they were both convicted of compulsory white slavery and sentenced to the penitentiary. But before they served a day, Torrio reached Governor Len Small, a Thompson puppet. He owed Torrio and his friends big favors; he had been indicted soon after becoming governor for embezzling $600,000 while state treasurer; bribery and intimidation had persuaded the jury to acquit him. Now Small repaid the favor. He pardoned the Guziks—and in the next three years, he would grant pardon or parole to almost 1000 convicted felons.

The first challenge to Torrio's peace, prosperity and cooperation came in the summer of 1923, when Spike O'Donnell returned from Joliet. Determined that he and his brothers would cash in on Prohibition like everyone else, he began hijacking Torrio's beer trucks and tried to muscle in on the Saltis-McErlane territory. The gangs followed the Torrio dictum of cooperation. Striking back, they killed at least eight of the O'Donnell troops and Spike himself barely escaped a couple of times. In a few months, he had had enough. "I've been shot at and missed so often I've a notion to hire out as a professional target," he sighed and departed Chicago.

The O'Donnells, despite the blood and the expense, had been only

Sometimes, liquor was spectacularly disposed of.

an annoyance. Another problem was not so easy. Thompson's term was over and Chicago was about to get a new mayor, a reform Democrat this time, named William E. Dever. He was going to see to it that the laws were obeyed and he told his new police chief, Morgan A. Collins, "I will break every police official in whose district I hear of a drop of liquor being sold."

At first, Torrio refused to believe it; he'd heard the same thing too often to be taken in. But he wanted to make sure, so he offered Collins a $100,000-a-month payoff to forget Dever's orders. Collins, instead, raided and padlocked the Four Deuces. Torrio later offered $1000 a day just to overlook the movement of 250 barrels of beer a day; Collins answered by raiding breweries, speakeasies, brothels and gambling dens around the city and locking up over 100 gangsters (in the process, old Mont Tennes, ruler of the race wire and the city's handbooks, decided it was time to retire and turn the business over to younger hands).

This hurt, but not all that much,

for new speaks, new brothels, new gambling houses, new breweries and distilleries sprang up as fast as the old ones were closed. But none of this made Torrio happy, for it was expensive. So he decided to look for a haven, a place from which his empire could be run without impunity, with no worry about official harassment. His eyes turned to the suburban town of Cicero, just west of the Chicago city limits. It would be the first—but not the last—American community to fall completely under the control and be at the total mercy of the underworld.

A lower-middle-class suburb of 60,000, mainly first- and second-generation Bohemians who worked in the factories of southwest Chicago, Cicero was, within its own terms, a relatively free and easy town. Its president, as the mayor was called, was an amiable lightweight named Joseph Z. Klenha; he did nothing without first checking with the Klondike-O'Donnell Gang, political boss Eddie Vogel and onetime prize fighter turned saloonkeeper, Eddie Tancl, who ran Cicero. The people liked to gamble on occasion, so slot machines, but only slot machines, abounded, the operators sharing the take with Vogel. The people liked to have a beer or two after the day's hard work and, Prohibition or not, they were not to be denied that pleasure. So there were plenty of illegal saloons operating out in the open. As for other vices, there were none.

In October of 1923, Torrio changed all that. Leasing a house on Roosevelt Road, he turned it into a brothel and installed a score of his girls. Cicero citizens were irate and the police quickly raided the house, closed it down and locked up the girls. Torrio said nothing, only opened a second house, with the same result. Again, Torrio did not complain and Cicero officials were certain they had turned back the invasion. It was a mistake they would regret, for they had done just what Torrio wanted. He called his friend and hireling, Cook County Sheriff Peter M. Hoffman, and two days later, a squad of deputies moved in and impounded every slot machine in Cicero.

There was no misreading the message, and emissaries went to Torrio to treat for peace. If he would get the sheriff to return the slots, they would open up Cicero to him. Torrio agreed not to bring in his whores; all he wanted was the franchise to sell all the beer in Cicero except for those small areas ceded to Klondike O'Donnell, to run all the gambling—and he would bring in a plethora of games in addition to the one-armed bandits—and the right to set up his headquarters in the town.

The conquest and capitulation of Cicero had been quick and easy, with no violence or bloodshed, just as Torrio wanted it. He decided that now he could afford to take a vacation. With his mother, his wife, Anna, and more than $1,000,000 in cash and securities to deposit in foreign accounts against future need, he sailed for Italy, returned to his birthplace, where he was greeted as a conquering hero, someone the youth of the town should

emulate, for he had left poor, returned rich and was even building his mother a luxurious villa for her last years.

Behind, he left his expanding empire and a man to oversee it, a man sometimes known as Al Brown but becoming even more notorious under his real name, Alphonse Capone. Born in Brooklyn in 1899, six years after his family's arrival from the slums of Naples, and one of nine children, Capone made his mark on the streets early, with fists, club and gun. He had worked as a bouncer for Yale at the Harvard Inn and there one night had earned the nickname Scar-

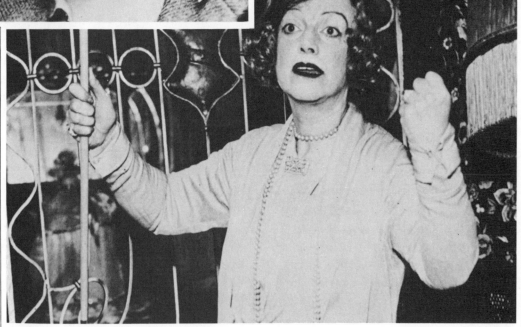

Miss Georgia Hopley (top left) was the only female Prohibition agent. Texas Guinan (bottom) was not the only female speakeasy owner.

face Al: A punk named Frank Galluccio took offense at some slighting remarks Capone made about his sister, whipped out a pocketknife and slashed Capone across the face; in an uncharacteristic gesture, Capone not only forgave Galluccio but some years later took him on as a $100-a-week bodyguard. Late in 1919, seeking refuge from a possible murder indictment, Capone had fled to Chicago and gone to work for Torrio as a bouncer in the Four Deuces. But Capone was ambitious. He was soon chief aide to Torrio.

Capone was the antithesis of the soft-spoken Torrio. Though his business was vice and crime, Torrio did not smoke, drink, gamble or womanize—he would remain a faithful and adoring husband until his death; he rarely swore and would not tolerate the use of obscenities in his presence; he spent his nights quietly at home with Anna, except on those rare occasions when he took her to a play or a concert. And he constantly preached against the evils of indiscriminate violence. There were, he said, times when force was inescapable, but such times were rare and when they did arise, only the minimal amount of force should be used (though sometimes, the minimal amount meant a killing). Violence, Torrio constantly preached, only led to more violence and trouble for everyone; persuasion, bribes, deals and compromise when necessary, meant peace and prosperity for all.

Capone, on the other hand, was a gross man with gargantuan appetites for food, liquor, gambling and women. His bets on horses, dice, roulette and other games of chance were rarely less than $1000 and sometimes as much as $100,000. And he was unlucky—he would later estimate that he had dropped more than $10,000,000 on the horses alone during his years in Chicago. (One of his bouts with a whore in his charge left him with syphilis, which went untreated, for Capone had a deathly fear of doctors and needles. He eventually died from paresis.) Capone believed in the maximum use of force and violence to gain his ends.

At first, in his initial experience as boss, Capone tried to follow the Torrio maxims. With Mayor Dever continuing to put the pressure on in Chicago, Capone moved the organization's headquarters to the Hawthorne Inn in Cicero, armor-plating it and keeping it constantly guarded. He repelled some attempted incursions by other gangs—with guns, of course, but not with undue force—and he added to the growing strength of the operation, bringing in his brothers Ralph and Frank, his cousins Charley and Rocco Fischetti, Frank "The Enforcer" Nitti and others.

And then events were set in motion that would mark the Chicago scene from that day on, would turn the city and its environs into a bloody battlefield claiming, before the Twenties were over, 1000 lives and causing even Charlie "Lucky" Luciano to exclaim after a visit, "A real goddamn crazy place. Nobody's safe in the streets."

Torrio returned from Italy in the spring of 1924, just as Cicero was about to hold a municipal election. Fearing that the citizens, resentful of the gangster invasion and influenced by the Dever reform movement in Chicago, might throw out the incumbents in favor of Democratic reformers, Vogel and Klenha went to Torrio with a new proposition. If he would ensure a victory for the Klenha slate, the town would be turned over to him. Any operation he wanted, except prostitution, would be granted absolute immunity from any interference, from the law or anyone else. What Torrio understood, and apparently the town fathers did not, was that violence would be necessary to fulfill Torrio's side of the bargain. So he turned that little job over to Capone.

And Capone accomplished it with a vengeance. Democratic candidates were beaten and threatened; Democratic voters were intimidated at the polls by gangsters holding drawn revolvers; ballots were seized and checked before the voter was permitted to drop them into the box. During election day's early hours, at least four persons were killed. The reformers sent out a plea for help and squads of Chicago cops poured in. All day, they engaged in running battles with Capone mobsters. At dusk, a squad car pulled up before a polling place at 22nd Street and Cicero Avenue. Standing outside with drawn guns were Al and Frank Capone and Charley Fischetti. A hail of bullets poured from both sides. Frank

Capone fell to the pavement, dead. Fischetti was captured—and quickly released. Capone fled down the street, ran into another squad of Chicago cops, held them off with revolvers in both hands until darkness came and he could escape. No charges were ever filed against him. But Al could take comfort in knowing that brother Frank had not died in vain. The Klenha ticket won with an overwhelming majority and Cicero, for a time, was the capital of the underworld. So completely was it dominated that later, in daylight and with a crowd watching, Capone would kick Klenha down the city-hall steps because the town president had displeased him.

Only one lonely voice continued to speak in opposition in Cicero, that of Eddie Tancl, whose hatred of the invaders was boundless, who had refused to go along with the compact, who refused to buy his beer from Torrio or his allies, who ignored their orders to get out of town. But he did not speak for long. Myles O'Donnell walked into his saloon and shot him dead. Myles was prosecuted for the murder—without success.

The guns and the blood in Cicero were only a prelude. The underworld peace that Torrio had labored for and achieved came to an end. The O'Banions and the Gennas were snarling and shooting. The Gennas had been flooding O'Banion's North Side territory with the cheap rotgut and underselling O'Banion. Even Torrio's remonstrances were unavailing. And then Angelo Genna lost $30,000 at a roulette table in the Ship, a casino

owned by Torrio and into which O'Banion had been cut for a small interest. Genna welshed on the debt. O'Banion demanded payment. Torrio told him to forget it. Instead, the volatile O'Banion called Genna and demanded that he pay up in a week. When Hymie Weiss and others told O'Banion to cool off, that he was only asking for trouble, O'Banion replied, "To hell with them Sicilians."

So the O'Banion Mob and the Gennas were on the verge of war. What was worse for the Irishman was that he had incurred Torrio's displeasure as well. The two had been partners in the Sieben Brewery for some time, and in May of 1924, O'Banion sent word to Torrio that he was

Capone grew fat and prosperous. His wife, Mae (left insert), could hide in rich furs and Al could take it easy in Biscayne Bay (right insert).

going to quit the rackets and retire to a ranch in Colorado. He was, he explained, simply afraid that he had pushed the Terrible Gennas too far and they'd get him if he didn't get out. Would Torrio be willing to buy O'Banion's interest in Sieben for $250,000? Torrio agreed and paid the money. To show how appreciative he was, O'Banion said, he'd help Torrio make one final shipment from the brewery.

That shipment was to be made on May 19. Torrio, O'Banion, Weiss and several others (Capone was in hiding; he had killed a man a few days earlier and was waiting until the witnesses were persuaded to change their stories) were at Sieben watching 13 trucks being loaded under the supervision of two local-precinct cops. Suddenly, the place was a hive of other cops, under the personal leadership of Chief Collins. The chief personally ripped the badges off the precinct cops and then hauled Torrio, O'Banion, Weiss and the others not before a city judge who would quickly spring them but before a federal commissioner. For O'Banion, this was a first arrest for bootlegging and, according to prevailing practice, he would get off with a fine. But Torrio had been picked up for bootlegging some time before and had paid a fine then. As a second offender, he could expect a jail term. Then, from a friendly cop, Torrio learned that O'Banion had tipped off Collins's office, setting up the raid and thereby not only reserving a jail cell for Torrio but clipping him for $250,000 plus what had been seized

Dion O'Banion died among flowers.

Hymie Weiss died next to a cathedral.

at Sieben. And the word got back to Torrio that O'Banion was telling friends, "I guess I rubbed that pimp's nose in the mud all right."

It was just too much. O'Banion had to be chastised and there was only one fitting chastisement for such a double cross. Torrio made common cause with the Gennas. All that held them back was the cautious voice of respected Mike Merlo, who headed the Chicago branch of the Unione Siciliana; he, even more than Torrio, deplored violence and its effect on his underworld friends. But Merlo was dying of cancer and his death would free Torrio and the Gennas. It would also provide the excuse for Torrio to once again call upon Frankie Yale, the Unione's national president.

Merlo died on November 8, 1924 (Angelo Genna was named to succeed him). The funeral was set for the tenth. Yale arrived in town for the ceremonies. And the orders for floral tributes poured into the O'Banion shop. Torrio bought a $10,000 mixed bouquet; Capone kicked in $8000 for red roses; the Unione itself anted up for a huge wax-and-flower sculpture of Merlo to be carried in a limousine behind the hearse. The night before the funeral, Angelo Genna called to order another massive and expensive tribute and told O'Banion he would send around a couple of guys to pick it up.

At noon on November 10, O'Banion was in the shop, waiting. In walked John Scalise and Albert Anselmi, two illegal immigrants from Sicily wanted for murder there and now working for the Gennas and Yale. "Hello boys," O'Banion greeted them. "You want Merlo's flowers?"

"Yes," one of the men replied.

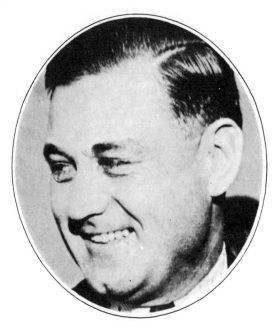

Bugs Moran did not die in a garage.

Then, inexplicably, O'Banion held out his hand; it was the first time anyone could remember his offering to shake hands; it would be the last. The hand was grasped. O'Banion was pulled forward, off balance. Before he could recover, guns were drawn and he was shot six times.

The farewell to O'Banion was orgiastic. "It was one of the most nauseating things I've ever seen happen in Chicago," said Judge John H. Lyle, one of the city's few courageous and honest judges at the time. The casket, rushed from Philadelphia, was of silver and bronze and cost $10,000; 26 cars and trucks were needed to carry the floral decorations, including garish ones sent by Torrio, Capone and the Gennas; there were three bands and a police escort; more than 10,000 people marched in the funeral train and 5000 more waited at

the cemetery; there were judges, aldermen and assorted other public officials. Hearing of it all, Yale would say to friends, "Boys, if they ever get me, give me a send-off that good." Three years later, they did.

But O'Banion's friend and successor as gang leader, Hymie Weiss, was determined that the fallen leader would be avenged, and he was certain he knew upon whom to wreak that vengeance—Torrio, Capone and the Gennas. Not willing to stand up as a target, Torrio took off for a vacation—unknown to him, he was trailed everywhere by Weiss gunmen, who never got the opportunity to get off a shot. In Chicago, the war was under way. An attempt was made to kill Capone as he drove through the city; it failed and Al promptly ordered an armor-plated, bulletproof car from General Motors. Other members of the gang, however, fell before Weiss's bullets.

By mid-January of 1925, Torrio was back, and he knew exactly where he could find safety. The federal bootlegging charges, growing from the Sieben raid, were finally before the court. Torrio pleaded guilty and, almost with a grin, heard himself sentenced to nine months in jail and fined $2500. He was given, as a prominent businessman, five days to clean up his affairs.

On January 24, he went shopping with his wife. At dusk, they returned to their Clyde Avenue apartment. Ann started for the apartment-house door. Johnny hung back to remove some packages from the car. A black

Cadillac stopped across the street. Inside were four men holding pistols and shotguns. Two leaped from the car (one was later identified as George "Bugs" Moran, killer and sometime clown prince of the O'Banion Mob). They dashed across the street and began firing at Torrio and his chauffeur. The chauffeur was hit in the leg. Torrio was hit four times—one bullet shattered his jaw, the others struck his right arm, chest and groin. Simultaneously, the two men in the car began firing across the street, lacing the Torrio limousine with bullets and shotgun pellets. One of the killers bent over to put a bullet in Torrio's head. His gun misfired and before he could fire again, a warning blast of the Cadillac's horn sent him hurrying away.

Within minutes, racked with pain, Torrio was in an ambulance on his way to the hospital. In the hospital, guarded by the best troops the shaken Capone could round up, Torrio proved to be not as seriously wounded as first thought, though he would bear scars on his jaw for the rest of his life and would never be without a scarf to hide them. He mended quickly. But when questioned about the assailants, he would say only, "Sure I know all four men, but I'll never tell their names."

Then Torrio went to jail. He was treated with the respect his wealth and power called for. Special furniture was brought in; the warden's office was his for the asking; he could make all the phone calls he wanted and he could have all the private conferences he desired. During these months, he came to a decision. All that he had built up so carefully was now coming down in violence and death and could easily mean his own death. He summoned Capone. "It's all yours, Al," he said. He was leaving Chicago, leaving everything behind, turning it all over to Capone to do with as he wished. All Torrio wanted was the peace and quiet of a retired businessman.

So Johnny Torrio, the mastermind of the Chicago underworld, left jail and was driven in a three-car motorcade to meet a train, a train that would take him to New York, where he would meet quietly with old friends and talk about the future, then board a boat for a long trip to Italy. But he would be back, and when he returned, his arena would be the whole country, for he would play a major role in forging a nationwide criminal alliance.

Now Capone was the boss. But not, as Torrio had been, of a semi-peaceful and cooperative underworld. There was war in Chicago and Capone was ruler of only one army, albeit the biggest and strongest, numbering between 750 and 1000 troops. Arrayed against him were the remnants of the O'Banion Gang, led now by Weiss and joined by other Irish, Jewish and Polish gangs who proclaimed their hatred of Italians. Their number and firepower nearly matched Capone's.

But Capone's gang was tightly knit. And he had the drive and ambition that others lacked and the unscrupulous amorality to see him to victory. He was determined to be Chicago's master.

To achieve his goal, Capone knew, he would have to smash his opposition unalterably, not with the Torrio technique of persuasion, treaties and compromise but in the manner he knew best, with violence. Initially and unwittingly, Weiss was of help, for with Torrio's departure, he turned his guns on the Gennas, sometimes allies of Capone but more often a threat. In a series of street-corner shoot-outs, motorcade battles and lonely ambushes during the spring and summer of 1925, Weiss's men gunned down Angelo, Mike and Tony Genna and a small army of their followers. It was the end of the Terrible Gennas. The surviving brothers fled the city, and when they returned a few years later, it was to a life of obscurity as importers of cheese and olive oil. The demise of the Gennas, and the murder in a barber's chair of their protégé Samuzzo "Samoots" Amatuna soon after, put the Unione Siciliana in Capone's pocket, for his *consigliere*, Tony Lombardo, succeeded to the presidency, all of which brought Capone new power and new troops.

He needed them, for the city rocked to the sound of gunfire in a seemingly endless battle between Capone and Weiss. In the summer of 1926, Weiss and one of his top gunmen, Vincent "Schemer" Drucci went to pay a call at the new Standard Oil Building on South Michigan; they were going to make a payoff to politi-

cal ward boss Morris Eller and assistant state's attorney and gangland funeral director John Sbarbaro. Instead, they met a carload of Capone gunmen. The street in front of the building, filled with people, was suddenly a war zone as bullets flew from both sides. The only casualty: a clerk grazed in the thigh. Later the same day, as Weiss and Drucci drove along Michigan Avenue, their car was strafed by a passing Capone car, but again, there were no casualties.

Weiss struck back. About a month later, he set up an ambush for Capone at a restaurant Al frequented near the Capone-controlled Hawthorne Race Track. A ten-car motorcade sped by. From each car protruded gun barrels. And from those barrels came the spit of bullets into the crowded restaurant. One Capone aide was wounded, and so, too, were three innocent bystanders. One woman's injuries were severe, and generous Capone paid the entire $10,000 hospital bill. He also paid for repairs to the restaurant and adjoining stores.

It wasn't that Capone minded the shooting; after all, he did it himself and it was one of the risks of the business. What he minded was all the bad publicity. Maybe the Torrio way was best, after all, he thought. So he sent word to Weiss, asking for peace and cooperation; there was enough for everyone. Not, Weiss replied, until Capone turned over to him O'Banion's killers: Scalise and Anselmi. "I wouldn't do that to a yellow dog," Capone snapped back.

The only thing Weiss would listen to, Capone decided, was gunfire, and gunfire that would end his career. An ambush team rented a room next door to the O'Banion flower shop, which Weiss still used as head-quarters. On October 11, 1926, as Weiss and four companions left a car to enter the shop, two waiting gun-men opened up with tommy guns and shotguns. Hit ten times, Weiss was dead before he fell to the pavement. A Weiss aide was also killed instantly. The two others, though wounded, re-covered. Directly in the line of fire was the Holy Name Cathedral. On its cornerstone was written:

A.D. 1874 AT THE NAME OF JESUS
EVERY KNEE SHOULD BOW
IN HEAVEN AND ON EARTH.

The fusillade that killed Weiss nearly obliterated the text, chipping off all but: EVERY KNEE SHOULD . . . HEAVEN AND ON EARTH.

So Weiss went to the cemetery, where he would soon be joined by Drucci, the victim of a policeman's bullet. And Capone said, "Hymie was a good kid. He could have gotten out long ago and taken his and been alive today."

And then, for a time, there was a semblance of peace. On October 21, 1926, Weiss's allies, frightened now of Capone's firepower, sued for peace and Capone granted it to them. He generously permitted the other gangs to split the spoils north of Madison Street, while everything south, and all the suburbs, would be his—a ter-ritory containing more than 20,000

speakeasies, uncounted numbers of gambling dens, brothels, and other rackets. "I told them," he would later say, "we're making a shooting gallery out of a great business and nobody's profiting by it.

PEACE CAME AT THE RIGHT MO-ment. For Big Bill Thompson was coming back. He cam-paigned on a platform of "What was good enough for George Washington is good enough for Bill Thompson. . . . I want to make the king of England keep his snoot out of America! Ameri-ca first, last and always!" and as-serted that "I'm wetter than the At-lantic Ocean. When I'm elected, we'll not only reopen the places these peo-ple have closed but we'll open 10,000 new ones." He was backed by a huge war chest, including a $260,000 con-tribution from Capone, who also sup-plied plenty of bribes, terror and mul-tiple votes. Thompson was swept back into city hall and Chicago was wide open again. Capone would later say that his payoffs to the police in the Thompson era averaged $30,000,000 a year and that half of the force was on his payroll. "Chicago is unique," said Professor Charles E. Merriam, University of Chicago political scien-tist and civic reformer. "It is the only completely corrupt city in America."

Thompson was good for business; the campaign investments paid off. But any hope of a lasting peace was bound to be an illusion in Chicago. No sooner had one group been conquered

The minestrone recipe that could have been worth $35,000.

than another rose to take its place. As the O'Banions regrouped, under Bugs Moran, and the Gennas disappeared, Capone was faced with a new challenge, from the nine Aiello brothers and their countless cousins who had succeeded the Gennas as bosses of Little Italy and who, unlike the Neapolitan Capone, were Sicilians and so full-fledged *mafiosi* with lines around the country (Capone was eventually made an honorary member of the honored society but never a full member). The Aiellos chafed when Capone's choice, Tony Lombardo, became president of the Chicago branch of the Unione over their choice, elder brother Joseph. They determined that both Lombardo and Capone, and anyone supporting them, had to go. They forged an alliance with Moran and they spread the word that they'd pay $50,000 to anyone who killed Capone.

All through 1927, there were takers. But most fell victim to the weapons of Capone's chief bodyguard, James Vincenzo De Mora, who went by the name of "Machine Gun" Jack McGurn. The Aiellos even tried poison, offering to pay the chef of a favorite Capone restaurant, Diamond Joe Esposito's Bella Napoli Café, $35,000 if he would put prussic acid in Capone's minestrone. The chef told Capone.

It was just too much, especially when Capone learned that Joe Aiello had brought in some outside gunmen to take care of both him and Lombardo from ambush. The police stumbled across the plot, finding first one stakeout, then another, and finally being led to Aiello. He was jailed. While in his cell waiting for bond to be posted, cars filled with Capone gunmen drove up and surrounded the jail. One of the gunmen was arrested and thrown into the cell adjacent to Aiello's. He whispered in Italian to the *mafioso* that his first step outside would be his last. The terrified Joe Aiello pleaded for police protection and got it, all the way to the railroad station and a train that carried him and several of his brothers to safety in the East. (Joe Aiello would return a few years later and at last succeed to the presidency of the Unione that he had always craved. But he would be no more fortunate in that office than his predecessors: Within a year, he would be caught in a cross fire from two machine-gun nests prepared by Capone.)

By the end of 1927, then, it seemed that Capone, from his luxurious and guarded headquarters, could look out over a city he ruled, having conquered it and achieved more by guns and violence than had Torrio by soft words and treaty. And Capone was famous. Torrio had never been more than a shadowy figure whose power and influence few realized. He had shunned publicity; the garrulous Capone wallowed in it. He loved it that every schoolboy knew his name and face. That wherever he went—in Chicago, Florida, anywhere—he was the center of attention. He gave interviews, trying to explain, but not apologize for, his actions. He had power and he was certain that to Chicago, at least, he was essential. When Thompson got virtuous— deciding when Calvin Coolidge announced he would not run that he would make a damn fine president

Calvin Coolidge decided not to run for a second term.

and the way to get the Republican nomination was by showing he was honest and was cleaning up Chicago—Capone just took himself off to Miami, Florida, where he bought his Palm Island retreat. "Let the worthy citizens of Chicago get their liquor the best way they can," he announced. "I'm sick of the job." Once Thompson renounced his White House dreams, the heat came off and Capone returned to pick up his life as Chicago's master and benefactor.

And benefactor he was, indeed. From the huge roll of bills he always carried in his pocket, he would peel off $10 tips for newsboys and boot-blacks, $20 for hatcheck girls or chambermaids, $100 for waiters. There was no end to his generosity. But then, he could afford to be generous. He was earning, the federal government would later estimate, more than $105,000,000 a year by 1928.

Capone had expanded far beyond liquor, gambling and prostitution; he had a lock on just about every racket in the city. By the end of 1928, according to the state's attorney's office, at least 91 Chicago unions and trade associations had fallen under the rule of the racketeers. They controlled everything from retail food and fruit to city-hall clerks to plumbers to bakers to carpetlayers to kosher butchers to movies and beyond. They collected initiation fees and monthly dues; in return, they offered employers protection from unions, unions the right to organize and to all, protection— from themselves. The cost to the public was enormous. When Capone moved in on the cleaning-and-dyeing industry, in order to raise the protection money, the merchants had to raise the price of cleaning a suit by 75 cents; when he moved in on the kosher butchers, the price of corned beef went up 30 cents a pound. By the end of the decade, the Mob's control was costing consumers in Chicago $136,000,000 a year, or $45 for every man, woman and child.

It was a good racket, and others besides Capone realized it. Bugs Moran, regrouping the shattered O'Banion-Weiss forces, was back on the attack. Trucks carrying liquor for Capone from the Detroit Purple Gang were repeatedly hijacked. Though dog racing was then illegal (Florida, in 1931, would be the first state to legalize it), dog tracks, dominated by Capone, flourished. Moran went into competition and even tried to burn down a Capone track. He tried to muscle into the Capone-dominated cleaning-and-dyeing industry. He set up ambushes and tried to kill Capone favorites like McGurn. And he never lost a chance to taunt Capone in public. "If you ask me, he's on dope," Moran said. "Me, I don't even need an aspirin." Capone, Moran would say, was "the beast."

By early 1929, Capone had had enough. He took off to Florida. But he was constantly on the phone with Jake Guzik in Chicago and several of his aides made quick trips down to see him. On February 14, Capone rose early, had his customary swim and then took himself down to the office of Dade County Solicitor Robert Taylor, for a chat about what he had been doing in Florida.

While Capone talked away the morning hours, it was Saint Valentine's Day in Chicago. At the S-M-C Cartage Company warehouse at 2122 North Clark Street, members of the O'Banion gang were waiting for a truckload of whiskey from a hijacker in Detroit. They were waiting, too, for the arrival of their leader, Bugs Moran. They were six hoodlums—

On St. Valentine's Day, in a garage on Chicago's North Clark Street, seven men were lined up against a wall and shot. Bugs Moran missed his appointment with death by only a few minutes.

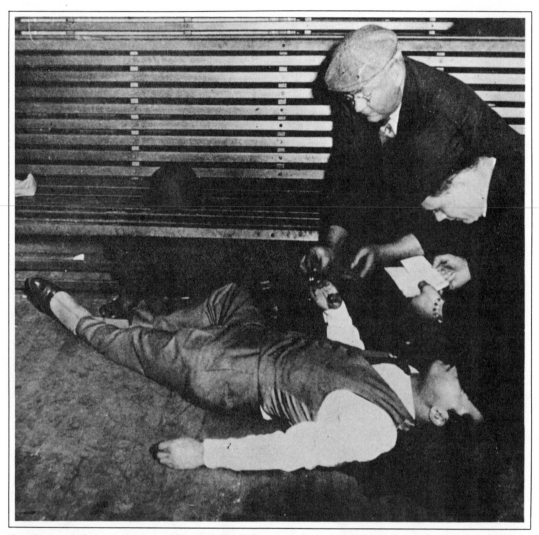

On the seventh anniversary of the 1929 St. Valentine's Day Massacre, one of the suspected killers, Machine Gun McGurn, was cut down in a bowling alley on Chicago's North Side.

Johnny May, Frank and Pete Gusenberg, James Clark, alias James Kashellek (he was Moran's brother-in-law), Adam Heyer and Al Weinshank. With them was Reinhardt H. Schwimmer, an optometrist and friend of Moran's who, though not a gangster, enjoyed the company of gangsters. And there was a dog.

A long black Cadillac, a police gong on its running board and a gun-rack behind the driver, pulled up outside. Moran, late for his appointment, was just turning the corner; he spotted the car, noticed its accouterments and, certain that a raid or a shakedown was about to take place, turned and hurried away.

According to witnesses, four men, two in police uniforms and two in civilian clothes, emerged from the car and started for the warehouse. A fifth man remained behind the Cadillac's wheel. The four disappeared inside.

One resident of Clark Street thought he heard the sudden clatter of a pneumatic drill going on and off in several short bursts, then the sound of an automobile backfiring twice. Two neighborhood women, drawn by the noise, looked out their windows and saw two men in civilian clothes leave the warehouse, their hands in the air, followed by two policemen with drawn guns. They got into the Cadillac and drove off. The women shrugged. It was just a raid.

And then the dog started to howl, a sad, mournful cry cutting through the silence. The dog would not stop. A neighbor went to investigate and fled, sick, to call the police. As best as anyone could reconstruct it, the seven men in the warehouse had been disarmed and lined up against the wall, and then cut down by submachine guns; all had been riddled in the head, chest and stomach. Two, May and Kashellek, had also been blasted in the face at close range by shotguns. There was blood everywhere, on the floor and all over the brick wall against which they had stood. Only one man could have described what happened. Somehow, Frank Gusenberg had survived. He would last a few hours. But all he would say was, "Nobody shot me. I ain't no copper."

No one was ever convicted of the Saint Valentine's Day Massacre. But Moran knew who was behind it. "Only Capone kills like that," he said. To which Capone, brought the news

at a gala party at his Palm Island mansion, replied, "The only man who kills like that is Bugs Moran."

Capone could joke, but the jokes had a gallows ring, not just for his victims but for himself. The slaughter on Clark Street had solved little, for Moran, the intended victim, had escaped. And the slaughter, at last, stirred a wave of public revulsion and disgust. And a cry for vengeance from Moran. The Aiellos had put a $50,000 price tag on Capone and, despite their flight in disarray, they had never withdrawn it. Now Moran said he would guarantee payment. And he found recruits willing to do the job. In 1928, Tony Lombardo had been gunned down in a crowd of shoppers on Madison Street, a fate that seemed destined for the Unione's Chicago leaders. (Joe Aiello, it was theorized, was behind that one.) After others who tried to hold down the job met the same fate, the new president became a Sicilian gunman named Giuseppe "Hop Toad" Giunta, and as his vice-presidents he named the O'Banion killers, Anselmi and Scalise. They decided to collect the Aiello-Moran bounty. But Capone, with spies everywhere, was quick to hear of their treachery. On May 7, at the Hawthorne Inn in Cicero, he gave them a banquet and when they had eaten and drunk to satiation, his aides suddenly surrounded them and tied them to their chairs. Then Capone personally picked up a baseball bat and with slow and cool deliberation, beat each one to death.

It might have seemed, then, that

despite the constant threats and the steady guerrilla warfare of his enemies, Capone still ruled with impunity. He dealt with his foes mercilessly and had little fear of official retribution—between 1927 and 1930, there were at least 227 gangland killings in Chicago, but only two assassins were every tried and convicted.

BUT THE TIMES WERE CHANGING, and so was the public temper. An era was coming to an end. For years, the public had read of the exploits of Capone just as avidly and with just as little moral concern or overt outrage as it had read of the exploits of the other public heroes of these years of wild wealth and moral stupor—Babe Ruth, Charles Lindbergh, Jack Dempsey, Red Grange. But the blood that stained Chicago's streets, the innocents—and there were many—who were caught in the cross fires, the indiscriminate and unconcerned violence, the mounting revelations about official complicity and corruption were beginning to have an effect on the city's and the nation's conscience. And the sudden end to that giddy era on the black Wall Street afternoon in October of 1929 did even more. Who had time any longer to be amused at tales of Al Capone and his millions when there was no money to pay the rent or put bread on the table, or even to buy a newspaper to read about him?

When Jake Lingle, a *Chicago Tribune* crime reporter, was shot down on June 9, 1930, and it was soon learned that he had been something else in addition to a reporter, that he had been a paid ally and an active member of the Mob with spreading interests in the rackets, even the kind of detached amusement with which the press had viewed Capone and the mobs (as long as they were around, there were plenty of good stories that would sell papers) ended. The press began to look harder and with more concern at the doings of the underworld, to demand action. And the wrath increased, and so did the demands for a wholesale cleanup.

Less than a month later, Jack Zuta, the Moran mob's expert on whorehouses, barely escaped assassination as he rode in a police car under official protection, and then was executed by five Capone gunmen. When Zuta's papers were examined, among them were found letters from a host of politicians asking for loans, thanking Zuta for favors and asking for more. Perhaps a few years earlier, in good times, it would all have been dismissed. But with the depression flattening the land, it was too blatant; the cries increased.

By the last years of the Twenties, even racketeers around the nation were becoming distressed by the Chicago odor; it was giving the whole underworld a bad name. And that odor, and the man responsible for it, was one of the subjects under discussion at a major national underworld conference from May 13 to May 16, 1929, at Atlantic City. There, under the protection of Atlantic City's su-

Madison Square Garden in New York was to become a target of the Mob, after the Prohibition Era.

preme ruler, the bootlegger-gambler-racketeer-politician Enoch "Nucky" Johnson, gathered the criminal powers of the nation—Frank Costello, Meyer Lansky, Lucky Luciano, Dutch Schultz, Louis "Lepke" Buchalter and others from New York, Max "Boo-Boo" Hoff and cohorts from Philadelphia, representatives from Cleveland, Kansas City, Detroit, Boston, everywhere. And Torrio, back home from Italy, operating now in cooperation with New York rulers, was an omnipresent figure, a respected elder statesman of the underworld. The conference dealt with cooperation and syndication in the bootlegging business, began charting a course for the day they all knew was coming, when Prohibition would end. And there was the problem of Capone and how to stem the mounting public outcry against the violence that had marked Chicago. There was, it was agreed, only one way. Capone would have to go, at least temporarily, and he would have to go with official connivance.

Though Capone at first resisted, he at last agreed and soon realized that the arrangements might actually suit him. Where better could he be protected from the vengeful Moran and his followers than in jail for a short spell? Arrangements were made with cooperative Philadelphia police. On his way home from Atlantic City, Capone was picked up for carrying a concealed weapon. The only thing that shocked him was what he got. He expected a vacation of a couple of months. Instead, he was given a one-year sentence in Holmesburg County Prison and served ten months in luxury.

But when he left prison in March of 1930, the world had changed. Prosperity was gone and depression had arrived, and with it a contraction of the income from the rackets. Worse, the federal government was now after him. If local officials would not deal with the underworld and if most federal laws were ineffective, there was,

Washington realized, one way of getting the mobsters—for violation of the income-tax laws. Under Elmer L. Irey, head of the Treasury Department's Enforcement Branch, the government took aim first at Chicago and, initially, at those under Capone. Ralph Capone got hit with a three-year sentence and a $10,000 fine for income-tax evasion; Jake Guzik got five years and $17,500; Nitti got 18 months and $10,000.

Then it was Al Capone's turn. The pressure on Irey to get Capone had come from as high as the White House itself. President Hoover kept pressing Treasury Secretary Andrew Mellon: "Have you got that fellow Capone yet? Remember, I want that man Capone in jail." And Mellon was passing the orders down to Irey and others in the IRS.

But it was no easy task. Capone never maintained a bank account, never signed a check or a receipt, never bought property in his own name. He paid for everything in cash and he kept his horde in a strongbox under his bed. So the tactic was to go after him on the basis of his net worth and net expenditures, to show that he had income, undeclared and on which no taxes had been paid. Stores were scoured to get records of purchases; hotels' and caterers' records were examined to see how much his parties had cost; the brothel operations were studied—even the towels that went to the laundry were counted in order to estimate income.

With the heat growing, Capone's lawyers went to the government and offered to settle up on back taxes on a reasonable basis. No deal. Then Capone, against the advice of everyone, hired five gunmen to kill the tax agents on his trail. The plot was discovered and a message was sent to Capone to call the gunmen off or they would be shot down on sight. Reluctantly, he did so. Next, he tried bribery, sending a message to Irey that he would hand over $1,500,000 in cash if the case against him were dropped or rigged in his favor. Again, no deal.

In the spring of 1931, Capone was finally indicted for failing to file tax returns and for evading taxes for the years 1925 to 1929. The government said it could estimate and prove only a fraction of his real income, but that fraction came to $1,038,655.84, on which he owed $219,260.12 in back taxes and $164,445.09 in penalties.

Capone's trial began on October sixth and lasted for ten days. The jury was out for eight hours and returned with a guilty verdict on five of the 22 counts against him. On October 24, Judge James H. Wilkerson sentenced him to 11 years in prison, fined him $50,000 and an additional $30,000 for court costs—the harshest penalties handed out up to that time for tax evasion. "You won't see me for a long time," said Capone as he was led away. He was right. First, he was jailed in Chicago; then, when his appeals had been turned down, he was transferred to federal prison in Atlanta and finally to Alcatraz, where he

remained until 1939. He was released a shattered man, his brain destroyed by the ravages of syphilis. He spent the remaining seven years of his life in guarded isolation on Palm Island. He would never return to take up his rule in Chicago. "Al," said Jake Guzik, not unkindly, "is nutty as a fruitcake."

But though Capone had gone—at first to prison and then to death—his organization remained and flourished. There were successors who adapted to new times, men like Charley Fischetti, his brother Ralph, Jake Guzik, Nitti, Sam "Momo" Giancana and others. For soon after Capone departed, a new world began. Franklin Roosevelt entered the White House and the law that had made Capone and his era was about to die.

The Prohibition era in Chicago, which was to be the model upon which all the Hollywood movies of gangsters would be based, had, however, been an exception, and a garish one. There had been other men, particularly in the East and New York, who had seen the gold in illegal booze and seized it. But they had done so without the flair for violence that had marked Capone and eventually brought his end. They had adapted to changing times with greater circumspection and so would last longer. And it would be they who came through the world of the Twenties to lead crime into a new world of organization.

SLICING UP THE BIG APPLE

THERE ARE NO COMMEMORATIVE plaques on the benches in New York's Central Park, but maybe there ought to be. The nation's elder statesman Bernard Baruch sat on one of them for years, holding court, philosophizing, advising, handing down judgments that would influence the direction of the nation and the world. And just inside the southern boundary of the park on 59th Street, there is another bench where, during the decade after World War I, an underworld elder statesman, Arnold Rothstein, held court, listened to propositions, philosophized and handed down advice.

On a bright warm day in the early fall of 1920, relaxing on his favorite park bench, Rothstein came to a deci-sion that would send tremors down through the years. Prohibition had been the law of the land for nearly nine months, but it was clear that the law was barely enforceable. There weren't enough federal or state agents and many of them were easily bribed political hacks. And much of the nation, particularly the big cities, showed no inclination to stop drinking just because the law said to. People were drinking just as much, and many would soon be drinking even more. Only now, instead of patronizing a neighborhood saloon or a gilded night club, they were drinking in the thousands of speakeasies that had sprouted since January 17 and that, though illegal, made little pretense of being anything but what they were and opened their doors to anyone who knew the passwords—"Joe sent me." And now, instead of buying stock for their private bars from neighborhood package stores, they were patronizing the neighborhood bootlegger. For liquor and beer and wine were still available, but not from legitimate businessmen; gangsters had moved in and were selling booze "right off the boat"—which could mean that it really came right off the boat; or maybe from an illegal distillery; or was good stuff that had been cut, reblended and rebottled, watered down; or came from a homemade still and was only a little better than poison.

During these early months, Rothstein—millionaire gambler, swindler, loan shark, fixer, friend and confidant of politicians and gangsters—had made no move to cut himself in for a piece of the action. He was essentially a loner, a man who wanted to run his own show his own way. But bootlegging, he saw early, was just too big and too complex to be controlled by a single man, or even by a single organization. Rothstein, however, was wary of developing an organization of his own, because he didn't trust the intelligence or balance of the labor pool he would have to draw upon: the underworld. He understood that with hoodlums competing for control, violence was inevitable, and he was a man who abhorred violence in most circumstances. He had no desire to cross the federal authorities, for he was certain that they would make a major effort to enforce the law, at least at its outset.

So Rothstein stood aside and let others open up the business and take the initial risks. Some he financed, provided with bail and lawyers when they were arrested (and, as security, in addition to the usurious rate of interest a Rothstein loan entailed, anybody who borrowed from A. R. was forced to take out a noncancelable insurance policy, with Rothstein as the sole beneficiary). But that was all. However, he watched and examined and thought. By the fall, he was convinced it was time for him to make his move. All he needed was the opportunity.

It came on the warm day in Central Park. A Detroit bootlegger named Max "Big Maxey" Greenberg had been running Scotch and other good whiskey across the Detroit River from Canada since January and had done well enough to buy a fleet of trucks and open a string of warehouses. But the competition for good whiskey from Canada was increasing, driving the prices up. Most of Greenberg's money was tied up in the stock on hand, in his trucks and storage depots, when he was approached by a contact in Canada who could guarantee a continuing supply of good whiskey. To secure the deal, Greenberg needed $175,000; he didn't have it. He went to his friend Irving Wexler: thief, sometime dope peddler and strikebreaker, now seeking to become a bootlegger and winning a reputation under the name "Waxey" Gordon. If Gordon could come up with the money, Greenberg would cut him in as a partner. But in 1920—within a year,

Arnold Rothstein and Big Maxey Greenberg met in Central Park.

it would all change—Gordon didn't have that kind of bank roll. He knew someone who did, however: Arnold Rothstein. Gordon took Greenberg to meet Rothstein at his bench in Central Park.

Rothstein listened to Greenberg's pitch and questioned him closely, his mind moving far ahead. When Big Maxey had finished, Rothstein turned him down. But Rothstein came back with a counterproposal. It was stupid, he said, to buy booze in Canada at the high prices caused by competition.

The way to buy it was to tie up the production of whole distilleries right at the source, in England and Scotland. Greenberg was intrigued, but that would take a hell of a lot more than $175,000. Don't worry, Rothstein told him. He would make all the arrangements and would, instead of lending Greenberg the money in cash, cut him in for $175,000, taking as collateral his trucks and warehouses—thus giving Rothstein immediate transportation and storage facilities—and, of course, as much life insurance as Greenberg could take out. And, in lieu of a finder's fee, Waxey Gordon would be given a small percentage of the new partnership, and thus his hoped-for start in the business. Greenberg and Gordon agreed with alacrity.

Rothstein set about the bootleg business not on a chaotic and random basis, as did most other early entrants, but with an approach copied from big business. He sent Harry Mather, a former Wall Street bucket-shop operator who had done jobs for him in the past, to England as his European agent. Mather was to tie up the output of good Scotch distilleries and make arrangements for shipping the whiskey to a point just outside the American territorial waters in the Atlantic. Within weeks of his arrival, he had bought 20,000 cases of good Scotch and leased a Norwegian freighter to haul the stuff to a point off Long Island.

At home, Rothstein pulled together the other threads of the business. He bought half a dozen fast speedboats to carry the booze ashore and, to make certain it got there with no trouble, he bribed the Coast Guard at Montauk Point not merely to look the other way when the freighter arrived but actually to help unload it onto the speedboats and even to carry some of it ashore in government cutters. At the landing zone, he had the Greenberg trucks, protected by tough gunmen, and in Long Island City and other points around Manhattan, he leased warehouses to store the merchandise. And he cemented contracts both with other bootleggers and with the better speakeasies in midtown to purchase the Scotch.

During the next 12 months, Rothstein's Norwegian freighter made 11 trips carrying booze to the man who had suddenly become the most important dealer in illegal liquor in the East. But as the ship set sail on its 11th voyage, Rothstein was tipped that a new officer-in-charge had assumed command of the Coast Guard station at Montauk and was going to take the ship when it started to offload. Rothstein urgently signaled the ship, diverting it to Havana, where an agent of a sometime Rothstein partner, Charles A. Stoneham, sportsman and owner of the New York Giants baseball team, took delivery and managed to smuggle the whiskey into the States another way (though Rothstein's partners, Gordon and Greenberg, were told that Stoneham had bought the booze at cost, so there were no profits from the trip).

Though the final voyage of the Norwegian freighter had been turned from a potential loss into the usual profit of more than $500,000 for Rothstein, it gave the gambler pause. He had in a single year made several million dollars out of rum-running—or, in his case, Scotch-running—but buying abroad and waiting for a shipment to reach the States tied up a lot of ready cash for months, and if, by chance, that shipment happened to be picked off by the federal men, the money was irretrievably gone. There were, he figured, quicker and easier ways to turn Prohibition into a buck.

Speakeasies could be closed (left) but the day when the good old neighborhood bar (bottom) would be open again was coming closer and closer.

Gambling casinos floating offshore were also drinking palaces. Once in a while, there was a raid.

Also, in his year as a whiskey importer, Rothstein discovered what he had suspected: Bootlegging was just too big for one man to control. There were too many people in it, all with big ideas about their own roles and their own power; the competition was intense; he could not command events nor the actions of other people. This was not the game Arnold Rothstein liked to play, so he decided to get out—of importing, at least.

After the freighter's final trip, he called in Gordon and Greenberg to tell them that it had been profitless —for them. And he told them he was quitting the racket; the business would be theirs after they paid up what they owed him, plus the usual high interest. They paid readily enough and without complaint. Then Gordon, with Greenberg receding into a secondary role as junior partner and aide, pyramided what Rothstein had started, becoming one of the leading illegal liquor importers along the Atlantic Seaboard and one of the biggest overall bootleggers in the East. By the end of the decade, he would be a multimillionaire, would own blocks of real estate in New York and Philadelphia, where he centered his empire, would live in a castle complete with moat in southern New Jersey, would own a fleet of ocean-going rum-ships, night clubs, gambling casinos. His Philadelphia distilleries would be cutting, reblending and rebottling booze for scores of other major bootleggers around the country for a share of their action.

But Rothstein, although no longer importing, was not completely out of booze. In his year in the business, he had put together an efficient organization, and while much of it had been turned over to Gordon, Rothstein was not willing to let it all go. He owned pieces of some of the best speakeasies and he held onto them, turning their back rooms into lavish gambling casinos. And he had in his employ a killer named John T. Noland, who adopted the name Legs Diamond (the Legs from his speed in fleeing from the cops during his petty-thieving days). With his brother Eddie, Diamond had worked for Rothstein as a strikebreaker and, when Rothstein moved into liquor, as a guard for the trucks. Now Diamond came to Rothstein with a new proposition. While a number of big and tough outfits were coming to the top in the bootleg business, the highways were still filled with hundreds of amateurs trying to make a quick buck. They had little power or little ability to retaliate if they ran into trouble. Diamond wanted Rothstein to turn him loose to prey on these amateurs; he and Eddie and their gang would hijack the trucks and turn the booze over to Rothstein to dispose of. Since Rothstein was into both wholesale and retail outlets for booze, he bought the idea and financed the Diamonds.

For a couple of years, it worked well. But by 1924, the amateurs were giving way more and more to the tough professional gangs. With soft targets scarce, Diamond went against Rothstein's orders and began to try his luck hijacking the professionals. One of those he picked on was William V. "Big Bill" Dwyer, an Irish ex-stevedore who, in partnership with a rising Italian mobster named Frank Costello, had moved to the top in the illegal liquor-importing business. Dwyer was the wrong guy to take on. He went to Rothstein and told him to call off Diamond or it would be open season on the hijacker. Rothstein, who was becoming weary of Diamond's penchant for violence, anyway, and of the whole uncontrollable bootleg racket, informed Dwyer that Diamond was running on his own and he wouldn't mind at all if Dwyer put a stop to him. Dwyer tried: In October of 1924, as Diamond drove down Fifth Avenue, a car pulled up alongside and pumped a load of shotgun shells at Diamond. Somehow, Legs received only minor wounds. Diamond, who would become one of New York's most conspicuous and flamboyant hoods, couldn't understand it. "I don't have an enemy in the world," he said. But the shots had their effect; The Diamond mob fell apart; Legs became little more than a feared outlaw among outlaws, everybody's target, who managed to escape both upper- and underworld retribution until 1931, when he was finally gunned down.

The shedding of Diamond was Rothstein's last direct involvement in bootlegging. He decided to let others take all the risks and remain, himself, strictly a peripheral figure. He would bankroll those who needed money at the usual high interest rates. He would, for a price, use his political muscle, which went to the top of Tammany Hall in the person of his close friend boss Charley Murphy and his heirs, to put the fix in when a bootlegger was arrested (and the fix was good; during the Rothstein years, of the 6902 liquor cases that went before the New York courts, 400 never went to trial and 6074 were dismissed).

Legs Diamond was one of the best known and most colorful hoodlums of the period. His girl-friend Kiki Roberts (page 68) was also fairly colorful but prettier. Legs became famous for surviving serious bullet wounds but someone finally hit the jackpot (bottom).

By the middle of the decade, Rothstein's importance in bootlegging was almost at an end. He had always wanted to be the top man in whatever he did, and that just wasn't possible in booze (and besides, he used to point out to friends, he himself didn't drink). He gradually turned his energies back to his first love, gambling—owning casinos and staying involved in some perpetual card game. His loan-sharking continued to prosper; he went heavily into jewel smuggling, a thriving business in good times, when the wives of the *nouveaux riches* were trading all their loose change for sparkling gems; and, in the last years of his life, he became more and more involved in narcotics; then a small but expanding business, sending his agent to Europe and the Near East to make purchases and supplying the big dealers in the underworld with the junk. In November of 1928, after welshing on losses of more than $300,000 in a card game, Rothstein's life came to an end; he was fatally shot at the Park Central Hotel on New York's Seventh Avenue (no one was convicted of the crime). In another couple of days, he could have paid off his losses with a flourish: He had bet heavily on victories for Herbert Hoover in the presidential election and Franklin Roosevelt in the New York gubernatorial race and when they won, he stood to collect nearly $600,000; further, even without those bets, there had been no need for Rothstein to welsh, for the initial accounting of his assets revealed an estate of about $3,000,000. And if he had really been tight, there were scores of friends in the underworld who would gladly have come up with the money for him.

As the years passed, Rothstein's influence remained strong and he was constantly sought for advice; the philosopher of the underworld, constantly preaching cooperation and the most limited use of force, unconcerned with ethnic or religious ties, but only with intelligence, imagination, ambition and nerve—he made use of anyone who could help him, unlike most underworld leaders, who seemed unable to break free of traditional ties and suspicions—Rothstein had drawn into his orbit all those who would lead the underworld in the years ahead. His ideas would influence their thinking and their actions.

IN THE FIRST YEARS OF PROHIBI-tion, three young hoodlums, then little more than hungry thugs, had been drawn into the Rothstein circle and were changed forever. They were a Calabrian named Francesco Castiglia, a Sicilian named Salvatore Lucania and a Polish Jew named Maier Suchowljansky. They would become infamous as Frank Costello, Charlie "Lucky" Luciano and Meyer Lansky.

Born in 1891 in Cosenza in the south of Italy, Costello was the oldest. He arrived in New York at the age of four and settled in the Italian community in East Harlem, where, though considered one of the neighborhood's brightest boys, he took to the streets after finishing elementary school and became leader of the 104th Street Gang, a bunch of young Italian hoodlums. Afflicted early with throat trouble—the result of a slipshod operation to remove tonsils and adenoids when a child—he never spoke much above a rasping whisper and that soft voice seemed to lend added authority and importance to whatever he had to say. In these early years, he was considered one of the toughest young hoodlums in the area. By the time he was 21, he had been twice arrested and twice freed on charges of assault and robbery. In 1915, though, at the age of 24, he went to prison for the first time—and it would be 37 years before he would see the inside of a cell again. He was convicted of carrying a gun and sentenced to a year. Released from prison, Costello promptly took up his old life. And he renewed a friendship he had made a year or so earlier, with Luciano, and teamed up with him in a steady parade of burglaries, robberies and other crimes. With Prohibition, his world and his outlook altered. For many Italians at that time, it would have been unthinkable to form close friendships and lasting partnerships with Jews like Rothstein, Lansky, Dandy Phil Kastel and others, with Irishmen like Big Bill Dwyer, even with Sicilians like Luciano. But Costello was an unusual man, unconcerned with background; he had married a Jewish girl named Loretta and would remain married to her for more than half a century, until his death.

Six years younger than Costello, Luciano was born in the poverty-stricken sulphur-mining town of Lecara Friddi in the Palermo district of Sicily. He had been brought to New York in 1906, where his family settled on the Lower East Side, in a district teeming not only with Sicilians and Italians but with Jews as well. His formal education, like that of most of the mobsters, ended with elementary school, though while there, he developed a racket he would later use to earn millions: He sold, for a penny or two a day, his personal protection to the younger and smaller Jewish kids who were being waylaid and beaten on their way to and from school. In the streets, Luciano was soon leading a gang of young Sicilian toughs through their ghetto. It was not long before he graduated to bigger things and was pushing narcotics, just becoming an underworld money-maker with the enactment of the Harrison Act, which ended the legal narcotics trade and forced thousands of people who had become addicted to legal opium-based patent medicines to turn—as Prohibition would cause drinkers to turn—to an illegal market to support their habit. In 1916, Luciano's career as a pusher came to a sudden end; he was arrested and sent to prison for a year—it would be 20 years before he would be in jail again. Back on the streets, he reassumed the leadership of his gang, teamed up with Costello and was soon joined, as well, by Lansky. As his reputation as a neighborhood tough with imagination grew, he came to the attention of older, powerful underworld leaders,

Francesco Castiglia,
better known as Frank Costello.

particularly those of the Sicilian Mafia. What set Luciano apart from most of his Sicilian friends were driving ambition, considerable native intelligence and shrewdness and little prejudice or suspicion of outsiders. He recognized the value of brains as well as courage. At a young age, he became a close friend of Lansky's and would remain his friend and partner almost until the end of his life.

Lansky was the youngest. He was born in 1902 in Grodno, in the Polish Pale of Settlement, then under Russian rule, and brought to New York's Lower East Side, with his younger brother, Jake, in 1911. Although he was small as a child and as an adult

would never stand more than a few inches above five feet, Lansky was, nevertheless, tough and belligerent, good with any weapon and seemingly always in the middle of a fight. While his education ended with the eighth grade, he was something of a mathematical prodigy; he combined this with mechanical aptitude, a penchant he shared with Luciano. Wherever he went, he was trailed by a taller, handsomer and four-years-younger Jewish kid named Benjamin Siegel, nicknamed Bugsy. The two were a team and would remain so, the leaders of a gang of young Jewish hoodlums. But when it was time to graduate from petty larceny into more daring and violent crimes, Lansky, with Siegel at his elbow, looked for those with brains, cunning and ambition to match his own. He found them in the older Costello and Luciano.

It was Prohibition that gave them, as it gave so many others, the chance to move up from the small time. And it was Rothstein who showed them the way. In recruiting strong arms and guns to protect Rothstein liquor shipments, Legs Diamond had, on occasion, made use of the services of Costello, Luciano, Lansky and their friends, and in so doing, he opened the door to the master. They knew Rothstein by reputation, knew that he was a man from whom they could learn what could never be discovered in the streets. And Rothstein had enough ego to be flattered by their respect and by their willingness to listen, ask questions, follow his advice. They were his pupils and he taught them well. He lectured constantly on the need for organization; free-lancers in the rackets were only looking for trouble, were always weak and at the mercy of the stronger, whether from the world outside or from the underworld. In organization (though he himself had always shunned it; what applied to others did not necessarily apply to him, he was sure), there was the strength and the ability to go after what was too big for the single man.

But Rothstein's ideas about organization far exceeded those commonly understood and practiced in the underworld. As they stood, he said, the gangs were ridiculous; ethnic exclusivity and rivalry were both stupid and wasteful. Make use of the best, organize the best, make alliances with anyone who could help, and to hell with where they came from. Look around at the way big businesses were run and copy their methods. That, Rothstein insisted, went beyond just selection of personnel, hiring and training of specialists, departmentalization and diversification, prudent use of money and time. It went to the creation of an image. Prohibition was giving the gangster an opportunity that might never come again, a chance to walk at least part way through the door to respectability and a measure of social acceptance as a good businessman, dealing in an illegal commodity, certainly, but a businessman nevertheless. All this could be blown if the image was only a grosser and richer reflection of the old portrait of the gangster. Let Capone and his Chi-

cago contemporaries dress garishly, flaunt their wealth and power openly, becoming the objects not merely of public fear but of public derision and amusement as well. The outward façade won more than half the battle, according to Rothstein, and he pointed to himself as an example. His pupils—and they followed his advice—should look only like the successful businessmen they were; they should dress in good clothes, but clothes from the same tailors and in the same conservative styles as the Wall Street bankers'; they should watch social leaders and ape their manners and their style; they should live quietly and conservatively, giving little indication of their wealth or power. They should avoid public display, notoriety or publicity as much as possible, remain in the background and let the light shine on somebody else, for when the light shone, so, too, did the heat. Look at Johnny Torrio; he had practiced these rules, had amassed great power and wealth, but few seemed even to know his name, while everybody knew Capone's, and this would eventually be Capone's undoing.

Rothstein also lectured on the limited use of force. And he taught them one thing more: Survival was dependent on alliances with those in political power. Cultivate them assiduously. Rothstein had the key to the doors, he would open them and let them through.

Beyond those doors, the young gangsters discovered a changed world. As money from booze poured

New York Mayor John O'Brien (left) made things easy for Tammany Boss James J. Hines (right).

into their pockets, they no longer had to seek favors from Tammany Hall; now Tammany leaders came to them, and so did the police; they could buy and own Tammany, and much more.

Using these contacts, Costello managed to corrupt the political world of New York even more than it had been corrupted before. He had already begun to make a number of contacts with contemporaries who had become ward leaders, and now, through Rothstein's influence, he widened his scope, began to forge deals with Tammany, with city hall,

with the police department that would, by the end of the decade, pour more than $100,000,000 a year in graft into official pockets up and down the line and would give the gangsters free rein to operate almost any racket in the city.

The moves to capture the allegiance of the politicians could not have come at a more opportune time for the racketeers. For Tammany was embroiled in a struggle for power. Boss Charley Murphy was coming to the end of his long rule; he would die in 1924. The heirs apparent were greedy, venal and eminently corruptible. They were James J. Hines, out of the traditional mold of Irish Tammany bosses. He had come up the long political ladder, and the closer he came to reaching his goal of power and wealth, the more desperate he became to achieve it, seeking support wherever he could find it. He bought the assistance of, and eventually sold himself to, almost every Irish mobster in the city.

Hines's chief rival was the first Italian to drive a wedge into the once solid Irish suzerainty over Tammany. He was Albert C. Marinelli. As Hines sought support, strong arms and votes from the Irish underworld, Marinelli turned to the Italian.

The struggle between Hines and Marinelli intensified and when Murphy died, the other powers in the Hall, rather than throwing in behind one or the other and so alienating the loser, turned to George W. Olvany as their new leader. But Olvany was a weak mediocrity who made little use of his power. So the struggle between Hines and Marinelli continued. Arnold Rothstein was friend to both, and to Olvany as well, and soon Costello became their friend and their benefactor, too. In the process, the Hall fell completely to the underworld. Before the end of the decade, both Hines and Marinelli not only would be on the payroll of the underworld that supported them but would also be partners with underworld leaders in some of their ventures—Hines with, among others, one Arthur Flegenheimer who adopted the name Dutch Schultz, and Marinelli with "Joe the Boss" Masseria, Luciano, Costello and others. As Tammany capitulated, so did the rest of the city's official complex, which took its cue from Tammany. Mayors, district attorneys, police commissioners and others would all be dependent on the underworld, afraid to move without first getting clearance from the organization. By 1932, a new mayor, John Patrick O'Brien, would tell the press when asked who his new police commissioner was going to be, "I haven't had any word on that yet." By that, he meant the word from Hines, Marinelli and the underworld.

Though there were parellels between New York and the Chicago of Torrio and Capone, there were also decided differences. Torrio had fallen victim to the violence that marked the Chicago scene, had been forced to flee for his life, leaving behind the brutality of Capone and a city strewn with the bodies of Dion O'Banion, Hymie Weiss, the victims of Saint Valentine's Day and hundreds more. The city had become a war zone, its street corners battlegrounds, its gutters often rivers of blood; Torrio's dicta of cooperation and peace were forgotten.

Such, though, was not the fate of New York. Perhaps the barons competing for power, most of whom had come under the Rothstein influence at one time or another, had listened and paid close attention to his words. Perhaps, too, New York was just too big for any one man or organization to control and there was a recognition of this simple truth. For whatever reasons, the city itself escaped the kind of ravages that filled Chicago. There were shoot-outs. Dutch Schultz was not above putting his enemies to a violent end, often in public and personally. In the early Thirties, he was embroiled in a running war with the young Irish killer Vincent "Mad Dog" Coll, in which the body count ran up to a score or more. Louis "Lepke" Buchalter's guns were often busy in the Garment District of Manhattan, where he was moving in on the rackets. Legs Diamond's count was high. Bootleggers had a nasty penchant for knocking one another over. Frankie Yale, the Brooklyn bootlegger–killer–

Unione Siciliane president, was cut down in his car on 44th Street in Brooklyn in 1928 by a submachine gun (the first time that weapon, a standby in the Chicago gang wars, was used in New York), but his killers, it turned out, had been sent from Chicago by Capone to pay off Yale for some double-crosses on liquor shipments.

But the body count in New York never matched Chicago's, even though the New York underworld was proportionately much larger. And though the city itself was the scene of many of the killings, there was a kind of circumspection about

Frankie Yale's funeral in New York was properly dignified but not as lavish as some Chicago productions.

New York did have its share of small-time hoods shot down in beer wars.

the murders. Most took place in lonely ambushes, in sparsely populated restaurants or speakeasies, on streets where there were few people about, at night, on back roads during a hijacking or after a one-way ride. The warfare, unlike Chicago's, tended to be private. The public was rarely involved, seldom caught in street-corner cross fire.

By the middle of the Twenties, the bootleg business in New York had been left to the strongest, and despite sometimes sudden and violent confrontations, they managed to cut the city up among themselves and maintain the power within their own provinces to repel attempted invasions. Aside from the older *mafiosi,* who were just emerging into the world at large, the bootleg rulers were mostly young, still in their twenties when Prohibition arrived and, if they survived the violent decade, only into their middle thirties when it ended. Though they were often rivals and bitter ones, they were often, too, friends and allies on a temporary or even a semipermanent basis. Their comparable ages and great ambitions both drove them apart and, particularly in the later struggles with the older gangsters from another generation, brought them together. Binding them, too, were common interests in turning Prohibition into wealth, and the lessons of Arnold Rothstein. Later, all this would enable many of them to work closely together to forge a national Syndicate that would make the underworld an organized business.

The Bronx was the realm of Dutch Schultz, a name he was later to regret: "It was short enough to fit in the headlines," he complained. "If I'd kept the name Flegenheimer, nobody would have heard of me." He was only 18 when Prohibition became law, but he had already served a prison term for unlawful entry (his rap sheet would eventually list 13 arrests, for every crime from disorderly conduct to homicide). Tough and merciless, Schultz fought his way to the top in his borough, eventually bossing an empire that would include liquor and beer, speakeasies, numbers, protection and assorted other rackets and would earn him millions every year. But Schultz was a miser. He paid those who worked for him as little as possible and would rage when anyone

had the temerity to ask for a raise; Otto "Abbadabba" Berman, a human computer who handled all Schultz's financial details and even worked out a method to rig the numbers so the payoff from the policy racket would be more astronomical than usual, had to threaten to take his valuable services elsewhere before Schultz agreed to pay him $10,000 a week.

Schultz never spent more than two dollars for a shirt or $35 for a suit, and rarely had them cleaned. "You take silk shirts, now," he once said. "I think only queers wear silk shirts. I never bought one in my life. Only a sucker will pay fifteen or twenty dollars for a silk shirt."

As Luciano, a meticulous dresser, later said, "Dutch was the cheapest guy I ever knew. The guy had a couple of million bucks and he dressed like a pig, and he worried about spending two cents for a newspaper. That was his big spending, buying the papers, so's he could read about himself."

But for all his parsimony, Schultz was willing to spend money to solidify, expand and protect his empire. He took Jimmy Hines in as a partner, thereby not only gaining Tammany's protection but also buying a piece of it. And he bought himself a piece of the Bronx Democratic organization, too, becoming such a power that boss Edward J. Flynn (later to be a major dispenser of patronage for Roosevelt), when sheriff of the borough in 1925, made Schultz a deputy sheriff. And Schultz, like all who rose to power, was merciless with his enemies; they had a way of dying or disappearing.

Thus, the Dutchman became the strong man of the Bronx and later, when he muscled in on policy, of part of Harlem as well.

Brooklyn was more populous and thus more profitable, so no man could hold complete suzerainty there. Until his death, Frankie Yale, with his base in the Unione, a tight organization, and his early entrance into rumrunning, had a major slice. Another slice belonged to a bright Jewish boy who aspired to culture and a more genteel life and thought the way to get it was through the riches of illegal booze, and who spread out from the Jewish ghetto into more of Brooklyn. His name was Abner "Longy" Zwillman. As the competition in the borough intensified, Zwillman, while maintaining a hold there, saw more riches and less trouble in the outlying districts and began to branch out into then-sparsely populated Queens and beyond into Long Island's Nassau County. He crossed the Hudson River to northern New Jersey, where he linked up with a rising young Italian mobster named Willie Moretti, who sometimes went by the more Anglo-Saxon name of Willie Moore. Together they controlled bootlegging in their province and moved into gambling with a string of back-room casinos that stretched down the Hudson from Fort Lee, directly across the river from Manhattan and easily reachable then by ferry. Through Moretti and growing out of his own bootlegging, Zwillman met and became friends and partners with his contemporaries, Luciano, Lansky, Costello and the rest.

Brooklyn, in the mid-Twenties, was becoming more and more a territory the young Italian gangsters were looking on as their own. A handsome young Italian named Joseph Doto—who took a name to match his good looks and vanity, Joe Adonis, or, to his friends, Joe A.—moved in from his original Manhattan base. The waterfront was gradually coming under the influence of a tough killer named Albert Anastasia, and a young and rising *mafioso* named Vincent Mangano was moving up in the wake of Frankie Yale.

But the real power and the real big money lay in Manhattan, which was split up a dozen ways among a dozen groups. In Harlem, just beginning to fill with blacks but still Italian ground, Ciro Terranova, a Mafia leader, gave the orders; in Little Italy in Lower Manhattan, other *mafiosi*, those who would be called the Mustache Petes—Joe Masseria, Salvatore Maranzano and others—controlled all the rackets, terrorized the people, warred on one another and were just beginning to edge into the outer world, a world still foreign to them and their methods.

The rest of the island, the world of the middle and upper classes, was the realm of the young mobsters who could adapt to this society and could deal with it on its terms. Costello, Luciano, Lansky and Siegel (soon joined by Adonis) worked closely together in midtown. They supplied good whiskey to the best speakeasies and to the best people and they cut themselves in for pieces of many of the speaks they serviced. They

Joseph Doto thought he was too good looking for such an ordinary name so he changed it to Joe Adonis.

worked together and they worked with others. Needing regular sources of supply, they struck up deals with Waxey Gordon, Max "Boo-Boo" Hoff and Harry Stromberg, alias Nig Rosen, who had become the bootleg powers in Philadelphia, a city vital to their success, for there Gordon and his friends ran a string of distilleries where domestic liquor was produced and imported whiskey was cut, reblended and rebottled. They came to arrangements with Enoch "Nucky" Johnson, the boss of Atlantic City, whose resort community was one of the prime landing zones for the imported stuff, and with Charles "King" Solomon of Boston, whose port was constantly busy unloading booze. In search of supplies to keep their growing list of thirsty customers happy, they bought from the Cleveland powers—Moe Dalitz, Morris Kleinman, Sam Tucker and Louis Rothkopf—

who were running a regular ferry service across Lake Erie from Canada. Lansky, as treasurer of the group in addition to other activities, was often dispatched on quick trips around the country to seek out new alliances and new sources of supply. He also went to Nassau, Bermuda, the other British islands and Cuba to tie up whiskey supplies there and to strike the toughest bargains, something at which he proved singularly adept.

Adonis, in partnership with Luciano and the others, put together what was called the Broadway Mob. Its territory was the great center of Manhattan and its clients were the class speakeasies—such places as Jack and Charlie's "21" Club, Jack White's, the Silver Slipper, Sherman Billingsley's Stork Club and the rest. In some they had a personal investment, to all they supplied only the best whiskey, "right off the boat"—which meant from Gordon's distilleries, from distilleries they took over, from their other sources, but not the rotgut that was being turned out in the thousands of stills in East Harlem, Little Italy and elsewhere. Not satisfied with only Manhattan, though, Adonis also branched out into Brooklyn and, backed by the growing reputations and might of his associates, was soon entrenched there. And he followed another pursuit that was to entrance him all his life: He became one of the master jewel thieves of the era.

Costello, meanwhile, was ubiquitous. Quiet, dignified, radiating success and power, he became the go-between for the underworld and the Tammany politicians, succeeding Rothstein in that role. But pulling the strings of politics was only one Costello role. Backed by a $40,000 loan from Rothstein, Costello went into partnership with Big Bill Dwyer as a rumrunner. By the middle of the decade, both had become millionaires. The government would charge Dwyer with evading more than $2,000,000 in taxes in just two years—taxes, that is, and not income. The partnership broke up in 1925, when both were indicted for bribery and rumrunning. Costello beat the rap and rose steadily upward; Dwyer, however, was convicted and sent to the federal prison in Atlanta. When he emerged, he decided to go straight, becoming a renowned sportsman who brought professional hockey to New York, opened race tracks around the country, in-

Burlesque houses, even the cleaned-up kind, were good anonymous meeting places for the Mob.

cluding Tropical Park near Miami, and eventually settled down in Miami to a life of rich respectability. But Dwyer's departure signaled more than the end of a single man; it also marked the end of an era; the influence of the Irish as leading underworld figures in New York went with him, and the Italians and the Jews now moved to the fore.

Dwyer, though, was only one of Costello's partners. Costello teamed up in brewery and bootlegging enterprises with Owney "The Killer" Madden, an English-born gunman who had served a term in Sing Sing for murder. Suave and smart, Madden was eventually sent down to Hot Springs, Arkansas, to oversee the Mob's growing interests in that wide-open resort town.

And Costello was into more. With a former Rothstein Wall Street operator and swindler named Dandy Phil Kastel, he branched out into gambling, gaining a near monopoly on the punchboards that infested every candy store in town, and the two soon secured a monopoly over the abundant slot machines. Later, Kastel would oversee the Costello interests in New Orleans.

Inseparable in these years, Lansky and Siegel not only worked closely with their friends and partners but also took off from the Legs Diamond trade. Bringing together the toughest Jewish hoods they could round up, they formed the Bugs and Meyer Mob. With their cars and guns, they were the protection service for the group's booze shipments, and they

were its hijacking arm. Selling their services to the highest noncompeting bidders on a free-lance basis, they would protect or hijack—it didn't matter which. The quality of their service was exceptional, but the price was high and soon, rather than paying Bugs and Meyer, many a bootlegger decided it would be a lot simpler and cheaper just to cut them in as partners. But they soon discovered that they were getting more than Lansky and Siegel as partners; they were getting Adonis, Costello and Luciano, too, which often meant that the original owners became servants or were forced out altogether.

To those who watched closely, it became evident that Luciano was emerging as the leader among these equals and as one of the rising young powers in the underworld. Behind Adonis in the Broadway Mob, there was Luciano. He had his own bootlegging going, too. He was involved with Costello in almost everything Costello did, and with Lansky and Siegel. He was in partnership with Zwillman and Moretti in a number of their deals and had a partnership, too, with Gordon. Schultz was his friend and, at times, partner. In the Garment District, he was working with Lepke and Lepke's strong gun, Jacob "Gurrah" Shapiro, and with the rising young Thomas Lucchese, known as Three Finger Brown, in union and management protection rackets, loansharking and all the rest. There seemed to be hardly an area of crime in Manhattan in which Luciano was not involved in some way. As his power and stature increased, he was wooed intensively by the competing Mafia rulers, particularly by Masseria and Maranzano. Though he worked at times with one and then the other, cooperated with them when need be, he delayed until late in the decade making the decision to join one. Before he would become an underling, even second man, he wanted his own power to be substantial enough to allow him to set the terms of a merger. And during this period of his rise, his power base lay in his partnerships with Costello, Adonis, Lansky and Siegel, in his dealings with the other young princelings.

THE LONGER PROHIBITION LASTED, the deeper seemed to become the thirst of Americans. Prices kept going up, both in the domestic market and at foreign sources of supply. Competition for those supplies among rival bootleggers intensified. In order to keep the customers happy, in order just to keep them, the bootlegger had to be able to fill his orders promptly and at a competitive price. In a time of mounting demand, this was not always easy. Through 1926 and 1927, hijackings increased sharply, and so did the almost concomitant casualties. Lansky might go to Nassau and buy all he needed from the Bay Street Boys, but there was increasing danger that somewhere between Atlantic City and the Philadelphia distilleries, or somewhere between the distilleries and the point of delivery, the ship-

ment might be hijacked. A deal could be struck with Dalitz and his Cleveland friends, with the Reinfelds, Bronfmans, and Rosenstiels in Canada, but there was no guarantee that the vital whiskey would ever reach its destination. The Bugs and Meyer Mob was constantly on the road, protecting the shipments of the partners, hijacking those of competitors. But this was a dangerous and costly game, cutting into the profits and the personnel and potentially bringing the East to the edge of a Chicagolike war. In a number of Eastern cities, the realization that there had to be a better way seemed to strike almost simultaneously.

Rothstein had always preached the absolute necessity of cooperation. So, too, had Torrio, his contemporary and his intellectual equal. Now Torrio was back from Italy; he had discovered that the climate there was nearly as treacherous as in Chicago, for Mussolini had declared that he was going to round up any American hoodlums he found in Italy and lock them in cages for public display before giving them what they deserved. Torrio packed his bags and set sail for home. In New York, he immediately renewed his contacts with his old underworld friends and promptly began to echo the Rothstein line that competition was bad for business and so was violence—just look at Capone in Chicago.

But what Rothstein and Torrio were talking about was not just cooperation among the gangs of a single city like New York. That would come eventually and was eminently desirable and should be worked for, but at the moment, it was only partially practical; the rivalries—ethnic, religious and generational—were just too deep to bring about more than a temporary truce. The cooperation they saw as attainable was sectional and, ultimately, national. Instead of everybody from every city competing with one another in search of booze, there should be some sort of merger. At the very least, a central buying office should be established that would take the orders from everyone, buy in huge quantities and, since there would be no competition, at reduced prices, then make sure everyone got his allocation. The buying office would make its purchases in Canada, England, the West Indies, from domestic distilleries, everywhere; it would make the shipping arrangements and handle trucking schedules. A member from every group that joined would serve on a kind of central committee to make sure that nobody got shortchanged. This kind of cooperation would benefit everybody; it would guarantee that every member got all the booze he needed at reasonable prices; it would sharply cut down on the number of hijackings, since they wouldn't be hijacking one another's shipments anymore and, in combination, their guns would be numerous enough to turn back any outsiders who tried.

At the end of 1927, that organization came into being. It was called the Seven Group—not a group of seven men but a group of powers. Its charter members included Luciano and Costello from Manhattan; Lansky and Siegel, the enforcers; Adonis from Manhattan and Brooklyn; Zwillman from Brooklyn, Long Island and northern New Jersey; Nucky Johnson from Atlantic City; Waxey Gordon and Nig Rosen from Philadelphia; and Torrio, as counselor, advisor, elder statesman and as a major underworld power in his own right. From this central core, alliances were formed with King Solomon in Boston, Danny Walsh in Providence, Moe Dalitz and his associates in Cleveland. Within the year, more than 22 gangs, from Maine to Florida and westward to the Mississippi River, were linked to the Seven Group and much of the bloody competition that had marked the first eight years of Prohibition came to an end (except in Chicago, which wrote its own special story for the decade) and the first tentative steps had been taken toward an interlocking criminal alliance of national scope.

But the underworld does not act in a vacuum unaffected by outside events. And there were some disturbing omens for anyone who thought that Prohibition had an unlimited future. Now that bootlegging was beginning to emerge from chaotic competition into monopolistic organization with increasing profits and peace for all, the realization began to seep in that Prohibition itself might be only a temporary national aberration, that liquor might well become legal again. The signs were there. Governor Al Smith of New York had for years made no secret of his disdain for the drys, his absolute conviction that Prohibition not only wasn't working but was actually deleterious to the nation. Now, in 1928, the Democrats nominated Smith to run for president against the Republican Herbert Hoover, and Smith carried his demand for an end to the noble experiment across ·the nation. In November, Hoover trounced Smith badly, but the reasons for the defeat were many—not just Smith's wetness. He was a Catholic in a Protestant country; he was a city boy—a Lower East Side New York City boy, at that, with the cigar, derby and accent—in a still essentially rural country; and he was a Democrat running against a Republican, and the Republicans had brought the nation eight years of unparralleled prosperity and good times.

But the indications were clear that Smith's demand for repeal of the 18th Amendment had not been rejected as fully as he himself. Indeed, if anything happened to the economy— and in the months before his murder, Rothstein was telling friends that he saw some very disturbing signs on Wall Street and around the country; farmers weren't doing well, he said, and were going broke, and trouble on the farms was eventually going to reach the cities; and, further, Wall Street was beginning to look to him like one big bucket shop, and he knew from experience that bucket shops could go on for only so long before collapsing—nobody was going to be able to stand in the way of the people's getting a legal drink. "Boys,"

Torrio told his friends in New York soon after the election, "we'd better start planning. I give Prohibition another four, maybe five years."

But planning for a new and unknown future was a vast and complex undertaking, far beyond the scope of a single organization. In the underworld in those months, there was increasing talk of the desirability of a national conference of underworld leaders, especially of those who had emerged with Prohibition and so were young enough to expect to lead crime into this unexplored territory. The proposals went around the nation and by early spring of 1929, there was unanimous agreement that such a conference ought to be held, and soon. Dalitz and his friends in Cleveland—which had been the scene of smaller meetings—offered to be the hosts. But the Cleveland cops, though on the pad, had developed the annoying tendency of picking up suspicious out-of-town mobsters they happened to spot and throwing them in the can for a few hours. Any major influx of out-of-towners would certainly mean a great deal of undesirable publicity and harassment. Dalitz's offer was politely declined. Then Nucky Johnson offered the sanctuary of his bastion in Atlantic City. What could be safer? Johnson ruled the town like a personal fiefdom. And, besides, if the conference were held at the beginning of the holiday season, when thousands were flocking to the seaside resort, who would notice a few extra visitors, even very rich ones?

On May 13, 1929, in their huge

limousines, with chauffeurs and armed bodyguards to protect them, the delegates began arriving, taking over the President Hotel on the boardwalk. Capone came from Chicago and brought along his financial advisor and, some thought, the real brains in his outfit, Jake "Greasy Thumb" Guzik. King Solomon drove down personally from Boston and Nig Rosen and Boo-Boo Hoff came up

from Philadelphia. From Cleveland there were Moe Dalitz, Lou Rothkopf and Chuck Polizzi (his real name was Leo Berkowitz; an orphan, he had been raised by the Polizzi family and had adopted its name; with his adopted cousin, Big Al Polizzi, he would become one of the leading Cleveland mobsters, the man who could deal with and be accepted by both the Jewish and the Italian or-

Governor Al Smith did not make it to the White House but his demand for repeal of the 18th Amendment worried the leaders of the underworld.

ganizations). The Detroit Purple Gang sent a large delegation headed by its boss, Abe Bernstein. Boss Tom Pendergast of Kansas City couldn't take time off to attend personally, but he sent a surrogate, John Lazia. Zwillman was there as the northern New Jersey power. And from New York came the largest and most prestigious delegation of all. It included Torrio; Luciano; Costello; Lepke; Adonis; Schultz; one of Costello's partners in the gambling and bookmaking business, Frank Erickson; Lansky, using the occasion to celebrate his honeymoon with his new bride, Anna Citron; Vince Mangano; Frank Scalise, a Brooklyn *mafioso;* and Albert Anastasia.

There were, however, some very prominent absentees, including Masseria, whose Mafia organization Luciano and Costello had finally thrown in with, on their terms, about a year earlier, with Luciano emerging as the number-two man to Masseria; and Salvatore Maranzano, who was still in bitter competition with Joe the Boss for Mafia rule. In fact, the list of delegates included not a single one of the older Mafia rulers around the nation, those the younger generation scorned as Mustache Petes. Perhaps, if invited, they would not have come, for they disdained outsiders, were suspicious to the extreme of anything they didn't know or understand, and this meeting was swarming with Jews and other non-Sicilians. But their very absence permitted Luciano, Costello, Adonis, Lansky and the others to form friendships and forge alliances that would, in a few years, propel them to the top of the new organization of the underworld and would spell doom for those who stayed away, uninvited.

The Atlantic City conference lasted three days, intermingling gaiety—Nucky Johnson was a lavish host, providing carloads of steaks, good whiskey, high-priced entertainers and a never-ending parade of willing girls—and serious business discussions. Rest periods found the gangsters strolling along the beach with their trousers rolled up around their knees, their shoes and socks in their hands, their feet washed by the lapping surf of the Atlantic Ocean.

For the first time in the history of American crime, the major leaders of the underworld were not only gathered in peaceful enclave but were looking to, and planning for, the future. The success of the Seven Group was held up as a model, and there was general agreement that as long as Prohibition lasted, this was the way to go; from that time on, there would be cooperation all across the nation in buying and dealing booze, an end to cut-throat competition. When Prohibition ended, as all were now convinced it would, there was the possibility of going legit. Money would be set aside for that day. Breweries, distilleries and liquor-import franchises would be bought and the control of liquor would remain right where it had been during the dry years. "After all," Luciano said, "who knew more about the liquor business than us?"

But going completely legitimate

was something, of course, that nobody at Atlantic City ever contemplated. Even with liquor out of the way, there were myriad other illegitimate enterprises into which they could move, and there were enterprises they were already in that could be expanded sufficiently to take up some of the slack. Some were strictly local, such as protection and union busting, even policy and other forms of minor gambling. While they were certain to grow, each outfit would handle its own without interference. But there were some that could easily mushroom on a national scale, require the cooperation and alliance of every organization and might end up even bigger than booze. Gambling was the major one, in casinos of all kinds and on horses and any other kind of sporting event. If Americans liked to do anything better than drink (putting sex aside, though sex, through the control of strings of cathouses, was still a good business for many), it was to gamble. And except on horses and then only at the tracks, gambling in most places in the United States was just as illegal as liquor. The mobs would begin to work out ways to give the public every opportunity to gamble, and would do so in cooperation where that was feasible, as, for example, in the dissemination of racing odds and results across the race wires, and deals would be worked out with Moses Annenberg, who controlled the wire syndicate.

The New York group, led by Torrio, Luciano and their friends, and backed by Dalitz and his friends from Cleveland and others, opened up a discussion of the unfortunate increase in underworld violence, particularly in Chicago. While violence and force were part of the business and were sometimes necessary, the way Capone was going at it, witness the Saint Valentine's Day Massacre, was just too much. This was hurting everybody, forcing the cops and the politicians to put the heat on. Something had to be done to get the heat off. Capone agreed and set up a deal. The most prominent of the nation's gangsters and the most voluble advocate of violence would stand an arrest and a short jail term on a minor charge as a sop to the public outcries.

Then, on May 16, the delegates packed and went home.

Before the next major steps could be taken and the national Syndicate could really come into being, those who stood in its way would have to be eliminated. Those of another generation and another background so wedded to their traditions that they could not see into the future, could not see the necessity of cooperation and peace and businesslike methods, the necessity of working as equal partners with those of different backgrounds, would have to follow the Irish into the garbage bin. They would not fade gracefully, so they would have to go violently.

Luciano, Costello and their allies went back to New York, to a war that was beginning.

WAR IN THE
4
UNDERWORLD

THE GANGLAND WAR THAT would end only with the death of the opposing commanders and the birth of a national underworld organization was set off in the last weeks of October 1929 not in some Mafia stronghold in New York's Little Italy but farther downtown, on Wall Street. The collapsing stock market ended a decade of exhilaration and Emile Coué optimism ("Every day, in every way, I am getting better and better") and of a frenetic search for pleasure. The euphoria of the Roaring Twenties gave way to panic and fear. Only weeks before, money had been plentiful; suddenly, paper millionaires were wondering where they could raise money for rent and food and whether the job would still be

there in the morning—or where they might find work.

No one was immune, not even those who had purveyed pleasure to the nation in the good times which had come to an end. The leaders of the underworld still had plenty of money; they had practiced a strictly cash business, had socked away millions of dollars (not in banks) and so had the capital to see them through anything. They became one of the few sources of cash to which desperate men could turn, and thus found themselves with the means to invade a thousand legitimate fields and corrupt them. Still, their vast reservoir of money was no longer being replenished by the steady rain of hard currency that had poured down on them during the golden years, and the future promised an extended drought. "There we were," said one major bootlegger. "We had been doing damn good, raking in the dough like it was grass out in the country, and all of a sudden it was all over. We got hit just like everybody else. Maybe not so bad, because we always got paid in cash and nobody I knew ever put a nickel in the banks or the stock market. But we got hit, too, and it hurt plenty. There was a time when things were really going good when some guy would try to weasel his way in a little around the edges of my territory. Sometimes I'd knock him over and sometimes I'd figure, what the hell, everybody's got to live and there's plenty for everybody and besides, the guy's a small-timer trying to turn a buck. So I'd give him a warning and let him alone. Why make a lot of trouble over a couple of cases? But after that thing on Wall Street, when the sales started dropping off and some of us had to start tapping the dough we salted away, I don't think anybody stood for any crap from anybody anymore. A guy set his foot inside my district and I cut it off for him."

Thus, as the national economy continued to contract, and the national mood turned from optimism to desperation, rivalries that had simmered for years finally came to a boil. It happened in every field of business, legitimate and illegitimate, but most violently in the bitterly competitive and fragmented Italian underworld, where the secret society, the Mafia,

was dominant. There the struggle for supremacy exploded like a capped pressure cooker. On one side was the army commanded by Guiseppe Masseria, known as Joe the Boss. On the other were the forces led by Salvatore Maranzano and dominated by his fellow immigrants from the Sicilian town of Castellammare del Golfo.

Masseria was a slob. Spaghetti stains always seemed to dapple his unvaryingly black vest and the front of his trousers; dirt and hair grease ringed the collars of his white shirts and he constantly exuded a rank, overripe aroma. Though never slim, his body had once been hard, muscular and agile, and though he never lost his surprising agility (which led many to call him the man who could dodge bullets), years of affluent living and a voracious appetite for pasta converted much of his body into rolls of fat. Even in his native Italian, he was barely literate, and he spoke English so haltingly that he used it rarely. He was an expansive man, his gestures florid, and he laughed often, the sound rising from deep in his immense stomach, his body shaking with the humor of it all—and he could find a source of laughter in anything from a crude practical joke on one of his underlings to the death of an enemy. To those who worked for him, he sometimes donned a benevolent air of the all-wise, omnipotent father, brooking no failure to meet his demands and severely chastising any sign of disobedience.

But Joe the Boss was no jolly fat man, no comic-opera clown. Most

Masseria was a slob, but through sheer cunning and cruelty, he became the New York Mafia boss.

times, his hard black eyes were cold and shuttered; but when his violent temper was aroused, they turned molten. A man of cunning and shrewdness, with overweening ambition and a monstrous ego, he had no pity toward those who crossed him or stood in his way.

Masseria had left Sicily in the early years of the century a grown man with strong Mafia credentials. Almost as soon as he settled in New York, he teamed up with Mafia ruler Ignazio Saietta, known as Lupo the Wolf, an extortionist and killer extraordinary who maintained in East Harlem a stable where his enemies were hung on meat hooks and then, still alive, fed to glowing furnaces. Working with Saietta in all the rackets that bled the Italian immigrants, Masseria soon became a recognized and feared power in Lower Manhattan's Little Italy. And when, in 1920, Saietta foolishly expanded his operations to include counterfeiting—with the consequences of capture, trial and a 30-year term in federal prison—Masseria emerged as one of the main contenders for the Mafia throne and the overlordship of the Italian-immigrant community.

With the advent of Prohibition, control of the country's Little Italys meant control of the wine-making vats and liquor stills that were common fixtures in Italian households. Those stills, especially, were an important source of bootleg booze, and the Mafia leaders who controlled their output not only enriched themselves by supplying raw alcohol to other bootleggers but could then wield power and influence far beyond their traditional ghetto fiefs.

And so Masseria's self-appointment as boss of the New York Mafia, and as ruler of the American Mafia as well, met with immediate challenge. His first rival was one Salvatore Mauro, who had been a bootlegger even before Prohibition and had rejected the authority of Masseria. That defiance was met with dispatch: Mauro was gunned down in the middle of Chrystie Street one bright morning in 1920.

A new rival promptly appeared in the person of Umberto Valenti, who considered himself the legitimate heir to Saietta and other Mafia rulers. More cautious than Mauro, Valenti and his faction kept up a running, sniping battle with Masseria all over Little Italy for more than a year and a half, all the while prudently keeping himself out of the line of fire. At first, Masseria considered Valenti no more bothersome than a pesky fly and gave the job of swatting him to underlings. When they proved unequal to the task, Masseria decided in May of 1922 that if he wanted the job done right, he would have to do it himself.

In these early years of Prohibition, a number of bootleggers, with the cooperation of pliant New York police, had established a kind of central exchange market in the streets of lower Lower Manhattan around police headquarters. Every morning, they would meet on the curbs and buy and sell needed supplies from one another, nodding to, and pressing bills into the hands of, the cops who emerged from headquarters during the day. It was there that Joe the Boss decided to lay a trap for Valenti. With two of his gunmen, he waited in a doorway on Grand Street, just south of police headquarters, and when Valenti showed up for his daily excursion in the market, along with his favorite bodyguard, one Silva Tagliagamba, Masseria and his men opened fire. They missed. Valenti and Tagliagamba pulled out their guns and returned the fire. For a couple of minutes, the bullets zinged up and down Grand Street. Four innocent

bystanders—two men and two women—incurred minor wounds. Valenti escaped without a scratch, but Tagliagamba was critically wounded and died a month later. When they could no longer ignore the nearby gun battle, the police finally began pouring out of headquarters. Masseria turned and ran—right into the arms of a cop. (His pistol was later returned; Masseria had a gun-carrying permit issued by a justice of the New York Supreme Court.) When Tagliagamba finally died at the end of June, Masseria was charged with his murder, then released on bail. The charges against him were filed away in some dusty corner of the hall of justice and soon forgotten.

Enraged at both the murder of his bodyguard and the failure of justice to avenge it, Valenti loudly declared that if the law wouldn't act he would do so himself. He had Masseria shadowed and, on several occasions, shots were fired; all missed. One afternoon, as Masseria left his apartment on Second Avenue, two Valenti gunmen were waiting across the street. They began firing at Joe the Boss, who ducked into a nearby millinery shop. The gunmen followed him inside, shooting all the time. They broke several mirrors and windows, destroyed some hats and put two bullets through the crown of Masseria's new straw boater. But Joe the Boss lived up to the legend that he could dodge bullets.

With the slugs coming that close, however, Masseria decided it was time to end such skirmishing. He sent

In 1931, Park Avenue was the scene of the very messy execution of Salvatore Maranzano.

emissaries to Valenti, asking for peace and a conference to decide the terms. Valenti agreed and Masseria invited him to an Italian restaurant on East 12th Street to celebrate the end of hostilities. At that dinner, Masseria was his most expansive self, proclaiming Valenti a brother, declaring that thenceforth they would work together in harmony. Then, his arm around Valenti's shoulders, he led his rival out to the sidewalk, stepped aside, raised his hand and a fusillade of bullets ended the challenge of Umberto Valenti.

Once again, Masseria was

charged with murder, once again he was freed on bail and once again the charges disappeared somewhere in official files, never to be resurrected.

For a time, Masseria seemed to reign supreme and secure. He tightened his grip on ghetto rackets, expanded his bootlegging business, strengthened his organization. Like his Mafia contemporaries, he considered his world the only world and had no use for anyone who wasn't Sicilian or at least Italian; when the bootleg business forced him to deal with someone outside the clan, he usually turned the negotiations over to one of his trusted aides. He felt no need for outside allies or partners and believed himself strong enough then to turn back any insider who had the audacity to challenge his rule.

One such rival was already emerging, a brighter and more patient man. He was Salvatore Maranzano. Born in Castellammare del Golfo, Maranzano was educated far beyond most of his underworld contemporaries. He had studied for the priesthood before finding his true vocation in the underworld and was a classical scholar, fluent not just in Italian but also in Latin and Greek (though his English was never more than passable). His home was filled with well-read books, many on the life and campaigns of Julius Caesar, to whom he constantly compared himself. To his uncomprehending associates and underlings, he would often quote long extracts from the Latin or Greek to make his point and to demonstrate his own superiority; then, as though suddenly noticing the blank looks, he would patronizingly translate into Italian or English.

A tall, ascetic, majestic man—"He looked just like a banker," said Mafia informer Joe Valachi decades later—Maranzano was a natural rival and threat to Joe the Boss. In his native Sicily, he became an important *mafioso* after abandoning his religious studies. But his undisguised ambitions earned him the animosity of older *mafiosi,* and when several of his depredations made him also the object of police scrutiny, he decided to seek a cooler climate. At the end of World War I, he emigrated to the United States and almost immediately established his own faction of the honored society. His self-confidence and commanding mien, his polished manners, his obvious learning and intelligence and his undisguised amorality, unscrupulousness and viciousness all combined to win him a devoted following in the Mafia. He moved in on bootegging, protection, the Italian lottery and a variety of other rackets in the ghetto and, in so doing, cut himself a slice of Masseria's realm. And he organized a lucrative immigration racket that brought him the subservience of a good part of the community: He arranged both legal and illegal emigration from Italy, for which he received not merely a high fee but also usurious interest rates impossible ever to pay. These debts he held over those who had come to him, exacting their loyalty and obedience under the threat of violence or deportation. Maranzano was, perhaps, the prototype of the American Mafia don, giving and taking, generous and penurious, benevolent and cruel.

Between Masseria and Maranzano there were increasing competition and enmity. Each aspired to the supreme rule, *capo di tutti capi,* "boss of all bosses," in the American Mafia. Masseria was the claimant and Maranzano the pretender. Their personalities clashed so directly that no entente between them was ever possible. Maranzano looked down on Joe the Boss as an uncouth, ignorant peasant. Masseria considered Maranzano a posturing, pompous jackal and, at least initially, no more of a threat than any other challenger.

Maranzano waited patiently and plotted coolly and secretly, certain that Masseria's own arrogance and greed would work to his advantage. At his peak in 1928 and 1929, Masseria had the strength and the well-armed troops, nearly 1000 of them; and through his own payoffs and contacts he was politically well protected. And Masseria had more: Because of his strength and his success, he was the acknowledged favorite of the other ruling Mafia *capos* around the country. Maranzano, as his only challenger, was an outlaw in the underworld, with a small army and little political influence.

There was no shortage of recruits for either army, however. With the advent of the fascist regime in Italy, scores of young *mafiosi* were scurrying to safety in the United States, driven from home by Mussolini's ruthless campaign against the Sicilian Mafia. As the exiled *mafiosi* reached America, they became willing and eager soldiers in the ranks of both Masseria and Maranzano, and of Mafia *capos* in other cities.

What neither Joe the Boss nor Maranzano understood, however, was that many of these younger Italians and Sicilians, particularly those who had grown up in America, had formed friendships and alliances with non-Italian gangsters during Prohibition and secretly despised the Mafia's aging leaders, who clung to the old country and the old ways. These Mustache Petes, who could not adapt to the new society, would have to be eliminated if the Italian underworld were to become a powerful and perhaps dominating force in American crime. The young were not yet strong enough to accomplish this themselves, but some began to anticipate that the Mustache Petes would eliminate one another.

That such a war was coming Maranzano never doubted, so he prepared for it. In conversations with older *mafiosi,* he would constantly disparage Joe the the Boss, building with eloquence on his sins. And he sounded out any likely recruit for his army, with the only proviso that he be a Sicilian, as the rules of the Mafia then dictated (by late in the decade, though, the collapse of the Mafia's chief rival, the Neapolitan-born Camorra, permitted recruitment among mainland Italians as well as Sicilians). He had no trouble winning the allegiance of a group of recent

The only evidence of some of the bloody skirmishes between mobsters would sometimes be an abandoned car in a lonely spot and some blood.

arrivals from his home town of Castellammare del Golfa. Among them were Joseph "Joe Bananas" Bonanno, rising rapidly in the Brooklyn organization, and Stefano Magaddino, becoming one of the most important *mafiosi* in Buffalo. Into his ranks, too, he pulled others disenchanted with Masseria, men like Brooklyn mobsters Giuseppe Magiocco and Joseph Profaci, who was already heading his own gang, and the Aiellos of Chicago, who by the end of the decade were throwing in $5000 a week to support the Maranzano cause.

This was the nucleus of the pretending group, but it was by no means powerful enough to take on Masseria.

So Maranzano continued his efforts to attract younger hoodlums who showed signs of independence or rebellion. He made a particularly forceful effort to win over Lucky Luciano, who would bring in Frank Costello, with his intelligence, imagination and political connections, and Vito Genovese, a tough and brutal young Neapolitan thug who was number one in Luciano's personal entourage. But all these efforts failed. Luciano politely declined Maranzano's repeated offers, as during these years he also declined Masseria's. By late in 1927, he had become a major underworld force in his own right through bootlegging, loan-sharking, protection, gambling of all kinds and a host of other rackets that extended far outside the Little Italys dominated by Masseria, Maranzano and other older *mafiosi*. However, as the pressures on him from both Masseria and Maranzano intensified, Luciano began to feel that unless he merged with one or the other, he would be caught in the cross fire of the developing struggle. At that moment, Joe the Boss was much the stronger and so the more likely victor in the coming war. At the same time, Luciano and his friends reasoned, Masseria's penchant for turning allies into enemies with his arrogance and greed would make him the more vulnerable to later overthrow Maranzano. So Luciano threw in with Joe the Boss, to help him win the war and then topple him in a palace coup.

At that moment, Masseria appeared invincible. He had his own army, he was backed by Mafia overlords around the country and now he had Luciano and his organization as well.

But this seeming invincibility was an illusion. In his rise to the top, Masseria had left behind a lengthy list of enemies, who, though not powerful by themselves, found mutual strength in joining the rising Maranzano rebellion. Also, there were the seeds of rebellion in Masseria's own organization. The young, like Luciano, were secretly working for his overthrow and their own ascension. And Masseria's own policies were turning even some of the older *mafiosi* against him.

Hostilities commenced with a series of sorties and skirmishes. Maranzano would hijack a Masseria liquor shipment and Masseria would retaliate in kind; a minor Masseria thug would be murdered and reciprocal action would be taken. It was a time of probing for weaknesses, of sporadic and inconclusive action and reaction.

THEN EVENTS OUTSIDE THE CLANnish circle of the Mafia intervened, bringing all-out war. In the fall of 1929, Wall Street crashed and the nation turned from an era of unparalleled prosperity to deepening depression. With business, including bootlegging and the other underworld rackets, in a sudden and sharp contraction, competition that might once have been ignored could no longer be tolerated. Joe the Boss began to put pressure on subordinates and allies for a bigger cut of their rackets, for a tighter accounting. Such demands, to which some acceded and others resisted, only increased the bitterness he had already engendered.

Greater income from his own organization was only one of Masseria's goals. He also determined to stamp out all competitors, particularly those like Maranzano, who had combined competition with threats. The first move took place far from New York. A native of Castellammare named Gaspare Milazzo had settled in Detroit, risen to Mafia *capo* and become a leading Midwestern advocate of the

President Herbert Hoover was in the White House when Wall Street collapsed in 1929. The collapse gave birth to the depression and to a stronger underworld organization.

Maranzano cause. Masseria gunmen tracked him down and killed him. If the murder was supposed to be a threat, it served merely to drive other Castellammarese tighter into the Maranzano network. So Masseria responded by declaring open season on any and all natives of that Sicilian town, ordering his gunmen to shoot them on sight. And, with the support of many national Mafia dons, he issued a death warrant on Maranzano personally.

Now outlawed and his life in jeopardy, the still-weaker Maranzano stepped up his attempts to court segments of Masseria's army and pull them into his own orbit. His initial target was Luciano, who had become Masseria's right hand as soon as he joined Joe the Boss's outfit and who more and more was becoming the most important figure next to Masseria in that group. Luciano's reputation and the awe he was inspiring among the underworld's common soldiers were enhanced when, in mid-October of 1929, he became the only gangster ever known to have returned alive from a one-way ride.

In the early-morning hours of October 17, a passing police car discovered Luciano, savagely beaten, slashed and bound, lying on the pavement of Hylan Boulevard on Staten Island. He was taken to the hospital, where 55 stitches were needed to sew him up. When he emerged, with permanent scars and a sinister drooping eyelid whose muscles had been severed, he was viewed with considerable respect and fear. He had told the police only that he would not say who had beaten him, that "I'll take care of this in my own way." Frustrated, the authorities charged him with grand larceny, for theft of a car. Luciano laughed and the charges were promptly dismissed.

The rumors about the ride were many: that he had been waylaid and kidnaped by some masked men who had beaten him and tossed him out of their car when he promised to pay them $10,000; that he had been picked up and kidnaped by a rival gang at the corner of 50th Street and Broadway and then beaten as a warning to stay away from their territory, and then dumped on Staten Island; that he had been seized by Maranzano's men at that Broadway corner and rescued at the Staten Island ferry by Meyer Lansky and Bugsy Siegel, who found him badly beaten and then drove him to Staten Island to create a mystery; that he had been beaten by federal agents who found him on a Staten Island pier, waiting for a shipment of whiskey or narcotics; that he had been beaten by a policeman, the father of a girl he had gotten pregnant. Luciano himself refused to give a satisfactory explanation, permitting the rumors to grow and, with them, his reputation as Lucky Luciano.

Though Luciano, in concert with his close friends Costello, Genovese, Lansky and others, had long been determined to dispose of both Maranzano and Masseria (preferably in that order) and take over himself, the Staten Island episode convinced him that the project was becoming urgent. Events of the next weeks would also persuade him to reverse his priorities and strike at Masseria first.

For, if the bid to Luciano had failed, Maranzano was making progress elsewhere, particularly in his approaches to Gaetano Reina. An educated and cultured man, Reina had less in common personally with his ally Masseria than with his supposed enemy, Maranzano, with whom he occasionally dined and enjoyed long talks about books, music and other common interests. Moreover, Masseria's demand for a bigger cut of Reina's rackets was becoming more insistent, so the course of conversations between Maranzano and Reina began to take a different tack. Secretly, they agreed that Reina would sever his ties with Joe the Boss and throw in with Maranzano. Such a move would start a flood of desertions from the Masseria cause and turn the battle to Maranzano.

While the meetings and the arrangements were clandestine, word of them soon leaked out to other young rebels in the underworld. Word also got back to Masseria. Such treachery, combined with Reina's adamant resistance to the dictates of the leader, threw Joe the Boss into one of his uncontrollable rages. He ordered Reina killed. On February 26, 1930, just after eight in the evening, Reina left the home of a friend in the Bronx. Waiting for him on the sidewalk was the Masseria killer, a shotgun in his arms. The assassin called to Reina and, as the older man turned, his head was blown off. As befitting a man of stature in the underworld, Reina had been shot from the front.

Masseria moved quickly to exploit the dispatch of the traitor Reina and assumed full control of his organization. Without consulting Reina's lieutenants, he appointed one Joseph Pinzolo—a personal lackey and an obese man whose appetite and gross behavior rivaled Masseria's—as the new boss of the Reina gang. Tom Gagliano, Dominick "The Gap" Pe-

trilli and Tommy "Three-Finger Brown" Lucchese refused to accept this dictate. They resumed the secret negotiations with Maranzano that Reina had begun and they plotted Pinzolo's overthrow. In September, the moment arrived. Lucchese invited Pinzolo to a meeting at his office, a legitimate front called the California Dry Fruit Importers, in the Brokaw Building on Broadway. Pinzolo walked into the office but not out. A stretcher bearing his body with two bullets in it carried him to the morgue. Lucchese was indicted for the murder, but, not unexpectedly, the charges were dismissed. (According to Valachi, the real killer was a former prize fighter turned gunman named Girolamo Santucci, who went under the name of Bobby Doyle; Lucchese, Valachi said, was not even present.)

With Pinzolo gone, Gagliano took control of the Reina Gang, with Lucchese and Petrilli his chief aides. Then Gagliano secretly and successfully concluded the negotiations with Maranzano. Masseria, for the moment, was not aware of the treachery and desertions, though the younger members of the hierarchy—Luciano, Costello, Genovese and others—not only knew about it but had supported the moves as advantageous to their own long-term schemes.

It was apparent to these younger mobsters, and to some of the older ones as well, that the Castellammarese War, as it came to be called, would not end until at least one of the main antagonists was killed. Joe the

Outside a Bronx apartment house lie the bodies of two Masseria soldiers, Al Mineo and Steve Ferrigno.

Boss, apparently still confident of his own invincibility, made few overt moves against Maranzano. In the fall of 1930, he managed to dry up one source of Maranzano's income by encouraging Chicago's Al Capone to rub out Joe Aiello—which he did in the grand Chicago manner. One October evening, Aiello stepped outside his expensive West Side apartment building and into the cross fire from two Thompson submachine guns and a sawed-off shotgun and died from 59 bullet wounds. But, for the most part, Masseria seemed content to pick off isolated and lower-ranking Castellammarese, to hijack Maranzano trucks and otherwise only nettle his rival.

Maranzano, the balance now tip-

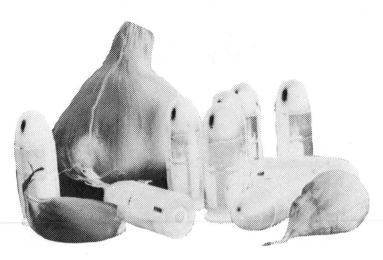

To make sure that the wounds would become infected, some of the gunmen rubbed garlic on their bullets—or so legend has it.

ping toward him, was less restrained. An ex-Capone gunman known only as Buster from Chicago had been imported to cut down Masseria's chief bodyguard and executioner, Pietro "The Clutching Hand" Morello and other Masseria associates. Years later, Valachi would describe how he, Buster, Profaci, Doyle, Nick "The Thief" Capuzzi and several other Maranzano gunmen rented an apartment in the Bronx directly across from that of Masseria underling Steve Ferrigno and for several weeks lay in wait for the mobster. During that watch, they missed an opportunity to get Masseria himself, when he showed up for a meeting, but on November 5, 1930, they nailed Ferrigno and Al Mineo when they emerged from the apartment; three shotgun blasts ended their careers.

There would be estimates later that more than 60 hoodlums were gunned down during the Castellammarese War, the casualties occurring not only in New York but also around the country, wherever supporters of Masseria and Maranzano met head on. By the early months of 1931, neither side had emerged victorious, but the bloodletting was bringing unwanted publicity and heat. In New York, Masseria's friends in the upper reaches of the police department called him in and ordered him to put an end to the killings, or the department's cops would be turned loose. Joe the Boss complied to the extent of ordering most of his gunmen to shoot only when shot at, though he still had some top guns out looking for Maranzano.

Maranzano, however, with a kingdom to win, would agree to no truce and kept his troops on the offensive. Other Mafia leaders around the country began to worry, and became impatient for a conclusion to the battle. As Capone's indiscriminate bloodletting in Chicago had brought unwelcomed heat on the whole underworld, so the Castellammarese blood bath was bringing official reaction against the Italian element. The elder dons tried to mediate. At a council just outside New York in the first months of 1931, they demanded an end to the battle. Masseria did not attend, sending word that he was already trying to do just that and that his men were killing only in self-defense. Maranzano, however, surrounded by bodyguards, did show up, made an eloquent assault on Masseria as a disgrace to the Mafia and a man who had committed uncounted crimes against everyone in the underworld. Then he demanded the revocation of the death sentence against him and its replacement by a death sentence against Masseria. The council agreed to the former but would not go so far as to order the death of one of its major rulers.

The situation, inconclusive and enervating, was ideal for Luciano and the younger gangsters. Only someone close to Masseria, a Judas, would be able to kill him, and Luciano and his followers were in that position. They put their plan into operation by striking a bargain with Maranzano. Luciano would see to it that Masseria was killed; in return, Maranzano would ensure that Luciano would take over as leader of the Masseria organization, that no reprisals would be exacted against those who had fought the Castellammarese and that peace and cooperation would be the rule in the Mafia thenceforth.

On April 15, 1931, after a hard morning's work at Masseria's fortress headquarters on Second Avenue in Lower Manhattan, Luciano invited Joe the Boss to lunch, suggesting that they take a long, leisurely drive out to Coney Island and dine at a favorite restaurant of the underworld, the Nuova Villa Tammaro, owned by a friend of gangsters, Gerardo Scarpato. A table was set for them in the center of the main dining room and Masseria ate with his usual gluttony, gorging himself on antipasto, spaghetti with white clam sauce, lobster *fra diavolo* and cream-filled pastries, and downing nearly a quart of chianti and a pot of black Italian coffee. Luciano, a modest diner, ate sparingly and sipped a glass of wine. By the time Masseria had finished his meal, the restaurant had emptied of the other diners. Luciano suggested a game of cards. Masseria agreed, though he said they should play for only an hour or so and then get back to the office for more work. Scarpato brought them a new pinochle deck and then left the restaurant for a quiet afternoon stroll along the beach.

For about 45 minutes, Luciano and Masseria played vigorously. Just before 3:30, Luciano excused himself, rose from the table and walked to the men's room. He had hardly closed the door when the front door of the restaurant opened and into the room walked Genovese, Joe Adonis, Albert Anastasia and one of Luciano's oldest and closest friends in the non-Italian underworld, Bugsy Siegel. They had come, according to the story, at the bidding of Luciano, had parked outside the Nuova Villa Tammaro and waited for a signal. When it came, they left their car and walked inside, leaving the motor running and Ciro Terranova behind the wheel, prepared for a quick getaway.

Once inside the restaurant, the four pulled out revolvers and began shooting; more than 20 slugs ricocheted around the room, six finding a target inside the body of Giuseppe Masseria. He slumped forward, face down on the suddenly blood-soaked white tablecloth, his right hand brushing the floor, dangling from it the ace of diamonds. As soon as they were certain Masseria was dead, the four killers raced out of the restaurant. But outside, a shaken and suddenly fear-ridden Terranova was frozen at the wheel of the car. Siegel pushed him aside, got behind the wheel himself and drove rapidly back to Manhattan.

When the echoes of the last shots and the fleeing footsteps had passed, Luciano strolled out of the washroom, studied the carnage in front of him and then telephoned the police. He waited for their arrival and explained to them that he had heard noises while in the toilet and "As soon as I finished drying my hands, I hurried out and walked back to see what it was all about." No, he said, he had not seen the killers and he had no idea why anyone would want to harm Joe the Boss.

Masseria's murder did not end the Castellammarese War; it only provided an interlude of truce. The end could not come until Maranzano had gone the same way. But in the weeks and months after Joe the Boss had been given the traditional gala send-off to the cemetery, Maranzano moved quickly and decisively to establish his supremacy in the Mafia. He proclaimed himself *capo di tutti capi,* and the title was formally bestowed, though not without some reluctance, at a conclave in Chicago at which more national Mafia rulers were absent than present. Then Maranzano held a formal coronation. There was a banquet in Brooklyn that lasted for days. All *mafiosi,* leaders and soldiers, in the New York area were invited to pay homage, and so, too, were *mafiosi* from around the country; those who couldn't attend sent substitutes. Maranzano, like the Caesar he had become, sat at the head table and to him ceremoniously came a parade of gangland overlords and underlords bearing gifts, envelopes stuffed with cash. Valachi would later claim that more than $100,000 was handed to Maranzano that night; others, higher in the honored society, would put the total at closer to $1,000,000.

Maranzano also gathered the members of the New York society in a Bronx meeting hall festooned with crosses, religious pictures, icons and other religious symbols. These were a cover in case some uninvited guest should appear, but they also reflected Maranzano's very deep and real religious convictions; he had, after all, once studied for the priesthood. More than 500 *mafiosi* attended. On a platform at one end of the room sat Maranzano, flanked by those who

"The one-way ride" (left), "the concrete overcoat" (right) and "the double-decker coffin" (top) were some of the Mob's favorite methods of disposal.

would be the princes in this new kingdom of the Italian underworld—Luciano, Gagliano, Profaci, Vincent Mangano and Bonanno.

Speaking in Italian, with an occasional lapse into Latin, Maranzano informed the hoodlums ranked before him that the chaos and the warring were over. From that moment on, the underworld (by which he meant the Italian-Sicilian underworld, for Maranzano gave little thought to any other segment) would be reorganized under his rule as *capo di tutti capi.* But, like the Caesar he imagined himself to be, he would thenceforth be above the battle; he would rule no separate gang but the whole thing. (From this eventually came the phrase Valachi would use in refer-

ence to the organization: Cosa Nostra, "Our Thing." The term acquired the status of a name probably because the Federal Bureau of Investigation and its director, J. Edgar Hoover, had for years insisted that organized crime was a figment of the imagination of crime writers, that the Mafia did not exist. In order to get Hoover off the hook, a new name had to be created, hence Cosa Nostra, though it bears about as much relevance to the organization as "doing your own thing.") Maranzano declared he would collect a share of everything reaped by all the mobs; later, he would tell the leaders how large a share, but it would be one befitting his stature as supreme ruler.

The Italian underworld, Maranzano said, would now undergo mergers and new alignments, out of which would come five New York "families"—a euphemism he coined to replace gangs or mobs. The families would control the world of crime under his authority; they would have noncompeting jurisdictions, both in territories and in spheres of operation, and each member at the meeting would belong to one of the families, each of which would be led by one of the five men ranked alongside him. Under each of these leaders, or *capos,* there would be an underboss, and under him would be several lieutenants, called *caporegimi* (according to Valchi), in charge of Mafia soldiers. Each man in the chain would be responsible to the leader a step above, who would himself be responsible for the actions of those below him. Rigid discipline would be the rule; every man, from bosses to soldiers, would obey the orders promulgated by Maranzano or suffer penalties, in some cases death. As for internal regulations, no man must ever, on pain of death, talk about the organization or his own family, even to his wife; he must never lust after the wife of another member; he must obey without question the orders of the leaders above him; he must never strike another member, no matter what the provocation. And Maranzano would be the supreme arbiter of all disputes, as he would be supreme in everything.

For the ordinary Mafia soldiers like Valachi, this was all stirring and somewhat frightening. But for those near the throne, it was considerably less than awe-inspiring. They had not fought a war, had not sacrificed troops, money, time and energy and conspired in the murder of a leader to relinquish all their power and independence. Maranzano imagined himself a Caesar and, like Caesar, he was surrounded by Brutus, Cassius, Casca and other plotters.

Those who ruled the families under Maranzano were all relatively young men who had a great deal more in common with one another than with him. They were men, too, who understood, as Maranzano did not, that the Mafia was only one element in the national underworld, and that its success required working closely and harmoniously with those other elements, the Jews, the Irish, even the WASPs where they held a major claim. Thus, rather than look to Maranzano, they began to look to Luciano for leadership, to him as the man who could lead them in a world that, as the depression deepened and repeal threatened, was radically changing.

Surrounded by bodyguards and ensconced in protected offices in the Grand Central Building at 46th Street and Park Avenue in New York, where he operated under a legitimate real-estate front called The Eagle Building Corporation, Maranzano, like Masseria before him, thought himself secure. He was not. Luciano, working closely with Lansky, was surreptitiously sounding out those other underworld leaders of his generation, seeking their support for a plan to kill Maranzano and escape retribution. Messages crisscrossed the country and secret meetings were held, including a major one in Cleveland early in the summer of 1931. From these conversations among the younger gang leaders came the decision that not only Maranzano must go but all the old Mustache Petes aligned with him, who were logs in the road to progress.

With this widespread support, a devious plan was worked out to penetrate Maranzano's elaborate defenses. It was Lansky who came up with the solution. The only people outside his own blindly loyal circle who might be able to get close to Maranzano, and get him alone, would be federal agents seeking to question him about taxes, bootlegging, immigration or one of his other rackets. He would have no reason to fear them. So a crew of Jewish gunmen, unknown to Maranzano or his close guards, would be imported, trained to look and act like federal agents and then sent to Maranzano's office. Their guise would gain them entrance and, once inside, they could do what they had come for and escape into anonymity.

On the surface, Maranzano seemed unaware of the cabal. His suspicions were apparently not even raised when, during the Cleveland meeting, Luciano, Lansky, Michele "Mike" Miranda—a Luciano triggerman at the time—their Cleveland hosts and several other visiting gangsters were picked up at a prize fight and booked as suspicious characters. Maranzano accepted Luciano's ex-planation that he had gone to Cleveland for the sole purpose of seeing the fights; after all, he was an avid fight fan who often traveled long distances for that purpose.

But if on the surface Maranzano was calm, underneath he was very concerned, indeed. He told Valachi and other confidants that he did not trust Luciano and his friends and that as long as they were alive, he was not safe. So he set in motion a counterplot to eliminate them. He drew up a list of those he considered his prime enemies—Luciano, Genovese, Costello, Adonis, Willie Moretti, Dutch Schultz, who was Luciano's close friend in non-Italian circles, and a number of others—and marked them for execution. And then, like those plotting against him, he searched for an outside gunman and hired the notorious young killer Vincent "Mad Dog" Coll to be the executioner.

It became a race to see who would kill whom first. But Maranzano was acting only on his suspicions. Late in the summer, Luciano had facts. He was tipped by a friend as to exactly what Maranzano planned. He was even told that he and Genovese would be invited to Maranzano's office for an important conference and when they arrived, Coll would be waiting with his guns. The invitation, then, would be the bell that set Luciano's own plot in motion.

It rang on September 10, 1931. Luciano and Genovese were requested to appear at Maranzano's office at two in the afternoon. Just before two, Maranzano waited for

One of the many unknown and unsung casualties of the Masseria-Maranzano War.

their arrival with his secretary, five armed bodyguards and Luciano's close friend, Tommy Lucchese, the underboss in the Gagliano family, who had dropped in unexpectedly. Lucchese had barely arrived when the door burst open and four men stormed in. They identified themselves as federal agents and demanded a conference with Maranzano in private.

Maranzano readily identified himself; he had never seen the men before and had no suspicion that they were anything but what they said, for his lawyers had warned him that he ought to expect agents to come calling one day. Maranzano's own identification was confirmed by Lucchese—who was there, as it happened, as the finger man in case of trouble.

The four "agents" pulled out revolvers and lined everyone up against the office wall, shaking down the men and relieving them of their guns. Two of the agents then shoved their guns into Maranzano's back and ordered him into his private office for questioning. Once inside, they set upon him, first trying to strangle him, then pulling knives to stab him to death, trying to commit murder with as little furor as possible. But Maranzano was stronger than he looked and fought back relentlessly; the killers had no choice; they pulled out their guns and blasted away. Maranzano collapsed with six stab wounds, his throat cut and four bullets in his head and body.

The two killers rushed out and, joined by the two who had remained guarding those in the outer office, fled

the scene. As they disappeared, Maranzano's bodyguards fled, too, in fear of their own lives and to avoid being found in the office with the corpse. As they raced down the stairs, one of them collided with Mad Dog Coll, on his way up to keep his appointment. He was told what had happened. With Maranzano's money in his pocket, no contract to fulfill and no one to accept a refund, Coll simply turned and walked away.

Through the early afternoon, Luciano, Genovese, Lansky and the other conspirators waited anxiously for the news and then proceeded according to plan. In later years, the rumors of what had happened on that night, which came to be called the "Night of the Sicilian Vespers" multiplied: Supposedly, Luciano's killers began a purge of Maranzano followers in New York and Luciano's allies followed suit all over the country, with more than 40 *mafiosi* falling before dawn. But no one has ever been able to compile a list, and the only clearly established victim of that purge was Scarpato, owner of the Coney Island restaurant where Masseria had met his end.

The death of Maranzano brought to an end the old ways and gave birth to crime as a fledgling national organization in which the Italian Mafia worked not alone but in concert with other elements in the underworld. Within weeks of the murder, a new criminal conclave was called, this time in Chicago. Despite his own mounting tax troubles, Capone was a generous host, providing accommodations, food, girls, entertainment and plenty of police protection at the Congress Hotel. Though it was essentially an Italian-dominated conference to proclaim Luciano's arrival as the most powerful Italian boss in the nation, there were observers and participants from the non-Italian underworld.

Those who went to that meeting went prepared to attend the coronation of Luciano as the new *capo di tutti capi*. The efficiency and dispatch with which he had handled the Masseria and Maranzano affairs, his ideas and outlook, his ambition and manner had brought him both fame and the respect of his underworld peers. But Luciano would have none of it. Knowing the fate of others who aspired to supreme rule and who publicly boasted of their new position, he categorically rejected the title and its implicit powers. He rejected, too, the envelopes stuffed with bills that were offered to him as the new ruler. What Luciano recognized was that in spurning the title publicly, in showing himself modest, just one of the boys, the power and the position would devolve upon him in fact. His demeanor would win him more than a formal title.

Luciano had discussed beforehand with Lansky and Costello just what he would do at the meeting, and now he outlined his ideas for the future—a nationwide gambling syndicate, legal liquor when Prohibition ended—ideas that were accepted with hardly a dissenting voice. There would be no more internecine warfare and, too, the days of total independence of one Italian mob from others and from the rest of the underworld were over. Everyone had better understand that cooperation and consolidation, a sense of order and business that emulated the great corporations were the orders of the day. This national combination would be ruled by a national commission on which the leaders of the major mobs would sit and at which all major policy decisions would be discussed and passed on. All members of the commission would be equals. Charlie Lucky would be the chairman (this decided by unanimous vote), but he emphasized that his voice and his vote would count for no more than anyone else's. While voting membership in the commission would be restricted to Italians, it was time to start bringing the Italian underworld into closer relationship with other groups, so some non-Italians—Lansky and Moe Dalitz, in particular—should sit at the meetings, have a voice although no vote. This was agreeable to Lansky and Dalitz, for they knew they could still guide policy and yet escape the heat; the Italians would be in the light, right out in front, and the overworld would soon forget that anyone but an Italian was a major factor in organized crime.

The makeup of the new ruling commission revealed the importance that the Italians, and organized crime in general, placed on New York. There were five New York members, the leaders of the five local Mafia families: Luciano, Mangano, Profaci, Bonanno and Gagliano. The two others were outlanders, Frankie Milano from Cleveland (where he worked closely with Dalitz) and Capone from Chicago. Capone's membership was brief; he was soon in prison and replacing him on the council was Paul "The Waiter" Ricca, who himself would later be succeeded by Tony Accardo.

That Chicago meeting at the Congress Hotel in the autumn of 1931 was a crucial one in the history of organized crime in America. Until then, the Mafia, or whatever one wants to call it, had been narrow and suspicious, operating on its own as a world unto itself. Now, under the prodding of Luciano and his youthful peers, it was emerging at last from the ghettos, from the Little Italys. It was

not yet ready to take its place as an equal with the other ethnic and/or heterogeneous groups in the criminal structure. Integration was by no means complete. But under Luciano, this could and would take place and the Mafia would enter the modern world. Within three years, it would finally join forces with the other outfits to form a truly national syndicate that would cut across all racial, sectional, ethnic and factional lines.

After the Chicago meeting, Luciano was at the top, boss, in fact, of the Italian underworld. He had changed it, modernized it and made it ready for the heady new times that were arriving, times when the nation would be in despair but in which the underworld would be in flower.

5
HAPPY DAYS
&
HARD TIMES

THE MOOD OF THE NATION IN THE first years of the Thirties was desperate. A fourth of the potential labor force, nearly 13,000,000 people, were looking for jobs by 1932, and that army of the unemployed was being swelled every day as businesses large and small gave up and closed their doors. Bread lines and soup kitchens were becoming fixtures in every American city. Hoovervilles, warrens of cardboard shanties, were springing up along river beds and railroad tracks and in vacant lots to shelter the homeless. A bonus army of thousands of jobless and hopeless World War I veterans descended on Washington to seek the aid of the federal government, only to be met and routed by the bayonets, trun-

cheons and tear gas of regular army troops commanded by General Douglas MacArthur. Banks were collapsing at an ever-increasing rate and carrying with them the hopes and the savings of millions. There was no money, not in the private purses of ordinary Americans nor in the state or federal treasuries, and the sources of revenue were fast disappearing. The melancholy anthem of the age was sung all over the country: *Brother, Can You Spare a Dime?*

With government seemingly unable or unwilling to meet the worsening crisis, many saw a developing potential for revolution. On one level, there was a crescendo of demands for action and change—radical and violent or moderate and peaceful; it didn't matter much which, as long as there were signs that someone was doing something. On another level, there was a demand, a necessity, for escape from the increasing wretchedness of life, if only for just a few hours.

The bankrupt administration of Herbert Hoover was swept out of office in the 1932 election by Franklin Delano Roosevelt, and he brought to Washington and the nation an infectious optimism, a frantic 100 days and more of action, a parade of needed reforms that, if not ending the depression, at least offered the hope that it would be ended.

Those who provided the country with its escapes and diversions had no less a stake in the survival of the system, though their contributions were of a different kind. By coincidence, they were made possible in some measure by the Roosevelt administration's rural-electrification programs, which brought the wonders of electricity to those who had never known it before. With the electric light came another wondrous invention: the radio. Like television two decades later, in the Thirties the radio became a necessity in even the poorest household. Every evening the family would gather around the little box with its lighted dial to forget reality and enter the world of Jack Benny, Fred Allen, Amos and Andy, Major Bowes, Fanny Brice as Baby Snooks, Cecil B. De Mille introducing the *Lux Radio Theater,* the whole distant world of drama and laughter and adventure. In the mornings and af-

ternoons, a housewife could go about her drudgery without thinking, her mind on the endless entanglements of *Young Doctor Malone, Our Gal Sunday, The Romance of Helen Trent, Ma Perkins, Pepper Young's Family* and all the rest of the soap operas. The world outside might be black, but inside the box all things were possible.

Amusement, change, total escape were even more satisfying in the darkness of the new talking-movie palaces, where, for a dime or a quarter, one could enter a convincing

Selling apples was one way to fight the depression (left); but some gave in, sleeping on benches or depending on public charity (below).

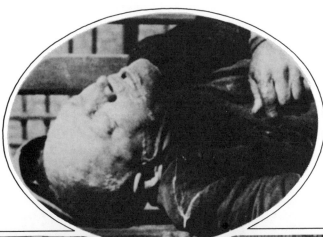

dreamland. On Wednesday nights there was bingo and on Saturdays a visiting celebrity, or maybe only the theater manager, might draw a number from a fish bowl and the lucky ticket holder would have a new set of dishes. Then the lights would dim and everything would be forgotten except those flickering black-and-white images on the huge silvery screen. It was a safe but exciting world: where Little Caesar was only Edward G. Robinson firing blanks, where the public enemy was Jimmy Cagney and Scarface was Paul Muni in makeup, where Boris Karloff and Bela Lugosi could create delicious shudders as Frankenstein's monster and Dracula, where Busby Berkeley

could work glamorous miracles along 42nd Street or with the Gold Diggers of 1933 and where the bulbous nose of W. C. Fields gleamed almost red in black and white.

But the escape provided by radio and movies, though vital, was an escape into a realm that even the most gullible knew (despite the publicized talent hunts and the exodus of pretty girls and handsome young men from the small towns to Hollywood's dream factory) was only a short flight for an hour or two before the return to reality. There were, however, other avenues of escape—some not so unreal, for they held out the possibility of power and riches. These were the dreams purveyed by the American underworld.

The survival of the American system was just as important to the criminals as to any other group. The underworld's roots were as deep in American society and tradition as the

Mobsters become part of celluloid mythology. Edward G. Robinson (top right), Humphrey Bogart (bottom left) and James Cagney (page 120) starred in movies thinly based on real gangland figures.

most honest patriot's, and many of its leaders, sensing this, became the most conservative of citizens. In later years, no single group was more patriotic or more virulently anti-Communist, more dedicated to the continuance of the American way of life without alteration. Major racketeers were easy marks for those who appealed to their love of country; their bank rolls were always open. (A dream of Meyer Lansky, a longtime conservative Republican, and Tommy Lucchese, a conservative Democrat, and a dream both realized, was to see their sons graduated from West Point and become commissioned officers.)

FOR ORGANIZED CRIME, THE CLImate of the depression was in some ways superior even to that of the Twenties. The racketeers were the dispensers of dreams and escape—in the form of alcohol, gambling, money, drugs and sex—and, by the early Thirties, they had enormous wealth and influence. Under the leadership of Lucky Luciano, Lansky, Frank Costello and their peers, the organized criminals were openly courted by politicians seeking their support, their allegiance and their dollars. They were too powerful even to display concern over the growing reform movement that was demanding an end to politically protected crime.

The time had come, it seemed to many, to do something about the corruption that had flourished in New York, and in most of the nation's cities, since the start of Prohibition. It had been one thing for city officials, judges and police to flout the laws openly, take payoffs and live high during an era of boom and prosperity. But it was another thing entirely for these same public servants to conduct business as usual during the depression, when joy had given way to desperation. The most blatant forms of venality could no longer be endured, and even the most blasé and jaded began to demand at least some semblance of honesty in civic government. As the new decade began, the scandals of the administration of New York's wastrel mayor, James J. Walker, and his Tammany allies and sponsors, such as Jimmy Hines, had reached the point where even the blind were forced to see.

Early in 1931, Roosevelt, then New York's governor but already beginning to sound like a presidential candidate, and the New York appellate court appointed a commission to take a searching look at what was happening in the nation's largest city. The commission was headed by Judge Samuel Seabury, who not only sought to open some windows in the back rooms and let in light but no doubt relished the opportunity to expose the corruption of Tammany Hall, which had cost him a governor's race more than a decade earlier. All through 1931 and 1932, hardly a day went by without some major disclosures from the commission. The Seabury hearings were an unending serial of payoffs, bribery, venality, corruption and

Judge Samuel Seabury was the head of a commission that fought the tide of gangsterism in New York.

crime, developing the almost unbreakable link between Dutch Schultz, Luciano, Costello, Louis Lepke Buchalter and other underworld figures and the political world of Hines, Tammany Hall, Mayor Walker and various police commissioners.

Though the publicity was certainly undesired, the gangsters assumed the heat would soon die down and it would again be business as usual—especially considering the political events of the time. The Democratic National Convention would open in Chicago at the end of June 1932. Its nominee for president would almost certainly be swept into the

White House over the forlorn and discredited incumbent, Herbert Hoover. The convention's choice seemed to be between Governor Roosevelt and the standard-bearer from 1928, Al Smith. (In the big cities, no one gave a moment's thought to the third contender, John Nance Garner, speaker of the House of Representatives; after all, he was from that land of cowboys and Indians, Texas, which the cities didn't even think of as part of America.) Both were New Yorkers and, to appear as viable candidates to the convention, both had to control their home state's delegation. Smith, with his easy, garrulous manner, his Lower East Side accent, his loyal party record, was the traditional Tammany favorite. The patrician Roosevelt, with his Harvard education, upper-class accent, Hyde Park manner and personal wealth, was, to those in the city, only a charming and somewhat suspicious unknown.

Tammany's control of a large bloc of city delegates to the convention made it, then, the object of fervent dealing on the part of both Smith and Roosevelt backers; and since control of Tammany rested not just in Hines and his rival leader, Albert Marinelli, but also in their underworld allies, the political trading necessarily had to include them. Early in 1932, the problem for Roosevelt seemed to be the pressure generated by the Seabury investigation. As long as Tammany and its underworld allies were under fire, Roosevelt could not count on their support.

Roosevelt denounced civic crime,

Franklin D. Roosevelt, as governor of New York, also fought against organized crime.

graft and corruption in ringing terms, lauded Seabury and his fellow commissioners for their work and then, mildly, said that he did not think a strong enough case had been made against Walker or anyone else to warrant legal or executive action.

The statement, and Roosevelt's refusal to authorize any action, did just what it was intended to do. Hines promptly announced that he was backing Roosevelt for the presidency and would lead a large delegation to Chicago in the governor's behalf. But Tammany's underworld associates were not yet ready to make a total

Huey P. Long (left) introduced the one-arm bandit in Louisiana, with some help from the Mob. New Orleans became a stronghold of illegal gambling, in spite of rather perfunctory raids (right).

commitment. They hedged their bets. Marinelli proclaimed his allegiance to Al Smith and his intention to lead a Smith bloc to Chicago.

Hines and Marinelli were taking orders, and those who were giving them also attended the convention. At the Drake Hotel, Luciano took a large suite for himself and Marinelli. Down the hall, Costello took an equally lavish suite for himself and Hines. And, in between, Lansky had his own suite, where the underworld's beneficence was dispensed to all willing delegates and where Lansky was prepared to mediate, to entertain and to explore new worlds out in the hinterlands.

In that late-June week there was no pretense of observing the doomed 18th Amendment, of drinking secretly. Liquor was for sale openly to any delegate who wanted it. There were well-stocked bars doling out free booze to all comers in Lansky's, Costello's and Luciano's suites, night and day. It was during an extended drinking bout in Lansky's suite that a florid politician from Louisiana named Huey Long, the Kingfish, proposed that Lansky and his friends take gambling and slot machines to New Orleans and the other parishes, and so provide amusement for the natives and riches for the Kingfish. It would take time to make all the arrangements, but then millions would be extracted from Louisiana.

And in Luciano's suite, it was decided that Smith had no chance and that Tammany and the underworld would throw their support to Roosevelt. After all, they were con-

fident the governor was, as Walter Lippmann had written, "an amiable man with many philanthropic impulses, but he is not the dangerous enemy of anything. He is too eager to please. . . . Franklin D. Roosevelt is no crusader." With Roosevelt as the candidate and with Roosevelt in the White House, it seemed certain, they would have nothing to worry about.

But with the nomination in his pocket, the New York governor proved less compliant than expected. Ever since he had denounced corruption, he had been under steady public pressure from Seabury and from New York City Congressman Fiorello H. La Guardia to take action. Now he did just that. Tammany's record and reputation were liabilities in the campaign and Roosevelt proceeded to dump the machine. Echoing La Guardia's constant refrain, he thundered that public office was indeed a public trust, the highest of public trusts. Those holding office, like Caesar's wife, must be above suspicion. If suspicions were aroused, the officeholders must allay them. They must answer all questions put to them by responsible investigators or get out of office. If there were questions about the sources of Walker's money, then let Walker answer those questions. Seabury could ask away and the answers had better be satisfactory.

Judge Seabury promptly haled a parade of Democratic city politicians and officeholders before the commission and grilled them relentlessly about their underworld connections, about caches of money that were sud-

Jimmy Walker was mayor of New York, colorful, elegant, charming and quite corrupt.

denly turning up. Walker, for one, was less than cooperative; his manner suddenly became subdued and evasive, and Roosevelt announced his intention to throw him out of office. Before he could, Walker sent him a telegram: "I HEREBY RESIGN AS MAYOR OF THE CITY OF NEW YORK . . . JAMES J. WALKER." And before anyone quite knew what had happened, he was on a boat for Europe with his showgirl mistress. (When he returned years later, the scandals were just old memories and he was greeted with nostalgia by New Yorkers who fondly remembered "the good old days.")

But the flight of Walker and the revelations about his aides had little

immediate effect on the masters of the underworld. While the rest of the nation was suffering, the underworld was in the midst of one of its great booms. It was expanding wildly in every direction, seemingly without check, though some of the directions had long been charted.

By the late Twenties, sagacious men like Arnold Rothstein and Johnny Torrio had been predicting the eventual demise of Prohibition, especially if the national economy were to suffer a sharp downward turn. At the Atlantic City meeting in 1929 and especially at the 1931 Italian-dominated session in Chicago, the leaders had begun to consider the increased likelihood of legal liquor and its effect on their empires. As the depression worsened, the public's demand for a legal glass of beer or shot of booze became a deafening roar that could not be ignored. In the euphoria of the Roosevelt ascendancy, the new Democratic Congress in March 1933 legalized the manufacture and sale of light beer and wines. Less than nine months later, Prohibition was dead at the age of 14. On December 5, Utah became the 36th state to ratify the 21st Amendment to the Constitution, repealing the discredited 18th.

When that day came, those who had made their fortunes in bootlegging or in Canadian booze—great amounts of which had made its way to the United States during Prohibition—were ready to move in on the newly legitimized United States industry. Going legit was, of course, an obvious move. Samuel Bronfman became one of Canada's richest and most respected men as owner of Seagram, and Lewis Rosenstiel, who numbered among his close friends both Lansky and John Edgar Hoover—he would eventually create and endow the J. Edgar Hoover Foundation—became one of the United States's most renowned philanthropists and industrialists as head of Schenley. (Rosenstiel and Schenley, from which he retired in 1968, have consistently denied his underworld background.) But if there were some who with repeal tried to escape their unsavory Prohibition backgrounds, there were others who played both roles. Costello and his longtime partner in gambling, Phil Kastel, set up Alliance Distributors, which became the exclusive United States agent for Scotland's Whiteley Company, producer of King's Ransom and House of Lords Scotch; and by the mid-Thirties, Costello and Kastel bought a controlling interest in J. G. Turney and Son, Ltd., the British holding company for Whiteley. Torrio took control of Prendergast and Davies Company, Ltd., another major Scotch importer and wholesaler, and among those fronting for him in that company was Herbert Heller, Rosenstiel's brother-in-law. Lansky, Luciano, Bugsy Siegel, Joe Adonis, Costello and their friends all had shares in

Walker was eventually replaced by Fiorello La Guardia (right), who was just as, or perhaps more, colorful but a great deal more effective in fighting crime.

Capitol Wine and Spirits, a major importer and distributor of French wines, Scotch, Canadian and domestic whiskies. Schultz and just about everyone else got into the legal beer-brewing business. After 1933, there was hardly a major bootlegger who didn't have a piece of one legal distillery or another, and through the years liquor has remained a mainstay of the Mob.

But bootleg booze, despite repeal, remained a lucrative business. During the campaign to legalize drinking, some bright young men in the new Roosevelt Administration had what they considered a brilliant idea. Prohibition had clearly demonstrated that there was no way of stopping drinkers from drinking. The underworld had cashed in on that for billions of dollars. Now that liquor was going to be legal again, why shouldn't the financially hard-pressed federal and state governments cash in on this with high excise taxes?

Those who conceived this plan thought they had discovered a new Golconda that would pour billions into public treasuries (as, indeed, would eventually be the case). But excise taxes that would raise the price of booze as much as 50 percent meant large profits in the illegal manufacture of untaxed liquor. All over the country, the Prohibition bootleggers became repeal bootleggers, setting up huge clandestine stills and bottling plants. Perhaps the biggest and most famous was Molaska.

Just ten days before Utah ratified

the 21st Amendment, the little company called Molaska Corporation was registered in Ohio. Molaska's president was one John Drew. His real name was Jacob Stein and he was a disbarred New York attorney who had been a close friend a decade before of Gaston B. Means, one of the prime movers in the Ohio gang brought to Washington by President Warren G. Harding. Working with Means back in 1922, Stein had gotten the FBI director, William J. Burns, to release government bonded whiskey into his bootleg pipeline, through payoffs to Burns, Attorney General Harry M. Daugherty and the Republican Campaign Committee. Now Stein, or Drew, as he was calling himself, had reemerged as president-in-name of Molaska. But he was only a front, as were the other publicly identified officers, including one Moses Citron of New Jersey, the assistant treasurer. The real owners of Molaska were the underworld powers: Lansky, who was Citron's son-in-law; Moe Dalitz, Sam Tucker, Chuck and Al Polizzi of Cleveland; Pete Licavoli of Detroit; Adonis; Longy Zwillman and others.

According to its incorporation papers, Molaska had been set up for the ostensible purpose of manufacturing dehydrated molasses (hence its name) as a sugar substitute. Its source of molasses was almost limitless. During Prohibition, as he scoured the Caribbean in search of bootleg booze, Lansky had made friends with just about every corrupt politician in the area. He had become particularly close to Fulgencio Batista, and when Batista emerged as Cuba's strong man, Lansky rode alongside him. Batista guaranteed Lansky as much molasses as he would ever need. (And this was just one of the many deals that, in the decades ahead, that partnership would parlay into millions.)

But Molaska had no intention of using any but a small part of the Cuban molasses as a sugar substitute. Its real aim was to turn out bootleg booze. Huge stills elaborately concealed underground and complete with escape tunnels, were built in Cleveland and Zanesville, Ohio, in Elizabeth, New Jersey, and at least 13 (no one is really certain how many) other locations in the East and Midwest. Molaska's product, which cost two dollars a gallon wholesale and retailed for $2.50 a quart, found a ready market all over the eastern part of the country and as far west as Kansas City. The customers were not just ordinary drinkers who were looking for good cheap liquor but also a host of legal distilleries in which the underworld had some interest. These merely bottled and labeled the Molaska liquor and then sold it, at a price higher than strictly bootleg booze but, even with excise taxes, considerably lower than competitive legal liquor made and sold by non-Mob distilleries.

More is known about Molaska than about other illegal operations, because Molaska eventually became gargantuan and attracted official attention. Early in 1935, agents of the Internal Revenue Service's Alcohol and Tobacco Tax Unit closed down the stills in Zanesville and Elizabeth. The one in Zanesville, they estimated, was the largest illegal still ever discovered in the United States; it contained at least $250,000 worth of equipment and had the capacity to turn out 5000 gallons of 190-proof alcohol every 24 hours. And the Elizabeth still, agents said, was turning out enough booze "to flood New York and New Jersey with illicit alcohol."

Though the raids ended these two operations, it is unlikely that they discouraged the underworld from its continuing bootleg activities. But as a major activity, bootlegging soon lagged far behind gambling, fast emerging as the biggest money-maker in the underworld portfolio. With the Wall Street collapse and the depression that followed, the chances almost vanished for a quick killing anywhere. But there was still the chance, the long one, to buck the odds and come out rich through gambling, and the underworld provided any and every game of chance that any sucker wanted: a bet on the horses (or any sporting event) at plush horse parlors or with neighborhood bookies, backed and banked by the organization; a bet on the numbers; a coin in a slot machine; a chance from a candy-store punchboard; and, for those with a little more cash, roulette wheels, crap tables, blackjack games and other pastimes at the casinos the Mob was beginning to open around the country.

There was hardly a resort area anywhere in which Mob money

wasn't building clandestine casinos, usually with the support of paid-off local officials. During Upstate New York's social event of the summer, the Saratoga horse meet, the casinos boomed, the wheels spun and the chips and money of the nation's elite poured into the pockets of Luciano and Lansky and Costello, who ran the games. In the mid-Thirties, with the backing of Huey Long (whose share of the take may have reached $20,000,000 or more before his assassination), Costello and Kastel not only took the slot machines to New Orleans but they opened the Beverly Club, which was soon awash in the money of rich Southerners and vacationers; Lansky built and opened the Colonial Inn, the Club Greenacres and other places north of Miami. Owney Madden was running a string of casinos for the Mob in Hot Springs, Arkansas, which was becoming not merely a resort for the rich but a sanctuary and a playground for the rulers of organized crime. Zwillman, Luciano, Costello, Willie Moretti and others held controlling interests in an uncounted number of casinos that flourished along the New Jersey strip down the Hudson across from the Manhattan. The Cleveland mobsters such as Dalitz, in association with Lansky and Luciano and others, were taking over wide-open Covington, Kentucky. Wherever the rich traveled in search of pleasure, there the Mob either was waiting or soon followed with the games to amuse them and take their money.

But the Mob's gambling was not just for the rich. There was something for the very poor, too. Since the Twenties, the numbers—the policy racket—had been ubiquitous in Harlem; it was the chance for the poor blacks, at the risk of only a penny, a nickel, a dime, a quarter or even half a buck, to suddenly have their pockets filled with cash. Almost everyone played every day, and with the economic collapse extending poverty to millions of whites, the racket spread rapidly to every poor neighborhood in almost every city in the country.

For the bettor, it was painless. Who would miss a penny or a nickel a day? For that penny, he could select any combination of three numbers up to 999, and if he won—the winning number was based ordinarily on the betting totals from a combination of races at some horse track, and so was theoretically unfixable—he would get a payoff of 600 to 1.

For the operators, policy was almost unimaginably profitable and without major risk. After all, the real odds on a numbers bet were 999 to 1 and not the 600-to-1 payoff. In 1931, for instance, the Harlem policy banks were grossing $35,000 a day and paying out to winners only $7700 a day. Even with their overhead—commissions, salaries, police- and political-protection payoffs and the like—they were reaping a profit of more than 50 percent. And by 1933, in the depths of the depression, there were estimates that policy in New York City alone was grossing more than $300,000 a day, or over $100,000,000 a year. Including the rest of the country, that figure could be multiplied at least ten times.

Costello, who had grown up in East Harlem, always maintained some control over the rackets there, though his real interests were elsewhere. Policy was raining money also onto Luciano and Lepke and others in New York and onto the Cleveland Syndicate and every other major mob in the nation. But in the early Thirties, the biggest numbers operator in New York, and in the whole country, was Schultz. It was said that by 1933, he was cleaning up $20,000,000 a year from the numbers alone.

In the Twenties and Thirties, the ganglords had discovered an important source of revenue in Harlem: the numbers.

Schultz had moved in only a couple of years earlier. Backed by the counsel of his lawyer, J. Richard "Dixie" Davis, and the political muscle of Tammany boss Hines, who became his partner, Schultz muscled in on the Harlem operators around 1931. Self-employed numbers bankers Wilfred Brunder, Big Joe Ison, Henry Miro, Alexander Pompez and others were suddenly forced into either retirement or the employment of Schultz. Once he had taken over, Schultz put the mathematical genius of Otto "Abbadabba" Berman to work to figure out ways to increase the take. In a series of devious maneuvers (including the involved one of using his aides to suddenly increase the bets on the vital races to manipulate the pay-off number), Berman managed to further reduce the pay-out and increase the profits by 10 percent or more. His genius was copied by others, though nobody else seemed to have his ability.

For people who didn't want to bet the numbers or who thought they were not enough, there were options. Bookies inhabited every neighborhood, often as the owners of candy stores or small groceries looking for a way to make ends meet; most of them used the central bookmaking banks controlled by Luciano and his allies in New York, by the heirs to Capone in Chicago and by the leading mobsters elsewhere. Costello and Kastel had a lock on the slot machines and punchboards, and when the new mayor, La Guardia, went on a rampage against them, personally wielding an ax to

break some of the slots seized in raids, they merely took up the offer made by Long and moved them down to Louisiana.

The money generated by gambling and other rackets was mounting almost faster than anyone knew what to do with it, and when combined with the millions that had been salted away during Prohibition, the underworld during the depression probably had the biggest stash of liquid assets in the nation. It was money waiting to be put to work to earn even more money in an upward-spiraling cycle. It was available, at a price, to any businessman who wanted and needed it, who was willing to seek out the underworld's loan sharks, who was willing to pay the usurious interest rates—50 percent, 100 percent or more—or, failing that, to take on a partner. Shylocking developed into one of the surest, simplest and most important of the underworld's enterprises. "Loan-sharking, sometimes called 'juice,' is believed to be the second most important source of income for criminal syndicates," said former Attorney General Ramsey Clark. And, as the then-acting chief of the Justice Department's Organized Crime Section, Martin Loewy, noted in 1971, "Organized crime is not ordinarily short of cash. When business is slow, it leaves room for organized crime to take over. What starts out as a creditor ends up as a partner."

That was exactly what occurred in the early years of the depression and continues to this day. The technique is simple. The shylock lends whatever is needed at the usual usurious interest rate. Every week, the collectors go around for payment of both principal and interest. A classic example is a man who borrows $1000 for ten weeks; each of those ten weeks, he pays the shylock $150; thus, in just over two months, the loan shark has not only recouped his original $1000 but has added $500 to it, all of which goes back onto the street in the form of new loans.

If, however, the borrower is short and cannot come across, the trouble begins. In the old days, the optional payment would be a pound of flesh, and this occasionally is still exacted as a warning to other defaulters. But after the Wall Street debacle, the shylocks' clientele expanded to include many respectable men in business and industry who had nowhere else to turn and loan-sharking took a new twist. Luciano, Lansky, Lepke, Costello, Schultz and the other racketeers with imagination and hoards of cash moved into the banking business in a major way. They understood that beating or killing a recalcitrant borrower was simply wasteful: It didn't ensure that the money would ever be repaid and it left behind a bitter customer who might go to the authorities and thereby endanger an almost completely riskless business (police and court records indicate that shylocks are rarely arrested and even more rarely convicted). They also understood that most of their new customers had collateral—their businesses. And so developed the pattern in which a defaulting debtor was no longer beaten; he merely wound up with a new partner.

Having a gangster as a partner was not always as bad as some have described it, depending on the mood and the immediate objectives of the new partner. In some cases, the racketeer's sole desire was to get back his capital and more. So, through a variety of maneuvers, the business would be milked dry and driven into bankruptcy. But if the business provided a nice cover for the racketeer, it was usually in his interest not merely to keep it going but to make it succeed, to make it pay off with high profits—which a gangster could sometimes do when no one else could. The underworld had its contacts and its payoffs, ensuring that city inspectors would overlook various code violations that otherwise would necessitate costly repairs. And not infrequently, the new partner would invest money in new machinery and equipment that would increase both efficiency and profits.

Then, of course, there were reciprocal deals and interlocking arrangements. Gangster control of a variety of companies in numerous industries opened many opportunities to buy supplies and services cheaper than legitimate competitors could. Also, a company's shipments could be guaranteed safe and speedy handling, for the gangsters often controlled trucking companies, a natural outgrowth of their heavy involvement in trucking during the old bootleg days. And if they controlled local unions (the price paid for their organizing help), they could negotiate sweetheart contracts.

With loan-sharking as either the key or the wedge, the underworld soon managed to infiltrate or take over many corporations in many industries. Adonis, for instance, was for a time the leading Buick dealer in Brooklyn as proprietor of the Kings County Buick Company; he owned Automotive Conveying Company of New Jersey, which Ford paid millions to ship cars from its Edgewater, New Jersey, assembly plant all over the East; he also owned, among other legitimate and semilegitimate enterprises, a major cigarette distributorship and a large vending-machine operation. Moretti, too, controlled cigarette distribution, laundries, trucks and other businesses. Lansky, in addition to his liquor, gambling and other illegal operations, controlled a company called Manhattan Simplex (later, Emby), which distributed Wurlitzer jukeboxes; Lucchese, Albert Anastasia and others were able to list their occupation with taxmen and other officials as dress manufacturer, with factories in New York, Pennsylvania and elsewhere. Joe Bonanno not only owned a garment factory in Brooklyn but, like Costello and many others, was putting his money in real estate. The underworld would eventually control office buildings, apartment houses and other choice properties in every major city. Some of the industries the underworld found easiest to penetrate were amusements of all kinds, including theaters, movie-equipment manufacturers and

distributors; automobiles, particularly distributorships; baking; cigarette distribution; drugstores and drug companies; electrical-equipment manufacturing; construction; flowers; foods, especially meats, seafood, dairy products, fruit—all the perishable commodities that required quick and efficient handling to avoid spoilage and loss; garments; gas stations and garages; hotels; import-export businesses of all kinds; insurance; jukeboxes and other coin-operated machines; laundries and dry cleaners; liquor; loan companies and bonding agencies; news services, especially those specializing in racing information; newspapers; oil; paper products; race tracks; radio stations; restaurants; real estate; shipping; steel; stevedoring; transportation.

Corporate infiltration was only one side of the coin. Along with it went infiltration and take-over of unions, especially those in major urban centers or in industries in which the gangsters were deeply entrenched. The Teamsters, for one, were an early target. During the Twenties, the gangsters had become some of the biggest trucking operators in the nation, controlling huge fleets used to transport the illegal booze to market, and with repeal they turned to hauling every conceivable kind of merchandise. But, for Teamster organizers, moving in on underworld-controlled companies to try to sign up drivers was no easy task. So deals were worked out. The price of unionization was control of Teamster locals and a voice in the Teamsters' international union. The underworld influence in the Teamsters became so strong that union pension funds and other hoards found their way into gangland hotels and other operations, and the relationship between top Teamster officials and the leading underworld rulers such as Dalitz and Lansky was deep, abiding and very friendly. So corrupt, in fact, did the leadership of the union become that eventually the A.F.L.-C.I.O. found that it had no choice but to expel the Teamsters from the house of organized labor.

The Teamsters was just one union that fell, to a greater or lesser extent, under gangland control. Another classic example occurred in New York's Garment District. For years, the International Ladies' Garment Workers Union and the Amalgamated Clothing Workers of America had been unsuccessfully attempting to organize the sprawling industry of small loft factories piled one upon the other in the teeming area of the West 20s and 30s in Manhattan. The attempts had been beaten back consistently. Manufacturers entered into alliances with underworld strong men such as Lepke and Luciano and Lucchese to ensure that organizers never crossed their thresholds. And when the underworld began taking control of countless factories, the danger to union organizers only increased.

But gradually there came the realization that more profit and power could be attained by playing both sides, and soon Lepke, Lucchese,

Luciano and the rest were not just making dresses, coats and suits but pinning a union label on them. What seemed of greatest interest to the garment-center union leaders such as Sidney Hillman, David Dubinsky, Jacob Potofsky and others during the late Twenties and Thirties was not the wages or working conditions of the laborers but putting a union card in their pockets and extracting dues from them. If it didn't cost the manufacturers much, if it guaranteed labor peace, if it enriched the racketeers and increased their powers, then they were not averse to coming to the aid of the I.L.G.W.U. and the Amalgamated. Soon the ranks of garment-union organizers were swelled by the hirelings of Lepke, Luciano and the rest—tough thugs and killers such as Jacob "Gurrah" Shapiro, Charlie "The Bug" Workman and Abe "Kid Twist" Reles.

So the garment industry was organized, but the price was high. Numerous locals fell under the absolute control of the underworld and the corrupting influence marched all the way into union headquarters. Dues were siphoned off into the pockets of the gangsters and honest garment manufacturers found themselves forced to pay additional extortion money to Lepke, Lucchese, Luciano and their friends to avoid strikes and slowdowns, while their competitors down the street, owned or controlled by the very same men, had no such labor problems.

And then there is the incredible story of the Mob's move into the mo-

An associate of Frank Nitti, Willie Bioff, put the squeeze on the movie industry.

tion-picture industry. It began in 1932, when George E. Browne, the business agent of Local Two of the International Alliance of Theatrical Stage Employees (I.A.T.S.E.), linked up with one Willie Bioff, extortionist, hoodlum and business associate of Frank Nitti and other Capone mobsters, of Luciano, Lepke, Costello, Zwillman and many more. Browne's local had jurisdiction over motion-picture projectionists and, times being not the best, more than half the local's 400 members were out of work. Bioff and Browne came up with an idea of how to turn that unemployment into golden linings for their personal pockets. They set up a soup kitchen to feed the destitute projectionists and then proceeded to

squeeze theater owners for contributions to support the kitchen. It was all pretty small time until the two decided to take on Barney Balaban, head of the Balaban & Katz theater chain.

Bioff and Browne showed up at Balaban's office one morning and demanded that he restore a pay cut he had imposed on his theatrical employees a couple of years earlier when the depression hit. When Balaban resisted, the two gave him an alternative. They would forget the demand if Balaban would kick in $7500 a year to operate the soup kitchen. "Barney," Bioff later testified in court when the law finally caught up with him, "turned out to be a lamb. When he agreed to our suggestion, I knew we had him. I told him his contribution would have to be $50,000 unless he wanted real trouble. By that I meant we would pull his projectionists out of the theaters. He was appalled, but we turned on the heat. He finally agreed to pay us $20,000."

It had all been so simple that Bioff and Browne decided that a single local was not enough, that they could make millions if they could capture the international. To support that bid, there was the underworld. In Chicago, Nitti, Paul DeLucia and other rulers of the Capone empire put the pressure on voting unionists to cast their ballots for Browne as the new president of I.A.T.S.E. In New York, the Browne slate had behind it the muscle of Lepke, Luciano and Zwillman; Dalitz, Frankie Milano and the Polizzis put the same kind of heat on union members in Cleveland

and elsewhere in the Midwest. The electioneering was direct and blunt, and successful. When the I.A.T.S.E. convention was held in Louisville, the underworld's enforcers were ominously present, strolling slowly among the delegates and passing out messages. When it came time to vote, Browne was elected president unanimously.

His first move was to appoint Bioff his "personal representative." And then the two decided to take over the whole movie industry, at least to the extent of extorting a fortune from it. They demanded a payoff from the theater chains in Chicago; if the theaters didn't pay up, Browne threatened to strike them with the demand that they hire two projectionists instead of the one they then had to employ. The gambit worked; the theaters came across with $100,000. The only problem for Browne and Bioff was that their Mob backers began demanding a bigger share of the take; instead of a 50-50 split, the mobsters demanded 75 percent, leaving Browne and Bioff to share the remaining 25 percent. That fazed the union leaders for only a moment; they told the theater owners they were taking a cut of the profits and then, to keep their incomes as high as they had been before the new split, told them to cut the wages of their projectionists and fire some of their stagehands.

Success in Chicago propelled Bioff and Browne ever onward. They turned to New York and with no difficulty at all took the Loew's theater chain for $150,000, the price for calling off a strike. But the biggest stake was still ahead—Hollywood itself. In 1936, I.A.T.S.E. had few members in the West Coast movie studios, but that didn't deter Bioff and Browne or their gangland backers. They demanded that I.A.T.S.E. be given jurisdiction over movie-studio labor. The studios resisted. The Mob reacted by striking and closing every movie theater from Chicago to St. Louis. The theater owners, led by Balaban, howled in anguish and the studios capitulated.

Controlling Hollywood labor was the wedge. Bioff called on Nicholas M. Schenck, president of Loew's and spokesman for the industry, and informed him: "You have a prosperous business here. I elected Browne president of this union because he will do what I say. I am the boss and I want $2,000,000 out of the movie industry."

Schenck was stunned. "At first I couldn't talk," he said. "But Bioff said, 'You don't know what will happen. We gave you just a taste of it in Chicago. We will close down every theater in the country. You couldn't take that. It will cost you many millions of dollars over and over again. Think it over.'"

Think it over was what Schenck did, along with Sidney Kent of 20th Century-Fox and Leo Spitz of RKO, and they decided that wisdom dictated the payment, immediately and in perpetuity. The first money was paid in New York, at the Hotel Warwick. Schenck and Kent took $75,000 as the initial installment in a satchel and then were forced to stand around and watch while Bioff and Browne dumped their loot onto a bed and slowly, carefully counted it.

The movie industry got its high-priced peace and Bioff and Browne and their Mob friends got their fortunes. This went on for several years, until Joseph M. Schenck, brother of Nicholas and 20th Century-Fox chairman of the board, ran afoul of the law. After neglecting to report several large items on his income-tax return, he was indicted for and convicted of tax evasion, and in return for a reduced sentence, he decided to tell the government of his underworld dealings. His tale led to the indictment of the extortionists. Browne and Bioff were both convicted and sent to prison, where they decided to do a little singing of their own about their Mob backers, some of whom were also indicted. Faced with another term in prison, Nitti decided that was too much. He committed suicide. DeLucia and several others wound up behind bars.

But that didn't happen until 1941. In the meantime, the Mob was thriving. Its legitimate businesses were booming, it was capturing union after union and its illegal enterprises were pouring money into the coffers faster than even a computer could count it. By the middle Thirties, such racketeering opportunities were clear, indeed, to the leaders of the underworld and gave increasing urgency to tightening the links that had been forged at Atlantic City in 1929 and at the Italian-dominated Chicago conference in 1931.

IN A SERIES OF MEETINGS DURING the next three years—in Chicago, Cleveland and at several places in New York, including the 39th-floor suite of the Waldorf Towers, where Luciano lived in luxury under the Anglo-Saxon alias of Charles Ross—there was born what some have called the Combination, others the Outfit, still others the National Crime Syndicate or just the Syndicate. Almost every important underworld figure in the nation, either in person or by proxy, took part in these discussions and decisions.

Much of the impetus behind these sessions came from Johnny Torrio, the underworld's elder statesman though still in his fifties. But Torrio had plenty of backing and many allies—men with strong voices and firm ideas of their own who saw, as he did, the need for national cooperation and were determined to bring it about. There were Luciano from New York and his powerful friends, Adonis, Costello, Lansky, Vito Genovese, Bugsy Siegel, Lepke. There were Dalitz from Cleveland, who usually traveled under the name Moe Davis, and Dalitz's friends in both the Jewish and the Italian underworlds. There were Costello's New Orleans partner, Kastel, who was discovering gold in southern slot machines and gambling, and Kid Cann, born Isadore Blumenfield, from Minneapolis–St.

WANTED

LESTER M. GILLIS,

aliases GEORGE NELSON, "BABY FACE" NELSON, ALEX GILLIS, LESTER GILES,
"BIG GEORGE" NELSON, "JIMMIE", "JIMMY" WILLIAMS.

On June 23, 1934, HOMER S. CUMMINGS, Attorney General of the United States, under the authority vested in him by an Act of Congress approved June 6, 1934, offered a reward of

$5,000.00

for the capture of Lester M. Gillis or a reward of

$2,500.00

for information leading to the arrest of Lester M. Gillis.

DESCRIPTION

Age, 25 years; Height, 5 feet 4-3/4 inches; Weight,
133 pounds; Build, medium; Eyes, yellow and grey
slate; Hair, light chestnut; Complexion, light; Occupation, oiler.

All claims to any of the aforesaid rewards and all questions and disputes that may arise as among claimants to the foregoing rewards shall be passed upon by the Attorney General and his decisions shall be final and conclusive. The right is reserved to divide and allocate portions of any of said rewards as between several claimants. No part of the aforesaid rewards shall be paid to any official or employee of the Department of Justice.

If you are in possession of any information concerning the whereabouts of Lester M. Gillis, communicate immediately by telephone or telegraph collect to the nearest office of the Division of Investigation, United States Department of Justice, the local offices of which are set forth on the reverse side of this notice.

The apprehension of Lester M. Gillis is sought in connection with the murder of Special Agent W. C. Baum of the Division of Investigation near Rhinelander, Wisconsin on April 23, 1934.

JOHN EDGAR HOOVER, DIRECTOR,
DIVISION OF INVESTIGATION,
UNITED STATES DEPARTMENT OF JUSTICE,
WASHINGTON, D. C.

June 25, 1934

During the depression, the free-lancers had their chance, too. Baby Face Nelson was one of the independents.

Paul. The Philadelphia strong men, such as Harry Stromberg, better known as Nig Rosen, all favored the plan, and so did Zwillman and his partner, Moretti, from northern New Jersey. King Solomon and, after Solomon died, Hymie Abrams usually attended to voice the desires of the New England mobs, and Anthony "Little Augie" Carfano, who had moved to Miami, usually appeared to lobby for the idea that he should have suzerainty there. Kansas City's Boss Tom Pendergast was kept informed of all developments, though he was so deeply involved with federal and

state authorities during these years that he couldn't spare the time to attend any of the meetings; his organization was in chaos and his underworld aide, John Lazia, convicted of tax evasion in 1934, was threatening to sing until machine-gun bullets sealed his lips. Torrio had decreed

Clyde Barrow (far left) and Bonnie Parker (left) were two criminals who made their names and reputation outside of organized crime. It paid off too: People lined up to view the bullet-ridden body of Bonnie (top).

that no formal invitation be extended to the Chicago mobs; his own experiences with these had convinced him that the Chicagoans were just too uncivilized to engage in polite discussions with perspicacious men. But he did permit Chicago to send observers to the meetings, usually Paul "The Waiter" Ricca, who was generally considered, along with Jake "Greasy Thumb" Guzik, the smartest racketeer in the old Capone organization.

The purpose of these meetings, of course, was to implement the decisions of the 1931 Chicago conference, to forge closer ties among all the mobs, whatever their ethnic makeup, in cities across the country, and to agree on the rules by which they could not only coexist, as in the recent past, but at least partially merge.

And the signs looked good that such hopes could be realized. Luciano frequently pointed out that the days of jealousy and clannishness in the Italian underworld were over. The assassinations of Giuseppe Masseria and Salvatore Maranzano, for which he took due credit, had already begun to bring the Mafia, or the Unione Siciliana, as he preferred to call it, out of the darkness of its provincialism to work cooperatively with everyone. When the underworld cartel was finally established, Luciano stressed, the Italians, too, would abide by the rules and disciplines of the national commission (on which, of course, he and other powerful Mafia figures would sit).

Luciano, Adonis, Lansky and others often referred to the success of the Seven Group (the organization established in 1927 to ensure cooperation among the seven major powers) as an example of what interethnic cooperation could accomplish, and after 1933, Lansky and Dalitz held up the Molaska operation and the joint gambling ventures as examples of how profitable interregional cooperation could be.

Zwillman's point, which he

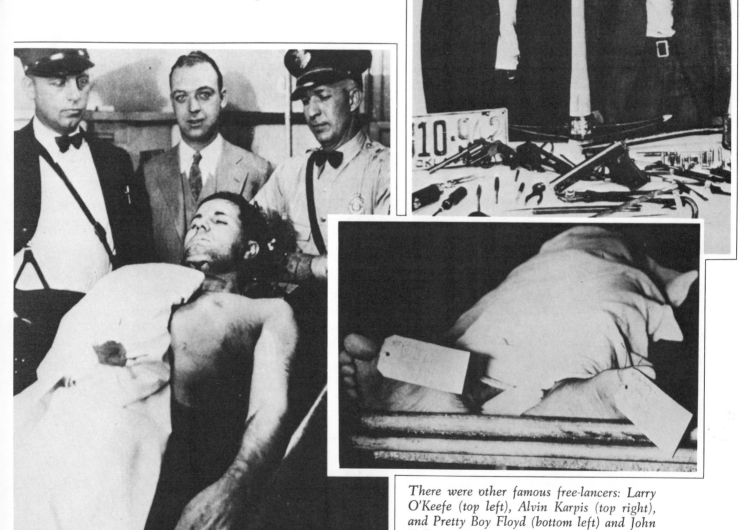

There were other famous free-lancers: Larry O'Keefe (top left), Alvin Karpis (top right), and Pretty Boy Floyd (bottom left) and John Dillinger (bottom right), both standing still for posterity.

raised time and again, dealt with public relations—the need for underworld leaders to present and comport themselves as good and responsible businessmen. It became something of an obsession with the New Jersey racketeer, who was forever denouncing the violence of the Dutch Schultz–Mad Dog Coll warfare and the rise of the free-lance criminals such as John Dillinger and his bank-robbing, chopper-waving, trigger-happy friends. Such adventurers had to be put down, he often said; they were bad for business, as was gangland feuding; and as good businessmen, he and the others must stress discipline, cooperation and organization. Nor should they neglect to enhance their images as public-spirited citizens. As examples, he cited his own offer of a reward for the capture and conviction of the kidnapper of the infant son of Colonel Charles A. Lindbergh, and Madden's offer of his own personal services at no cost.

Through these continuing discussions, the determination to establish a national Syndicate became fixed, and in the workings of the new Roosevelt Administration—the National Recovery Administration, with its national board and its regional district boards—the underworld found a model for its own organization. By 1934, the Syndicate was following this route, setting up its national commission, or board of directors, to decide overall policy and arbitrate all disputes. Under it were regional boards; the country was di-

vided into districts with a regional commission in charge of all organized crime in its territory, and with territorial lines inviolate. In those areas, such as the West Coast and Miami, where the organization was just getting started, joint ventures should be undertaken.

To enforce these agreements, the national commission adopted an idea that Lepke had long been advancing. During Prohibition, the Bugs and Meyer Mob had been the enforcers for their partners and for the Seven Group. Lepke proposed a similar enforcement arm, directed by him and Anastasia and composed of professional killers who would work under contract to the national commission and to regional and local organizations. It was a plan that met with approval, except for two minor objections, voiced by Dalitz and Lansky. They noted that when a politician or a reporter was killed, the inevitable result was bad publicity and a wave of civic reform. Thus, politicians and journalists should be declared off limits. With these necessary exceptions, Lepke's scheme led to the establishment of what would become known as Murder, Incorporated.

Such elaborate plans could not be implemented in a single day or week; that took years and many arduous meetings. But by 1934, the Combination was becoming a reality.

At the same time, however, the heat on the underworld was increasing through a series of scandals and disclosures and would soon result in staggering explosions.

THE HEAT'S ON

BY THE EARLY THIRTIES, IT seemed that nothing could halt the spread of underworld power. Most of the country's major cities and many of the smaller ones were, in important ways, controlled by criminals. Politicians and police took money and orders from the racketeers; businessmen facing bankruptcy during the depression had nowhere else to turn for cash, and so fell under their control; unions sought their services and became their servants. There were times when the entire nation seemed at the mercy of the Mob.

But the specter of government by gangsters also inspired the first major reform efforts by federal, state and local authorities. The federal effort was led by Elmer Irey and his associates at the Internal Revenue Service. When all other tactics seemed unavailing, there was still the possibility of sending gangsters to jail for income-tax evasion. In New York, long-ignored civic corruption was suddenly in the spotlight of the Seabury Commission. And a little later, the city itself would join the drive against the underworld when a new mayor, Fiorello "Little Flower" La Guardia, and his reformist fusion administration came to power.

Under the spur of President Herbert Hoover and Treasury Secretary Andrew Mellon, Irey had kicked off the federal drive in Chicago in 1929. He had collected enough financial evidence to send Ralph and Al

Taxes became a fate worse than death to many mobsters.

Capone, Jake Guzik, Frank Nitti and others to prison. In Kansas City, his agents had brought about the disgrace, if not the total collapse, of the Pendergast machine. And in New York, the multimillionaire bootleggers and racketeers were being put under the tax microscope. The initial target was Waxey Gordon.

There was little affection for Gordon in the fledgling national crime Syndicate. His control of illegal distilleries in Philadelphia, New Jersey, New York and elsewhere, and his hold on foreign sources of supply, had given him a degree of independence and power that forced almost everyone to come to him. Moreover, requests for deals with Gordon usually resulted in his demanding a partner-

ship, and his tough, arrogant manner further alienated his business associates. In Philadelphia, he had feuded long and bitterly even with his allies, men such as Nig Rosen and Boo-Boo Hoff. Perhaps more serious, the enmity between him and Meyer Lansky had deepened over the years. By the end of the Twenties, they would rarely speak to each other or sit down together in the same room. Lucky Luciano, Joe Adonis, Longy Zwillman and his partner Willie Moretti, Tommy Lucchese, even Lansky's oldest friend and longtime partner, Bugsy Siegel, all of whom had tried to work with both, found it increasingly difficult to keep the peace between the two seemingly indispensable men. They wanted no showdown, but if one were to come, they would side with Lansky. The "Little Man," as the 5'4" Lansky was often called, had brains and ability, kept his ambitions to himself and preferred to stay in the background as a man who would not challenge the power of anyone else. Even more than Frank Costello, Lansky seemed content to guide obliquely by suggestion and subtle persuasion. So Gordon's vitriol against Lansky won him no points in the organization. And he lost points in the early Thirties when he made himself another powerful enemy in Dutch Schultz, as each began invading the other's brewing domains in anticipation of legal beer.

Gordon, with his wealth, power and ostentation, was as natural a target for Irey's taxmen in the East as Capone had been in the Midwest,

Willie Moretti.

Tommy Lucchese.

and, according to some underworld sources, the Irey investigation was secretly abetted by Gordon's multitude of enemies. Through Lansky's brother Jake and others, the taxmen were quietly fed information and leads about Gordon's sources of income. In a number of private underworld meetings, the decision was made not to deal with Gordon by the old, violent methods, though some, especially Schultz, favored such action. To kill Gordon, the wiser counsel went, would only result in more bad publicity at a time when too many bodies were already littering the landscape, so the undoing of Waxey Gordon would be left to the government.

But Schultz could not resist taking one last blast at Gordon, and in April 1933, he sent a crew of killers after the bootlegger. As they went in

the door of Gordon's room at the Carteret Hotel in Elizabeth, New Jersey, Gordon escaped. Not so lucky were two of his aides, who were both gunned down.

Schultz's failure to get Gordon was his last chance. The government's tax case had by then been fully developed and put in the hands of a young United States attorney in New York. He was a small man with a mustache, an immense ego and outsized political ambitions, a small-town Michigan Republican who had become a Wall Street lawyer before entering public service. His name was Thomas E. Dewey. As a prosecutor of businessmen, financiers and industrialists indicted for financial peculations, Dewey was something less than brilliant; he seemed unable to convict prominent citizens. With gangsters, however, it was different. He seemed

Benny "Bugsy" Siegel (top left), Meyer Lansky (bottom left), Waxey Gordon (right).

then a vengeful tiger with an instinct for the jugular. Within five months of his appointment as an assistant United States attorney in 1931, he did

what prosecutors had been trying to do for years: convict Legs Diamond. Unfortunately, Diamond never served a day; while free on bond pending his appeal, he was murdered in an Albany, New York, rooming house, probably by the Schultz Mob.

In 1933, Dewey was named interim United States attorney and personally took charge of the tax-evasion case against Gordon. His presentation was masterful, replete with histrionics, self-righteousness and scorn. Gordon, he told the jury, had a real income in excess of $2,000,000 a year, was spending more than $6000 a year in rent, owned vast amounts of property, including several homes with lavish furnishings, spent money on innumerable luxuries and then had the gall to file income-tax returns declaring a net income of only $8125 a year. The jury was convinced. Gordon was convicted in December 1933, fined $80,000 and sent to prison for ten years. That was the end of Waxey Gordon as a major underworld figure. (Released just in time for World War II, Gordon immediately got into the black market and ended up back in prison. When next on the streets, he returned to an occupation of his youth, pushing drugs, and by the late Fifties was back in prison once more.)

With Gordon out of the way, the next target for the IRS and Dewey was Schultz. This upset the Dutchman and gave rise later to his plaint that the cops were after him, that he was notorious only because his name fit the headlines; better he should have remained Arthur Flegenheimer. For by this time, Schultz was, indeed, a household name, constantly in the headlines as the Seabury investigation and others dug deeply into his

racketeering and his relationship with politicians. But worse for Schultz, though he didn't know it yet, was the fact that he had also become a target for his sometime partner in the underworld.

The Dutchman had an unpopular penchant for trouble and violence. He had fought Gordon for control of the beer business in New York and New Jersey, while almost simultaneously warring with "Mad Dog" Coll, the young Irish killer and beer runner who had left Schultz in the late Twenties to form a rival gang. The struggle lasted about a year and filled the streets, alleys and rivers with bodies from both sides—nobody was ever sure how many, since the Castellammarese War was going on about that time and there were other internecine battles as well.

For a short time in the middle of the Schultz-Coll War, there was a truce, but only because Coll was out of commission. A car filled with his gunmen had roared through East Harlem prepared for a shoot-out with some of Schultz's troops in residence at a social club. Coll's men sprayed the area with bullets, hitting several nearby children and killing a five-year-old boy. That outrage finally compelled the police to intervene. Coll was picked up and charged with murder. His trial was something of a farce. Coll's lawyer, Samuel Leibowitz (who would win the reputation as the nation's most vindictive hanging judge when he sat on the county-court bench in Brooklyn), riddled and ridiculed the state's case and Coll won a directed verdict of acquittal.

But this was Coll's last hurrah. No sooner was he back in circulation than Schultz was after him. Coll's older brother, Peter, had already been gunned down on a Harlem street. Coll replied by shooting several Schultz hirelings. Schultz stepped up the attack and Coll went into hiding but was tracked down to a rooming house in Manhattan's Chelsea district. On February 8, 1932, he left his room to

Mad Dog Coll (right insert) was precisely that. His war against Dutch Schultz filled the streets with blood.

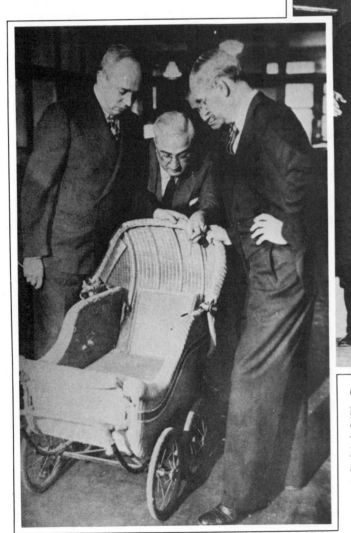

Children were caught in the cross-fire and one five-year-old boy was killed. Coll's lawyer, Samuel Leibowitz (in the camel-hair coat), later known as a "hanging" judge, made a farce of the trial and Coll was set free.

make a telephone call at the corner drugstore. Schultz's killers waited until he closed the door of the phone booth, then riddled it, and its helpless occupant, with submachine-gun bullets.

The Dutchman's victory was something of a disappointment to his underworld friends Luciano, Lansky, Costello and Louis "Lepke" Buchalter. For them, Schultz had become an object of concern and envy. His successes in battle and in captur-

Coll didn't enjoy his freedom very long. Schultz's gunmen caught up with him in a phone booth in a West 23rd Street drugstore.

ing the Harlem policy racket made many fear that he would soon be casting eyes on their domains. Furthermore, they themselves were coveting the Schultz empire and would not have objected if Coll had eliminated the main obstacle to their taking it over.

When Coll failed, the next hope was the federal government. In the waning days of his presidency, Hoover, pleased with the early successes of his treasury agents, began to pressure them to go after Schultz as well as Gordon; and in January 1933, Dewey presented enough evidence to a federal grand jury in New York to indict the Dutchman for failing to file

Mad Dog was mourned only by his bride (top right), buried on a bleak February day and left as his only legacy the bullets used to kill him (bottom insert).

tax returns for 1929, 1930 and 1931. In those years, the government charged, his provable taxable income from bootlegging alone amounted to $481,637.35, and he was thus in arrears for $92,103.34, plus interest. It appeared to be an airtight case; the government could not lose.

But Schultz was a different breed from Capone, Gordon and the rest. Where they had readily surrendered to authorities upon indictment and gone to trial, Schultz had new interests in policy, in restaurant protection and in breweries that needed his personal attention. That attention could best be given while he was a free man, so he went into hiding, at least officially. With the overt and covert assistance of bribed police and politicians, he managed to remain at large, even travel about, despite more than 50,000 WANTED posters prominently displayed all over New York. He lived openly at a number of apartments around the city, receiving friends, associates and those public servants on his payroll, and he did not abandon his night-clubbing nor his regular visits to Polly Adler's brothel.

By mid-1934, nearly a year and a half after the indictments had been handed down (and by which time Republican Dewey was out of the U.S. attorney's office and temporarily practicing law on Wall Street), Schultz's flouting of the law had become too blatant to ignore. Franklin Roosevelt's secretary of the treasury, Henry Morgenthau, put the heat on federal and local officials. FBI Director J. Edgar Hoover ordered his agents

to bring in Schultz without delay, and New York's new reform mayor, La Guardia, who had ridden into office on the promise to "throw the bums out," directed his new police commissioner, Lewis J. Valentine, to get his men off their asses and after the Dutchman.

Schultz turned to his supposed friends for help, not suspecting the kind of help they really wanted to give him. At that moment, though, they helped him hide out and he offered to cough up $100,000 as a settlement if the government would withdraw the indictments. Like his predecessor in the Hoover Administration, who had turned down a much more generous $400,000 offer from Capone, Morgenthau refused. "We don't do business with criminals," he said.

The search for Schultz intensified, and with the then-trigger-happy FBI involved, Schultz decided to avoid any confrontation. On a cold November day in 1934, he walked into the Albany office of United States Commissioner Lester T. Hubbard and said, "I'm Arthur Flegenheimer. I am under indictment in the Southern District of New York. I wish to surrender."

In the following months, Schultz, free on $75,000 bail, toiled at preparing his defense. The last thing his battery of lawyers wanted was a trial in New York City, where Schultz was notorious. La Guardia's campaign against the underworld and the continuing Seabury revelations had finally caused citizens to withdraw some of their tolerance toward glamorous gangsters. A change of venue was requested and eventually granted.

The trial was scheduled for April 1935, in Syracuse. The government's case, built with diligence by Dewey and his staff before they returned to private practice, was handled by John H. McEvers, special assistant to Attorney General Homer Cummings. McEvers paraded witness after witness before the jury to lay out the details of Schultz's bootleg empire and the amounts of cash that flowed into it. There seemed little possibility that the government would lose, particularly when Schultz entered no denials. His defense took only three hours to present. There was the startling admission that the government was, if anything, understating his bootleg income. But, the defense contended, Schultz had not filed tax returns because his lawyers had told him he didn't have to, that income from illegal sources could not be declared for tax purposes. When this advice proved wrong, Schultz claimed, he had made his offer to come across with $100,000. As he explained it outside court (and the jury was not unaware of the remarks), "I offered $100,000 when the government was broke and people were talking revolution and they turned me down cold. . . . Everybody knows I am being persecuted in this case. I wanted to pay. They were taking it from everybody else, but they wouldn't take it from me. I tried to do my duty as a citizen—maybe I'm not a citizen?"

The jury debated for two days before coming back to court to inform the judge that it was hopelessly deadlocked, seven to five for conviction.

But the government was not ready to give up. A second trial was called for July in the isolated upstate town of Malone, near the Canadian border. Schultz arrived in town a week before the trial. At home, he was a miser. In Malone, he became a gregarious and extroverted spendthrift. He toured the bars and taverns every night, standing all the customers to free drinks. He made lavish contributions to local charities and went to major social events with the mayor, other politicians and prominent businessmen. An outraged local clergy, ranting about his corrupting influence, managed to get his bail revoked and he was lodged in the local jail, but he had made a deep impression on Malone and, according to rumors, had enriched a number of its influential citizens.

So a climate had been established. The trial was almost a replay of the one in Syracuse, and Schultz's attorneys informed the jury that he intended to "do my duty as an American citizen" and pay over the $100,000 he had offered, no matter what the outcome. Again, the jury debated two days, returning to court to announce that it had reached a unanimous verdict. Schultz was not guilty. Federal Judge Frederick H. Bryant was horrified. "Your verdict," he told the jury, "is such that it shakes the confidence of law-abiding people in integrity and truth. It will be apparent to all who followed the evidence in this case that you have reached a verdict based not on the evidence but on some other reason. You will go home with the satisfaction, if it is a satisfaction, that you have rendered a blow against law enforcement and given aid and encouragement to the people who would flout the law. In all probability, they will commend you. I cannot."

The Schultz case was one of few failures that government had or would have in prosecuting racketeers for tax evasion. Even the quiet man, Johnny Torrio, behind the scenes, fell victim to the charge in 1939 and wound up in Leavenworth. But Schultz, as in so many ways, was the exception.

News of the acquittal was received with considerable shock back in New York City, and not just by city officials. Schultz's underworld associates were also shaken. During the time since his surrender, they had been operating on the assumption that Schultz was finished and had begun cutting up his empire among themselves, with help from inside the Dutchman's kingdom. As Schultz's tax troubles and future prospects worsened, his senior lieutenant, Abraham "Bo" Weinberg, the man who kept the books and who knew intimately every business secret, had become increasingly restive. Schultz was drawing off large sums from his policy, protection and the other rackets to pay for his defense, and this did not make Weinberg happy. What particularly worried him was his own

future once Schultz departed for good and his empire became spoils for the rest of the underworld.

He took his problem to his old and good friend Zwillman. To Zwillman he offered to open the books on all the operations and turn over the organization intact, thereby avoiding a war that would almost certainly shatter the empire he had worked so hard to build. In return, he wanted a percentage of the take and a job as overseer of the business, doing what he had done so long.

As a member of the national Syndicate and as a friend and partner of most of the other underworld leaders, Zwillman could not very well take over by himself. He took the Weinberg package to his compatriots and they grabbed it eagerly but still insisted on splitting it up: Zwillman got all the New Jersey interests; Costello and Lansky took the restaurants and protection; and Luciano, as *de facto* chairman of the board, was cut in for a piece of everything. As for Weinberg, he worked for the whole Syndicate, coordinating the Schultz operations, with Zwillman his contact man for the group.

It was all fine as long as Schultz was away and preoccupied with staying out of jail. But after his acquittal and return to New York, he was less than appreciative of the way his interests had been protected by his erstwhile friends. Initially, there was little he could do in the way of reprisal. Some of what had been seized was returned with the explanation that his friends had merely been managing

General John Thompson displays with pride (right) the 1921 model of the gun that did so much for organized crime. He couldn't have guessed its future criminal notoriety. The 1920 model (below) had the buttstock removed; an earlier model (bottom right) used ammo belts instead of clips.

it in his absence. Schultz had to buy this; he was still under constant harassment by La Guardia and Valentine and could hardly make a move without being picked up for questioning. So he began spending more and more time in New Jersey, cultivating his interests there. In New Jersey, he found himself potentially embroiled with Zwillman, who had become a major political and underworld power in the state, and again Schultz bit the bullet. The two had been long-

time friends and business partners and Schultz still had hopes of moving into some new ventures in partnership with Zwillman.

But Weinberg was another matter. Schultz knew that his operations could not have been so quickly gobbled up and so efficiently run without the help of Weinberg. And Weinberg was not high in underworld circles, and was not protected. One warm September evening in 1935, Weinberg left his office after a day's work, possibly to meet Zwillman. In any case, he was never seen again. The story goes that Schultz himself was waiting, put a bullet in Weinberg's head, his feet in concrete, his body in the Hudson River.

While the dispatch of Weinberg must have been personally satisfying to Schultz, it did not solve his problems. Nor did it permit him to reconstruct his sundered empire. He was now the prey of many and the traps were being set.

Former Federal Prosecutor Dewey was setting one of them, as part of the cleanup drive that had been begun some years earlier with the formation of the Seabury Commission. That panel's revelations had driven Jimmy Walker to exile in Europe, had created enough public disenchantment to propel La Guardia into the mayor's chair. But though La Guardia was mayor and his police commissioner, Valentine, was telling the cops, "I'll promote the men who kick these gorillas around and bring them in. And I'll demote any policemen who are friendly with gangsters," it took longer for the spirit of reform to infest the district attorney's office. To avoid any such contagion, Jimmy Hines had put up a candidate for D.A. named William Copeland Dodge—"stupid, respectable and my man," Hines said of him—and Dodge won narrowly. However, once in office, Dodge proved himself equally responsive to the demands of La Guardia, the press and the reformers and empaneled a special grand jury to investigate corruption, graft, policy and

William C. Dodge preceded Thomas E. Dewey as New York County D.A.

other evils. Then, of course, he refused to do anything about the evidence it uncovered. The grand jury gave up, but it wired Governor Herbert H. Lehman and demanded a special prosecutor, asserting that it was hopeless to work with Dodge. Lehman came up with a list of four prominent Republicans. One after another, the four declined. A fifth Republican lawyer, Tom Dewey, was suggested and he accepted with alacrity.

REACTIVATED PROSECUTOR Dewey moved into special quarters early in 1935. Working slowly and carefully with a staff of bright young attorneys and investiga-

Carlo Gambino.

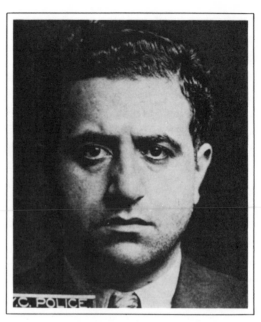

Albert Anastasia.

tors, he began accumulating evidence. Schultz was of no special interest initially, because the federal government had him. But once he was acquitted in Malone, Dewey publicly announced that Schultz was his prime target. The rumor spread that Dewey was set to indict Schultz in connection with the restaurant rackets and that this case would be unbeatable. But there was another rumor, as well. Dewey, it was whispered, was gathering evidence that would put Schultz in the Sing Sing electric chair for the 1935 murder of one Jules Modgilewsky, sometimes called Jules Martin or Modgilewsky the Commissar, one of Schultz's restaurant enforcers with whom he had had a falling out. (A few years later, Schultz's sometime lawyer, close advisor and confidant, J. Richard "Dixie" Davis, then on trial for crimes

growing out of the association, told the full story of that snowy March evening near Albany, how Schultz, with Davis watching, had pulled a gun in a hotel room and killed Modgilewsky on the spot.)

As the rumors spread, Schultz's underworld friends worried considerably. If Schultz were convicted and confronted with a long stretch in the penitentiary, would he take some of his friends with him in trade for a reduced sentence? Or would he, if acquitted again, declare total war to recover his empire? Either way, a living, breathing Schultz was a danger to everyone.

To make things worse, Schultz also was spouting the need to kill Dewey, proclaiming with nearsighted logic that Dewey's demise would solve his immediate problems and the future problems of others. Schultz even had a plan for the assassination and he turned to Albert Anastasia for help, asking Anastasia to stake out Dewey's Fifth Avenue apartment to see how easy it would be to get to him. Anastasia obediently did just that, but he did more. Concerned about the reaction of his friends at the top of the organization, he discussed the Schultz proposal with such rising young aides as Carlo Gambino, who did not take kindly to the idea of a hit on a prosecutor and convinced Anastasia to carry word of the Schultz plot to Luciano and the other leaders of the Combination. Such news was upsetting, indeed, coming so soon after the Syndicate had established firm rules against the killing of public officials and newspapermen. There was only one recourse. Schultz had to go, and the contract was given to the Lepke-Anastasia enforcement arm of the Syndicate. One of the top killers in the outfit, Charlie "The Bug" Workman, a longtime Garment District enforcer, was given personal responsibility for the job.

On October 23, 1935, Schultz went to a favorite hangout, the Palace Chop House and Tavern, in Newark. With him in a back room were two bodyguards, Abe Landau and Bernard "Lulu" Rosenkrantz, and the wizard of the numbers, Otto "Abbadabba" Berman. Late in the evening, Schultz left the table to go to the men's room. As he closed the door behind him, the front door of the Palace opened and Workman and another killer entered. On their way to the back room, one of them opened the men's-room door

and shot the man at the urinal while the other fired at the men in the back room. A quick survey identified Landau, Rosenkrantz and Berman, but no Schultz. Then the killers went back to the toilet. There was the Dutchman—the first man they'd shot, simply as a precaution against an attack from behind.

Schultz lingered until the next day, received the last rites of the Catholic Church and issued a long and delirious soliloquy with such admonitions as, "Mother is the best bet and don't let Satan draw you too fast." Then he was gone. Six years later, Workman was arrested and tried for the murder. In the middle of the trial, he suddenly pleaded guilty and was sentenced to life in prison. (In 1964, he was paroled and returned to New York, a shy, quiet man. When last heard of, he had become a notion salesman in the Garment District he had terrorized so many years before.)

Upon the Dutchman's death, the detailed records he had kept in his miserly concern over every penny spent fell into the hands of the authorities. Dewey would use them and other evidence to prosecute the underworld's political allies. In the next four years, he managed to snare Davis, and then used him as a witness to land the biggest Tammany tiger of them all, Jimmy Hines, who ended up in Sing Sing for four years.

Moving against Hines and the political hacks of Tammany Hall was only one facet of the Dewey campaign that would put him in the district attorney's office, the governor's mansion and, twice, on the campaign trail for the White House. Once Schultz was gone, the next target of the special prosecutor was the chairman of the national crime Syndicate, Charlie Lucky. For years, Luciano had followed the examples of Torrio, Lansky and Costello and had lived quietly according to the principle out of sight, out of mind. Most of his troubles with the law had come early in his career. Twice he was deeply involved in narcotics, and that stigma would remain

with him the rest of his life. In 1916, he had been arrested as a runner and sent to a prison farm. In 1923, he was arrested again by federal narcotics agents, who trapped him with heroin in his pocket. He maneuvered his way out of trouble that time by directing the agents, in exchange for dismissal of charges, to a large cache of heroin in a trunk hidden in a basement closet on Mulberry Street in Little Italy. But from that time on, he remained clean, or as clean as a rising underworld overlord could ever be, his record dotted with arrests only for traffic violations, concealed weapons and

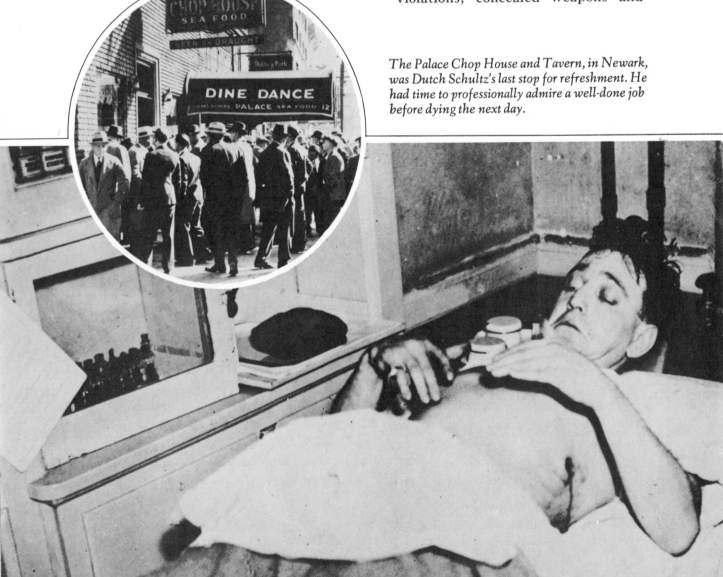

The Palace Chop House and Tavern, in Newark, was Dutch Schultz's last stop for refreshment. He had time to professionally admire a well-done job before dying the next day.

bootleg counts, all of which were dismissed or nulled with small fines.

Even after the murders of Giuseppe Masseria and Salvatore Maranzano made him the most powerful underworld leader in the nation, Luciano remained a shadowy and slightly sinister figure about whom much was whispered and little was known. He was seen with beautiful showgirls most often with the dancer Gay Orlova, making the rounds of the best midtown speakeasies. He enjoyed the best seats at major sporting events. Unlike most of his underworld associates, he never married, opting instead for a nomadic existence in the best hotels, from the Barbizon Plaza to the Waldorf Towers. His reputation was that of a sportsman, gambler, bootlegger, whose private clients inhabited society's upper strata and who often invited him to their golf clubs and parties.

Luciano had a growing reputation as one of the major underworld powers, but the true extent of his influence was little realized until he was singled out by La Guardia. As soon as he took office, La Guardia denounced Luciano as the city's leading hoodlum and ordered his arrest. He was, in fact, picked up by friendly cops but promptly released, because there were no charges on which he could be held. If nothing else, the arrest caused the kind of publicity La Guardia craved and Luciano detested.

After La Guardia's attack, Luciano became for New Yorkers something more than just another mobster, and after the murder of Schultz, he found himself in the middle of the spotlight. Dewey promoted him to the top of the list of those he was determined to send away. But it was no simple matter for the boy prosecutor to nail the underworld's board chairman. Unlike Schultz, Luciano was no maverick, running wild and on his own; instead, he was the complete organization man, a model corporate executive. The Italian underworld, the Unione Siciliana or the Mafia, for want of a better name, had been restructured under his command—for though theoretically he ruled but a single family, it was to him that all the families looked for guidance. By the mid-Thirties, there were many strata of managers between Luciano and the actual commission of crimes. Maybe Luciano gave the orders from his headquarters at the Waldorf Towers, in the Claridge Hotel, in a small midtown office on Broadway, in the back rooms of a dozen inconspicuous restaurants—but, like the dictates of any corporate executive, they filtered down through the chain of command before they were executed. To tie Luciano directly to any racket or crime seemed almost impossible.

The deeper Dewey's staff dug into the various rackets, from protection to numbers and all the rest in which they knew Luciano to be involved, the more hopeless the task seemed. Charlie Lucky had covered himself well.

As one promising investigation after another collapsed, a sense of frustration filled the special prosecutor's office. But late in 1935, one area began to show promise. Assistant District Attorney Eunice Carter had been given the thankless job by District Attorney Dodge of prosecuting the endless parade of whores picked up in the brothels and on the streets of Manhattan. Though she won few convictions—the magistrates' courts, where such trials were held, were perhaps the most corrupt in the city —Mrs. Carter observed some rather striking coincidences. On the witness stand, most of the prostitutes told almost identical stories, how they were poor working girls from out of town who just happened to be visiting a friend when arrested; they were all represented by the same law firms; if they were fined, the same bondsmen appeared with the money; and hovering in the background was always the same disbarred lawyer, Abe Karp, who was known to have close contacts in the underworld. Soon Mrs. Carter decided she was dealing not with free-lance purveyors of joyless sex but with a huge and tightly controlled organization. She took her suspicions to Dodge, who ridiculed them. But down the street at Dewey's office, she found a receptive audience. Dewey hired her away from Dodge and put her to work with two of his brightest young attorneys, Sol Gelb and Murray Gurfein (now a United States district judge in New York), who soon confirmed that the whores were, indeed, organized. Wherever they looked, the same names kept reappearing: Ralph "The Pimp" Liguori, a small-time punk who controlled scores of prostitutes and wielded more power than

his reputation indicated; Benny Spiller, a loan shark who supplied money for defense and fines; Tommy "The Bull" Pennochio, a man with a reputation for at least some financial acumen, to whom much of the prostitution money appeared to flow; and a middle-level organization hoodlum named David "Little Davie" Betillo. For Dewey, Betillo was the key; he was known to be a member of the Luciano organization, though exactly how high up nobody was certain.

More and more Dewey staff members were assigned to the investigation. There seemed no doubt that a vast prostitution ring had been uncovered—Dewey would later estimate that it controlled 200 brothels throughout the city, employed 1000 prostitutes and grossed more than $12,000,000 annually. What the investigators were determined to prove was that the ring did not stop with Betillo but reached to the very highest echelons of organized crime and even to Luciano himself. As yet, there was no evidence of this and some doubt that it could be developed, for it seemed unlikely that anyone of Luciano's stature would deal directly with prostitutes, madams and pimps, any more than he would deal directly with underlings in any other racket.

But by early 1936, enough evidence had been developed to make an overt move. On February first, in coordination with Commissioner Valentine's special squads of police, Dewey's staff raided brothels all across the city, picking up more than 100 prostitutes, pimps and madams, and round-

Good-time girls were natural targets for the underworld prostitution rings.

ing up, too, Liguori, Pennochio, Betillo and others.

Once these low-level workers had been arrested, Dewey's investigators installed them in rented offices and hotel suites and began round-the-clock grillings. To those under questioning, it soon became apparent that they were of no concern to Dewey; he was after much bigger game—namely, Luciano. As potential witnesses, they were made some promises in exchange for a little testimony. If they would talk about the ring and about

Jean Bell (top left) had been branded "C. L." for Charles "Lucky" Luciano (top right). She and other mistreated young ladies.testified at Luciano's trial. Between them and Tom Dewey, he didn't have a chance.

Charlie Lucky, all charges against them would be dropped, immunity would be granted and, once Luciano was locked away, they would find that their lives would take a sudden change for the better.

At first, Luciano himself displayed little concern over the stories that Dewey was out to get him or over the roundup of men like Betillo, Pennochio and Liguori, who had worked for him in a variety of enterprises. That they might be involved in prostitution did not seem unlikely. The combination of the depression and the end of Prohibition had sent scores of middle- and low-level hoodlums scrounging for new sources of income. Some had gone into narcotics, others into prostitution and a dozen other illegal activities. But Luciano was certain that nobody could link him with these more-or-less-independent enterprises, for, he strenuously maintained, no such link existed—especially with prostitution.

So Luciano was less concerned over what Dewey's investigators might uncover concerning prostitution than with what they might come up with in other areas—or manufacture for the purpose of prosecuting him. Early in March 1936, these suspicions were confirmed when informers revealed to Luciano that some unspecified charges were about to be lodged against him. Luciano decided not to wait around to find out what kind of charges and, one step ahead of the detectives, he beat a hasty retreat to Hot Springs, Arkansas, an underworld sanctuary where

he could relax, gamble and wait for things to cool off. Owney Madden and his paid-off politicians and police were supposed to see to that.

On April 2, Luciano learned exactly what Dewey had in mind for him. A blue-ribbon grand jury in Manhattan indicted 12 persons for running the prostitution racket. Betillo, Pennochio and Spiller were, of course, among them. So was one Charles Lucania, as the indictment incorrectly read, charged with 90 (later reduced to 62) counts of compulsory prostitution. Dewey immediately announced that Luciano was public enemy number one in New York and demanded his arrest on sight.

But Luciano was nowhere to be found. A Bronx detective in Hot Springs on another case was strolling along the Bath House Promenade when he came upon Luciano in friendly conversation with Herbert Akers, the resort community's chief of detectives. Word was flashed back to Dewey, who publicly demanded that Hot Springs and the state of Arkansas arrest Luciano and return him to New York for trial. Luciano was, indeed, arrested, but then released on $5000 bail put up by two of Madden's better casinos, the Southern and the Belvedere clubs. It was obvious he enjoyed the protection and the sanctuary of the city.

Dewey was incensed. "I can't understand how any judge could release this man on bail," he said. "Luciano is regarded as the most important racketeer in New York, if not in the country. And the case involves one of the largest rackets, and one of the most loathsome types of crimes." Embarrassed by the outcry, Arkansas Governor J. Marion Futrell ordered Luciano's arrest. Once again, the racketeer was lodged in the Hot Springs jail, but there he was given complete freedom of movement, use of the telephone and rooms for private conferences with his corps of legal advisors, headed by a former assistant United States attorney named Moses Polakoff (who would provide legal counsel for a host of other top racketeers, including Lansky, in the years ahead). They decided to fight extradition and to counter Dewey's public pronouncements with some of their own. "Back of this action is politics," declared Luciano to reporters at a press conference. "I may not be the most moral and upright man alive, but I have not, at any time, stooped to aiding prostitution. I have never been involved in anything so messy."

There was a stalemate. As long as Luciano remained in Hot Springs, there was little chance of extraditing him, and he showed no inclination to leave. Dewey continued to press the governor and State Attorney General Carl E. Bailey and Arkansas became the object of considerable national scorn. Eventually, Bailey ordered Luciano brought to Little Rock for an extradition hearing before Governor Futrell. The Hot Springs sheriff refused to honor the order. Finally, Bailey dispatched a troop of Arkansas Rangers with orders to storm the jail

if the sheriff wouldn't hand over the racketeer. The sheriff capitulated.

In Little Rock, Luciano tried another ploy to block extradition. One of his underlings offered Bailey $50,000 to permit Luciano to remain in Arkansas. It was a bad move. At the hearing before the governor, Bailey stormed, "Arkansas cannot be made an asylum for criminals. Officers of Hot Springs seem to have issued an invitation to criminals to come to that city, where they are told not to worry, that they will be given protection and that they will not be compelled to return to answer for crimes committed elsewhere. The money these criminals pay for protection is blood money, from their murdered victims and from women. We are trying to make it impossible for that class to spend its filthy money in Arkansas."

And so Luciano, handcuffed, was shipped back to New York, where he soon posted $350,000 bond and began planning for the trial. His battery of lawyers included Polakoff, George Morton Levy, one of the country's most respected trial lawyers, and Francis W. H. Adams, who had succeeded Dewey as United States attorney in New York and who two decades later would become New York City's police commissioner. The trial, which lasted more than three weeks, began in New York Supreme Court in Manhattan on May 13, 1936. In the jury box were 12 substantial New Yorkers. On the bench was a socially prominent jurist and symbol of moral rectitude, Justice Philip J.

McCook. Dewey, ever eager to enhance his own reputation, handled the prosecution himself.

The line Dewey would follow was set in his opening statement. "The vice industry," he asserted, "since Luciano took over, is highly organized and operates with businesslike precision. It will be proved that Lucky Luciano sat way up at the top, in his apartment at the Waldorf, as the czar of organized crime in this city. Never did Lucky or any codefendant actually see or collect from the women. Luciano, though, was always in touch with the general details of the business. We will show you his function as the man whose word, whose suggestion, whose very statement 'Do this' was sufficient; and all the others in this case are his servants."

And how was Dewey to prove this? During the three weeks devoted to the prosecution's case, he paraded 68 witnesses before the court. Forty were simple laborers in the vineyards of vice who had never seen or heard directly from Luciano, though they could point to Liguori, Pennochio, Betillo and most of the others as directly involved in the business. But they set a proper stage. They described the seamy story of prostitution, of being enticed into the ring, of being held almost captive in brothels, of being forced to turn over so much of their money to madams, pimps, doctors, lawyers and bondsmen, so that they considered themselves fortunate to keep $25 a week after servicing scores of men every day. They described how they were turned on to addictive drugs, which were then given or withheld as inducement to make them perform up to prescribed standards (and all declared that thanks to Dewey and his staff, they had received treatment and were now free of addiction).

At first, nothing implicated Luciano. He sat relaxed at the defendants' table and chatted easily with reporters outside the courtroom. But Dewey had been painstakingly creating a picture of such misery and degradation that the jury was only waiting for the first mention of Luciano to believe anything said about him. That word came, initially, from an incorrigible thief named Joe Bendix, brought down from Sing Sing, where he was serving a mandatory life sentence for a career of robbery and burglary. Luciano, he declared, had personally offered him a job as a collector for the prostitution ring, and had boasted of how he controlled it.

If Bendix gained yardage for Dewey, Cokey Flo Brown scored at least one touchdown. A prostitute, madam and drug addict, she suddenly appeared in court in a shabby, ill-fitting blue dress, worn shoes, disheveled dark hair, looking like a small, lost and defenseless waif who had been ill used by society. She had met Luciano, she declared, on a number of occasions, had been at one meeting with him when he asserted, "I'm gonna organize the cat houses like the A&P," had attended another when he told the whorehouse managers to use strong-arm methods to bring the madams, bookers and girls into line. "First you got to sit on them," Cokey Flo quoted Luciano, "then you got to step on them. Talking won't do no good. You got to put the screws on." He had, she said, ordered the girls threatened, beaten, forced to use narcotics. The points Cokey Flo scored mounted when she would not be shaken under cross-examination.

And more points were scored by Nancy Presser, a faded belle who had entered the profession at 13, had risen to high-priced call girl and mistress of Gordon, Schultz, Adonis, Masseria and more, and had at last fallen into the hands of Liguori, who had lodged her as a common laborer in a two-dollar Harlem crib. Luciano, she asserted, was an old and close friend, and he had rescued her from this low point in her life, calling her one day and summoning her to his Waldorf Towers suite for the first of many visits. "When Charlie called me over, he'd give me a hundred dollars, but we'd just talk. That's all. We never went to bed." During her hours with Luciano in his bedroom, Nancy said that she had listened in on his conversations with Betillo and others about the prostitution ring.

If all this sounded somewhat unlikely, Dewey was prepared to demonstrate that Nancy was telling the truth. He led her through a detailed description of the Luciano quarters, including the furniture and the arrangements. But during cross-examination, Nancy's eye for fine detail proved to be somewhat astigmatic and her memory more than a little muddled. Her description of the suite was at considerable variance with its true arrangement ("She's not an interior decorator" was the way Dewey dismissed that problem). And then there was her testimony that she had entered and left the Waldorf Towers late at night on all her many visits without ever seeing any employees, without ever being stopped and questioned by anyone; she had just walked in, gotten on the elevator and ridden up to the 39th floor. That was surprising, since the hotel manager testified to the Waldorf's tight security arrangements; there was always somebody on duty inside the entrance and all visitors were checked and announced before being permitted to enter. And then, not only was Nancy unable to describe the hotel or the location of the elevators, she wasn't even quite sure where the Waldorf was, except somewhere on the East Side near Park Avenue.

Did this damage Dewey's case? Not at all. The jury and the judge seemed more concerned with the personal plight of Miss Presser than with what was being done to her story.

To some observers at the time, and to many who examined the court records later, the case against Luciano—if not against Betillo and the other codefendants—was beginning to emit an offensive odor. That odor became even ranker when Dewey led witness after witness into declaring that she had been threatened if she testified against Luciano, and the court, over strenuous defense objections, let those statements go into the record and the jury's ears. And it was ranker yet when Frank Brown, an assistant manager of the Barbizon Plaza, where Luciano had lived as Charles Lane, was called as a prosecution witness. He crossed up Dewey, declaring that he had been intensely interrogated by Dewey staff members who demanded that he identify photographs of the other defendants as frequent callers on Luciano. Brown testified that when he could not do so, one of the Dewey staffers "warned me about jail if I didn't tell the truth. There were three or four in the room. They were very insistent about my identifying the pictures. When I said I couldn't do it honestly, they threatened me. They hinted that Mr. Dewey was very powerful and could do as he liked."

But the blue-ribbon jury preferred to believe the testimony presented by the prosecutor and not the holes poked in it on cross-examination or the complete denial by Luciano. Indeed, Luciano turned out to be his own worst witness, being forced by Dewey to admit a life of crime and association with almost every notorious underworld figure in the country. If the jury retained any doubts, they were dispelled by both Dewey and Justice McCook. In his seven-hour summation, Dewey accused the defense of using every trick and "all their evil means" to break down the testimony of his witnesses because "they dare not face the truth." Luciano, he declared, had committed "a

shocking, disgusting display of sanctimonious perjury—at the end of which I am sure not one of you had a doubt that before you stood not a gambler, not a bookmaker, but the greatest gangster in America." McCook drove the final spike, telling the jury that it did not need to find that Luciano had ever dealt directly with the prostitutes, madams or anyone else in order to find him guilty—only that he had in some manner received some of the proceeds of prostitution. And then, to show his own feelings, he concluded, "The crimes of which these men are accused are vicious and low and those who would aid and abet such crimes are not to be met in polite society."

Within six hours, the jury's verdict was in: guilty on all counts. McCook sentenced Luciano to 30 to 50 years in state prison, the longest sentence ever handed down for prostitution.

In what can only be considered an arrogant confession, Dewey afterward crowed, "This, of course, was not a vice trial. It was a racket prosecution. The control of all organized prostitution in New York by the convicted defendants was one of their lesser rackets. . . . The prostitution racket was merely the vehicle by which these men were convicted."

The question of whether Dewey suborned perjury to convict Luciano has never been resolved. Luciano himself maintained to the end of his life that while he was involved in many kinds of crime, prostitution was not one of them; that he had been framed by a prosecutor who could get him no other way. Luciano's statement may be self-serving, but some persons close to Dewey in those days have privately indicated that Luciano's contention is very close to the truth. Further, there are some pieces of circumstantial evidence supporting this. The witnesses who testified damagingly against Luciano were, indeed, well rewarded. Not only were the charges against them dropped and immunity granted but when the trial ended, Cokey Flo Brown, Nancy Presser and a couple of the others were sent, at the expense of the state, for indefinite vacations to Europe, returning only with the outbreak of the war. All would, a few years after the trial, declare in depositions obtained by Luciano's lawyers, that they had lied on the stand and that they had been prepared and rehearsed in those lies by Dewey's staff. The appeals courts, however, preferred to credit their original testimony and not their retractions.

Dewey could take pleasure in the way the case enhanced his own reputation, providing him a springboard to higher and higher office. And the city could take some satisfaction in the fact that the underworld's board chairman seemed to be out of commission, locked far away in Clinton State Prison in Dannemora, New York. Yet even from his cell, Luciano continued to rule, to give orders, to maintain his power. He left behind an efficient and powerful organization and he left it in the care of some very efficient managers—Adonis, who was the link with

Vito Genovese went to Italy for what he thought would be a short visit.

the Italian underworld; Costello, who lived in all worlds; and Lansky, who was the link between the national Syndicate and Adonis.

Vito Genovese might have been one of the heirs, but Don Vitone, as he was often called, had too many troubles of his own. As one of Luciano's chief lieutenants and already one of the biggest narcotics dealers in the underworld, he was next on Dewey's list for prosecution.

Ironically, what really spelled trouble for Genovese was a small-time badger game. As Joe Valachi and others have detailed, soon after his return from a honeymoon trip to his native Italy—he had fallen in love with Anna Petillo and then murdered her husband so he could marry her— Genovese had been brought a super-sucker by a small-time punk named Ferdinand "The Shadow" Boccia. The sucker, a Brooklyn merchant, was lured into a card game with Genovese and a fellow thug named Michele "Mike" Miranda, who would later rise high in the Genovese underworld family. They took their victim for $60,000, then offered him a chance to recoup: They would sell him a machine for $100,000 that manufactured real ten-dollar bills. The idiot bought it and Genovese was ahead $160,000.

Then Boccia came around, looking for the one-third cut he had been promised for setting up the deal. Genovese, who sometimes made the penny-pinching Schultz look like a spendthrift, decided on a different payoff. He hired two hoods named Willie Gallo and Ernest "The Hawk" Rupolo to kill Boccia, which they did. Then he paid Rupolo $175 to kill Gallo. Rupolo, however, was unequal to the task, managing only to wound Gallo in two tries. Understandably put out, Gallo turned Rupolo in to the cops and then gave testimony that sent him away on a 9-to-20-year sentence.

This was all quite upsetting to Genovese. Dewey was after him on a number of grounds, and now he feared that Rupolo, in the solitude of his prison cell, might consider revealing the whole Boccia murder plot. Genovese decided to take a vacation. He packed $750,000 and some clothes in a black satchel, kissed Anna goodbye and boarded a ship for Italy, where he hoped to find sanctuary with the friends he had made on an earlier trip, friends who were high in Mussolini's Fascist regime. Genovese envisioned only a short stay, but he reckoned without world events that would extend his visit to 1945 and deprive Dewey of this trophy.

But the flight of Genovese was merely an annoyance; in 1937, the ambitious prosecutor, on the strength of his Luciano conviction, was elected Manhattan district attorney. With Luciano in the clink and Genovese in exile, Dewey set his sights on the next biggest gangster in New York, Louis "Lepke" Buchalter. But what would emerge from the Lepke investigation would surprise and shock not only ordinary citizens but even the most sophisticated law-enforcement officials. And it would add a new name to the American lexicon: Murder, Incorporated.

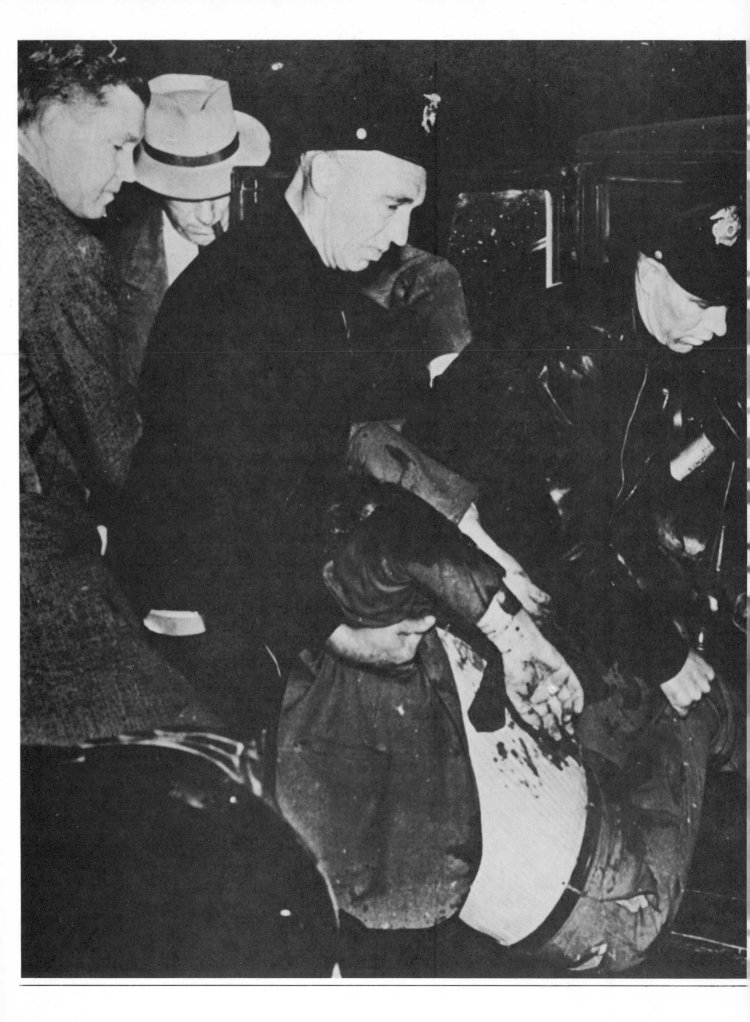

CHAPTER SEVEN

MURDER, INC.

MARCH 22, 1940, WAS LIKE most days at the Brooklyn district attorney's office on the fourth floor of the borough's Municipal Building. There were 100 or more cases in various stages; some attorneys were getting set for court appearances, others were just beginning the painstaking research that might lead to indictment. At 5:30, as much of the staff was preparing to go home, a call came for Burton Turkus, chief assistant district attorney. A dark-haired, dark-eyed, obviously pregnant woman in a beige coat with a wolf-fur collar had walked into the outer office and was demanding an interview. Turkus went out to meet her and recognized her immediately. Her name was Rose Reles. She told

Turkus, "I want to talk to the district attorney personally." William O'Dwyer, a former county-court judge, had just been elected chief prosecutor of Brooklyn. The assistant D.A. led Mrs. Reles directly into O'Dwyer's office. "My husband," she nervously announced, "wants an interview with the law."

Her husband was Abe "Kid Twist" Reles, a small, squat, hard-eyed thug, and the law had been practically salivating to talk to him, without much expectation of doing so. Reles was not the kind of hoodlum who turned into a canary. In 1940, he was 32 and had been in trouble more than half of his life. His rap sheet ran over several pages and listed 42 arrests in the previous 16 years—six for murder, seven for assault, six for robbery or burglary, and others for possession of narcotics, vagrancy, disorderly conduct—almost every crime in the book. And he had already served six prison terms without emitting so much as an implicating whisper.

So Reles was a tough guy who had never cracked before and who nobody thought would crack now, in the early months of 1940, despite a new murder charge against him. The charge had come about through bizarre circumstances: A small-time crook named Harry "The Mock" Rudolph was sitting on Rikers Island in the East River serving time for a minor crime that didn't even warrant the train trip up to Sing Sing or one of New York's other major prisons. While in his cell, Rudolph fretted, fumed and then, for reasons not even he could later explain, started talking of some crimes he knew about, particularly the 1933 murder in Brooklyn of an old friend, a no-account thief named Alex "Red" Alpert. That seven-year-old murder had so faded into obscurity that the detectives who went to interview Rudolph had to check the files first to make sure there had, indeed, been such a crime and then to check out the circumstances. What little the yellowed records showed was amplified by Rudolph, who then gave the police the names of the killers: Reles, Martin "Bugsy" Goldstein and Anthony "Dukey" Maffetore, all three of whom were known quite well to the cops— Goldstein had been arrested 34 times,

Maffetore 15, their records rivaling Reles' Without corroboration, the Rudolph story was not enough to convict, but it was enough to get indictments and the O'Dwyer office did just that, charging Reles, Goldstein and Maffetore with the murder of Alpert. Hoping that at least one of them would crack, confess and implicate the others, the three were lodged in separate jails in different parts of the city. Then, under the direction of Turkus, the Brooklyn prosecutor's staff began rigorous interrogations that covered practically every unsolved crime in the previous decade in Brooklyn.

It was Reles, the toughest of them all, who finally broke. The word from his wife sent Turkus scurrying to Manhattan, where Reles was sprung from his isolated cell at the Tombs. Like Rose, he refused at first to talk to anyone but O'Dwyer. In the privacy of the district attorney's office, he declared that he was completely unworried, that he could never be convicted of anything, because all O'Dwyer had was the testimony of Rudolph, and under New York law, the testimony of an accomplice must be corroborated "by such other evidence as tends to connect the defendant with the commission of a crime" and/or the testimony of a nonaccomplice. O'Dwyer had neither.

Why, then, had Reles demanded the interview? He was concerned that a lengthy investigation might well turn up corroborating evidence to support Rudolph's story and that at any trial his record would certainly

Abe Reles (left) and Martin "Bugsy" Goldstein (right) shown at the time of their arraignment.

turn both judge and jury against him. Some years earlier, when he had been convicted of a relatively minor crimė, the judge had said, "Reles is one of the most vicious characters we have had in years. I am convinced he will eventually either be sentenced to prison for life or be put out of the way by some good detective with a couple of bullets."

Reles knew, too, that many of the gangsters who had cooperated with crime buster Thomas E. Dewey, the famous special prosecutor who became Manhattan district attorney, had received immunity from prosecution and the chance to start a new life. Reles was certain that the new Brooklyn district attorney, competing for headlines with Dewey, would be just as receptive and no less generous to anyone who could advance him professionally. So he had come to O'Dwyer to strike a bargain. "I can make you the biggest man in the country," he declared.

Then he lapsed into silence. He would talk no more unless the room were cleared and he were strictly alone with the D.A. O'Dwyer agreed. In their private conference, Reles presented O'Dwyer with nonnegotiable demands. He wanted what Dewey had given his witnesses—immunity from prosecution, dismis-

sal of all charges pending and the guarantee that once he had kept his promises he could walk out the door a free man. If O'Dwyer would do all that, he would tell everything he knew and would testify fully in court; otherwise, he'd silently go back to the Tombs and take his chances. O'Dwyer hedged for a moment, talked to Turkus nervously and then accepted.

Reles was immediately put under round-the-clock police guard in a suite at the Hotel Bossert in Brooklyn, near O'Dwyer's office, and later moved several times, ending up at the

The Garment Center in the early Forties.

Half Moon Hotel at Coney Island. Each day, he was taken to the office, where he poured forth a torrent; the first gush, to be followed by many more, lasted 12 days and filled 25 stenographic notebooks.

"I can tell you about fifty guys that got hit," Reles boasted. "I was on the inside." (According to Turkus, by the time Reles finished, he had talked about more than 200 murders all around the country, murders of which he had personal knowledge. O'Dwyer was somewhat more modest in his recollections: he said that Reles cited only 83 murders.) Reles told his enthralled listeners he would provide witnesses, sometimes an accomplice and sometimes even a nonaccomplice, to corroborate his stories, and he promised also to show Turkus where to find corroborating evidence.

Then he began to give the details. "He had the most amazing memory I have ever encountered," Turkus said. "He could recount minutely what he ate at a particular meal years before, or where he was and with whom, and all without a single reference or reminder of any kind. And investigation proved him entirely accurate, down to the last pinpoint check, on every detail he mentioned. . . . The Kid rattled off names, places, facts, data on one manslaughter after the other, days on end, without once missing up. He recalled not only the personnel involved but decent people who had an unwitting part in some angle of the crime." Reles also spewed out everything he knew about organized crime—how the Mob had taken over the Garment District, both the manufacturers and the unions, and how it maintained its control through extortion, threats, bribery and murder; the intimate workings of the underworld's juice-loan operations. He was a limitless font of knowledge and data about a score of rackets and a legion of hoodlums who specialized in intimidation, assault and murder— Harry "Happy" Maione, Harry "Pittsburgh Phil" Strauss, Frank "The Dasher" Abbandando, Seymour "Blue Jaw" Magoon, Vito Gurino, Albert "Allie" Tannenbaum, Charlie "The Bug" Workman, Louis Capone (no relation to Al), Emanuel "Mendy" Weiss, Maffetore and Goldstein.

But what made Reles so valuable was not this parade. He had been a man in the middle ranks, between the bosses and the troops; he had taken orders and transmitted them to others; he had been a trusted aide of Louis "Lepke" Buchalter; he was privy to the thoughts and decisions of such top men as Albert Anastasia, Benny "Bugsy" Siegel, Joe Adonis, Charlie "Lucky" Luciano, Vince Mangano and others. "We are like this with the Purple Mob," he told Turkus, holding his fingers together as he cited the terrors of Detroit. "We work with Bugsy Siegel in California and with Lepke and the troops he's got. We are with Charlie Lucky. With the Jersey troop, too, and Chicago and Cleveland."

If anyone at that time still had doubts that crime had been organized and that on the national scene there was an interlocking directorship,

Reles dispelled them. He and his group of enforcers and killers were employed directly by the national Syndicate, but their services were also available, on a contract basis for a fee, to any member of the Syndicate anywhere in the country. They provided custom murders with any weapon—a gun, a knife, an ice pick, a bomb, a garrote—and they would even rob or hijack to order. Their work was so good and so efficient, Reles boasted, that "all the big shots were satisfied."

Reles opened a door and the authorities rushed in eagerly. Armed with his testimony, and with evidence he showed them where and how to get (including long-missing bodies buried in Sullivan County in the Catskills), O'Dwyer's office and the Brooklyn police swept up almost everyone Reles named and proposed for many a one-way ride to the electric chair. This inspired more singing, and the star of the new crooners was Allie Tannenbaum, whose own string of murders was as long as Reles's, maybe even longer. In exchange for his evidence and testimony, he, too, was promised immunity and eventual freedom. (After his performance, Tannenbaum faded from view, abandoned his occupation as hired killer and later turned up as a respectable salesman in Atlanta.)

And so the murder prosecutions began and, as Reles had predicted, quickly transformed O'Dwyer from a little-known D.A. into a famous crime buster, a man to equal Dewey. All of which caused concern, but also amusement, in the higher ranks of the underworld Syndicate, particularly among Frank Costello and his friends; they had supplied thousands of dollars and crews of hard-nosed workers for O'Dwyer's campaign and, for reasons of their own, would continue to support his political interests in the future.

With Reles the star witness, Maione and Abbandando both went to the electric chair for the brutal murder of a loan shark named George "Whitey" Rudnick—they had stabbed him 63 times with an ice pick and knives, shattered his skull and then, for good measure, strangled him. But, as Reles explained it, Rudnick had earned his fate; he had been a stool pigeon and Lepke had ordered his end.

Reles was the lead canary, too, when Pittsburgh Phil Strauss and Bugsy Goldstein got the chair for garroting and cremating a small-time gambler named Irving "Puggy" Feinstein. Just why Feinstein was killed Reles wasn't too sure. The murder, he said, had been done on orders from Anastasia, who had been given the contract by Mangano, co-boss with his

Allie Tannenbaum sang and won his freedom.

brother Phil of the Brooklyn family in which Anastasia was chief lieutenant. All Reles knew was that "This guy crossed Vince in something." Inexplicably, nobody bothered to follow up this enticing bit of testimony. Neither O'Dwyer nor anyone else ever asked either Anastasia or Mangano what they knew about Feinstein.

It was Reles, backed up by Tannenbaum, who pinned the murder of Dutch Schultz on Charlie Workman. When Workman heard all the testimony, he changed his plea to guilty and got off with a life sentence instead of the chair.

But these were all small-timers, as far as the prosecutors were concerned. They made headlines and reaped some good publicity. But Dewey had gotten Luciano, and if O'Dwyer were to match him, he had to nail somebody of like stature in the underworld. The man he was racing Dewey for now was Louis Lepke.

His mother had called him "Lepkeleh," an affectionate Yiddish diminutive meaning Little Louis. But when people talked about Lepke, they did so not with affection but with fear. By late in the Thirties, with Al Capone and Luciano in prison and Schultz buried, Lepke was perhaps the most notorious criminal in the United States, the object of a massive manhunt spurred by offers of rewards for his capture dead or alive.

Buchalter had been born in 1897 on New York's Lower East Side, one of several children of poor Jewish immigrants who were barely scratching a subsistence out of a small hardware business. As a child, he earned himself a reputation as a proficient sneak thief who pilfered from every neighborhood candy store. He was still a child when his father died and most of the family moved west, to Denver. Lepke stayed behind, living with one relative and then another, and finally quitting school and going out on his own. On his own meant following a career in crime; by the time he was 18, he had been arrested three times for burglary and had served a two-month sentence at the Cheshire Reformatory in Connecticut. Within the next four years, operating in and around New York City, he was arrested several more times and served two sentences in Sing Sing. But after that, it would be 20 years before he would see the inside of a cell again. Despite 11 subsequent arrests for crimes ranging up to and including murder, between 1919 and 1939 his record was not stained by a single lasting conviction.

The fortune to be made in booze had attracted most of the young hoodlums his age at the beginning of Prohibition. But not Lepke. He and another young thug, Jacob "Gurrah" Shapiro, took a different route to wealth and power. Both relished the use of strong-arm methods—the blackjack, the gun, the bottle of acid, the knife, anything that would lead to a flow of blood. As one associate of the time commented, "Lep loves to hurt people."

In the early Twenties, they linked up with a third young advocate of violence, Jacob "Little Augie" Orgen (who was shot down in 1927), and set up shop as strikebreakers for hire to Manhattan garment manufacturers fighting the International Ladies' Garment Workers Union and the Amalgamated Clothing Workers of America. They were so good at their work that soon they were serving both sides, hiring out also as union organizers and then taking control of union locals.

Racketeering in one industry quickly leads to racketeering in others, as Lepke and Shapiro were quick to perceive. Bread was a common necessity, but bread made stale by long delays in deliveries was not good for much more than stuffing turkeys. So Lepke moved in on the bakery-drivers' union and then put the pressure on the bakers to pay up, a penny or more a loaf, to get their products delivered fresh to market. The bakers paid. Lepke moved on. Working with Willie Bioff and the Chicago Mob to gain control of the movie-projectionists' union, he extorted millions from motion-picture moguls. By the mid-Thirties, his industrial racketeering had spread clear across the New York economic scene. He was extorting, threatening, controlling to one degree or another, on his own and in combination with others, the leather business, the handbag makers, the shoemakers, the milliners, taxis, poultry, cleaning and dyeing, restaurants and more. There were official estimates that legitimate businessmen were paying Lepke between $5,000,000 and $10,000,000 a year for the right to operate without interference.

This much had been known or suspected for several years. But not until Reles started singing did the authorities begin to appreciate Lepke's position in the Syndicate and his role as chief enforcer of discipline and internal policy. It was to Lepke that his peers turned when the need arose to enforce underworld rules, and his efficiency in doing so won him the title The Judge.

Yet there were indications that Lepke would not retain his power and stature for long. Unlike Meyer Lansky and Costello, or even his ofttime Garment District partner Tommy Lucchese, Lepke was not content with a life in the shadows. He relished the spotlight and loved reading about himself in the newspapers. He lived lavishly and conspicuously, almost courting attention. Thus, when Luciano went off to Dannemora, it was only natural that Lepke would be the next target for the ambitious Manhattan Prosecutor Tom Dewey.

Lepke's troubles stemmed not merely from Dewey. There were others who wanted him just as badly, including the federal government. So tight was Lepke's noose around several industries that the Justice Department had succeeded in indicting him and Shapiro for restraint of trade in violation of the antitrust laws. In 1936, both were convicted, sentenced to two years and fined $10,000. Shapiro took the rap and went to prison, and then picked up an additional term when later convicted of extorting bakers. But Lepke appealed, went free on $3000 bond and then disappeared while the courts listened to his lawyers. A federal appeals court overturned his conviction in 1937.

But the heat on Lepke was still intense. A grand jury, directed by the Manhattan district attorney, indicted Lepke and Shapiro for bakery extortion; the Justice Department announced that it was rewriting the antitrust indictments with the intention of bringing him to trial on new racketeering charges; and the Federal Bureau of Narcotics entered the picture as well. It had uncovered evidence that Lepke was the man behind a massive narcotics-smuggling enterprise that involved extensive bribery of United States customs agents and had managed to smuggle at least $10,000,000 worth of heroin into the country from the Far East.

Surrounded by so much trouble all at once, Lepke decided to extend his vacation—not a vacation from business or even from New York but merely from public view. In 1937, he sought help from his close friend Anastasia, who sheltered him in several places in Brooklyn during a two-year nationwide manhunt. More than 1,000,000 WANTED posters were distributed all over the country. Dewey, calling Lepke "the worst industrial racketeer in America," announced that he would pay $25,000 to anyone who brought the gangster in, dead or alive. And J. Edgar Hoover, apparently alarmed that so many others— Dewey, Narcotics Bureau Director Harry Anslinger, New York City Police Commissioner Lewis Valentine—were stealing the headlines from him, chimed in with a $5000 reward for "the most dangerous criminal in the United States," although the only claim the FBI had to him was as a fugitive from justice suspected of crossing state lines. There were rumors that Lepke was hiding out in Florida, Arkansas, California, Chicago, that he had left the United States and was in Cuba, Poland, the Far East.

But nobody could flush him out, and as the search intensified during 1938 and into 1939, investigators took the extraordinary step of questioning his friends in the underworld. An

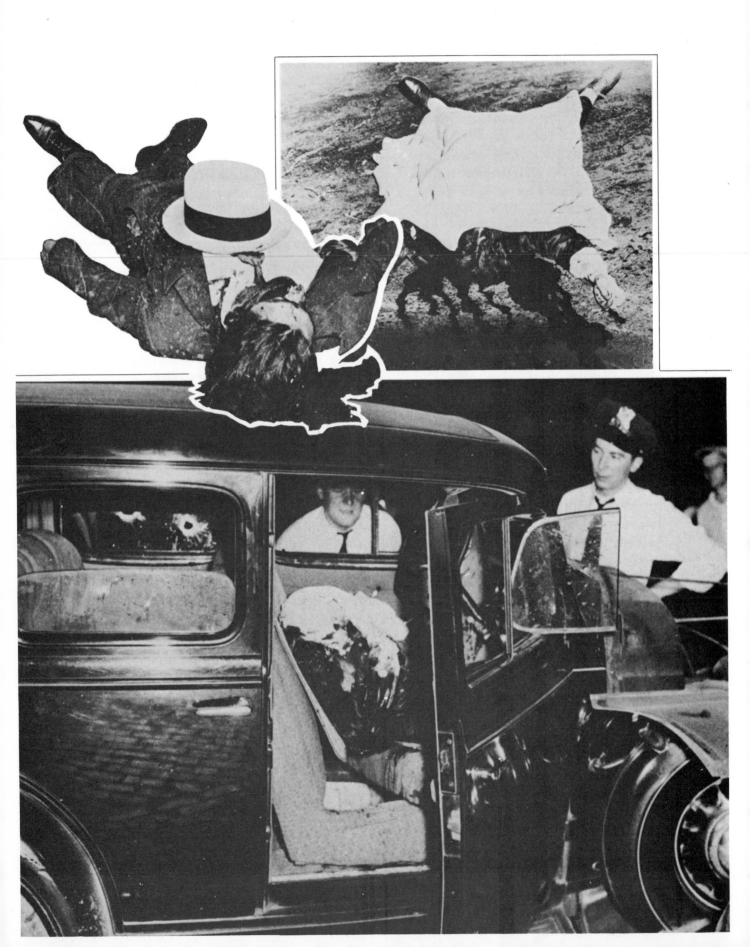

agent went to Havana to see Lansky, then in the process of developing his Caribbean gambling empire with the aid and partnership of Cuban President Fulgencio Batista. Lansky dismissed the federal man with a smile; it had been years since he had seen Lepke, he said, and all he knew about the wanted man was that he wasn't in Havana. When Costello was interviewed, he, too, professed complete ignorance. Longy Zwillman was called before a special grand jury in Newark. "I know Lepke for a long time," Zwillman said, "but I haven't seen him in three, four years. So far as I know, he was a pleasant fellow and clean morally." The investigators even went up to Dannemora to talk to Luciano. He laughed at them.

But a good many people knew exactly where Lepke was and what he was doing, and that his continuing underground existence was beginning to make him paranoid. He saw signs in every word and action that others were trying to encroach on his domain, and he was taking steps not merely to repel the invaders, real or imagined, but to strengthen his own position at others' expense. At times during these years, Reles served as Lepke's chauffeur and bodyguard, and he told of the night in 1938 when he drove Lepke from his hideout to a Brooklyn meeting attended by Anastasia, Lucchese, Willie Moretti, Jerry Catena, Zwillman and several others. Lucchese had demanded the session and he wanted to know what Lepke was doing in the Garment District. When Luciano had been around, Lepke had always been cooperative. But now Luciano was in Dannemora and Lepke was tightening his personal control of the garment industry, even from his hideout, and trying to squeeze out Lucchese and others who had worked so closely with him through the years. And he was doing the same thing in his other rackets. Lucchese demanded that Lepke start respecting the old agreements, especially since these were backed by

Murder, Incorporated eliminated them—thoroughly if not always neatly.

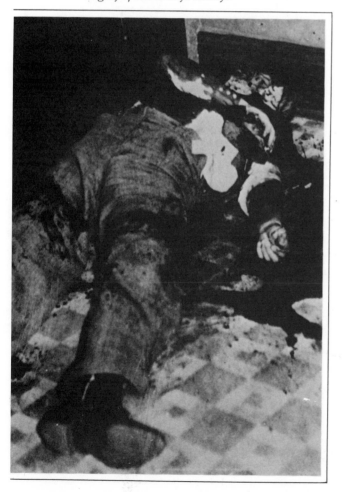

the national Combination, but Lepke refused to listen. He took the position that everyone was trying to cut *him* out. "Nobody moved in on me while I was on the outside," Reles quoted him as saying, "and nobody's gonna do it just because I'm on the lam. There's no argument. The clothing thing is mine." And with those words, Lepke rose from his chair, stalked out of the room and ordered Reles to drive him back to his sanctuary.

There, surrounded by his and Anastasia's guns, Lepke continued to rule his empire and muscle in on friends he believed were trying to take it for themselves. And he was trying to cover his tracks. It was his theory, voiced often and loudly, that while Dewey and the federal government could both build up strong cases against him, those cases would collapse without the testimony of certain vital witnesses. So, Reles explained to Turkus, "Lep gave us eleven contracts for witnesses when he was on the lam. We knocked off seven of them."

It became a race between Lepke's killers and the forces of the law. Could Lepke be tracked down and captured while there were still live witnesses to testify against him? Hoover sprang FBI agents from other jobs to pursue Lepke; agents of the Narcotics Bureau intensified their hunt; Dewey's men and special squads of Valentine's New York City police devoted full time to the search.

Then another tactic was tried—heavy pressure on Lepke's underworld colleagues. Bookies who had been operating comfortably, paying off police and politicians, were suddenly being raided and jailed; well-protected betting banks and numbers operators now found cops camped on their doorsteps. Underworld figures of any note were rousted, brought in for questioning, harassed continuously. The authorities deliberately fostered the rumor that the heat would continue, would be stepped up even more, that the gangsters would no longer have room or time to breathe, let alone operate, unless the Lepke problem were brought to a satisfactory conclusion. When some civil liberties groups protested to Mayor Fiorello La Guardia about the unconstitutional harassment by police, he summoned Commissioner Valentine to the meeting, turned to him and said, "Lewie, these people claim you violate the Constitution."

Valentine replied, "So do the gangsters." With that, La Guardia sent the civil libertarians packing.

And when another group came to complain that mobster Ciro Terranova was being prevented from even entering the city, La Guardia told Valentine, in the group's presence, "Terranova has a perfect right to come into New York City. Let him come in, by all means. Wait until he gets to 125th Street—and then go to work on him." Whether La Guardia's actions were part of the pressure to bring about the surrender of Lepke or just the mayor's well-known style of law enforcement is impossible to say. But such harassment had its effect, especially when the word spread that

La Guardia knew how to apply the pressure on the Mob.

the heat would dissipate once Lepke was in the hands of authorities.

For Lansky and Costello, and for others as well, this was an opportunity to solve a number of problems with a single stroke. Both had worked with Lepke since the early Twenties and had grown to despise his violence, braggadocio and contrariness. Moreover, if he were put away, the heat presumably would be turned off; not only would business return to normal but Lepke's empire would be thrown into the hopper to be parceled out among the other leaders.

So, in secret council with Lucchese, Zwillman, Moretti, Adonis and other leaders, Lansky and Costello argued that Lepke must be per-

suaded to come out of hiding and surrender. If he could not be so persuaded, they said, then the problem would have to be solved in the classic Lepke fashion—kill him. The only voice to defend Lepke, to argue that he had served the Combination too long and too well, was that of Anastasia, who would soon win the public title Lord High Executioner of Murder, Inc. Not only were Anastasia and Lepke old friends and partners in the enforcement/murder business but Anastasia hated Lansky. He could not abide the man's display of knowledge, his polished manners, his superiority, his preachments against force, his condescension toward Anastasia in particular and Italians in general.

Despite Lepke's liabilities and the power of Lansky, nobody wanted to go to war with Anastasia; but somehow he had to be persuaded. The one man he might listen to was Luciano, who had been the boss when he had been free and who still wielded power from his isolated cell in Dannemora. Costello took the problem directly to Charlie Lucky in the Dannemora visiting room, where the two hammered out a plan. What Lepke most feared was falling into the hands of Dewey. On the basis of Dewey's prosecution of Luciano and his general demeanor, Lepke was convinced that the racket buster would send him away forever and, indeed, Dewey was proclaiming that he had enough on Lepke to put him in prison for 500 years. Lepke was less concerned over the federal indictments. He knew he was certain to be convicted in federal court, but he was sure that even on a narcotics charge, he would get off with only a couple of years. So the plan was to persuade Lepke that a deal had been struck with the government; if he turned himself in to federal agents and stood trial for narcotics, the feds had promised they would not turn him over to Dewey.

Now a go-between had to be found who could convince Lepke that such an arrangement had been made, and Lansky had just the man. His

Some of the bodies were hidden in peculiar places.

name was Moe "Dimples" Wolensky, a shady character who had worked in gambling enterprises at various times for both Lepke and Lansky, who was trusted by everyone who knew him and who was known to have contacts with the law. Wolensky was sent to Lepke's hideout with the message that the national Syndicate had worked out a fix with J. Edgar Hoover. If Lepke would surrender personally to Hoover (thereby embellishing the G man's reputation, which was suffering from competition and continuing failure to track Lepke down), Dewey would never get his hands on him.

Lepke bought this idea. But Anastasia didn't. He continued urging Lepke to hold out; as long as he was free, he was safe; in the hands of the authorities, anything could happen. Once more, Luciano intervened. Through Adonis, he sent word to Anastasia that the deal was set, that business demanded Lepke accede to it and that Anastasia, despite his misgivings, go along. At last, Anastasia agreed and even took a hand in the melodramatics that followed. Contact was made with Walter Winchell, the gossip columnist of the *New York Daily Mirror* and a close friend of Hoover's. Winchell was advised that he could share in the glory if he would get in touch with the FBI director and help work out the details of the surrender.

Just before ten o'clock on August 24, 1939, a sweltering Manhattan summer night more than two years after Lepke had disappeared, a car driven by Anastasia stopped at 101

Walter Winchell, a close friend of J. Edgar Hoover.

Third Street in Brooklyn, picked up a passenger wearing his coat collar upturned and large sunglasses to hide his face. Anastasia drove rapidly across the Brooklyn Bridge into Manhattan. At Fifth Avenue and 28th Street, he slowed, spotted a parked car and pulled to the curb a short distance beyond. The rear door of his car opened, the passenger stepped out, paused for a last word with Anastasia and then walked rapidly to the waiting parked car. When he reached

Lepke (top) walked into a neat trap set by W. Winchell, J. E. Hoover and the Mob.

it, Winchell, behind the steering wheel, leaned across and stared at him intently. Then he turned to his stocky companion in the back and said, "Mr. Hoover, this is Lepke."

Hoover nodded, reached across and opened the rear door, motioning Lepke to enter. "How do you do," he said brusquely.

"Glad to meet you, I'm sure," Lepke said as he slid into the car next to Hoover. Any pleasure he might have felt at the meeting immediately vanished. With Hoover's first words,

Lepke discovered that there was no fix, no deal, at least where he was concerned—or that Hoover either wasn't admitting to a deal or didn't know about one. Lepke was informed that he would be tried promptly by federal authorities on the narcotics charge. Lepke expected that. Then, to Lepke's horror, Hoover said that after the trial, he would be turned over to Dewey for prosecution on bakery-racket charges. "I wanted to get out of that car again as soon as I heard," Lepke later said. But that was impossible. For, as Winchell turned on the car lights and started the engine, a fleet of cars, filled with FBI agents, pulled out of every side street and nearby parking space, surrounded Winchell's car and escorted it to the FBI offices.

(If Lepke had been taken, so, too, had Dimples Wolensky. As soon as they learned that the deal was a phony, Lepke's friends began to search for him. The search took time, but in 1943, on orders of Anastasia, Wolensky was shot down on a Manhattan street corner.)

Within a month of his dramatic surrender, Lepke was convicted of narcotics conspiracy and sentenced to 14 years in federal prison at Leavenworth. Hardly had sentence been pronounced when the shaken gangster was turned over to Dewey, who saw him as another stepping-stone on the road to Albany and, ultimately, the White House. Using all the legal legerdemain at his command, Dewey tore the stunned Lepke to shreds in the courtroom and obtained a sentence that matched Luciano's—30 years to life. Then Lepke was returned to Leavenworth to serve out the time he owed the federal government before paying his even greater debt to the state of New York.

BUT THERE WAS MORE TO COME for Lepke, and for Anastasia and Siegel. By now, Reles was singing his song in Brooklyn to ambitious O'Dwyer, whose political objective was the city-hall chair occupied by La Guardia.

On the basis of evidence supplied by Reles and Tannenbaum, O'Dwyer in May of 1940 demanded that the federal authorities turn Lepke over to him to stand trial, along with Mendy Weiss and Louis Capone, for murder. The murder was that of a Brooklyn candy-store owner named Joseph Rosen in 1936. Rosen had once been an uncooperative trucker in the Garment District and Lepke had put him out of business. Instead of accepting this gracefully, Rosen started telling friends he was going to take his grievances to Dewey, and word of this soon got back to Lepke. According to Reles, Tannenbaum and a couple of other canaries, Lepke gave the Rosen contract to Weiss, Capone and Strauss, and the three fulfilled it in Brooklyn one morning in September 1936 by filling Rosen's body with 17 bullets.

Turkus prosecuted Lepke, Weiss and Capone in the fall of 1941, with Tannenbaum as the key witness. Reles had been scheduled to testify but was to die mysteriously before his opportunity came. He didn't die soon enough to save Lepke, however, especially with Tannenbaum still warbling. Lepke, Weiss and Capone were all convicted and on March 4, 1944, the three died in the Sing Sing electric chair.

Reles's death did save Siegel and Anastasia, however. His testimony was the key to putting both in the death house.

In the course of their narratives, Reles and Tannenbaum had talked

(Top) William O'Dwyer mapped out the attack on Murder, Incorporated with assistant Burton Turkus.

(Bottom) Lepke and his codefendants Mendy Weiss and Louis Capone were found guilty and sent to the electric chair in 1944.

often about the demise of a one-time Lepke enforcer named Harry Greenberg and variously known as Harry Schacter and Harry Schober but more familiarly called Big Greenie. When the heat was on Lepke early in 1939, Greenberg took off for the cooler climes of Canada. Unfortunately, he soon ran short of funds and hinted to the boys in New York that if he didn't get some money, he might decide to return for a little talk with Dewey.

That was a mistake, and Tannenbaum was given the contract to correct it. By the time he reached Canada, however, Big Greenie had disappeared. He surfaced a little later in California, where Siegel had taken up residence in 1937 as the local overlord for the national Combination. In those days, the West Coast was still considered virgin territory, and who better to deflower it than the great underworld lover, Siegel? He had traveled West several times, had liked the climate, the women, the easy money of the movie colony. He had talked constantly about its potential and had found open ears among his Syndicate associates in the East, particularly Zwillman, who was in love with Hollywood and with one of its biggest stars, Jean Harlow. So Siegel went west, where he was an immediate success and an immediate celebrity, becoming close friends with scores of Hollywood personalities, including George·Raft, Wendy Barrie, Clark Gable, Gary Cooper, Cary Grant and many more (some of whom would later put their money into Siegel enterprises).

Celebrity that he was, Siegel was first and foremost a member of the Syndicate, privy to its lore and responsive to its bidding. When he learned of the fugitive Greenberg's presence in California, he hurried East to confer with Adonis, Zwillman and company. Siegel offered to take on the contract himself. But Tannenbaum had been awarded it, so he was dispatched West, with Siegel's help and logistical support. In Tannenbaum's possession were two guns stolen from a New Jersey warehouse and delivered to him personally by Zwillman as he boarded his plane. Once in Los Angeles, Tannenbaum made a couple of tries at Greenberg but failed. So Siegel brought in another gunman, one Frankie Carbo (who later would come to prominence as the manager of several boxing champions and contenders). On November 22, 1939, Tannenbaum drove Carbo and Siegel to 1804 Vista Del Mar in Los Angeles shortly after dark. A second car, driven by a friend of Siegel's, no gangster himself but a thrill seeker who relished the company of the notorious, a man named Champ Segal, parked a short distance down the block. Each night, adhering to a fixed schedule, Greenberg made his only trip out of doors, a short drive to pick up the newspapers. He had already left when Siegel, Carbo, Tannenbaum and Segal arrived. As they waited, Big Greenie's old Ford turned the corner and pulled up in front of the house. As Greenberg stepped out, a door of the waiting car flew open, Siegel and Carbo stepped out, pulled

There were plenty of women in Bugsy Siegel's life. Among the better known ones were Hollywood socialite Dorothy diFrasso (left) and movie actress Wendy Barrie (right).

out the two guns Zwillman had sent West with Tannenbaum and emptied them into Greenberg.

Why Carbo and Tannenbaum participated is easily explained; they were, after all, hired killers doing their job. Not so easily explained, though, is why Siegel decided to participate and dirty his executive hands with the actual commission of a violent crime. A couple of years later, Los Angeles County Deputy District Attorney Arthur Veitch offered his own theory to a grand jury seeking to indict Siegel. "In gangster parlance," he declared, "Siegel is what is known as a 'cowboy.' This is the way the boys have of describing a man who is not satisfied to frame a murder but actually has to be in on the kill in person."

It was more than a year later that Tannenbaum told the story of the murder of Big Greenie to Turkus. It was good and convincing, but not convicting, for Tannenbaum had been an accomplice. But then, as usual, there was Reles, a nonparticipant, to come through with corroboration. He said he knew all the details from the very beginning. Turkus turned the evidence over to California authorities and then, with O'Dwyer's approval, flew Reles and Tannenbaum to Los Angeles to testify before the grand jury. Five murder indictments were returned, against Siegel, Carbo and Segal as participants and against Lepke and Weiss as the men who had given out the contract.

When the police went to arrest Siegel and Carbo, they were nowhere to be found. When they finally picked

Siegel up at his Beverly Hills mansion some months later, he professed no concern. His scores of Hollywood friends visited him regularly in jail, where he was permitted almost complete freedom, and on several occasions he even walked out of the jail to spend a night on the town. Then in December 1940, the newly elected Los Angeles County District Attorney, John Dockweiler, moved for dismissal of all the indictments. He announced that he had learned that a prime witness had lied, so he didn't have a solid case. What others learned was that Siegel had contributed $30,000 to Dockweiler's campaign. (It was later rumored that Siegel became so impatient at Dockweiler's delay in dismissing the indictments that he demanded a refund—and got it.)

If Dockweiler had no desire to prosecute, others wanted to very badly. Requests were made to O'Dwyer to ship Tannenbaum and Reles back to the Coast for a new grand-jury appearance and new indictments. At first, O'Dwyer refused. There were too many other calls for their services in his own jurisdiction, he explained, and he didn't want them 3000 miles from Brooklyn, where they might get lost. The California authorities persisted, and finally in September 1941, O'Dwyer relented to the extent of letting Tannenbaum but not Reles make another trip west. New indictments were obtained, this time naming only Siegel and Carbo, and once more Siegel went underground. But not for long. Suddenly, in October, he turned himself in. Then even more suddenly, in November, Reles—and the case against Siegel—went out a sixth-floor window. Once more, Dockweiler asked for dismissal of the indictments and Bugsy went free again to build the Syndicate's empire on the West Coast. (Carbo was later tried for the Greenberg murder, but the jury, after deliberating for 53 hours, could not reach a verdict.)

The death of Reles also sprang Anastasia. Throughout his marathon ramblings, he had frequently described Anastasia as the man who not only ordered killings but participated in some of them. Tannenbaum, too, talked constantly about Anastasia. Unfortunately, much of what they said was only rumor that they could not substantiate. Anastasia had been good at covering his tracks. He had, it seemed, slipped up only one time, but what Reles knew about that incident could have sent him to the electric chair.

For a number of years, Morris "Moishe" Diamond, the business agent for a teamster local, had been resisting the encroachment of the racketeers into his Garment District bailiwick. By early 1939, he was so distressed by the gangster take-overs that he started threatening to talk to Dewey. Anastasia wasted no time. He not only ordered Diamond's extermination but personally gave the order to shoot when Diamond was cornered on a Brooklyn street in May 1939. One of those present had been Tannenbaum.

Reles had not been there, but he could corroborate: He knew the par-

John Dockweiler became Los Angeles County district attorney—with the help of Bugsy Siegel.

ticipants and had heard their accounts of the killing, he had been present when the murder was planned and, most important, he had heard Anastasia give the orders.

It seemed to be O'Dwyer's big moment. Not only was he ready to convict Lepke but he was about to get Anastasia as well—and make Dewey look like a small-timer by comparison. His office, O'Dwyer announced, had the "perfect murder case" against Anastasia, and he ordered the arrest of the underworld's Lord High Executioner. Only Anastasia, predictably, couldn't be found. Embarrassed,

O'Dwyer issued his assurances that as soon as Anastasia was arrested, he would be tried, convicted and sent to the electric chair.

But before anyone could arrest the fugitive, Reles took his mystery flight and the case collapsed. On Wednesday morning, November 12, 1941, Reles was comfortably ensconced in his bed in room 623 at the Half Moon Hotel at Coney Island, waiting for his summons to appear at the Lepke trial. As usual, his door was open. He had his regular guard—18 men, divided into three shifts, had been assigned to protect him. Sometime before seven in the morning, the hotel's assistant manager thought he heard a thud on the extension roof beneath Reles's room but paid no attention to it. Sometime close to seven, a detective looked into Reles's room and the Kid was in bed, asleep. At ten after seven, Detective Victor Robbins checked. This time, the bed was empty, the window was open and Reles was gone. He rushed to the window and looked down. What he saw, 42 feet below on the extension roof, was the twisted body of Reles, fully dressed, two knotted bed sheets nearby.

Expressing shock and dismay, O'Dwyer ordered Police Captain Frank Bals, head of the O'Dwyer investigating staff and the man responsible for the safety of Kid Twist, to determine what had happened. This took Bals only a couple of hours. There was nothing unusual in the fact that Reles was alone in his room, Bals said, just as long as he was checked regularly by his guards, according to the normal routine. (Not so, Tannenbaum would later assert; he and Reles had never been alone while in custody; guards were always present, even when they were asleep.)

Reles's death, Bals concluded, was regrettable, but it was just an accident. Bals theorized that it could have come about in one of two ways. Reles had been attempting to escape, ergo the knotted bed sheets, and had fallen to his death when the sheets had given way. Considering that freedom was the last thing Reles needed, Bals's second possibility was equally plausible: Reles, a notorious practical joker, may have been trying to pull a good one on his protectors by sliding down the sheets to the fifth floor and then sneaking up the stairs and shouting "Peekaboo, I see you" at the cops. A third theory, which did not consider the knotted bed sheets, was advanced by other police officers in Brooklyn: Reles, stricken by his conscience and fearful of his future, had simply committed suicide.

Those, at least, were the official theories. Few believed them, not even members of the police department. There were plenty of rumors that made a lot more sense. The one that has lasted longest and the one that New York City police officials even today seem to unofficially believe is that the Organization paid handsomely for the murder of a dangerous informer. The Mob had plenty of friends, tightly held through the payment of regular stipends, both on the police force and in O'Dwyer's

The Half Moon Hotel in Brooklyn, from which Reles sang his last song and took his last flight.

office—enough friends that it could arrange to have Reles and some knotted bed sheets thrown out just about any window in town.

The cops who had been assigned to guard Reles were put back in uniform and sent out to walk a beat. That was their punishment. And when O'Dwyer became mayor of New York City in 1945, Captain Bals was appointed a deputy police commissioner. One of his jobs, high underworld sources maintain, and many high po-

lice officials believe today, was disbursing the regular payoffs from the Mob.

In any case, Reles was dead and so was the "perfect murder case" against Anastasia. But even worse were the indications that the old alliance between the politicians and the underworld was as strong as ever, maybe even stronger. It seems that during the 19 months O'Dwyer had been bragging about his case against Anastasia and supposedly looking for him, the district attorney had never bothered to obtain an indictment against him for the Diamond murder and had actually forbidden anyone on his staff to do so. O'Dwyer's explanation was that since Anastasia was a fugitive from justice at the time, there was no sense in seeking an indictment until he had been apprehended.

A few months after Reles's fall, O'Dwyer took a leave of absence from the D.A.'s job to enter the army (from which he would emerge in 1945 as a brigadier general, something of a hero, a political power and Tammany's candidate for New York City mayor). He left behind the final disposition of the Anastasia affair, a disposition based on a memo from Captain Bals: "In the case of Anastasio [Anastasia's real name], legal corroboration is missing . . . On November 12, 1941, Abe Reles, who was under police guard in the Half Moon Hotel, Brooklyn, attempted to escape, and fell five stories, being instantly killed. This not only seriously hampered the investigation but deprived the state of his testimony and information. At the present time, the only testimony adducible against Anastasio is that of accomplices."

(In 1945, a Brooklyn grand jury had what may have been the final legal word on the Reles affair, though its impact was negligible. It charged that there had been "negligence, incompetence and flagrant irresponsibility" in the way the Anastasia case had been handled by O'Dwyer. "The undisputed proof is that William O'Dwyer [was] in possession of competent legal evidence that Anastasia was guilty of first-degree murder and other vicious crimes. This proof admittedly was sufficient to warrant Anastasia's indictment and conviction, but Anastasia was neither prosecuted, indicted nor convicted . . . The consistent and complete failure to prosecute the overlord of organized crime . . . is so revolting that we cannot permit these disclosures to be filed away in the same manner the evidence against Anastasia [was] heretofore 'put in the files.'")

So Anastasia surfaced, returned to Brooklyn and was soon strutting about his waterfront domain with renewed confidence, aggressiveness and invincibility. He did not, however, remain there long. He was drafted into the army and, as a technical sergeant, trained GI longshoremen at a camp in Pennsylvania from 1942 to 1944. In return for his services, the United States government granted him American citizenship.

Within a month after Reles was buried, the United States was in the war, and while much of the nation deprived itself in the drive for victory, the underworld fattened itself at the old games and at new ones. There were opportunities to gain a measure of respectability with a show of patriotism. There were opportunities to try to spring the boss, Luciano, from his prison cell to serve the war effort. And beckoning, too, in the years ahead, were the sun-washed shores of the Caribbean and the sandy cities of Nevada.

FOR VICTORY, VICE AND VEGAS

A FOREBODING SPREAD ACROSS the United States in the early months of 1942. Since the cataclysm at Pearl Harbor, the news had been all bad and was getting worse: The Japanese, so long underrated as a military power, had smashed through the Philippines, the islands of the western Pacific and were bringing much of Asia under the umbrella of their Greater East Asia Co-Prosperity Sphere. Europe and much of North Africa were captives of Hitler's new order, and although the blitzkrieg had been stopped at the gates of Moscow by winter snows, few considered this more than a temporary halt to the Nazi advances. In the United States, President Roosevelt might talk confidently of ultimate victory and the

people might believe, but so far there was only disaster. And the enemy was coming closer. German U-boats prowled the Atlantic Coast and that winter the beaches were stained with oil and other flotsam, testimony to the loss of ships, lives and vital cargo. A band of German agents was landed one night by U-boat on the eastern tip of Long Island and, though quickly captured, the audacity of the landing did nothing to calm the national nerves.

The worse the reports, the greater the fear of fifth columnists and saboteurs. That fear sent government forces swooping down on all Japanese on the West Coast, herding them into isolated internment camps. In the East, although few overt actions were taken against Germans and Italians, their loyalty also was suspect, especially by many in the military who viewed any foreigner as a potential enemy agent and who waited with dread for an expected outbreak of sabotage.

Some of those fears had already seemed realized. On February 11, 1942, the night sky over blacked-out Manhattan burst into flame. Berthed at a Hudson River pier, the French luxury liner *S.S. Normandie*, interned at the fall of France and then requisitioned by the United States, was being converted into an Allied troopship capable of transporting an entire division. Now she was in flames; she burned for days, then rolled over and died. Despite a series of investigations, the cause was never satisfactorily fixed, though there were many theories: sparks from a welding torch in the hands of a careless ship fitter; flammable debris littering the vessel igniting spontaneously; a saboteur's match.

If no one was able to explain the cause, the spark that gutted the *Normandie* did have an immediate consequence, and one that could not have delighted the American underworld more. To navy officials in Washington and at the headquarters of the Third Naval District in Lower Manhattan, the destruction of the *Normandie* rekindled long-held suspicions about the lack of security along the New York waterfront. Many of the longshoremen and others in the fishing and shipping industries that ringed the harbor were Italians—immigrants or the sons of immigrants. If these men felt greater loyalty to Italy than to the United States, then the waterfront was swarming with potential saboteurs, agents who could foment strikes and other troubles to tie up the port at a crucial phase of the war, who could commit acts of destruction, who might feed information to the Germans lying offshore, who might even use their fishing boats to supply those submarines. How could there be any security along the waterfront, especially when the docks were the bastion of the underworld and men such as Albert Anastasia, the lord high executioner of Murder, Inc., and his brother, Anthony "Tough Tony" Anastasio, one of the most powerful leaders of the International Longshoremen's Association?

Such fears inspired one of the most bizarre episodes of World War II. It was called Operation: Underworld, and the nation's leaders of organized crime—Meyer Lansky, Frank Costello, and, above all, Charles "Lucky" Luciano—saw in it the keys that would unlock the gates of Dannemora prison, where Luciano had already spent more than five years of a 30-to-50-year sentence as the boss of organized prostitution. From them, through their legitimate contacts, the navy received a subtle message that Italian racketeers not only were loyal Americans but were in a unique position to offer the country much help against its foreign enemies.

The idea was as farfetched as it

Frank S. Hogan succeeded Thomas E. Dewey as Manhattan district attorney.

was offensive, but the navy was desperate and a young reserve officer in Naval Intelligence, Lieutenant Commander Charles H. Haffenden, was assigned to investigate the feasibility of enlisting the underworld and its leaders in the war effort. Haffenden was a strange choice, for he knew little about the New York waterfront and even less about the underworld. Having no idea where to start, in April 1942 he turned for help to the office of Manhattan District Attorney Thomas E. Dewey. The racket buster himself was too busy to deal with Haffenden directly—his political activities occupied almost all his time; he had already lost the 1938 New York gubernatorial race to Herbert

Lehman, had made a serious but unsuccessful bid for the 1940 Republican presidential nomination, and now, with his eyes still on the White House, was again engaged in an all-out effort to capture the governor's mansion in Albany. So Dewey turned Haffenden over to two key assistants, Frank S. Hogan (already anointed to succeed Dewey as Manhattan district attorney, an office in which he would reign until 1974) and Murray Gurfein (a Dewey aide during the Luciano trial in 1936 and later to become a U.S. District Court judge).

Hogan and Gurfein had just the man for Haffenden to see—Joseph "Socks" Lanza, the semiliterate but all-powerful ruler of the Fulton Fish Market. "Joe Zox," as his friends called him, was so absolute a dictator that no fish went into or out of the city-owned market without payment of tribute to him—ten dollars from every boat arriving and $50 from every truck departing—and no stall operated without his paid-for approval. No one challenged Lanza, for he had met challenges in the past with sudden violence and had managed to beat both murder and gun indictments. During the mid-Thirties, he had even been able to maintain his control while serving a federal sentence in Flint, Michigan, for conspiracy to monopolize the fresh-water fish industry in New York. Furthermore, his influence reached into both the world of politics and the world of organized crime, in which he was a leading figure. His brother-in-law, Prospero Vincent

Viggiano, was a powerful Tammany district leader; one of his closest friends was Albert C. Marinelli, long one of the absolute monarchs of Tammany Hall; he had been partners in a number of operations with Joe Adonis, Luciano and Costello, who had been best man at his wedding in 1941.

But as the war began, Lanza was in trouble. The American Federation of Labor, finally fed up with his extortion and strong-arm activities, had thrown his United Seafood Workers Union out of the house of organized labor. And Dewey's office had him indicted for shaking down a Teamster local. Even these troubles, though, had not yet shaken his control over the fish market and the fishing fleets that daily sailed from New York out to the open sea. He was, then, the ideal man for Haffenden to contact.

Lanza responded quickly. In fact, underworld sources maintain he had been told to expect the call and had rehearsed his responses. He agreed to meet with Haffenden, but not in public; if they were seen together, he said, it might be taken the wrong way by his friends, what with the rash of informers like Abe Reles and Allie Tannenbaum. He would meet Haffenden at midnight on a park bench near Grant's Tomb.

The meeting went as scheduled and Lanza could not have been more helpful, perhaps hoping that his cooperation would lead Dewey to deal more kindly with him when his case came to trial. (It didn't: He eventually pleaded guilty and was sentenced

Joseph "Socks" Lanza controlled the fish market in New York.

to seven and a half to 15 years in prison.) He agreed to do everything in his power to combat sabotage and fifth columnists, authorizing Haffenden to put intelligence agents and communications devices on fishing vessels and trucks and throughout the fish market.

But at a second meeting soon after, as Haffenden asked for further cooperation, Lanza declared that his own powers were strictly limited. He had no control, he said, over the longshoremen nor over a hundred other areas where the government might want help. There was only one man who could weld the entire American underworld, and the entire Italian-

and Sicilian-American community, into a patriotic force devoted to the Allied cause: Charlie Lucky.

Back went Haffenden to Gurfein for advice and assistance. Gurfein called Luciano's attorney, Moses Polakoff. Polakoff hedged, suggested that instead of sounding out Luciano immediately, it might be wise for Gurfein to explore the matter with one or two of Luciano's closest friends. Gurfein agreed. A breakfast meeting was arranged at a hotel overlooking Central Park and Polakoff arrived with Lansky.

NEARLY TWO DECADES LATER, while seeking haven in Israel from a variety of American indictments, Lansky gave his version of that breakfast. Gurfein, he said, "explained the situation to me. I went immediately to see Frank Costello, telling him the story and asking what does he feel about it. Frank was patriotic and felt that help should be given. So we made up a white lie and we decided that we will tell Charlie Lucky that if he will be helpful in this case, it might help him to get out of prison."

Though nothing had been done without his knowledge and approval from the very inception of Operation: Underworld, Luciano was not about to appear overeager. When the call came asking him to meet with Gurfein and navy officials, he initially refused. He would talk with nobody, he said, as long as he was in Dan-

nemora; he wanted a more congenial environment. So he was moved, first temporarily to Sing Sing for the initial conferences, and then more permanently to Great Meadow Prison, north of Albany, the country club of New York State penitentiaries.

In this more relaxed atmosphere, Luciano agreed to do all he could to help the United States win the war. But, he informed Gurfein and the navy, in order to do his best, he would need easy access to his friends in the underworld to get his orders out and around the country. At Great Meadow, Luciano was given a private office for use during his secret meetings and permission was granted throughout the war years for a steady procession of mobsters to visit him for private discussions. Among those who arrived regularly were Lansky, Costello, Adonis, Willie Moretti, Tommy Lucchese, Mike Miranda, and Lanza, until he, himself, went to prison.

If they talked about national defense, they also talked about a lot more, for they were concerned primarily with the Syndicate in its wartime search for wealth. They may all have been self-professed patriots, but there was nothing in their definition of patriotism that said they couldn't make a buck out of the war (and in this they differed little from many legitimate businessmen). And there were plenty of ways to do it, especially since many Americans wanted to continue enjoying the amenities of life despite shortages, rationing and the laws. As it had during Prohibition, the Mob was both willing and

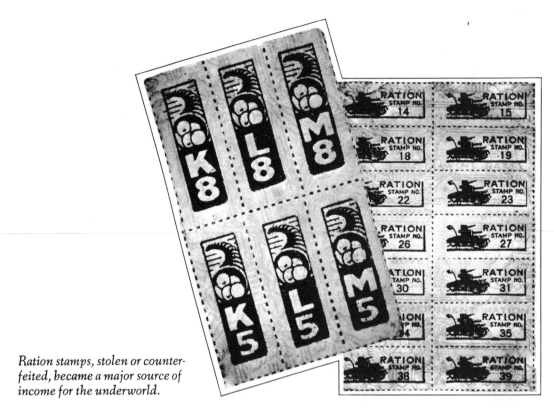

Ration stamps, stolen or counter-feited, became a major source of income for the underworld.

determined to supply the demand. People wanted ration stamps so they could buy meat, other foods, gasoline, tires and other rationed goods; the underworld provided millions of stamps to those who would pay for them—stamps pilfered in raids on federal depots, purchased from dishonest government officials, counterfeited.

Not only did the racketeers supply the stamps, they soon supplied the rationed commodities themselves and thus made further inroads into legitimate business in the course of building a black market. Led by Lucchese and Anastasia, they used wartime shortages to tighten their grip on the garment industry. Because of the scarcity of beef, the meat industry became the target of a power drive by

Carlo Gambino, until then only another ambitious and rising hoodlum in the family run by the Mangano brothers and Anastasia. Assisted by such tough and violent lieutenants as Paul Castellano (who would later emerge as partner of Gambino's brother Paul in the huge Pride Wholesale Meat Company) and Sonny Franzese, Gambino organized the meat purveyors in Brooklyn, then spread his influence across New York. Under his rule, the industry was tightly controlled and paid off handsomely. The butchers knew that the dollars going into Gambino's pockets not only ensured an end to any trouble but also guaranteed a steady supply of choice cuts of meat (since Gambino and his friends had moved into wholesale meat packing, as well) and all the ration stamps they needed. For the customers, it meant that at Mob-controlled markets they could buy all the meat they wanted, with or without ration stamps—at prices well above the legal ceiling.

Meanwhile, Lansky, Costello and others had found another enterprise equally suited to their talents. As a kind of patriotic gesture to show that they, too, would make sacrifices to the war effort, they had shuttered their gambling casinos in Havana and other places difficult to reach because of travel restrictions and even closed some of their fancier operations in the United States—but in reality to concentrate their efforts on black-marketing. Gasoline and tires were even harder to get than meat or clothes—unless you knew somebody. So the Syndicate moved in, buying through fronts hundreds of gas stations that never ran dry, and made no great fuss about ration stamps. And the same stations always seemed to have plenty of recapped tires for sale at a price. There were millions to be made by profiteering in shortages during the war, and the Mob and its friends made them.

It was such operations and how to continue them in peacetime that mostly concerned Luciano and his visitors during those years at Great Meadow, in sanctuary provided by the state of New York at the request of the United States Navy. But Luciano did give at least some thought to his government assignment. He ordered dock workers and the underworld to cooperate with the military and, in fact, there were very few acts of sabotage along the American waterfront or in any other area under Mob control during the war years. But were such dictates from Luciano really needed? It seems most unlikely that longshoremen or the leaders and rank and file of American organized crime might have aided national enemies whose victory would have meant their own undoing. Indeed, through the years, few have more stridently proclaimed their devotion to the United States—or reaped more from the American system—than the gangsters.

It was also claimed that Luciano dispatched orders to the Sicilian-American community to give the military any photographs and postcards of the Sicilian landscape to aid in topographic studies of the island; and that Luciano persuaded the powerful leaders of the island's Mafia to assist the Allied landings in 1943. But Luciano had not been in Sicily since 1906, when, as a child of nine, his family emigrated to the United States. Though he had risen to become perhaps the most powerful ruler of American organized crime, the ties between the American underworld and the Sicilian Mafia were, at best, remote, and if Sicilian criminals helped, it was because they decided it was in their own interest. For years they had been under attack, threatened with extermination by Mussolini; it only made good sense to aid those who would topple the Fascist dictator and restore the old system.

SOME YEARS LATER, THE NAVY'S coordinator of Operation: Underworld, Commander Haffenden, would dismiss the racketeer's contribution. "Luciano was like all other informers we used in our intelligence work," he said. "He did no more than any good American citizen would have done. I can't set him up on a pedestal as having done anything great, because he rendered only normal cooperation." But at the time, Haffenden had lauded Luciano for making a "great" contribution to victory. And Gurfein had declared, "There is no doubt that Luciano did wield a tremendous and peculiar influence in the underworld and, from what I understand, he did do some good in creating this underworld counterespionage system." No one, however, would discuss the details of Luciano's work.

Such secrecy was useful. It permitted Luciano's parole, without much explanation, by Dewey, who had sent him to prison in the first place.

In the possession of Luciano's lawyers were sworn affidavits from the major witnesses at his 1936 trial stating that they had lied under oath and that their lies had been concocted in Dewey's office under threat of prosecution on other charges. An appeals court had rejected similar affidavits in 1938, but then Luciano was a recently convicted felon, the heralded boss of the American underworld and a name with which to frighten children. By 1942, he had been in prison long enough for his notoriety to subside, while Dewey himself had become highly vulnerable. He was a national figure, a candidate for high state office and a potential president. Charges that he had suborned perjury, even if untrue, would certainly not have helped his image as the white knight in shining armor shattering the rackets and bringing to the state and the nation honesty and good government.

According to underworld stories, a deal was struck. The affidavits would be filed away to gather dust and Luciano would not appeal for a new trial. A large bank roll—some have put it at $250,000 or more, with Luciano subscribing a major part—would be secretly put at the disposal of Dewey's campaign organization. And the muscle of the Mob would cut down the normally overwhelming Democratic majorities in New York City to help ensure Dewey's victory. In exchange, Luciano would later receive his freedom.

In November 1942, Dewey was elected governor, then reneged on a promise he had made not to seek the Republican presidential nomination in 1944. To Luciano's relief, he lost heavily to Roosevelt and returned to Albany.

On May 7, 1945, the very day the war in Europe ended, Luciano's petition for executive clemency was dispatched to the governor. Dewey turned it over to his state parole board, its members all his appointees. At the hearings, there were general statements to the effect that Luciano had performed noble and, because of security, necessarily secret labors for the Allied cause. The board unanimously recommended parole.

On January 3, 1946, Dewey announced his agreement with the board's recommendation. The gangster would go free, but he would not be permitted to remain in the United States. "Luciano," Dewey said, "is deportable to Italy. . . . Upon the entry of the United States into the war, Luciano's aid was sought by the armed services in inducing others to provide information concerning possible enemy attack. It appears that he cooperated in such efforts, though the actual value of the information provided is not clear. His record in prison is reported as wholly satisfactory."

Some years later, Dewey amplified that statement in an interview with an editor of the *New York Post*. He said, "An exhaustive investigation . . . established that Luciano's aid to the navy in the war was extensive and valuable. Ten years is probably as long as anybody ever served for compulsory prostitution. And these factors led the parole board to recommend the commutation, combined with the fact that Luciano would be exiled for life under law."

On February 9, 1946, Luciano had his final look at the city where he had grown up and whose underworld he ruled. He was hustled aboard a converted Liberty ship, the *S.S. Laura Keene*, and sent to Italy. In the hours before the scheduled noon sailing, all his old underworld friends and a score or more of politicians went to the ship for a farewell party. Also on

Lucky Luciano went home again—deported by the U.S. government.

hand was a small army of reporters hoping for a final word at a shipboard press conference promised by the United States Immigration and Naturalization Service. But when they arrived, they could only stand in the bitter cold 100 yards distant, watch the curtained limousines arrive and depart and try to guess what was going on. In their way stood a gang of longshoremen, armed with sharpened baling hooks; they had been massed by Anastasia and Anastasio to protect Luciano and his well-wishers from prying eyes. When the newspapermen turned to members of District Attorney Frank Hogan's staff for intervention in their behalf, they received no help. The authorities were not anxious to participate in a clash between reporters and dock workers.

As the *Laura Keene* cast off, several of the dock workers yelled, "So long, Charlie . . . you'll be back." That was exactly Luciano's intention. He had left all his holdings in the hands of Lansky, Costello and Adonis, but he did not intend that this gift should be permanent. He had already set in motion plans for his return, if not directly into the United States, then at least close enough to American shores to resume control of the American underworld and fend off any rivals.

Perhaps the most ambitious of these rivals was his old lieutenant, Vito Genovese. As Luciano was leaving, Genovese was about to reemerge after an absence of nearly a decade and make his play for the throne. In 1937, with New York authorities closing in on him for racketeering and murder, Genovese had put more than $1,000,000 into a satchel and fled to Italy. On his honeymoon trip there a few years earlier, he had become acquainted with a number of officials in Mussolini's government; now he sought them out again and curried their favor to guarantee himself a

certain degree of comfort during his visit to his native land—a visit, he soon realized, that was going to be prolonged by a world war.

His personal safety and comfort, Genovese decided, lay in a public espousal of the Fascist cause, and with a flourish he handed over $250,000 to build a Fascist party headquarters. Later, when war broke out, he further demonstrated his loyalty to Mussolini by financing and supervising construction of a munitions factory. For all his public efforts, Mussolini personally awarded Genovese the title of *commendatore*.

But Genovese feathered his Italian nest with more than money and patriotic gestures. He made friends in high places and did favors for the right people, including *Il Duce* himself. In 1943, the Italian dictator was particularly incensed at the anti-Fascist writings of a political *émigré* named Carlo Tresca in his New York Italian-language weekly, *Il Martello*. Genovese promised to deal with this problem to Mussolini's complete satisfaction. Though the war was on, Genovese managed to get a contract back to New York, and one day in 1943, Tresca was shot to death on Lower Fifth Avenue.

Perhaps Genovese's closest friend in the government was Mussolini's son-in-law, the Italian foreign minister, Count Galeazzo Ciano. Imagining himself the ultimate sophisticate, Ciano constantly searched for new pleasures as old ones paled, and he eventually discovered cocaine. Genovese became his personal supplier. He asked little money and used his influence with Ciano to make contacts not just in the Italian narcotics racket but directly at the source, in the poppy fields of the Middle East. With Ciano's protection, he became one of Italy's biggest and richest narcotics dealers.

By 1944, HOWEVER, THE FOR-tunes of fascism had collapsed. Italy surrendered and Mussolini was in flight (he was caught in the north and executed by partisans early in 1945). The prisons were filling up with those who had been high in the regime or who had cooperated with it, and those not yet captured were the object of massive hunts as war criminals. But not Genovese. Almost as soon as Americans occupied the country, he turned up at the headquarters of the Allied military governor, Colonel Charles Poletti, a former lieutenant governor of New York and one-time acting governor. The bilingual Genovese was promptly hired as an official interpreter on Poletti's staff, working out of the huge supply base at Nola.

That job, however, was merely a cover for his real activities. He became the biggest black-market operator in occupied Italy, with the overt and covert cooperation of a number of high army officials. He dealt in medicines, cigarettes, liquor, wheat, food of all kinds, clothing, anything stocked at army supply depots to which he had ready access. His position in the inner circles of the military government gave him freedom of movement, freedom from immediate suspicion and an open door to the supplies pouring into Nola and the other bases.

And in his pockets, Genovese carried testimonials to his great loyalty and dedicated service to the United States. From Captain Charles L. Dunn, Nola's provisional officer; from Major E. N. Holmgreen, the civil-affairs officer; from Major Stephen Young, there were warm references to Genovese's "invaluable" contributions as an interpreter and advisor, to the fact that he was "honest . . . trustworthy, loyal and dependable . . . worked day and night . . . exposed several cases of bribery and black-market operations among so-called civilian personnel . . . is devoted to his adopted home, the U.S.A. . . . served without any compensation whatever."

But there was at least one man who was not quite so ingenuous. Sergeant Orange C. Dickey of the army's Criminal Investigation Division was assigned to investigate the disappearance of large quantities of vital supplies from Nola, Foggia and other military depots. Almost immediately, he began to come across the name Genovese on papers diverting shipments, assigning trucks, allocating supplies. Dickey looked further, found two Canadian soldiers involved in black-marketeering; they told him that whenever they delivered truckloads of supplies to Italian civilian middlemen, the password was, "Genovese sent us." Dickey dug deeper

"Vito says he's running a special next week on Jeeps."

and came up with the most disturbing information of all. The interpreter working deep within the American military government, with access to military secrets and with the confidence of high officials, was suspected by Counterintelligence of being a German spy, a suspicion based on his long history of close ties with Italian Fascists.

Dickey reported his findings to Captain Dunn and others in the summer of 1944. He was ordered to drop the investigation. He went to Rome to see the officers of the American military government. They told him Genovese was of "no concern" to them. But Dickey persisted. In August 1944, on his own hook, he walked into headquarters at Nola and arrested Genovese as a black-market operator and suspected enemy agent. Still, the American military in Italy refused to press the case. And from his cell, Genovese continued to run his black-market operation and to receive a steady parade of visitors, his old army friends and supporters.

In frustration, Dickey wired the FBI in Washington, informing them of Genovese's arrest and asking if he was wanted in the United States.

The past that Genovese had fled returned. Ernest "The Hawk" Rupolo, one of the killers Genovese had hired to murder a man named Boccia, had long been fretting in prison, serving a sentence for another murder Genovese had hired him to commit, one that had misfired. Rupolo had decided to talk about the Boccia murder and gave Brooklyn authorities

not just the facts but a corroborating witness, a cigar-store salesman and sometime underworld hanger-on named Peter LaTempa, who had been around when the details of the killing were discussed. A murder indictment naming Genovese had been secured and when Dickey's message arrived, Brooklyn authorities advised the FBI that someone did, indeed, want Genovese.

The army could have tried Genovese on the charges filed against him by Dickey. Instead, it dropped them and ordered Dickey to take Genovese back to New York to face capital charges. Genovese, of course, was not anxious to make the voyage. "At various times," Dickey later said, "I was offered many things. At one point, I was offered a quarter of a million dollars to let this fellow out of jail." When Dickey refused the money offers, Genovese tried other enticements: gifts, jobs, anything else he desired. Still Dickey refused. Genovese then threatened him and his family. Dickey still would not be deterred. He took Genovese back to New York and turned him over to the police.

Genovese was jailed in Brooklyn while the district attorney's office prepared its case. On January 15, 1945, however, that case collapsed. At his own request, LaTempa was being held in protective custody in Brooklyn. He was not a well man. That evening, he was stricken by a severe attack of gallstones. Several pills dissolved in a glass of water were taken to him for his pain. Within minutes, there was no corroborating witness against Genovese. According to a toxicologist who performed the autopsy, LaTempa had been given enough poison "to kill eight horses." (Soon thereafter, Rupolo, the other witness, was freed; he lived for some years awaiting gangland retribution and in August 1964, he vanished. A few weeks later, his body surfaced in Jamaica Bay, weighted with concrete, mutilated by an ice pick and bullets that had blown off the back of his head.)

Brooklyn authorities continued to hold Genovese for more than a year, hoping to secure new evidence that would permit bringing him to trial. When at last, in June 1946, they were forced to turn him loose, an angry judge said to him, "Genovese, by devious means, among which were terrorizing of witnesses, kidnaping them—yes, even murdering those who could have given evidence against you—you have thwarted justice time and again."

Genovese was welcomed back into the high councils of the Syndicate at a series of parties thrown by his old friends and he moved rapidly to take control, in Luciano's name, he asserted, of the exiled leader's organization. He also began a series of encroachments into the Brooklyn domain of Philip and Vincent Mangano and their feared underboss Anastasia, and into the territory of Joe Bonanno. Moreover, he argued for rapid expansion of narcotics operations as a sure way to make everyone rich and provide plenty of work for the ordinary soldiers.

But Genovese's intended victims prepared to resist his take-over, even if it meant an underworld war such as had not been waged since the Castellammarese struggle. And other leaders prepared to fight his increasing emphasis on narcotics, convinced that the profits were not worth the trouble junk would cause. The Organization, they said, had evolved into an orderly business, supplying the illicit needs and desires of society. It provided services and products that hurt nobody and, consequently, many politicians and police were willing to look the other way, provided they received their share.

But narcotics were universally disapproved, would guarantee new crackdowns and new heat on the underworld. So they wanted no part of heroin or other drugs.

Genovese's ambitions split the old Luciano family. During his decade in Italy and Luciano's in prison, its regent had been Costello. He was a benevolent, tolerant and generous ruler who did not impose his views on others and did not foment trouble with his peers. He had worked quietly and assiduously, cultivating friends, contacts and allies in every stratum of society, had become such a political power that he could name judges, city councilmen and other officeholders, and the word around Tammany Hall on any new appointment or important decision was, "Clear it with Frank." As a result, Costello had won great respect and power throughout the underworld and, with Lansky, was considered the wisest, most intelligent and judicious leader. It would be no easy thing for Genovese to topple him should Costello decide to resist.

Perhaps there was only one man who could heal the splits before they tore the Syndicate apart. That was Luciano himself, and late in November 1946, he was on hand, ready to do some knitting and to reassert his own authority. With a legal Italian passport and visas for half the countries in Latin America, Luciano turned up one afternoon at the Hotel Nacional in Havana, registering under his own legal name, Salvatore Lucania, in a suite reserved for him by Lansky. And within a few days, he had settled down as though he never intended to leave, in a villa in the exclusive Miramar suburb. He was even able to demonstrate a legitimate reason for his presence in Cuba: Soon after his arrival, he purchased a small percentage of the casino at the Hotel Nacional from its owners—Lansky and his good friend Fulgencio Batista, the one-time Cuban strong man who, living in Miami and preparing for a comeback, was a major power behind the regime of President Ramon Grau San Martin.

Luciano summoned all the major chieftains of the American underworld to Havana for the first full-scale convention of the Syndicate since the early Thirties. Just before Christmas, mixing with the other holiday fun-and-sun seekers, they began to arrive, by plane and boat, singly and in pairs. From New York, there were Costello, Adonis, Genovese, Anastasia, Bonanno, Lucchese, Moretti, Miranda, Augie Pisano, Joe

Profaci and his brother-in-law and anointed heir, Joseph "The Fat Man" Magliocco; from Chicago came Tony Accardo, the reigning ganglord, and the Fischetti brothers, Charlie and Rocco, cousins of Al Capone, who by then was out of prison and dying of advanced paresis only 90 miles away at his Palm Island mansion off Miami Beach; Carlo Marcello and the Syndicate's New Orleans gambling czar, "Dandy Phil" Kastel, came from Louisiana; Santo Trafficante arrived from Florida; there were several from other cities and, of course, Lansky, who had made all the arrangements at Luciano's request.

Had anyone noticed or commented upon the arrival of such a galaxy of racketeers, there was an ostensibly legitimate reason for the assemblage: a party at Christmas to honor an Italian boy from New Jersey who had become the idol of the nation's bobby-soxers and yet had never forgotten his old friends. His name was Frank Sinatra and he flew to Havana with two old friends, the Fischetti brothers. While the gang leaders came bearing cash-stuffed envelopes for the returning boss— estimates of the total money run from $200,000 all the way up to several million—Sinatra had a few tokens of his own to dispense. Some years later, a gold cigarette case would turn up in Luciano's possession engraved:

TO MY DEAR PAL CHARLIE, FROM HIS FRIEND, FRANK SINATRA.

For more than a week, from Christmas through New Year's, the visiting mobsters partied long and worked hard. They gave their allegiance to Luciano as the chairman of the board of organized crime, the man to whom they would turn for advice, counsel and major policy decisions. They agreed to cooperate, to end feuds and growing rivalries, to respect one another's jurisdictions and to keep the peace. They discussed narcotics, but in an atmosphere charged with recrimination, tension and bitterness. Luciano always maintained that in the councils his was the strongest voice in opposition to narcotics; he had learned, he said, by bitter experience, with his prison term in 1916 and his arrest in 1923, that narcotics was a racket that didn't pay off because of the peril involved. And his views were shared by Lansky, Costello, Lucchese, Stefano Magaddino (the Syndicate's Buffalo boss) and a few others. So divided was the discussion that eventually the subject was tabled, with no decision on an Organization policy; each ruler would follow his own dictates.

And then there was the distressing affair of the Organization's West Coast viceroy, Benjamin "Bugsy" Siegel. During the war years, Siegel had begun to have visions of a new empire, one that would mine gold out of the desert. Gambling was legal in Nevada, but the attraction then was Reno. Las Vegas was only a sleazy oasis, offering a couple of greasy spoons, a few slot machines and some gas stations catering to tourists on their way to Los Angeles. Siegel dreamed of Las Vegas as a great me-tropolis, a gambling paradise unmatched anywhere in the world. He began to lay plans for a luxury hotel and casino that would open up the town. His enthusiasm was infectious and he persuaded his underworld partners to back him. When Lansky, the Mob's treasurer and financial genius, announced his support, the money flowed in.

Siegel named his dream hotel the Flamingo and, to decorate it in the most lavish manner, he gave a free hand and an unlimited bank roll to his mistress, Virginia Hill, who at one time or another had shared beds with almost the entire underworld hierarchy, including Adonis, Costello, the Fischettis, Accardo and Frank Nitti. But Siegel knew he would need more than a hotel, however spectacular, and desert gambling to woo the customers from Reno. His lure, in addition to the tables, would be the best food, the best accommodations and the greatest entertainers, all at such low prices that no high roller could afford to stay away.

With an initial building budget of $1,500,000, Siegel handed the construction contract to the Del E. Webb Construction Company of Phoenix (Del Webb would later become part owner of the New York Yankees). Though both labor and materials were still scarce, Siegel's Flamingo had little trouble getting all it needed; it required only a little Mob muscle in the right places. Ground for the Flamingo was broken in December 1945, and it did not take Siegel long to discover that his insistence on quali-

Lily St. Cyr was one of the first stars to play Las Vegas.

ty—concrete walls, imported·woods and marble, special sewer lines for every bathroom—was wrecking his original budget. Time and again, he went back to Lansky and his other underworld partners for more money, and time and again, though not without some grumbling, they gave him what he needed. When he needed still more, he began to hit up his friends and acquaintances in Beverly Hills and throughout the motion-picture colony, holding out the promise of enormous profits when the Flamingo finally opened. But with the constant delays and mounting expenses—the Flamingo would eventually cost more than $6,000,000—the Organization began to fret. Promises were not enough.

The Flamingo's financial backers were angry at Siegel, and he had also incurred the wrath of Accardo, the Fischettis, Murray "The Camel" Humphreys and others in the Chicago underworld. One of Siegel's major assignments on the West Coast had been to handle the Mob's betting operations, in partnership with Jack Dragna, the leader in Southern California until Siegel turned up. For the bookies to operate, they needed a racing wire to give them instantaneous track results. The dominant wire in the country then was Continental Press Service, based in Chicago and owned by James M. Ragen, who had succeeded Moses Annenberg as the country's racing czar when Annenberg went to prison. Ragen's independence was not something the Mob could tolerate, so it decided to go into competition, setting up the Trans-American Publishing and News Service. Siegel was given the responsibility for ensuring its success in the West. With muscle, threats and a little violence, Siegel did exactly that. Soon he had a lock on nearly all the bookies in his area and was charging them up to $100 a day for his service, which they could not do without.

But, with Ragen still around, the Chicago Mob was not yet satisfied. It offered to buy Ragen out; he figured that even if he sold, his former competitors would not let him live long enough to enjoy the profits. He refused the offers. So, in June 1946, Ragen was gunned down as he walked along a Chicago street. Though hit by several bullets, the marksmanship had been poor and he ended up in a hospital under round-the-clock police guard. In September, Ragen suddenly died; an autopsy revealed that he had been poisoned by mercury.

With Ragen gone, the Chicago Syndicate took over Continental and told its West Coast partner, Siegel, to close up Trans-American. He refused, then demanded $2,000,000. Harsh words flew back and forth, and the men in Chicago decided to play for time.

Thus, in Havana during Christmas 1946, there were men very unhappy with Siegel—his partners in the Flamingo and his partners in Trans-American. Siegel was not invited to the meeting, was not even told about it, but he was well aware of his unpopularity and felt the need to improve his underworld relations. Though the Flamingo was still unfinished, he decided to demonstrate how right his predictions had been and announced that it would officially open on December 26. George Jessel would be master of ceremonies, with entertainment provided by Xavier Cugat's orchestra, Jimmy Durante and an army of beautiful girls. Siegel's close friend George Raft would be on hand to greet the customers. Unfortunately, as things turned out, there were few customers for Raft to greet. The night was cold and rainy, grounding the planes that Siegel had chartered to bring in gamblers and Hollywood celebrities. Few tried to find alternative means of travel.

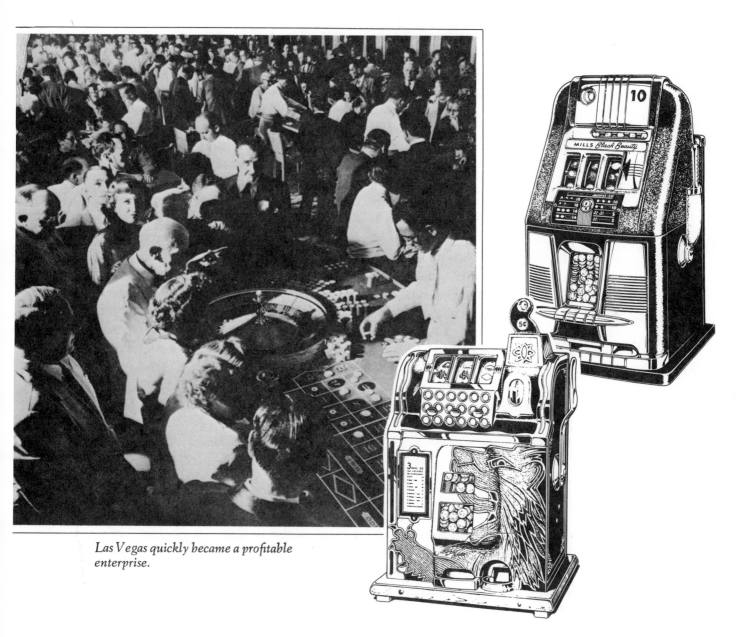

Las Vegas quickly became a profitable enterprise.

The debacle of the Flamingo's opening night did not endear Siegel to his old friends, and then came disturbing news from his oldest and closest friend, Lansky. Siegel was not only a flop as an impresario but, Lansky said, he was a thief as well. Lansky had learned that Miss Hill was making frequent trips to Europe, depositing several hundred thousand dollars in cash in a numbered account in Switzerland; the cash had come from the Flamingo's building fund.

Nobody, not even an old and trusted comrade like Siegel, steals from his underworld friends and gets away with it. Siegel's execution was ordered, but first he would be given time to try to prove that his Nevada dream might actually come true.

In mid-January, the Flamingo closed while finishing touches were added. The corporation was reorganized and Siegel found himself reduced from majority ownership to no more than a 10-percent partner. But he worked hard to get the Flamingo ready for a new opening, perhaps unaware of the Havana decision on his future or perhaps aware of it and hoping to produce a success that would cancel the contract. In March, his labors were complete and the Flamingo reopened, but with no better fortune than the first time. It seemed as though every gambler who showed up at the tables had an incredible run of luck. The losses piled up. Checks made out by Siegel to Webb and others in payment for work on the hotel-casino bounced and Siegel grew increasingly edgy. One night, Webb arrived at the hotel to pick up a payment. Siegel, he said, "was a remarkable character. Tough, cold and terrifying when he wanted to be—but at other times a very easy fellow to be around. He told me one night when I was waiting for my money that he had personally killed twelve men. But then he must have noted my face or something, because he laughed and said I had nothing to worry about. 'There's no chance that you'll get killed,' he said. 'We only kill each other.'"

In May, Siegel seemed to relax. There had been no overt moves against him and the casino finally was turning around; that month it cleared

$300,000. But it was too late. Word had reached Lansky and others in the Syndicate that not only had Siegel accelerated his work on the hotel but he had also accelerated his skimming, had now siphoned off at least $500,000, had dispatched Virginia on another European trip, and there were rumors that he was preparing to follow her there.

Early in the morning of June 20, 1947, Siegel returned to Los Angeles from Las Vegas. He visited his favorite barbershop and seemed in a relaxed and cheerful mood as he talked about the glowing prospects of the Flamingo and the imminent arrival from the East of his two daughters. From the barbershop, he went to see his lawyer. In the evening, he had dinner at Jack's Café on the beach with a friend, Allen Smiley, and Virginia's brother, Charles "Chick" Hill, and his girlfriend, Jerri Mason. Just before ten in the evening, they returned to the Beverly Hills mansion at 810 North Linden Drive that Siegel had rented in Virginia's name.

At 10:45 P.M., Siegel and Smiley were relaxing in the living room, talking and reading the newspapers. Suddenly, a fusillade from a .30-caliber carbine, fired by an assassin standing in the bushes outside the living-room window, blasted through the room. One bullet tore through Siegel's head, ripping out his eye and tossing it across the room. Four more slugs struck his body, cracking his ribs and piercing his lungs. Three more missed, shattering small objects around the room and burying themselves in the wall. At the first shot, Smiley dove to the floor and escaped injury.

Almost the minute Siegel collapsed dead on a sofa, three men walked into the Flamingo in Las Vegas and announced that they were taking over. They were all longtime workers in Lansky's fields: Morris Rosen, Gus Greenbaum and Morris Sidwirtz, better known as Moe Sedway. And in Los Angeles, Jack Dragna

promptly assumed command of the Syndicate operations on the West Coast.

The murder of Siegel, never solved, prevented him from seeing his Las Vegas dream come true. In the decade that followed, the city flourished: Hotel-casinos, whose garish architecture and lavish decor were

Virginia Hill (top right) was in Europe when Bugsy Siegel became a homicide statistic.

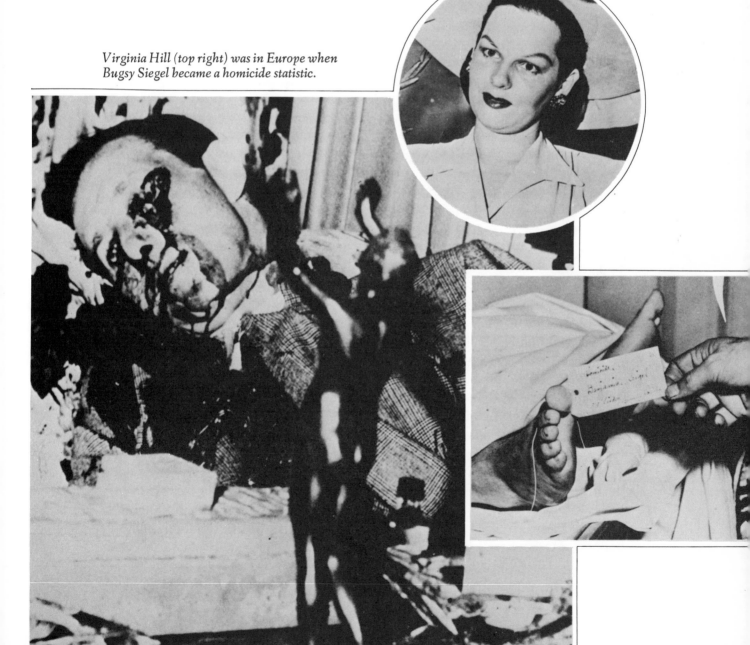

matched only by places in Miami Beach, rose one after another along the Strip pioneered by Siegel, each trying to exceed the others in entertainment, food, accommodations and gambling facilities. Behind almost every one was underworld money and control, with the mobsters both competing and cooperating with one another. The biggest guessing game in Las Vegas was who really owned what, though it was assumed that Lansky had a piece of everything.

Within a year of Siegel's murder, Lansky's money financed the Thunderbird. When the Desert Inn opened two years later, it was widely heralded as the culmination of the dream of a long-time "clean" gambler, a man named Wilbur Clark, who reputedly was free of Mob connections. As it turned out, the Desert Inn was actually financed and 74 percent owned by Moe Dalitz, then the Syndicate's Cleveland overlord, and his friends and associates from Prohibition days, Morris Kleinman, Sam Tucker, Lou Rothkopf, Thomas Jefferson McGinty, and others. When the Sands opened its doors in 1952, the money and control belonged to men whose names rarely appeared on the record: Lansky, Adonis, Costello, New Jersey mobster Joseph "Doc" Stacher, Florida and Kentucky bookie Eddie Levinson, Minneapolis crime leader Isadore Blumenfeld, better known as Kid Cann—and 9 percent belonged to Frank Sinatra. The Sands's official greeter was a man named Jack Entratter, who had been a bouncer at the Stork Club and the

Copacabana in New York and for a time had been the front man for the real owners of the Copa—Costello and Adonis.

The Sahara opened the same year as the Sands, and on the record it belonged to three small-time Oregon gamblers. But they got their stake from the Chicago–New York–Cleveland Syndicate money men. It was the Chicago Mob—Accardo, the Fischettis and Sam "Mooney" Giancana—that ended up owning the Riviera casino and then hired Greenbaum, one of the Lansky trio who had taken over the Flamingo at Siegel's death, to run it. (In 1958, Greenbaum earned his employers' displeasure, for reasons never fully explained. So he was fired in the usual way: He and his wife had their throats cut one night at their home in Phoenix.)

The Dunes brought riches to Raymond Patriarca, the Syndicate's Rhode Island boss; the Stardust was another annuity for Dalitz; and the Tropicana kept Costello and his partner Kastel from want. And, of course, there was Caesars Palace, whose architecture and decor were supposed to evoke images of ancient Rome but inspired comedian Alan King to remark, "I wouldn't say it was exactly Roman—more kind of early Sicilian." Financially ensconced in the Palace were Patriarca, Accardo and Giancana; Jerry Catena, one of Genovese's chief lieutenants; and Vincent "Jimmy Blue Eyes" Alo, a Lansky associate. But perhaps the biggest stake in the hotel-casino was held by James R. Hoffa and the Teamsters Union's pension fund, and that was only one of the union's holdings in the gambling capital. Before Hoffa was through investing Teamster pension funds in Las Vegas, he had seeded more than $50,000,000 into the city, mostly in the form of permanent loans. Caesars Palace itself received more than $10,000,000 in Teamster money and the rest went into several hotels and casinos (including the Landmark, the Fremont and the Dunes); Dalitz's favorite charity, the Sunrise Hospital; two golf courses and a miscellanea of downtown business properties.

As the years went on, other unlikely people began to work the Las Vegas money mines. In the mid-Fifties, the Parvin-Dohrman Company (headed by Albert B. Parvin, a one-time interior decorator who had laid the carpets for many of the big hotels) bought the Flamingo. In the Sixties, it bought the Fremont and then sold the Flamingo to an investment syndicate headed by Miami Beach hotel man Morris Landsburgh (the Eden Roc), who, as it happened, was an old friend of Lansky's. Parvin then paid Lansky a $200,000 finder's fee for having turned up Landsburgh and used remaining Flamingo assets to set up the Albert Parvin Foundation to provide fellowships for students from underdeveloped countries. (On the foundation's board sat Robert F. Goheen, president of Princeton University, Robert Maynard Hutchins, head of the Center for the Study of Democratic Institutions, and U.S. Supreme Court Justice William O. Douglas.) Landsburgh and his friends soon tired of the Flamingo, about the time the government began its investigations of his New York–London charter gambling flights and of his part in Las Vegas skimming operations, for which he, Lansky and some others were later indicted. So the Flamingo was sold again, this time to Kirk Kerkorian, a former nonscheduled airline operator who now heads Metro-Goldwyn-Mayer.

But the most unlikely figure of all to hit Las Vegas was billionaire recluse Howard Hughes. In an effort, perhaps, to own a state of his own, or maybe just to get back into an old-time love, show business, or maybe just because he thought there was money to be made, Hughes started buying up Las Vegas in the mid-Sixties, taking over a number of the Mob-owned hotels and other properties. In rapid succession he bought the Desert Inn, the Sands, the Castaways, the Frontier, the Landmark, the Silver Slipper, Alamo Airways, North Las Vegas air terminal, the Krupp Ranch and television station KLAS-TV. Before Hughes finally fled the spotlight turned on by the Clifford Irving hoax and the lawsuits of his former chief of staff, Robert Maheu, he had served at least one beneficial purpose. Though the Organization never completely abandoned the Las Vegas gold fields, its influence and control began to wane with the increasing dominance of Hughes. Before, there had been a widespread feeling that only the mobsters could run casinos profitably; the Hughes operations proved that this was only a Mob-perpetuated myth. And the arrival of Hughes also pushed some Nevada officials out of their easy chairs to take a closer look at the casinos that they had long claimed could not be controlled.

Finally, the Las Vegas transition gave the lie to the old idea that, given the opportunity, the wise men of organized crime can and will run a business honestly. Gambling in Nevada is both legal and, even after the heavy taxes that nearly support the state, enormously profitable. By most estimates, tourists spend around five billion dollars in Las Vegas every year and casino profits average about 20 percent of that. But an honest count has never satisfied the Syndicate. Almost from the start, a percentage of the casino take—perhaps as much as 20 or 25 percent—has been skimmed off the top, carried away in satchels by Mob couriers to Lansky and other underworld financiers. That skim has formed the basis for one of the Mob's most successful ploys, the "laundry" business. Much of the money was deposited in numbered Swiss accounts, where it disappeared and was "laundered," returning to the United States in the form of loans to other Mob enterprises (which, of course, claimed the interest as tax deductions) or for investment in, hence further control of, legitimate businesses.

Just how much has been skimmed off the top in Las Vegas through the years few are even willing to guess. But in 1969, Lansky, Landsburgh and several others were indicted, charged with skimming $36,000,000 from the Flamingo alone between 1960 and 1967.

Siegel could never have imagined the riches that would pour into the Mob treasury when he first broke ground in the Nevada desert. Neither could those who handed down his death sentence at Christmas 1946. The place envisioned as the future gambling capital of the Western Hemisphere was Havana, where the Mob's money was moving in a flood, right along with the American tourists suddenly freed from the wartime travel restrictions and seeking pleasure in the Caribbean sun.

Cuba, at that moment, seemed the ideal spot from which Luciano, with the help of his old friend Lansky, could resume his direct rule of the American underworld while waiting, hopefully, for the day he could return to New York. With a legal passport, visas and residency permit, and with a legitimate stake in the casino at the Hotel Nacional, Luciano had every reason to feel secure.

He reckoned without Harry Anslinger, director of the U.S. Treasury Department's Bureau of Narcotics. Anslinger was convinced that Luciano, despite his protestations to the contrary, was the brains behind the burgeoning international drug traffic, was the man responsible for the sharp increase in the flow of narcotics into the United States. When word reached Anslinger that Luciano was luxuriating in Havana, he blew. He sent a formal demand to Cuban president Grau San Martin that Luciano be thrown out, stating that he had no business in the Americas and was a positive danger to the security of the United States as long as he remained.

At first, the Cubans did no more than politely acknowledge the demand. Benito Herrera, chief of the Cuban Secret Police, shrugged that Luciano "has maintained contact with certain interests in the United States and he has been receiving money from business interests, which allows him to live lavishly. But so far as we have ascertained, there is no evidence that he is mixed up in any illicit business in Cuba." And the Cuban minister of the interior, Alfredo Pequeno, noted that while Luciano "is a dangerous character and a perjurer . . . his papers are in perfect order." Luciano had spread his money around Havana to good purpose.

But Anslinger would not relent. He went to President Truman and argued his case so forcefully that the president gave him the power to take whatever steps he thought necessary. Anslinger promptly announced that until Luciano was shipped back to Italy, the United States would send no more medical drugs or supplies to the island. With no facilities to manufacture their own, the Cubans capitulated. Late in February 1947, Luciano was arrested and thrown into the Tiscornia Immigration Camp in the steaming swamps across the bay from

Havana. Then his friends in the Cuban government tried to strike a deal. They would expel Luciano, to be sure, but to Venezuela, which had offered to grant him residency. Anslinger would not hear of it. If Cuba wanted drugs and medicine, then Luciano had to go back to Italy and nowhere else.

At last, Luciano himself gave in. Early in March, he boarded a Turkish freighter, the *S.S. Bakir*, for the long, slow voyage back across the Atlantic. He would never again come so close to American shores. But until his death in Italy in 1962 from a heart attack, he would continue to play a dominant and often decisive role in the workings of the U.S. criminal Organization he had done so much to create.

And now that the Organization had completed its transition to peacetime operations, Luciano, through couriers, was ready to settle back and reap the rewards of Las Vegas, Havana and the other gambling centers, to exploit the boundless opportunities opening up in the postwar world. The violence and notoriety of the Thirties, the sensational Murder, Inc., trials of the early Forties belonged to an era that most people wanted to relegate to history, and now that the Syndicate had learned how to operate stealthily in the shadows of legitimate business, mobsters envisioned a future of harmony, prosperity and invisibility. That vision soon was shattered by a very junior senator from Tennessee named Estes Kefauver, who would shed new light on the American underworld.

9

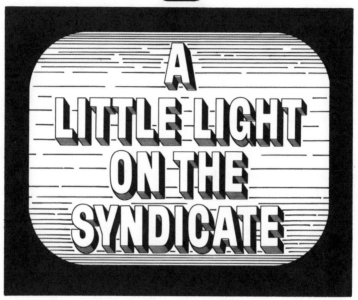

A LITTLE LIGHT ON THE SYNDICATE

MIDDLE AGE IS THE TIME WHEN men who have reached the pinnacles of their chosen professions begin to receive the public recognition, esteem and other rewards that accompany wealth and power. So it was in the late Forties and early Fifties for a small group of very wealthy businessmen, mainly Italian and Jewish, who, along with the 20th Century, had reached their middle years. They were the men who had helped create and who ruled a shadowy organization that had no formal title but was called, depending on who was doing the calling, the Syndicate, the Combination, the Mafia or any one of a dozen other names and whose influence on the entire nation was profound and ma-

levolent. But that part of their lives was concealed as much as possible and rarely discussed, especially by those who had come to them often for help and had repaid past favors with public tributes. On the surface, at least, these were men who wielded great power in half a hundred industries and whose careers had been marked by unselfish labors for scores of charities and community betterment projects.

Thus, in 1949, a group of prominent Italian-American Catholics petitioned Pope Pius XII to award the title Knight of St. Gregory to a Brooklyn businessman who had done much to earn his community's gratitude. His name was Joseph Profaci. He had arrived in America as a poor boy from

Sicily and had become the nation's leading importer of olive oil and tomato paste, majority owner of no fewer than 20 legitimate businesses, generous donor to every Catholic charity that approached him, benevolent employer of hundreds of fellow Italian-Americans. But Profaci was also—as an angry Brooklyn district attorney, Miles McDonald, insisted in a successful effort to block the papal knighthood—one of the nation's top racketeers, head of one of the major crime families in New York and longtime practitioner of the crafts of extortion and murder.

Thomas Lucchese, a quiet, conservative dress manufacturer who owned half a dozen factories in New York and Pennsylvania, was a tireless worker for charity in his spare time. When he called on his friends to buy tickets to dinners for favorite causes, a sellout was assured. At one such dinner, 22 New York State judges, presiding over courts at every level of the judicial system, sat at tables he sponsored. Some were so fond of Lucchese that they even tried to return the favors. His hotel bills in New York and on several trips to Washington were picked up by Armand Chamkalian, assistant to U.S. Attorney Myles Lane. But then, Lane himself and New York City Police Commissioner (and later a federal judge) Thomas F. Murphy were close personal friends of the manufacturer, dropping by his home now and then for lunch or for cocktails. And another close friend, the late Congressman Vito Marcantonio, helped

Lucchese realize a long-held dream: the appointment of his son to West Point, even though Lucchese was a political conservative and Marcantonio a radical, winning elections as the candidate of the American Labor Party. To these people, Lucchese was merely a very rich businessman who, as he often said, had held office in only one organization—the Knights of Columbus. What was ignored was Lucchese's real position—as the boss of another of New York's major crime families, as partner in the Garment District rackets from the early Thirties with Louis "Lepke" Buchalter, and as a close friend of the exiled Syndicate ruler, Charles "Lucky" Luciano.

When the B'nai B'rith, the Zionist Organization of America and other Jewish organizations held fund-raising campaigns, among their most successful money raisers were two eminent Jewish businessmen—the liquor-automotive-steel magnate from New Jersey, Abner Zwillman, and the liquor-real estate-television tycoon from Miami and New York, Meyer Lansky. Both, it was said, had done more than just raise money. In 1948, when the newborn state of Israel was battling for its life, they had used their influence to purchase stocks of weapons and to make sure that those arms were expeditiously loaded aboard ship in New York harbor, even though such activities were illegal. But then, Zwillman and Lansky had plenty of muscle along the waterfront. They were perhaps the most powerful Jewish racketeers in the country and Lansky, particularly, had emerged as the financial wizard of the organized underworld.

PERHAPS THE LEADING FUND raiser for the Salvation Army in New York was the vice-chairman of its men's division, a quiet, retiring real-estate and investment specialist named Frank Costello. When the charity held its annual dinner at the Copacabana nightclub (owned, as it happened, by Costello and another charity-conscious industrialist named Joe Adonis), Costello was selling tickets all over town, and most of his friends wore tuxedos to the $100-a-plate black-tie affair. Those friends included Hugo Rogers, Manhattan Borough president and leader of Tammany Hall; state supreme court

Senate hearings linked gangsters to a number of famous nightclubs.

justices Morris Eder, Samuel Di Falco, Anthony Di Giovanni, Thomas Aurelio; and many more from the worlds of politics and business. When Costello invited friends up to his Central Park West apartment or out to his summer place at Sands Point on Long Island for a quiet drink and some small talk, the guest list might have included Rogers and other Tammany leaders, New York's Deputy Fire Commissioner James Moran, even Mayor William O'Dwyer himself.

But then, who in New York had cultivated the power elite and had amassed power himself as had Costello? All of Tammany's leaders—from Christy Sullivan to Michael Kennedy, from Rogers to Carmine DeSapio to Frank Rosetti to Bert Stand—were beholden to him for favors done, for funds raised, for votes delivered. When there were appointments or nominations to be made, they turned to Costello for advice and approval, and for thanks.

"Good morning, Francesco," said Aurelio over the phone on the morning of August 23, 1943, only minutes after he had received the news that he would be the Democratic nominee for state supreme court justice. "How are you, and thanks for everything."

"Congratulations," Costello replied. "It went over perfect. When I tell you something is in the bag, you can rest assured."

"It was perfect," Aurelio said. "It was fine."

"Well, we will all have to get together and have dinner some night real soon."

"That would be fine," Aurelio said. "But right now I want to assure you of my loyalty for all you have done. It is unwaving."

Unfortunately, somebody was listening in. Manhattan District Attorney Frank Hogan had obtained a court-ordered wiretap on Costello's phone. When the transcript of that conversation was made public, the outcry resulted in disbarment proceedings against Aurelio. They failed; he remained on the ballot and went on to win election to the state supreme court in November and, thereafter, publicly demonstrated his continuing devotion to Costello by showing up at the racketeer's favorite charity dinners every year.

The power of Costello, Profaci, Lucchese, Lansky, Zwillman, Adonis and others at the top of the American underworld—so long the object of only frustrated shrugs from those municipal officials who professed any concern at all—had, however, begun to fascinate the junior senator from Tennessee, Estes Kefauver. Early in 1950, the nation's capital was the scene of two gatherings held almost simultaneously, the American Conference of Mayors and the United States Attorneys Conference. Kefauver was invited to speak at both meetings, but mainly he listened. At the mayors' meeting, he heard De Lesseps Morrison of New Orleans, Fletcher Bowron of Los Angeles and others express the despairing opinion that organized crime had become so pernicious in America's major cities that it was out of control and local authori-

Senator Kefauver led the investigation of organized crime.

ties were powerless to do anything about it. But at the United States Attorneys Conference, Kefauver heard another story: that there was no serious organized-crime problem in the nation, that, indeed, there was no national organization, only a disparate collection of hoodlums who should present no problem to aggressive municipal authorities.

These conflicting views disturbed the senator. Somebody had to be right and somebody wrong, and Kefauver happened to be in a position to find out who was which. He sponsored a resolution to create a Special Senate Committee to Investigate Organized Crime in Interstate Commerce, and when that committee was organized in May 1950, Kefauver was named chairman. The five-man panel also included Democrats Herbert R. O'Conor of Maryland and Lester C. Hunt of Wyoming, and Republicans Charles W. Tobey of New Hampshire and Alexander Wiley of Wisconsin. It was a strange group to investigate organized crime. Not a single one of the senators was from a major city or even from an essentially urban state, the places where the underworld operated most actively and with almost complete impunity. To cynics in Washington at the time, the composition of the Kefauver Committee seemed a sure indication that its in-

quiry would be just another of those periodic and cursory Congressional probes, filled with a lot of bombast and very little substance.

Kefauver, however, intended otherwise. Despite his own proclivities for drinking and wenching, the lanky, drawling Tennessean saw himself as a staunch guardian of moral standards, especially when it came to those in the public realm. Behind an ingenuous manner he had an inquiring mind—some called him a Rhodes scholar in a coonskin cap—and he was resolute in his aim to expose the influence of the underworld on American life, both for his own edification and in the public interest (though he soon perceived that his committee

Senator Kefauver's five-man panel included Senator Herbert R. O'Conor, Senator Lester C. Hunt, Senator Alexander Wiley and Senator Charles W. Tobey.

also was the perfect vehicle in which to ride to higher office if he so desired, which he did).

But for Kefauver to succeed, he would have to break some new ground. He did not have—as, a decade later, the McClellan Committee would have, in the person of Joe Valachi—a prime witness, an informer from the inside who would bare his breast and recite all the dreadful secrets of the Syndicate. But Kefauver had other things going for him; mainly, a staff that was determined to gather all the facts it could and to expose those who had concealed themselves for years behind a façade of respectability. Even had Kefauver so desired, there was no holding back such aggressive and ambitious lawyers and investigators as chief counsel Rudolph Halley or associate counsel Joseph Nellis. And President Harry Truman offered his help; he made the hitherto confidential income-tax returns of the racketeers available to the committee, a gift that opened a thousand avenues of search.

Perhaps even more important, though, was television. TV was just then reaching American homes in significant numbers, and the decision was made early to permit the cameras to focus on the hearings. The result was the most enthralling daily serial of the times, captivating and fascinating viewers as nothing out of Washington had ever done before and as only the army-McCarthy and the Watergate hearings have done since.

In the 16 months of its existence, from May 1, 1950, to September 1,

1951, the committee heard more than 600 witnesses, from minor hoodlums to major racketeers to officials on every level of government. It took testimony in 14 cities—Washington, Tampa, Miami, New York, Cleveland, St. Louis, Kansas City, New Orleans, Chicago, Detroit, Philadelphia, Las Vegas, Los Angeles and San Francisco—and it put on public display the enduring link among crime, politics and business.

Wherever the committee went, the television cameras followed, and the senators luxuriated in the glare of the hot lights and in the public adulation. They became instant stars, at least some of them. The unemotional and judicious manner of Kefauver brought him such an outpouring of acclaim that he nearly captured the Democratic presidential nomination in 1952 despite the near-unanimous opposition of all the party bosses, from Truman on down, and he did succeed in winning the party's vice-presidential nomination four years later. His cool and judicious manner, so ideal in a committee chairman, was, however, disastrous in a political candidate; Kefauver was, perhaps, the dullest orator on the public platform in modern times.

The aging Senator Tobey, who wore a green eyeshade and a look of moral outrage at the stories he heard—such things just didn't happen in New Hampshire—became something of a national pet. His office was flooded with letters and telegrams from thousands of admiring Americans who agreed with his every sentiment, who applauded his characterization of the racketeers appearing before the committee as rats and vermin and who, as seemingly disregardful of the Constitution as Tobey, agreed with his feelings toward lawyers who represented gangsters: He asked Moses Polakoff, Lansky's attorney, "How did you become counsel for such a dirty rat as that? Aren't

Senator Tobey's green eyeshade captivated the American public (top left). Senator Kefauver's authority brought him close to a presidential nomination (bottom).

there some ethics in the legal profession?"

"Minorities and undesirables and persons with bad reputations are more entitled to the protection of the law than are the so-called honorable people," Polakoff replied in anger. "I don't have to apologize to you."

"I look upon you in amazement," Tobey said.

Then there was Rudy Halley. His pointed questions, delivered acidly in a high, lisping, nasal voice, seemed to entrance the witnesses, who appeared uncertain whether to be frightened, angered or amused. But baiting the underworld elite did not hurt Halley's ambitions. Though he failed in one try to become New York City mayor, he did win an election later as president of its city council, the city's second-highest office.

The witness side of the committee table had its bit players and stars too, though the roles were anything but relished by those who were forced to play them. Indeed, many in the cast did their best to avoid making any entrance at all. When Joe Nellis arrived in Cleveland one day to pave the way for the committee's appearance and to hand out a fistful of subpoenas, the city's criminal hierarchy simply vanished. Moe Dalitz, Morris Kleinman, Louis Rothkopf, Sam Tucker, Samuel "Gameboy" Miller, John and George Angersola and others decided that Nellis's visit somehow coincided with their need to take vacations. Later, after warrants for their arrest had been issued, most wandered in and innocently ex-plained that they had been unaware anyone wanted to talk to them. Then they sat in stony silence, or pleaded the Fifth Amendment's guarantee against self-incrimination, or voiced complete ignorance of all the committee wanted to talk about.

The same thing happened in Chicago. The usually omnipresent Charles and Rocco Fischetti, Murray "The Camel" Humphreys and Jake "Greasy Thumb" Guzik were nowhere to be found. Later, rather than go to jail, they, too, put on the masks of wronged innocents and sat at the witness table and denied everything or, as Guzik did, refused to answer because any replies might tend to "discriminate against me." Only Charley Fischetti avoided the questioning; before he could appear, he had a fatal heart attack.

Then there were some who, surprisingly, were never called, even though they were on the committee's list of potentially important witnesses and their names kept coming up in the questioning of their friends and associates. Tommy Lucchese, for one, was ignored, and nobody later could figure out why. When Vito Genovese learned that he might be forced to sit under those bright lights, he took himself off for a long vacation in the Caribbean sun until the hearings ended; nobody ever went looking for him. But Nellis did talk to Genovese's estranged wife, Anna, who told him she hadn't seen the gang boss since Christmas, when he had arrived at her home with a present and said that he would be out of touch for a while.

The Senate hearings went from city to city.

During his absence, he told her to use whatever money she needed from the "steel box in a safe in our house. I have a key. There's a pile of money in it and a bunch of papers. . . . It comes from his gambling and the rackets and the bums he runs around with." Then Anna told Nellis, "I know what he's doing, too, running them numbers and morphine and whatnot." It was a tantalizing bit, but as far as the committee knew, Genovese was then only a second-level hoodlum, and it went after bigger fish.

Even without Genovese, Lucchese and, until they turned up, the rulers of Cleveland, Chicago and other cities, the committee had plenty of big names and big scandals with which to make headlines and shock the public. At one time or another, the television cameras were focused on Costello, Adonis, Lansky, Zwillman, Willie Moretti, Albert Anastasia,

Carlos Marcello, Santo Trafficante, Frank Erickson, Paul "The Waiter" Ricca, Tony Accardo, Phil Kastel, Mickey Cohen and many others. Not that most of them had anything to say. Flanked by their high-priced lawyers, they volunteered nothing, professed innocence, answered few questions and, for the most part, painfully recited from rote or from written cards their refusal to answer on grounds of possible self-incrimination.

Their appearance, though, was all the committee really wanted. It had no illusions that it would obtain any useful colloquy from the Syndicate's chieftains. They were merely the vehicle for Halley, Nellis and the senators to put what had been uncovered on the record, usually with a long recitation of facts prefaced or concluded with "Isn't that so?"

Albert Anastasia (insert) and Joe Adonis (top right) briefly became television stars. The hearings were a TV sensation.

There seemed no other way to detail the corrupting influence of organized crime on American society.

It mattered little that Zwillman, when he finally came out of hiding to testify, constantly invoked the Fifth Amendment or answered a few questions with disarming innocence and ignorance. The questions themselves told the public that he, along with Joseph Reinfeld, had been among the founders of Browne-Vintners after Prohibition, owning 50 percent of the liquor-importing firm, and that Zwillman had made a fortune when it was sold in 1940 to Seagrams for $7,500,000; that he was associated, as well, with Reinfeld Importers, Ltd., exclusive distributor and importer of Gordon's Gin, Haig & Haig Scotch and Piper Heidsieck Champagne; that he owned many legitimate companies in such businesses as cigarette-vending and laundry machines; that he had a General Motors truck franchise that could secure contracts with New Jersey municipalities even though his bids were consistently higher than competitors'. Even more disturbing to the uncommunicative Zwillman, though, were the revelations about his political power in New Jersey, from his close friendships with the bosses of Jersey City and Newark to his influence on state politics. During the 1946 gubernatorial campaign, for instance, the Republican governor, Harold G. Hoffman, personally solicited Zwillman's support, and in 1949, Zwillman offered $300,000 to the Democratic candidate Elmer Wene if Wene would let him name the state's attorney general (the offer was declined).

Like so many others, Zwillman had initially evaded service of the committee's subpoenas and his friends in the underworld were confident that when he did appear, Longy would maintain silence. Not so with Zwillman's long-time partner and a major Syndicate leader, Willie Moretti. By 1950, Moretti was suffering

Willie Moretti talked a lot but said little.

from advanced paresis, a souvenir of his youthful gambols that left him with syphilis, which he had never had treated. There were increasing periods when his mind wandered, when he was overly garrulous and indiscreet. Among his friends there was a growing fear that should he sit before the Kefauver Committee, he might, in his ramblings, say things better left unsaid. Every effort was made to keep Moretti and the com-

mittee from ever coming together; he was sick and under doctor's care; he was on vacation; he was unavailable because of business emergencies. Such tactics did not keep the committee from pressing and eventually Moretti had no choice but to show up.

Moretti turned out to be a garrulous witness indeed—hard to turn off. But while his words flowed freely, there was little substance to them. Certainly he knew almost every leading racketeer in the nation. But he didn't know them as racketeers. They were "well-charactered men" and he had run into them at the race tracks. It was, after all, only natural that men of substance should gravitate together. He himself was a successful businessman, proprietor of several going concerns, including U.S. Linen Supply in New Jersey. Rackets? "Everything is a racket today . . . everybody has a racket of their own." Mobs? "People are mobs that make six percent more on the dollar than anybody else does." Political influence? "I never made no contributions—only my voice."

Like any good show, the Kefauver traveling circus began slowly, in medium-sized and large cities around the nation, and built to a climax in New York, with appetites whetted for really big disclosures. But what had emerged from the hearings in the hinterlands was no less important, or, to many, less shocking.

In Ohio, for instance, the Syndicate, led by Dalitz and his friends, seemed impervious to periodic cleanups. When their control over Cleveland was threatened in the early Forties by a reform combination of Public Safety Director Eliot Ness, Prosecutor F. T. Cullitan and Judge Frank Lausche, Dalitz and his partners simply moved their gambling operations across the city lines out into the counties. When Lausche moved into the statehouse as governor and attempted to crack down on the gangsters all over Ohio, they jumped across the state line into northern Kentucky. "In

the Ohio-Kentucky communities in which wide-open gambling has been carried on by the Syndicate and local hoodlums," the committee found, "officials are strangely afflicted with the inability to see the obvious, a disease which seems to strike law-enforcement officials in wide-open communities everywhere. The police chief of Newport, Kentucky, was probably the only adult in the city who did not know that there were wide-open gambling houses in his community. . . . The casinos were so unconcerned with the possibility of interference with their operations that they advertised openly in the Cincinnati papers." When the Kefauver Committee arrived, the casinos temporarily shuttered. But the Beverly Hills Club, for one, also passed out fliers announcing that it would reopen for business as usual the day after the committee was expected to pass into history.

What intrigued the senators in Miami was the success of the S. & G. Syndicate: It had nearly a monopoly on bookmaking in that resort area, maintained bookie concessions at 200 hotels and grossed an estimated $30,000,000 to $40,000,000 a year, with a net profit of between $4,000,000 and $8,000,000. Once, S. & G. had been an independent concern, owned by five Miami-area bookies. In 1949, it suddenly acquired a sixth partner, Harry Russell, a longtime member of the Capone organization in Chicago. For his full partnership in the multimillion-dollar gambling empire, Russell paid $20,000—

and, as chance would have it, within a couple of months, S. & G. bought a yacht from Accardo, head of the Capone Mob, for $20,000.

But then, the original five partners were in no position to quibble, for just prior to Russell's appearance, S. & G. was having trouble. When Fuller Warren took office as governor of Florida in January 1949, he had appointed W. O. Crosby as a special investigator. It happened that one of Crosby's closest friends was William H. Johnston, who owned race tracks in Chicago and Florida. According to the Kefauver Committee's second interim report, he was an old associate of the Chicago Mob and had contributed $100,000 to Warren's campaign. As special investigator, Crosby dropped in on Dade County Sheriff James Sullivan and asked for his cooperation in cleaning up the gambling in the Miami area—meaning the gambling controlled by S. & G. Suddenly S. & G. suffered a series of raids on its bookies and, at the same time, was cut off from the Chicago Mob's Continental Press Service racing wire, without which it could not operate. Two weeks later, Russell bought his partnership in S. & G., the Syndicate bought Accardo's yacht, the raids stopped and the wire service was turned on again.

S. & G. boomed as never before and the underworld began to broaden its influence in the Miami area, moving in on resort hotels and other enterprises. Since wide-open gambling was obviously the key to the underworld's encroachments, a number of reform groups appealed to Sheriff Sullivan and to Sheriff Walter Clark of adjacent Broward County (which harbored Lansky and plush casinos like the Colonial Inn and the Greenacres Club) to do something. Both merely shrugged and explained how difficult that would be.

Indeed, it would have been difficult for them. As the Kefauver Committee noted, "Sheriff Sullivan's assets increased during his five-year term from $2500, which was his net worth as given in a bank loan, to well over $70,000. . . . His deputy, whose purchase of a new Cadillac in 1949 caused Sullivan a certain amount of uneasiness, retired after four years to a farm for which he paid $26,000, although his salary was never more than $4200 a year. Both Sullivan and his deputy distrusted banks and testified to keeping large amounts of cash in their homes in a tin box, an old fishing box or in a blanket. . . . Sheriff Clark of Broward County made a very large fortune by participating in the profits of gambling ventures and as a partner in the Broward Novelty Company, which operated an illegal *bolita* and slot-machine business. The gross income of this company from 1945 to 1947 was more than $1,000,000."

Did such revelations accomplish anything? Sheriff Sullivan was investigated by a Miami grand jury and suspended from duty. Governor Warren promptly reinstated him, though Sullivan resigned soon after. As for Warren himself, he flatly refused to testify before the committee, citing separation of powers and state rights.

BUT THERE WAS NOTHING UNIQUE about the Miami story. It was repeated with variations in almost every city the senators visited. In Missouri, the committee learned about Charles Binaggio, Kansas City's gambling boss, and his Mafia friends Tony Gizzo (who owned the franchise to distribute Canadian Ace Beer) and Joe and Vince di Giovanni (who ran the city's liquor-dealers association and held exclusive franchises to distribute Schenley's, Seagrams and several other brands of liquor). They wanted Kansas City wide open and believed the best way to open it was to back the gubernatorial aspirations of Democrat Forrest Smith. When he won, Smith was unwilling to go as far as his underworld supporters hoped, and some of them blamed Binaggio. In April 1950, Binaggio was murdered along with another Syndicate strong man, Charles Gargotta—just two of 16 unsolved gangland murders in Kansas City during the period.

In Chicago, it was as if nothing had changed since the days of Scarface Al Capone and Frank "The Enforcer" Nitti, though now the Mob was run with a little bit more sophistication by Accardo, the Fischettis, Guzik, Ricca, Humphreys and an up-and-coming hoodlum named Sam "Mooney" Giancana. It was in Chicago that the national racing wire was centered, and it was there that almost all the nation's slot machines and other coin-operated devices were made. Policy and every other form of gambling flourished as though legal; only one policy operator had gone to

jail in years, while a couple of others had been slapped on the wrist with $25 fines.

As elsewhere, the Mob in Chicago had it easy because it owned the police and the officeholders. "Certain members of the state legislature," the Kefauver Committee concluded, "particularly those living in districts most heavily infested by racketeers, vote against legislation designed to curb gangster activities . . . and associate freely with their gangster constituents." Police Captain Dan Gilbert, chief investigator for the state's attorney's office in Cook County and also known as the world's richest cop, gave the committee his and, he implied, other policemen's views of the situation. Gilbert testified that he himself placed illegal bets, explaining, "I have been a gambler at heart." He agreed that raids could be initiated by his office on bookies in the city, but admitted that this had not been done since 1939.

Tampa was ruled by Trafficante, who didn't like the police nosing around in his business—which included gambling, narcotics and other rackets. The city's history included dozens of gangland murders and bombings, but no one would have known it from the police files, which had a way of mysteriously disappearing. And when it came to gambling, no one ever got convicted. Perhaps Sheriff Hugh L. Culbreath was too busy elsewhere, for, according to the Kefauver Committee, his net worth grew from $30,000 to more than $100,000 during his term in office.

In New Orleans and throughout Louisiana, the senators kept stumbling across the names of Costello, Kastel and Marcello, the Tunisian-born (of Sicilian parents) ruler of the local Mafia. Together, they ran the slot machines that infested the state, the lavish casinos such as the Beverly Club in New Orleans, the pinballs, the wire service, everything—though Marcello, because his friends had certain compunctions, enjoyed a personal monopoly over narcotics. Of course, these men had a little help from their friends. One was Angelo Gemelli, a New Orleans cop assigned to check on pinball operators and arrest those who tried to pay him off. The committee learned that he also moonlighted as a member of the executive committee of the pinball association and received 10 percent of everything he collected from members for dues, initiation fees and protection money.

But, if you looked at it from the viewpoint of the Louisiana officeholders, it was really quite simple. As Jefferson County Sheriff "King" Clancy put it, he didn't enforce the gambling laws in his parish because more than 1000 people, most of them old and underprivileged, were employed by the casinos there. A close-down would have thrown them out of work and cost the parish and the state a lot of welfare money. Beauregard Miller, the town marshal of Gretna, didn't enforce the law because "Without gambling, the town would be dead." Of course, such altruism did have its rewards. Both

Clancy and Miller turned out to be very rich, as was the New Orleans chief of detectives, who somehow managed to sock away $150,000 in a safe-deposit box on a salary of $186 a month.

In Detroit, more fascinating than political corruption itself were some of the convoluted dealings between big business and the underworld. Ford Motor Company, for example, had made some strange alliances. In the East, the exclusive contract to transport Fords from the Edgewater, New Jersey, assembly plant had been awarded to the Automotive Conveying Company of New Jersey. Who controlled that company? Joe Adonis. And the contract to haul cars from the Detroit-area plants had been awarded to the E. & L. Transport Company. Who was the majority stockholder of E. & L.? Anthony D'Anna, long-time partner of Detroit's Mafia boss, Joe Massei. But then, D'Anna had been a good friend to Ford for years; in fact, since 1931, and a particularly good friend of Henry Ford's alter ego and chief of staff, Harry Bennett. The two had met when Bennett called D'Anna to his office, the Kefauver Committee said (but could not prove), "to instruct him not to murder Joseph Tocco, who had a food concession at a Ford plant. . . . Bennett entered into an agreement that D'Anna would refrain from murdering Tocco for five years in return for the Ford agency at Wyandotte. As a matter of record, Tocco was not murdered until seven years after this meeting. Also as a matter of record, D'Anna did become a 50 percent owner in the Ford agency at Wyandotte within a matter of weeks after the meeting." Subsequently, D'Anna bought into E. & L., which then got the Ford hauling contract. After Bennett left Ford's employ, even to the time of Kefauver's arrival, D'Anna retained that contract, just as Adonis retained his in the East.

THEN THERE WAS SARATOGA, THE watering hole of New York society. For more than a quarter of a century, the spa had been as wide open during its racing season as any town in the country, filled with everything from back-room bust-out joints to lavish casinos catering to the high rollers who had not lost enough during a day at the track. Among the most famous: the Chicago Club, Delmonico's, Smith's Interlochen, Piping Rock, Arrowhead and Newman's Lake House. Among the proprietors: Adonis, Lansky, Costello, Luciano and Lefty Clark from Detroit. Though just up the road from Albany, where the most famous of racket busters, Thomas E. Dewey, occupied the governor's mansion, nobody had ever bothered the resort's gambling complex before Kefauver. Walter A'Hearn, a Saratoga detective, told the senators that during his 19 years on the police force, he had never made a gambling arrest and, while a frequent visitor to many of the clubs, had never ventured farther than the dining rooms. If he had, he said, he

was certain he would have been out of a job. But A'Hearn did not completely close his eyes to what was going on. During the height of the season, he and his partner, with the knowledge of Police Chief Patrick F. Rox, were paid ten dollars a night to escort cash from the casinos to the bank.

If the local police had done nothing, why, then, had the state police failed to intervene? That question was put to the superintendent of the New York state police, John A. Gaffney. Well, Gaffney explained, in 1947 he had authorized a survey of gambling in Saratoga and, after studying the results, had come to the conclusion, "This looks like a sizable operation." But, after all, "It's been going on for 25 years to my knowledge."

"In other words," Kefauver said to him, "you just knew you just weren't supposed to do anything about it."

That's right, Gaffney agreed, and then he added that when you get to be head of the state police, you're savvy enough to leave gambling in Saratoga strictly alone and say nothing about it to Governor Dewey. Otherwise, he said, he would have ended up "out on the sidewalk."

Dewey himself refused to testify before the committee, would do no more than file formal statements through his counsel, though he did say that if the committee gave him enough advance notice, he might grant the senators a few minutes in his private office. So the committee never heard from the governor about his view of Saratoga or other matters,

Tony Anastasia was well cast as a tough New York labor racketeer.

such as his decision to release Luciano from prison. But the exposure of the Saratoga situation did force Dewey to act. The gamblers were ordered not to open for business during the summer of 1950 and they stayed closed—for a time, at least.

But the big show for Kefauver was still to come. That took place in New York, and at last the real stars took their turn on the stage: Virginia Hill, the underworld's sweetheart; Costello, the underworld's prime minister; William O'Dwyer, former New York City mayor, ambassador to Mexico and the underworld's good friend.

Virginia Hill was both the sex symbol and the comic relief among all the heavies. She had left Alabama at 17, a girl with long legs, big bust, constantly changing hair style and a wiggle that said she must have been good in the bedroom. That she was. In the 16 years between her arrival in Chicago in time for the 1934 World's Fair and her trip to the Kefauver Committee room, she acquired and discarded husbands and lovers like they were baubles from a five-and-dime. First there was Joe Epstein, big-time bookie and tax expert for the Capone Mob, and after him there were the Fischetti brothers, Accardo,

Humphreys, Nitti, Gizzo, Marcello, Adonis, even Costello, until she found her true love in Benny "Bugsy" Siegel. By the time of Kefauver, though, Siegel was dead and Virginia had gone on to become the bride of an Austrian ski instructor named Hans Hauser.

But Virginia was more than just a good bedfellow to the Mob. Those she had slept with had entrusted some of the Organization's most cherished secrets to her, and they had used her, too, to pass on a great deal of the Mob's cash. But before the senators, in a flowing black dress and floppy hat, she played the dumb Southern belle. "I never knew anything about their business," she insisted to Halley. "They didn't tell me about their business. Why would they tell me? I don't care anything about business in

So was Virginia Hill as a hard-boiled dame and a comic relief.

the first place. I don't even understand it. . . . If they ever started to talk about anything, I left, because I didn't want to know." When Halley expressed some incredulity, Virginia shrugged, "Maybe it's impossible, but it's true."

As Virginia left the committee hearings, she was surrounded by reporters and photographers who badgered her all the way out of the building. Suddenly she turned and threw a right cross to the jaw of *New York Journal-American* reporter Marjorie Farnsworth and screamed at the rest of the press, "You goddamn bastards. I hope an atom bomb falls on all of you."

With that, Virginia disappeared. For some years, she wandered Europe with her husband, so wary of the surveillance of American tax men that she rarely touched the horde Siegel had entrusted to her care in numbered Swiss accounts. Several times she attempted suicide; and then, in March 1966, she swallowed a handful of sleeping pills, lay down in the snow near Salzburg and died.

For Costello, the summons to appear before the Kefauver Committee as its star witness was a shattering blow. He had spent years attempting to build an image as a kind of elder statesman—of what kind, he never specified—and public benefactor. He had learned to dress well and conservatively, to speak softly, to use his power sparingly. He had even gone to a psychiatrist and sought to mix with a better class of people. In the councils of the underworld, his had been the voice of moderation and caution, and his advice almost invariably had led to success and increased power. Now he faced publicity and disaster.

The publicity was partly his own doing. Fearful of national exposure, Costello wanted nobody to hear his words and was even more determined that if forced to speak, at least nobody outside the committee room should see his face. Citing his right to privacy under the Constitution, Costello refused to appear before the committee if the television cameras were present, threatened to walk out and not return, regardless of the consequences, unless the committee complied with that demand. It did, but only to the point of agreeing that his face should not be on-camera. The victory, then, was a pyrrhic one. His husky voice whispered into the microphones and across the nation while the cameras held tightly on his hands, which—nervously clenching and unclenching, rapping, tapping, toying with cigarettes—hypnotized viewers and brought Costello all the publicity and notoriety he had fought so hard to avoid.

Costello was one of the most uncooperative witnesses to appear. He would not produce demanded papers; he stormed out of the room when the questioning grew increasingly tough (and was cited for contempt of Congress); he sought refuge in the Fifth Amendment; he hedged, delayed, changed stories, dissimulated. He insisted he was only an honest businessman, owner of some land and buildings on Wall Street and elsewhere in

A whole nation was fascinated by Costello's nervous and jittery hands.

Manhattan; one-time partner (with Adonis) in the Copacabana; investor in oil wells; partner, with two other businessmen named Adonis and Lansky, in the Consolidated Television Company and in another firm that made infrared broilers. Perhaps in the old days he had been a gambler, a slot-machine operator, a bootlegger, but those days were long in the past.

The committee's investigators, however, had learned much about Costello. Under the pointed questioning of Halley, he was forced to admit to some other major sources of income and positions of power. "He admits as much as he thinks he has to and does not hesitate to change his story to suit the occasion," the committee said. Senator Tobey called some of his testimony "the tale of the flying saucers." And Costello himself said that maybe he was boasting when he told some political friends at his home that he had a financial interest in the Scotch he was serving them and denied any connection with Whitely Distributors, the English company

Costello was not a happy witness (top right). When the questions got too rough, he stormed out of the hearings (bottom).

that made King's Ransom and other brands of Scotch.

The Costello hands, though, were most active and nervous when Halley began to fire at him some of the data gathered by the staff—Costello's 20 percent interest in the Beverly Club in New Orleans (in partnership with Lansky, Kastel and Marcello), plus a $1500 monthly salary for acting as talent scout and good-will ambassador; his 30 percent interest in Saratoga's Piping Rock Casino (with partners Lansky and Adonis); control of the Louisiana Mint Company, which ran the slot machines in that state, in partnership with Kastel; a $15,000-a-year stipend from the Roosevelt Raceway on Long Island, a major New York trotting track, partly owned by Costello's lawyer-friend George Morton Levy, for services rendered in keeping bookies away (that payment was terminated when the IRS disallowed it as a track business expense). Though Costello insisted that he had been out of the bookmaking racket for years, the committee had reasons to believe otherwise. There was, for example, his long and continuing friendship with George Uffner, a major New York bookie who listed a phone in his own name at Costello's home. And there were Costello's dealings with Frank Erickson, the East's leading bookmaker. Erickson had lent Costello money for business ventures, had given him investment advice on oil wells and had been Costello's weekly golf partner, along with Levy and a onetime IRS agent who had quit the government job

when his $200 investment in Levy's Roosevelt Raceway began to return $4000 a year in dividends.

Even more distressing to Costello was the detailing of his relationship with Tammany Hall. He was willing to admit that he knew most of the leaders well "and maybe they got a little confidence in me." But that was only natural, because he had lived in the city and in the same district for so many years. He had never voted, belonged to a political party nor made a political contribution, he said, and after the debacle over the nomination of Judge Aurelio in 1943, "With me, they sort of curb their conversation, because they know I am against it, I don't want to hear about it no more." It was only a coincidence that a lot of his friends were constantly getting elected to office or being appointed to high positions. He had nothing to do with that kind of thing. And he had no idea why Tammany boss Hugo Rogers would say, "If Costello wanted me, he would send for me." And as for former Mayor O'Dwyer, he knew him just as he knew a lot of people—he liked him, thought he had been a good mayor, but that was all.

When Costello walked out of the hearing room for the last time, he knew full well he could never return to the clandestine councils of the underworld Syndicate and continue to guide organized crime in the paths of moderation. The future would be one of constant legal battle. He was cited for contempt and sentenced to 18 months in prison, his first term since before World War I. On top of that, he was indicted and convicted for income-tax evasion and received another term. By the time his appeals were heard and his sentences were served, much of the Fifties would pass, the Organization would turn in a different direction and he would lose his position of leadership.

PERHAPS THE MOST TRAGIC FIGure to appear before Kefauver, though, was O'Dwyer. Once he had been a crime-busting district attorney and a liberal mayor. Now he was a discredited man with a shattered reputation. His administration had been riddled with scandals and corruption; he had abruptly resigned from office less than a year after winning reelection, hoping to find distant sanctuary as the American ambassador to Mexico. But the Kefauver Committee exhumed his past. And so, perspiring heavily, mopping his red face continuously, he became a nervous, devious witness, trying to defend himself as best he could. His best was not very good and he left the hearing room a disgraced man.

The senators dug deeply into O'Dwyer's political career, and what emerged was a portrait of an ambitious man who did more than merely cut a few corners on his way up. O'Dwyer boasted to the committee of his successful prosecution of Murder, Inc. Noted the committee: "Of the men whom O'Dwyer identified as the Big Six [Adonis, Lansky, Siegel, Luciano, Zwillman and Moretti], all were

friends or associates of Costello. . . . None of the top six were prosecuted or even touched in the investigation, with the exception of Bugsy Siegel, who was indicted in California and in whose case O'Dwyer refused to produce Abe Reles as a witness at the trial . . . as a result, Siegel never was tried."

O'Dwyer insisted he was not to blame for that failure, nor for the failure to indict or prosecute Anastasia. The blame was that of subordinates to whom he entrusted such details, especially after he took a leave of absence to enter the service during World War II. But those subordinates were men appointed by O'Dwyer, men in whom he had complete faith. They included Frank Bals and James Moran.

A police captain, Bals had been chief investigator on O'Dwyer's Brooklyn district attorney's staff, the man responsible both for the protection of Murder, Inc., stool-pigeon Abe Reles and for the investigation into his death—which Bals perfunctorily labeled an accident. So convinced was O'Dwyer of Bals's honesty and efficiency that as mayor he appointed Bals the city's seventh deputy police commissioner. With a staff of 12, Bals's assignment was to gather information about gambling and corruption in the police department. But, according to committee staff members, Bals told them (though he would later deny this) that his job was actually somewhat different. He and his men were really the bagmen for the police department, collecting from the gamblers and then dispersing the funds throughout police headquarters. Bals held the job just long enough to qualify for a pension of $6000 a year—$1000 more than he had ever earned as a working police captain.

Moran's association with O'Dwyer also dated from the old days in Brooklyn. Though he had absolutely no legal training, O'Dwyer had appointed him chief clerk in the district attorney's office, which gave Moran power to open and close investigations and initiate grand-jury hearings. And, as a kind of extra duty, he handled all of O'Dwyer's personal finances. Once O'Dwyer became mayor, he appointed Moran deputy fire commissioner and then, just before taking off to Mexico, made him a lifetime member of the Board of Water Supply, a job usually reserved for an engineer. As the committee noted, "This is the same Moran who was visited regularly in his office in the fire department by Louis Weber, a well-known policy racketeer . . . to whom John Crane, president of the Uniformed Firemen's Association said he gave $55,000 of the funds of the association as a gift because it was necessary to do so in order to keep Moran's friendship . . . who probably knows more than any other about New York graft." Moran was also the man who lied so blatantly before the Kefauver Committee that he was convicted of perjury and packed off to prison for five years.

The committee's interest in O'Dwyer went deep and spread wide.

The underworld controlled the New York docks and the senators were puzzled as to why the mayor had never tried to clean up the area. O'Dwyer himself acknowledged, "There was never any doubt in my mind that Anastasia owned that waterfront."

The committee noted that O'Dwyer "could point to no accomplishments . . . except the shifting around of police officials assigned to the docks."

When it came to investigating the stories of widespread police corruption, O'Dwyer's record was equally dismal. When his successor as Brooklyn D.A., Miles McDonald, had begun investigating payoffs to cops, O'Dwyer had characterized it as a witch-hunt, though he told the Kefauver Committee that perhaps McDonald was right when he estimated the payoffs to average at least $250,000 a week. But, O'Dwyer maintained, he had vigorously investigated all such charges during his tenure in City Hall, and he pointed to the assignment of Bals and to an investigation by Judge John J. Murtagh, then the city's commissioner of investigations.

What Bals did was obvious. As for Murtagh, he told the senators that he had questioned every ranking police officer and 500 cops about their financial status, and while "I don't believe the cops are honest . . . nothing turned up." In fact, he said, the only corruption he had been able to uncover had been something that existed while Fiorello LaGuardia was mayor.

O'Dwyer, flustered under fire, became a symbol of civic corruption.

Then there was the matter of O'Dwyer's friends—such as Costello, whose home O'Dwyer visited and where he ran into the ranking hierarchy of Tammany, as well as the prominent gambler and old acquaintance Irving Sherman. But, O'Dwyer explained, he had actually sought out Costello during the war to ask his help in driving gamblers off an army base. He was, indeed, very surprised to see politicians and gamblers in the apartment. Had he done anything about that, the committee asked? No, O'Dwyer reluctantly ad-mitted, even though he had spent years in office castigating various politicians for associating with gamblers. And, the committee continued, wasn't it true that O'Dwyer had actually filled his administration with men recommended by those very politicians and men who were very close to Costello? That was just a coincidence, the former mayor said; his appointments had nothing to do with Costello; he had made them because the men had "special knowledge of the subject," were the lesser of two evils or because "there are things you have to do politically if you want cooperation."

Despite all the evidence, O'Dwyer insisted that he and Costello were only casual acquaintances. The same could be said for Adonis; he remembered meeting him some years earlier, but it had been just a passing exchange, and it was just another coincidence that a number of his major appointees happened to be friends of Adonis's. (When questioned on the same subject, Adonis took sanctuary in the Fifth Amendment.) The relationship with Irving Sherman was not so easy to dismiss. He was an old friend and, through the years, a constant companion, a man who had often helped O'Dwyer in many ways. But, O'Dwyer said, he knew Sherman as a shirt manufacturer and those other witnesses must be mistaken in their testimony that they had seen him in Sherman's casino. Yes, he had heard that Sherman was a close friend of Costello's, Adonis's, Lansky's and Siegel's, and might even have been a collector for Costello and Adonis, but he was sure that Sherman had never asked for a favor, had never asked him to go easy on the bookies.

Throughout his testimony, O'Dwyer's memory proved hazy or contradictory, especially when put against that of others. For example, he could not remember a meeting on the porch of Gracie Mansion with John Crane during which the political support of the firemen was offered to him. Crane testified to that meeting and said that he had given the mayor both verbal and concrete evidence of

that support—a manila envelope containing $10,000 in cash, which O'Dwyer took with thanks.

When finally dismissed by the committee, O'Dwyer was a broken man. He went back to Mexico to serve for a little while longer as ambassador and then, before his death, to fade into a kind of obscurity, his name a symbol of civic corruption, of the underworld's hold on the nation's largest city. In its characterization of him, the committee was scathing: "A single pattern of conduct emerges from O'Dwyer's official activities in regard to the gambling and waterfront rackets, murders and police corruption, from his days as district attorney through his term as mayor. No matter what the motivation of his choice, action or inaction, it often seemed to result favorably for men suspected of being high up in the rackets. . . . The tendency to blame others for the ineffectualness of official efforts to curb the rackets and the ensuing corruption had also turned up very often at every stage of O'Dwyer's career. . . . His actions impeded promising investigations. . . . His defense of public officials who were derelict in their duties and his actions in investigations of corruption, and his failure to follow up concrete evidence of organized crime . . . have contributed to the growth of organized crime, racketeering and gangsterism in New York City."

This was the climax. After O'Dwyer, though the committee sputtered along for a time, both the senators and the nation had begun to lose interest. The United States was embroiled in a seemingly endless war in Korea and for many it was easier to work up a wrath over Communists killing American soldiers than it was over somebody booking bets down at the neighborhood candy store. And Senator Joseph R. McCarthy had begun waving around pieces of paper—"I hold here in my hand . . ." —saying they were lists of Communists in high places. In the wake of the convictions of Alger Hiss, William Remington, the Rosenbergs and others, McCarthy played on the public fear of domestic radicals who might be next-door neighbors aiding the Communist cause. The rude men with Italian surnames who spoke in broken English and only ran gambling casinos, paid off the politicians (who could never be trusted anyway) and murdered one another were no longer so interesting or fearsome as the subversives lurking under every bed.

So national attention shifted. The Kefauver Committee cranked out a fistful of recommendations, some exemplary, some dubious, some forgotten, some enacted into law—recommendations that included the organization of a racket squad in the Justice Department, strict federal checks over gambling casinos and other forms of wagering, the outlawing of the use of communications media to transmit gambling information, restrictions on the interstate shipment of slot machines and similar equipment, increased penalties for the sale of narcotics, stepped-up efforts to deport gangsters. Then it

passed into history.

Within months, the Syndicate was operating almost as though Kefauver and his fellow senators had never existed. Almost, that is, for there were some changes. The public had been made aware of organized crime as never before, and though now diverted temporarily, Americans would never again be so ignorant or so passive. In the years ahead, a wave of reform would sweep through a number of cities and, while never killing the Organization, at least would cripple it.

And the Kefauver hearings led to convulsions within the underworld hierarchy. Costello would spend the next several years in and out of prison. The power of Adonis was squelched. For years, he had been one of the ruling circle, regent for some of Luciano's American interests and member of the Combination's board of directors, able to summon the country's top gangsters to meetings in his back-room headquarters at Duke's Restaurant in Cliffside Park, New Jersey. But after Kefauver, public officials at all levels began to persecute and prosecute. Duke's was closed. The state of New Jersey indicted Adonis for violation of the state's gambling laws and built such a strong case that he pleaded guilty. In 1951, he went to prison for the first time in his life, receiving a two-year sentence and a $15,000 fine. That was just the beginning. New York also indicted him for gambling violations; contempt of Congress charges were lodged against him for his perform-

Joe Adonis decided to go back to Italy. It was better than prison.

ance before the Kefauver Committee; perjury charges and deportation actions were brought, on the ground that he had lied to several bodies by declaring that he had been born in Brooklyn rather than in a small town outside Naples; the Internal Revenue Service revealed that it was investigating him for income-tax violations. It was all too much. Faced with a choice between years in jail and deportation, Adonis left the country. Just after New Year's Day in 1956, he boarded the Italian luxury liner

Moretti had become a danger because of his apparently failing mind. He was retired.

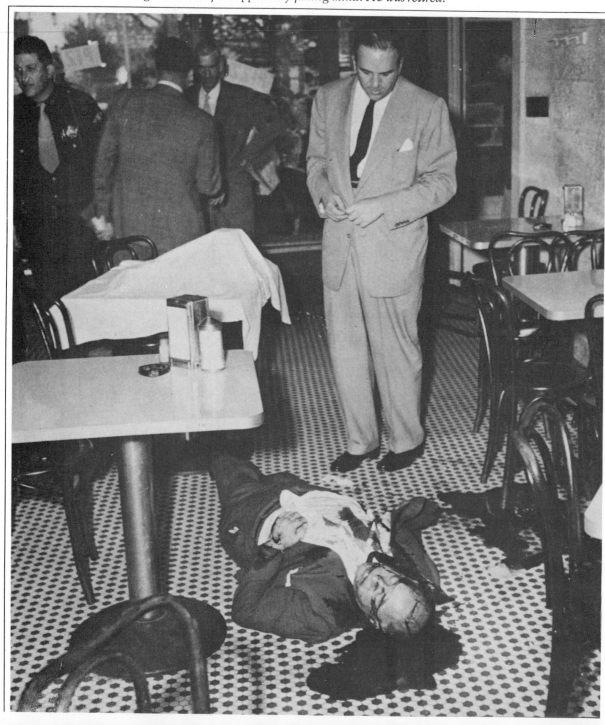

Conte Biancamano and set sail to join Luciano in Italian exile (though he would live in Milan, Luciano in Naples, and the two would rarely meet).

For Zwillman, the rackets and even legitimate businesses were pushed aside as the government filed income-tax charges that he would be fighting the rest of his life. His old partner, Moretti, had troubles of his own. In the months following his appearance before the committee, Moretti's health continued to deteriorate and there were rumors, assiduously spread by Genovese in his struggle toward the top, that Moretti had gone completely around the bend. By late summer of 1951, under the prodding of Genovese, the Syndicate council reluctantly came to a decision: Moretti would have to go, both as a protection for the Syndicate and as a favor to him. On October 4, Moretti left his New Jersey mansion for an early luncheon meeting at Joe's Elbow Room in Cliffside Park, the Mob hangout since the closing of Duke's. There, he joined four others. While the waitress was away getting menus, Moretti's friends pulled out pistols and shot him twice in the head, then calmly walked out of the restaurant. Like so many other gangland slayings, Moretti's was never solved. But, then, perhaps nobody wanted to solve it. As New Jersey racket buster Nelson Stamler remarked to a reporter as they stood over Moretti's body, "It was a good thing. Poetic justice, I'd call it."

In Brooklyn, Anastasia decided the time had come for him to take over the Mob of which he long had been underboss. In April 1951, he moved directly, murdering both Philip and Vincent Mangano, the heads of the family since the Thirties. Phil's body turned up in a vacant lot; Vince's was never found. And Anastasia was confirmed as the family chief. Then Anastasia took a short vacation; he pleaded guilty to income-tax evasion, was fined $20,000 and served ten months in jail.

Prison, in fact, loomed for many in the underworld hierarchy. Although the doors would actually close on very few, many of the bosses would spend the next few years doing their best to ensure freedom, for their appearances before the Kefauver Committee had brought contempt citations against Accardo, Rocco Fischetti, Guzik, Humphreys, Kleinman, Erickson, Pete Licavoli, Joe Aiuppa, Marcello, Kastel and others. Lansky finally saw the inside of a jail; he was arrested as a gambler in New York in 1952, pleaded guilty and served 90 days. Then he departed for Florida, which became his permanent home. During the next several years, more and more of his time was spent building a gambling empire in the friendly climate of Batista's Cuba and out in Nevada.

One man, though, was ignored. Nobody was after him. The time was ripe for Genovese to make his final drive for absolute supremacy over organized crime in America.

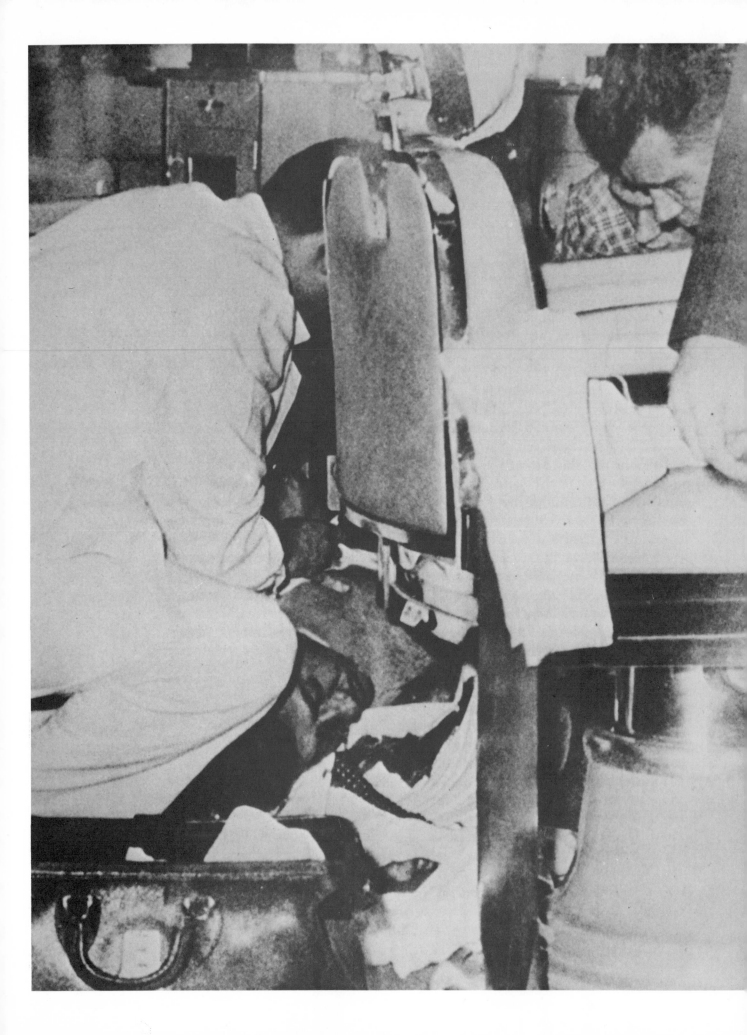

10
PERILS OF POWER

THERE IS AN OLD TRUISM THAT nobody retires from the councils of organized crime; the only way out is in a box. But Frank Costello, fretting away months in prison in 1956 and well aware that his legal battles were far from over, knew that such truisms are not necessarily truths. While old racketeers are usually no more willing to relinquish power and position than their counterparts in big business, there are some who have stepped down gracefully to spend their old age in wealthy retirement. In the years before his death (of a heart attack in Brooklyn) in 1957, nobody questioned Johnny Torrio's right to life as a rich pensioner, nor did anyone try to put a bullet in Al Capone's head when, sick and dying, he left Alcatraz and retired to his Palm Island estate in Florida. All along the Florida Gold Coast, in fact, old-time bootleggers and racketeers took their ease in the warm sun, far from the wars of their youth.

So it was that Costello, the publicly proclaimed prime minister of the underworld, decided that he, too, would retire and settle down to a life of well-earned ease as an elder statesman. When he walked out of prison in March 1957, he announced his decision to his intimates, certain it would meet with their approval. After all, he was 64, a millionaire several times over, with few worlds to conquer. He was also mentally and physically exhausted from the decades of struggle and he knew that ahead lay still

Willie Bioff tangled with some Mob rivals and lost the contest; he and his pickup truck went up in a blast.

more struggle, particularly with the tax-men and with the Immigration and Naturalization Service (which claimed he had lied about his criminal record when naturalized in 1925 and was trying to deport him to Italy). Costello wanted only a little peace and leisure time to enjoy his rewards, one of which was just about to begin paying off—the Tropicana hotel and casino in Las Vegas, in which he and his old partner, Phil Kastel, had a major stake.

If the decision initially surprised some of Costello's old friends, they soon came to understand it. At a specially called meeting in November 1956, the leaders of the Syndicate—Meyer Lansky, Longy Zwillman, Tommy Lucchese, Albert Anastasia and others—were in agreement: Costello was a founding member, had

long guided the Organization in the paths toward riches and respectability, had helped change the image of the racketeer from cheap thug to semirespectable businessman. Even in retirement, his counsel might still be needed. Thus, his request ought to be respected.

There were, of course, more selfish reasons. The continuing publicity that centered on Costello after the Kefauver hearings had made him a liability, bringing light and heat down on his associates. Further, Costello's empire was vast and lucrative. Much of it would go to old partners such as Lansky and Kastel, and some would go to Vito Genovese, who now would rule unchallenged as head of the old Luciano family; but there would be plenty left for others.

But there were objections. Genovese, for one, insisted that Costello would be too dangerous, even in retirement; but he was voted down, and when affirmative votes had been received from Joe Adonis and Lucky Luciano in their Italian exiles, the decision was binding: Costello could settle on his estate in Sands Point, Long Island, and concern himself mainly with clipping coupons and fighting the government.

Despite that decision, Genovese had other ideas and other reasons for wanting Costello out of the way. By 1957, his ambition to become the new Salvatore Maranzano, the new boss of all bosses—*capo di tutti capi*—and not merely of the Italian underworld but of the entire criminal syndicate, had become almost a mania. As long as Costello lived, he posed a threat to such plans: He had once been Genovese's superior in the Luciano family; after the war, they had been coequal regents when Luciano went into exile. But their ideas and methods were in sharp conflict. Costello's emphasis was on gambling of all sorts, on the infiltration of legitimate businesses, on making as few waves as possible, on cooperating with everyone, on benevolent rule. And he deeply abhorred narcotics, incessantly preaching and warning against involvement. By contrast, Genovese was abrasive, his rule dictatorial, and narcotics had long been one of his passions. He recognized the profit potential, scorned the risks and, under his guidance, the Luciano family became deeply enmeshed in dope traffic. So Costello's opposition to nar-

cotics and his differing policies made him, even in retirement, the natural rallying point for those who objected to Genovese's ironfisted rule and his heavy emphasis on drugs. And Genovese, despite the Syndicate decision, was determined to eliminate that source of opposition.

On the evening of May 2, 1957, Costello had drinks with a couple of friends—gambler Frank Erickson and fellow racketeer Anthony "Little Augie Pisano" Carfano—at the Waldorf's Peacock Alley. Then he joined some friends for dinner at L'Aiglon, a fashionable East Side restaurant. About 11 in the evening, Costello left, explaining that he was expecting an important telephone call from his Washington lawyer, Edward Bennett Williams.

As Costello's cab stopped before the Majestic Apartments at 115 Central Park West, a long black Cadillac pulled up behind it. While Costello was paying the driver, a gargantuan man in a dark suit, his gray hat low on his forehead, got out of the Cadillac and hurried into the Majestic. Apparently, Costello did not even notice him. A few seconds later, Costello walked through the door, held open by the doorman, into the foyer and headed for the elevators. He had nearly reached them when the fat man stepped out behind him from the shelter of a pillar, pulled out a pistol and aimed. Perhaps giving a last-minute heed to the old rule that a leader deserves to get it from the front, he yelled, "This is for you, Frank." Then he snapped off a shot at Costello's head, fled to the waiting Cadillac and sped off into the night, probably believing that Costello was dead.

But the gunman's last-minute shout had saved Costello's life. At the sound of the voice, he had turned instinctively and the bullet only grazed him, ripping a gash along the right side of his head just behind his ear. Dazed and bleeding, Costello was rushed to nearby Roosevelt Hospital. While the doctors patched his head, Manhattan detectives went through his coat pockets, and what they discovered only spelled more trouble. There was $800 in cash and a slip of paper with some writing on it: "Gross casino win—$651,284. Casino win less markers—$434,695. Slot wins—$62,844. Markers—$153,745.

Though Costello professed ignorance of the paper with the numbers, said he didn't even know how it had gotten into his pocket, the Nevada Gaming Control Board heard about it and did a little investigating. It discovered that the figures matched the gambling revenues for a 24-day period at the newly opened Tropicana. Costello turned sullen and, when summoned before a grand jury to explain, refused to talk. The result: another jail term for contempt of court and then another indictment for income-tax evasion.

Just who had shot Costello was no secret to either the underworld or the police. The gunman was a one-time prizefighter and Genovese thug named Vincente "The Chin" Gigante, a hulking man gone to more than 300

pounds of blubber. Though Costello refused to give police any information about his assailant, claiming he had never seen him and so could not possibly identify him, the Majestic's doorman had gotten a good look. On the basis of his description, police instituted a search for Gigante. But the gunman was nowhere to be found. According to Mafia informant Joe Valachi years later, "The Chin was just taken somewhere up in the country to lose some weight." When Gigante eventually walked into a Manhattan police station and ingenuously insisted he had just learned the cops were looking for him, he was back in fighting trim. It was a relatively slim and trim Gigante who went on trial for attempted murder. He was acquitted when Costello still refused to identify him and the doorman either couldn't or wouldn't.

The bungled assassination of Costello seemed certain to bring trouble to Genovese, for he had unilaterally disobeyed a council decision. A dead Costello could not have protested and, besides, the commission rarely intervened in internal family disputes. But a live Costello was a different matter. Not only was there now the possibility of a council action but Costello had plenty of friends who might, if he prodded them, decide to mete out fitting punishment on their own.

To counter this threat, Genovese desperately needed a strong show of support from his own lieutenants. He holed up in his mansion in Atlantic Highlands, New Jersey, and sum-

Vincente "The Chin" Gigante (insert) ambushed Frank Costello, seen here after the attack. He was acquitted when Costello refused to identify him.

Augie Carfano defied Genovese. Later, he and girl-friend Janice Drake (top right), a former Miss New Jersey, were found shot.

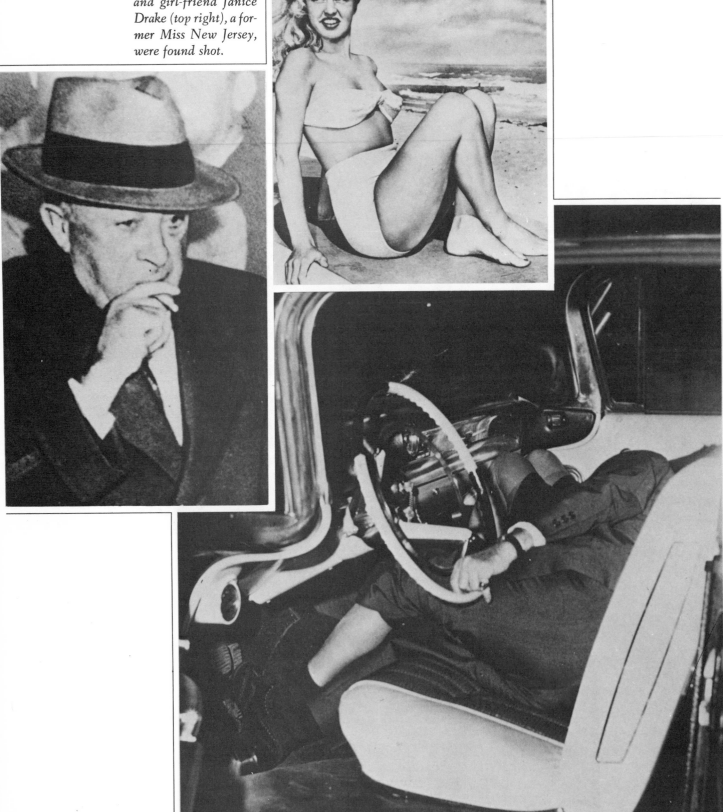

moned all the leaders to appear, to join with him in presenting a united front. Fearful, all but one, Augie Carfano, answered the call, and at this single defection Genovese was enraged. He ordered one of his aides, Anthony Strollo, better known as Tony Bender, to bring Carfano in, and told him that if he failed, he "would be wearing a black tie"—decked out for his own funeral. The reluctant Carfano finally arrived (his contrariness was repaid two years later, when he and his companion, former beauty queen Janice Drake, were shot to death in their car near New York's La Guardia Airport). To the full gathering of his lieutenants, Genovese stated flatly that he had ordered the shooting of Costello because Costello was plotting against him, that anyone seen even talking to Costello thereafter would be dealt with summarily, that the family now belonged to Genovese and nobody else, and that the new underboss would be Gerardo "Gerry" Catena. No one said nay.

Even with the solid backing of his own organization, Genovese realized that he still faced trouble if Costello decided to press the issue with the commission. But he did not, at least not formally. According to an underworld source, Genovese and Costello met secretly on neutral ground shortly after the shooting and reached an accord: Costello would not charge Genovese before the commission and would withdraw completely (as he had previously said he would do) from all family affairs; Genovese, in return, would stop shooting at Costello and would let him retire gracefully to enjoy the returns from his real-estate and gambling investments.

BUT THE ATTACK ON COSTELLO and the monomaniacal ambition of Genovese, now out in the open, signaled the end of the uncertain underworld peace that had existed for so many years, almost since the end of the Castellammarese War. The underworld was about to enter a decade and more of bloodletting that would equal or surpass the conflict of the Thirties.

Even the usually nonbelligerent Costello was caught up in the new era of violence. For, despite his surface timidity, he did not intend that the attack on him should go unavenged nor that Genovese should assume control unchallenged over the Combination he had labored to create. Costello, however, was wise enough to know that some of his old friends were no longer quite so reliable as they had once been. Lansky, for instance, obviously had personal ambitions and was standing aloof from the developing struggle within the Italian underworld, convinced that the battle would so decimate each side that he would emerge undisputed master of the Syndicate. Costello, then, could not depend upon Lansky unless Lansky saw some advantage in it for himself. Zwillman, too, might once have proved a valuable ally, but his fortunes had taken a decided downward turn since his appearance before the

Kefauver Committee—the taxmen were swarming around him and so were other legal officials, and it was taking all his energy to fight them off.

But Costello did have two formidable allies who shared his contempt for Genovese. One was Luciano, who even in Italian exile had immense power and influence; the other was Anastasia, perhaps the most violent and feared leader in the underworld.

Genovese, of course, was not blind to these threats. He was not particularly worried about a Costello in semiretirement, detached from the day-to-day affairs of the underworld and preoccupied with fighting to stay out of prison and avoid deportation. But he was very worried about Costello's friends, particularly Anastasia. The one-time lord high executioner of Murder, Inc., was the key. Luciano might come to Costello's aid, true, but despite the steady parade of couriers taking money and messages to him in Italy and returning with orders and advice, Luciano was essentially boxed in. By himself, he could do little from 5000 miles away; he would have to give orders to somebody on the scene he could trust implicitly, and that someone would necessarily be Anastasia.

In the late spring of 1957, danger to Genovese began to appear imminent. Word reached him that Costello had surreptitiously sent messages, contents unknown, to Luciano, and that Costello and Anastasia had been meeting secretly. Lacking the forces to mount a frontal attack on Anastasia, he set out first to cripple him, to isolate him from his associates and allies.

One of the most loyal lieutenants in the Anastasia family, the underboss and heir apparent, was 63-year-old Frank "Don Cheech" Scalise; he had been in the Organization since Prohibition, was a close friend of Luciano's, whom he visited several times in Italy, and was a power in his own right as a result of his control over the construction racket in the Bronx. Any plot against Anastasia would have to include Scalise in order to forestall his assumption of power in the family. The rumor was quietly spread (and it was one that Valachi would hear from Genovese himself) that Scalise had started a racket to sell memberships in the American Mafia for prices up to $50,000 to aspiring young thugs. This was something even Anastasia could not stomach and he reportedly flew into a violent rage when the rumor reached him. A second rumor quickly followed: that Scalise, long deeply involved in the narcotics traffic, had welched on his responsibility to reimburse some underworld partners when narcotics agents seized a shipment of heroin. Scalise was marked for death. On June 17, 1957, as he picked through some fruit at a favorite stand in the Bronx, two gunmen walked up behind him and put four slugs into the back of his head and neck.

Anastasia said nothing, but Scalise's brother, Joe, vowed revenge. When Anastasia continued to maintain his silence, Joe realized that

In happier days Frank Scalise (left) visited with Lucky Luciano in Italy.

maybe he had been a little precipitous and went into hiding. Soon, though, word reached him that all was forgiven and by early September, Joe was back at his old haunts in New York. Then, on September 7, he disappeared and was never seen again. According to Valachi, Scalise unwisely accepted an invitation to a party at the home of Jimmy "Jerome" Squillante, boss of the New York garbage-collection racket and a very good friend to Bender and to Genovese. Scalise was greeted by butcher knives and left as part of the garbage collec-

tion in one of Squillante's trash trucks. (Squillante himself did not remain on the scene long, either. In 1960, he was indicted on Long Island for extortion but disappeared before his case came to trial. According to underworld rumors, a bullet was put through his head, his body was loaded into the trunk of a car and the car put into a crusher that compacted it into a cube of scrap for melting down in a blast furnace.)

With the murder of the Scalise brothers, Carlo Gambino emerged as the number-two man in the Anastasia family. Genovese knew that Gambino had his eye on the Anastasia throne and was sure that anyone who helped him get there would earn his complete loyalty. An approach was made, and after several private meetings in late summer and early fall of 1957, Genovese and Gambino struck a bargain. Gambino would assist Genovese in the elimination of Anastasia and would make sure that nobody sought retribution. In return, Genovese would throw all his strength behind Gambino to ensure his easy assumption of rule in the Anastasia family and would even cut him in on some of the more profitable Genovese rackets.

Then, unexpectedly, the plot won a new ally—Lansky. Ordinarily, if Lansky had moved from his firm neutrality, it should have been against Genovese; from the earliest days, the two had barely tolerated each other, but Lansky detested Anastasia even more than he did Genovese. Almost from their first meeting, Lansky and Anastasia had despised each other, and not cordially. Lansky viewed Anastasia as an ignorant, impulsive, violence-prone thug who could never be civilized; Anastasia viewed Lansky as a moneygrubbing Jew, a condescending and devious intellectual always looking for the angles instead of direct action. It was, then, seemingly in Lansky's interest to let Genovese and Anastasia destroy each other.

But Anastasia had committed an unforgivable sin in Lansky's light. By 1957, Lansky was firmly entrenched in Cuba, his partnership with the

Dictator Fulgencio Batista opened up Cuba to the Mob.

island's president, Fulgencio Batista, stronger than ever. New casinos and hotels were springing up almost overnight to dominate the Havana skyline and the country's economic life. With his instinct for self-protection and self-aggrandizement, and for putting his associates firmly in his debt, Lansky had cut a number of long-time associates, including Santo Trafficante, Moe Dalitz and several Italian mobsters, in on shares in some of the casinos (and had even helped some old entertainers who were down on their luck: George Raft, for example, was hired to greet the folks at the Capri; later he would do the same thing in London at Mob-ruled casinos until he was thrown out of England). Genovese had made no moves in the direction of Cuba, which suited Lansky just fine. But Anastasia wanted in, and Lansky gave a firm no that was backed by Batista. Anastasia was unwilling to accept that response. He tried to move in secretly through some Cuban businessmen, even sought to circumvent Lansky by dealing with Lansky allies such as Trafficante. The word, of course, got back to Lansky, who decided to dispose of the troublesome Brooklyn gangster. When he learned of the germinating Genovese-Gambino plot, he sent word that he would back it, mainly by permitting some of his Cuban friends and gambling partners to string Anastasia along, to disarm him with false hopes and optimism.

The intricate plotting against Anastasia—to end his life and, simultaneously, deny Costello the gun that might endanger Genovese—accelerated. Gambino and Genovese decided not to use their own killers but to give the contract to fellow ganglord Joe Profaci, who was a good and close friend of Lansky's and of Trafficante's. Profaci turned the job of Anastasia's execution over to a

young thug named "Crazy Joe" Gallo, one of three brothers who relished such work.

Early on the morning of October 25, 1957, Anastasia was driven from his walled estate in Fort Lee, New Jersey, to the Park Sheraton Hotel on Seventh Avenue at 55th Street in Manhattan (as the Park Central, it had been home three decades before to Arnold Rothstein and it was there that he was murdered in 1928). At 10:15, while his chauffeur-bodyguard, Anthony Coppola, parked his new Oldsmobile in a nearby garage and then conveniently went for a short stroll, Anastasia entered the hotel barbershop, hung up his coat and sat down in chair number four, telling barber Joseph Bocchino, "Haircut." Then he settled back, closing his eyes as Bocchino draped a cloth around his neck, took a pair of clippers and went to work on the shaggy hair that apparently had not been cut in several weeks.

The barbershop door swung open. Two men, scarves across their faces, stepped quickly inside and pulled out pistols. "Keep your mouth shut if you don't want your head blown off," one of them snapped at the shop's owner, Arthur Grasso. Then they strode calmly down the aisle, stopped behind Anastasia's chair, raised their guns and began to fire. With the first shots, a wounded Anastasia leaped out of the chair. Disoriented, he lunged at the images of the two gunmen in the mirror in front of him. A second volley sent him reeling against the glass shelf under

Anastasia was shot in the barbershop of the Park-Sheraton Hotel on New York's Seventh Avenue.

the mirror, crashing to the floor amid a litter of broken bottles of hair tonic. As Anastasia lay on the floor, one of the gunmen took careful aim and shot him in the back of the head. Then the two hurried out of the shop onto Seventh Avenue and disappeared down the B.M.T. subway entrance at the corner. As they fled, they dropped their guns—one was found later in the vestibule of the shop, the other in a trash barrel on the subway platform. It had all taken less than two minutes. The gunmen had done their work and escaped. But despite their reputations, their efficiency and marksmanship left something to be desired. They had stood directly behind Anastasia, within a few feet of their target; they had fired ten shots; they had missed with half of them. Of the five shots that found Anastasia, one hit him in his left hand, a second in his left wrist, a third in his right hip, a fourth in his back. Only the final head shot, as he lay on the floor, was fatal.

In the confusion that followed the murder of Anastasia, Genovese moved quickly to consolidate his gains and to assume the crown of *capo di tutti capi.* With no fanfare at all, Gambino quietly assumed the leadership of the Anastasia family. Then Genovese summoned the leaders of organized crime throughout the United States to the first major underworld conference since the one in Havana in 1946. At the suggestion of

Buffalo boss Stefano Magaddino, Genovese altered his original idea of holding the meeting in Chicago and scheduled the session for November 14, three weeks after the fall of Anastasia, in the sleepy upstate New York hamlet of Apalachin, at the country estate of a Magaddino lieutenant named Joseph Barbara.

On the agenda were a number of pressing items: an official justification by Genovese to his peers of his attacks on Costello and Anastasia; a demand by Genovese that he be named boss of all bosses and receive, as tribute, cash-filled envelopes from the delegates; authorization of a massive purge to eliminate unreliable members of the Combination; the closing of books on the admittance of new members until the purge had created a tightly knit and loyal Organization; the formulation of an Organization policy on narcotics (for there was a growing belief that the massive antidrug drive by authorities was making narcotics too hot to handle).

What decisions the delegates might have made on any of these subjects is unknown; they never got a chance to vote or even to discuss the agenda. For one of the biggest blunders in the history of the Syndicate was to assume that 100 or more major racketeers could drive along a country road in an isolated area in their big limousines, many with license plates from distant states, all heading for the same place, and attract no attention.

In the days just prior to the conclave, Barbara went on a meat-buying and motel-room-reserving spree, and this sudden spurt of activity, signaling the arrival of a throng, aroused the curiosity of New York State Police Sergeant Edgar D. Crosswell. And when the Cadillacs and Continentals began driving up to the Barbara estate, Crosswell was more than intrigued. With his force of three state troopers, he set up roadblocks around the property, called for additional help and waited to see what would develop.

Hardly were the roadblocks in place, hardly had the racketeering galaxy begun to settle in, when a minor hoodlum taking a stroll along the Barbara driveway spotted the roadblocks and rushed back to the house to spread the alarm. Then ensued one of the most comic, and degrading, scenes in the annals of the American underworld. Scores of middle-aged and elderly gangsters, dressed in their hand-tailored suits, dived out windows, fled through doors and went crashing through the woods and underbrush in a desperate attempt to escape. Many did escape, including a lucky few who, instead of risking the wilds, sought shelter for several days in a cellar of the house, emerging only when the authorities had cleared out. But Crosswell, reinforced with additional troopers, managed to round up 60. It was a bag that stunned even the most sophisticated Syndicate watcher. In that haul were Genovese, Barbara, Magaddino, Trafficante, Profaci, "Joe Bananas" Bonanno, Cleveland boss John Scalish, Los Angeles boss Frank DeSimone, downstate Illinois mobster Frankie Zito, Philadelphia's

Apalachin was, in almost every aspect, a typical upstate New York hamlet.

Joe Ida, Colorado's Jimmy Colletti, Dallas leader Jimmy Civello and many more. In their possession was more than $300,000; it was to have been put in envelopes for Genovese; he would never get it now. Among those known to have been in attendance who somehow managed to elude the police were Sam Giancana of Chicago, Joe Zerilli of Detroit and James Lanza of San Francisco.

The result, in a number of ways, was devastating. Those who even tried to explain what they were doing at Apalachin said they were good friends of Barbara's, that they had heard he was recuperating from a severe heart attack and had dropped by to cheer him up. Others wouldn't talk at all, citing the Fifth Amendment right against self-incrimination. Such responses didn't satisfy authorities and a number of those picked up in the raid were charged with obstructing justice, tried and found guilty, fined and sentenced to prison, though all the convictions were later overturned on the grounds that a meeting in itself doesn't constitute a crime.

THE APALACHIN DEBACLE WAS shattering for Genovese. His dream of absolute rule came tumbling down in the ruins. Who among his fellow leaders would award unquestioning fealty to a man who had led them to such disaster? But more than just the dreams of kingdom were collapsing. Genovese's legendary ability to survive untouched was about to end, as well. His enemies—his estranged wife, his underworld foes, the federal government—were closing in upon him.

Anna Genovese had already provided an opening through which the government could take a hard look at Genovese. Suing for separate maintenance, she had gone to court to tell why she thought Vito could pay any amount of alimony she desired. Their house in Atlantic Highlands, she said, had originally cost $75,000, but Vito had plowed an additional $100,000 into it for renovations and $250,000 for furnishings—things like marble fireplaces and staircases, Oriental vases, Chinese teak furniture, Italian statuary, gold and platinum dishes. Anna had a closet full of gowns that cost between $350 and $900 each and another closet full of furs. Genovese, she said, "never paid less than $250 for a suit. He pays $350 for coats, $35 for shirts and $60 for shoes. . . . We lived very high . . . money was no object." Indeed, there never was a worry about funds. According to Anna, she kept the books all the years Genovese was in Italy, and from all his rackets, such as the Italian lottery, he was earning at least $40,000 a week (the federal government would later estimate the Genovese fortune to be in excess of $30,000,000). But life with the gangster, despite all the money, was no fun. Genovese, she

said, made no secret of his bevy of mistresses and, worse, he often beat her brutally.

When Anna got through complaining, the court granted her a meager $300 a week alimony and attorney's fees. Genovese loudly proclaimed that this was too much, for he was just a poor workingman who owned a few small businesses. As though to prove the contention, he sold his mansion and moved into a five-room clapboard bungalow on a quiet street in Atlantic Highlands, renting the house for $100 a month.

Genovese's friends were stunned when, despite her revelations, nothing happened to Anna; the underworld had fully expected Genovese to deal with her in a manner befitting an informant. But, for some inexplicable reason, he could not bring himself to harm the woman he had won years before by ordering the murder of her first husband. Some action, though, was necessary, if only to show that he had not turned soft and, perhaps, to warn Anna that her singing days had better end. The victim would be Genovese's one-time friend and Anna's constant companion, Steve Franse, in whose care he had left her while in Europe during World War II (and who had served, it appeared, merely as a cover for her dalliances with lovers of both sexes). As Valachi would later testify, Bender informed him that Franse was to be killed and the murder performed in a restaurant Valachi owned. Franse was lured there. Two Genovese killers were waiting. Franse was garroted and bru-

Vito Genovese almost made it to the real big time, but a 15-year prison sentence stopped his upward mobility.

tally beaten to death, then his body was dumped into the rear of his car, which was abandoned on the Grand Concourse in the Bronx.

This was an oblique revenge that did not save Genovese from the plots swirling around him. Anna's testimony had sent federal authorities scouring his books and records, hoping to pin, at the very least, a tax-evasion rap on him. What they wanted most, though, was evidence of involvement in major crimes, hopefully narcotics, that could send Genovese to prison for a good long time and then lead to his deportation. This thought also intrigued the growing ranks of Genovese's enemies in the underworld hierarchy.

In mid-1958, only six months

after the Apalachin fiasco, a two-bit heroin pusher named Nelson Cantellops, serving a five-year drug rap in Sing Sing, suddenly asked for an interview with federal narcotics agents. That Cantellops, a Puerto Rican nabbed for pushing junk on a Manhattan street corner, should have anything of major importance to say seemed unlikely; that he knew about high figures in the Mafia chain of command, that his contacts would reach as high as Genovese himself seemed impossible. But that was just what Cantellops claimed, and he told a good story—had it down so firmly in every detail that no amount of grilling was able to shake him or make him stumble. Either it was the truth, illogical as that may have seemed, or—as a number of persons in both law enforcement and the underworld firmly believe—he had been primed and rehearsed so thoroughly that he could not be broken. To the government, it didn't matter which, as long as Cantellops could help put Genovese in jail.

According to Cantellops, after a period as a lowly pusher, he had begun to meet some of the bigger, more important people and to do errands for them. Soon he was making heroin deliveries for "Big John" Ormento, an important Genovese lieutenant, and for Gigante, Costello's would-be assassin. He handled these deliveries with such dispatch that soon he was meeting even bigger men, including Natale Evola and Rocco Mazzie, two trusted Genovese aides, and finally Genovese himself. Then

came Cantellops's crusher: He had been in a car with Evola, Mazzie, Ormento and Gigante when Genovese personally gave the orders for his men to move in and take over narcotics distribution in the East Bronx.

On the basis of that testimony, 24 men, including Genovese, were indicted for narcotics conspiracy in July 1958. In the spring of 1959, 15 were brought to trial (the others had become fugitives and the objects of major manhunts). The star and only witness against Genovese was Cantellops. But his testimony was good enough for the jury, especially when the defense was unable to make him backtrack a step during intense cross-examination. All the defendants were found guilty. Genovese was sent to federal prison for 15 years. Gigante drew a lighter term. And Costello took time out from his own troubles to smile.

There is little doubt that Genovese, in the months between his arrest and his conviction, began to suspect that the federal authorities were getting at least covert assistance from his enemies in the Syndicate. If so, Costello would be deeply involved; but it was no easy thing to reach Costello. He was in and out of prison as though caught in a revolving door, he was battling denaturalization moves (which climaxed in 1961 with revocation of his American citizenship) and, when free, he was usually sequestered well out of harm's way.

But other enemies, such as Zwillman and Bender were not so well protected. There are stories in the underworld that Zwillman, as his troubles with the federal taxmen deepened, as liens were placed against his property, became so financially desperate that he approached Genovese for help—and was spurned. Zwillman made some angry noises to friends. Soon thereafter, Cantellops surfaced. There are some who saw a connection. One, perhaps, was Genovese. For on February 27, 1959, Zwillman was found dead in his West Orange, New Jersey, mansion. The official verdict: suicide by hanging. Which was surprising, in light of some of the details that later, unofficially, leaked out. Zwillman had been discovered hanging with wire around his neck under a rope, his body was heavily bruised, his hands were tied with wire. Some in the underworld say that the contract on Zwillman had been let by Gerry Catena, the underboss in the Genovese family.

Suspicions about Bender's trustworthiness also began to mount, for it was no secret in the councils of the underworld that his loyalty too often had been for sale to the highest bidder; Bender had survived the purges and the wars of the decades usually by switching to the winning side after the troubles started. On April 8, 1962, his luck ran out. That morning, as he left home, his wife said to him, "You better put on your topcoat. It's chilly."

Bender shrugged off the advice. "I'm only going out for a few minutes," he said. "Besides, I'm wearing thermal underwear." Then he disap-

peared down the sidewalk and disappeared from the society of crime. No trace of him has ever been found. But, according to underworld stories, Genovese had ordered his death and the contract was handed to a Jewish killer, a one-time boxer turned loan shark and killer by contract. When he got through with Bender, the body was dumped into a cement mixer and is now part of a Manhattan skyscraper.

No one is certain what ended Bender's career, but some have speculated that it grew from the failure of another devious plot, part of the Genovese revenge against those he believed had railroaded him to prison.

With Luciano dead, the victim of a heart attack in Naples in 1962, the imprisonment of Genovese left an opening at the top of the Italian underworld, at least in New York. The problem—and it would become ever more crucial over the next decade—was a lack of men truly capable of rule, men who had earned the respect and loyalty of their fellows. Age, death and double-dealing, especially the machinations of Genovese, had taken their toll.

Certainly, the regents of the Genovese family—Catena, Tommy Eboli and Mike Miranda—whatever their secret ambitions, had neither the stature nor the power to command others. They had enough trouble trying to keep order in their own organization and trying to placate a bitter Genovese, raging in federal prison. Until he finally sickened and died in 1969, and then was brought home to be buried in a Queens cemetery only a few hundred feet from the tomb of Luciano, they had to keep their ambitions in check.

One man who, had he tried, might have restored order and peace and assumed some kind of leadership was Tommy Lucchese, the most secret of the rulers of the five major crime families in New York. His credentials were impeccable. Since the Twenties, he had been high in the councils of the Organization; he had been a close and constant friend to Luciano, in death an even greater legend than in life; and through the years, he had run his family with considerable efficiency and little or no internal friction.

But Lucchese had never had such ambitions and, in his sixties, seemed to lack the stomach for the kind of fight that might be necessary to expand his power. He was content to run his own family and his own legitimate businesses, to tend to his widening interests in Florida in cooperation with his friend Lansky and to sit on the ruling board as one of the most respected voices of the Syndicate— partly because of his refusal to compete with others. He was preoccupied with fighting federal tax-evasion charges and government efforts to deport him to his native Sicily. Then, too, his health was deteriorating. Like many others who had risen high in the Organization, he was afflicted with a progressively debilitating heart ailment and, on top of that, he began to suffer dizzy spells. (In 1965, he would enter the hospital for surgery on a brain tumor, would never fully recover and within 18 months would die in his own bed at the age of 64.)

If Lucchese was not interested in more power, he did have a man to whom he was willing to throw his support. That was Gambino, whose son was married to Lucchese's daughter. But Gambino was a relatively new member of the national commission, anointed only with the murder of Anastasia, and he wisely chose not to push himself ahead too rapidly. Besides himself, there were only two obvious candidates to become *de facto* ruler, and looking at both Profaci and Bonanno, Gambino realized that within both were the seeds of their own destruction. Then it would be his time.

Profaci might have stepped forward; indeed, he was ruthless, powerful and experienced enough to have made the bid and perhaps won it. But he had too many troubles within his own family to be concerned about expanding his power outside. Rebellion was erupting and it would take all his efforts to put it down.

Joe Gallo, his older brother, Larry, and his younger brother, Albert "Kid Blast," had been ordinary soldiers and prime hit men in the Profaci army and as such, they had done yeoman service. It was they, or at least Crazy Joe, who had fulfilled the contract on Anastasia. And it was they who, in the fall of 1959, had meted out Profaci's form of justice— bullets in the head—to Frank "Frankie Shots" Abbatemarco, a Profaci policy banker suspected of holding back some of the take for himself.

The Gallos thought their good work should earn them some tangible rewards, such as control of gambling, loan-sharking and narcotics in Brooklyn's East New York section. Profaci, however, was anything but a generous man. He believed that sharing meant sharing with him; he demanded a cut of every racket his men were involved in, plus $25 a month dues from every member of his family. With hardly a nod, he turned down the Gallo request.

This did not make Joe very happy. "Any man who is strong enough to take something and hold it, he owns it," he was fond of saying, so the Gallos decided to do some taking and

holding. What they took in February 1961 were Joseph "The Fat Man" Magliocco, Profaci's brother-in-law and underboss; Frank Profaci, the boss's brother; and two powerful aides and bodyguards, Salvatore "Sally the Sheik" Mussachia and John Scimone. They also tried to take Profaci himself, but the ruler was tipped off and took a plane to Florida for sanctuary. The four hostages were secreted in separate Manhattan hotel rooms while the Gallos presented Profaci with their demands for a cut of the empire.

With an unusual shrug of surrender, Profaci acceded and promised no retribution. The hostages were re-

The Gallo brothers, Larry (left) and Joey (right), were good soldiers, but they wanted more than a good reputation.

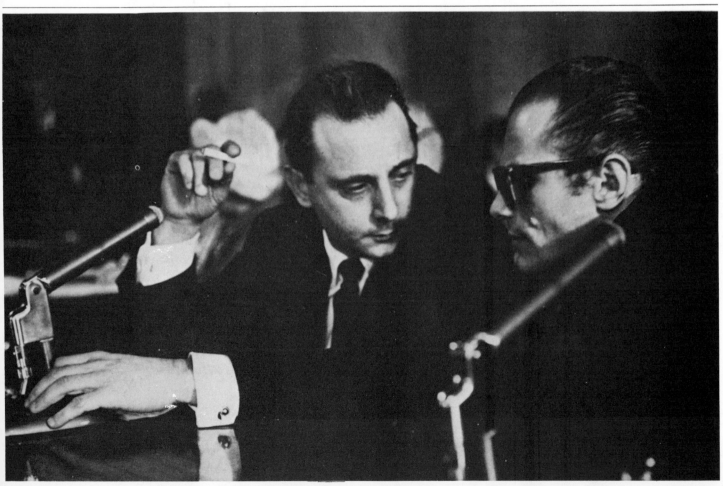

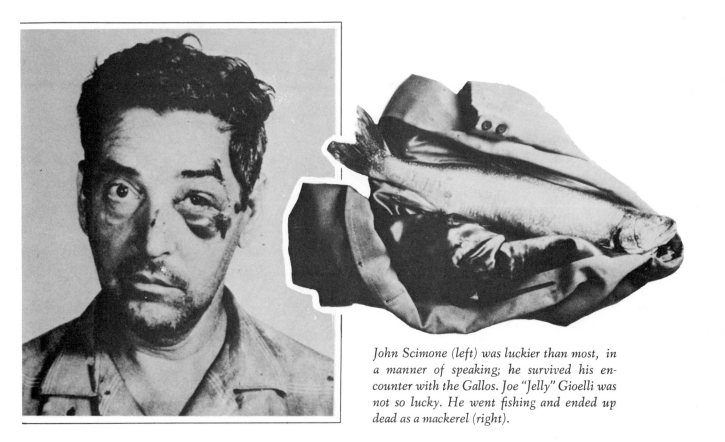

John Scimone (left) was luckier than most, in a manner of speaking; he survived his encounter with the Gallos. Joe "Jelly" Gioelli was not so lucky. He went fishing and ended up dead as a mackerel (right).

leased unharmed and the Gallos waited for their rewards. The payoffs that came, however, were in keeping with Profaci's reputation. In August of 1961, a top Gallo enforcer named Joseph "Joe Jelly" Gioelli went deep-sea fishing, an abiding passion of his. What returned from the trip was Gioelli's coat wrapped around a dead fish, dumped from a car near a favorite Gallo hangout in Brooklyn.

This was Profaci's first answer. Simultaneously, Larry Gallo got an invitation to meet Scimone at the Sahara Lounge in Brooklyn to hear some good news and get the first payment over a couple of drinks. The payment and the good news were a $100 bill

and a noose around Larry's neck as he sipped his whiskey. The only thing that saved him was the unexpected appearance in the bar's doorway of a cop making his rounds. When the cop inquired politely what was going on, a couple of shots were fired at him, one hitting his partner.

And so erupted the Gallo-Profaci War. Faced with far stronger and better equipped troops, the Gallos and about 25 of their allies holed up on the second floor of a brick-front building at 49–51 President Street in Brooklyn, soon nicknamed The Dormitory. There, surrounded by mattresses, an arsenal of weapons and a hoard of food, and lulled by the strains of

Larry Gallo's favorite Verdi operas pouring from a phonograph, they prepared to do battle. However, most of the casualties were the Gallo soldiers who made forays into the city; about the only real action on President Street occurred when a house nearby burst into flames and the Gallos raced up the tenement stairs to rescue a family trapped on the third floor. "We only done what any red-blooded American boys would do," Albert Gallo told reporters modestly, though he added, "With our crummy luck, I suppose we'll get arrested for putting out the fire without a license."

There were, however, two major casualties, though neither was a direct result of the war itself. The first was Joe Gallo. In December 1961, the cops arrived on President Street to remove him from his fortress to jail. Gallo had a big mouth and a penchant for wisecracks, and one day, while trying to shake down a café owner, who wanted time to think it over, he said, "Sure, take three months in the hospital on me." Unfortunately for him, three detectives were sitting at the next table. That wisecrack cost Crazy Joe a 7-to-14 year prison sentence.

The second victim was Profaci himself. Early in 1962, the boss fell ill. He was taken to the hospital and operated on for a massive cancer. It was too late. On June 6, Profaci was dead. His successor as head of the family was his brother-in-law, Magliocco, a weak and vacillating man incapable of commanding an army or maintaining the allegiance of his troops.

So the Gallo-Profaci War ground to an indecisive halt, with both sides claiming victory. For the regulars, the war, at least, was over, with the Gallos back in the fold, proclaiming loyalty. For the Gallos, there were the spoils that they had long demanded. They were given control of the rackets in East New York and for the next few years, under Larry's leadership, their power in the Profaci organization grew. But in 1968, Larry died of cancer and Albert proved incapable of running things with dispatch. The Gallo mob deteriorated, the remnants hoping for a renaissance when Joe walked the streets again.

The Gallos may have gotten their spoils, but the man who emerged with the real power in the Profaci family was a young and obscure *capo*, considered merely a minor gambler. His name was Joseph Colombo. At the start of the war, he had been considered so loyal to Profaci that the Gallos marked him for death. The plot failed, but Joe Gallo, for one, never considered him other than an enemy, even after he had done the Gallos a good turn: When Profaci died, it was Colombo who negotiated the peace and wrote the terms that gave the Gallos what they had fought for.

Colombo's most successful ploy, though, was yet to come. It was one that would bring him the blessings of Gambino and the mantle of leadership in the Profaci family. For it undid the only remaining rival to Gambino for leadership in the Italian underworld and, at the same time,

Profaci controlled the Brooklyn chapter of organized crime. His fate was not as swift as some of his victims'; he died of cancer.

deposed Magliocco as Profaci's successor.

Bonanno's ambitions had been waxing mightily, especially as all the old *mafiosi* died away. With the death of Profaci, he began to see himself as the boss of all bosses. Though the ruler of the smallest of New York's five families, his interests were wide and varied, running all the way from narcotics to legitimate garment manufacturing, and spreading from Brooklyn all the way to Tucson, Arizona, and into Long Island, the Midwest, Canada and the Caribbean. Bonanno decided the time had come to act on his ambitions, to eliminate in one move all who might stand in his way: Lucchese, Gambino, Buffalo's Magaddino and even the Los Angeles boss, DeSimone. Not certain he had the power to do this all by himself, Bonanno sought allies, and he turned particularly to Magliocco, an old and dear friend. Swayed by Bonanno's arguments, and by promises of a share in the spoils, Magliocco joined the plot and even agreed to assume the contracts for the murders in New York. He called Colombo and turned them over to him.

This was Colombo's opportunity. He saw that Magliocco was a sure loser; instead of fulfilling the contracts, he hurried to Gambino with a complete report. Now Gambino saw his own opportunity. He called an emergency session of the underworld commission, which included himself, Lucchese, Chicago's Giancana, Philadelphia's Angelo Bruno, Magaddino and a couple of others—with Lansky, in particular, kept constantly advised of the discussions and decisions. News of the treachery was very upsetting to the Italian overlords, bringing back unpleasant memories of the early Thirties and of the Genovese-inspired violence of the recent past. Magliocco and Bonanno were summoned to appear and explain. A quivering Magliocco arrived, quickly confessed the whole plot and pleaded for his life. Convinced that Magliocco lacked the guts to have conceived the plot on his own, had been swayed by Bonanno and was so ill that he wasn't going to live long anyway, the commission opted for mercy. Magliocco was fined $50,000 and stripped of his position. Within a few months, he was dead of a heart attack.

Colombo got the reward he had hoped for. With the blessings of Gambino, he was named to head the Profaci family, at just over 40 years of age, the youngest Syndicate leader and council member in the country.

Magliocco was Profaci's brother-in-law and his successor—but not for long.

"Joe Colombo? Where's a guy like that belong in the commission? What experience has he got? He was a bust-out guy [small-time gambler] all his life," gasped Sam "The Plumber" DeCavalcante, leader of a small New Jersey family, to his underboss, Frank Majuri, when he heard the news. (The FBI was listening in: It had bugged DeCavalcante's telephone, office and other hangouts.)

"This is ridiculous," Majuri agreed.

Then DeCavalcante added, "This guy sits like a baby next to Carl all the time. He'd do anything Carl wants him to do."

Still, Bonanno had to be dealt

Joe Bonanno was kidnapped, given some useful advice and—incredibly—released.

with. He was no quaking Magliocco. Instead of heeding the commission's summons, he vanished, hiding out first in California and then in Canada. He was spotted there and a second and stronger order for his appearance before the commission was issued. Once again, Bonanno ignored it.

It was time for drastic steps. On October 21, 1964, Bonanno was back in Manhattan, prepared to answer to a grand-jury summons. He had dinner that night with his lawyers, then accompanied one of them, William Power Maloney, back to the lawyer's Park Avenue apartment house. As they were saying good night, two men suddenly confronted Bonanno, shov-

ed him into a car, saying, "Come on, Joe, my boss wants to see you," and sped away.

When news of the Bonanno kidnapping broke, it was generally assumed he was dead. Only Luciano had ever returned from a ride. But somehow, and no one is certain just how, he persuaded the commission to spare him. Held for some time at a hide-out in the Catskills, Bonanno tried to strike a deal. He would retire completely from the commission, from the rackets, from his family, would settle down to a quiet life far removed from the underworld at his home in Tucson. In his stead, he proposed that his son, Salvatore "Bill" Bonanno, assume the leadership of the family. The commission rejected that proposal out of hand and told Bonanno that his family would pass into the hands of Gaspar DiGregorio, a relative of Magaddino's who was known to be loyal to both Magaddino and Gambino and who had the advantage of having no criminal record.

Bonanno had little choice but to accept the council's decision. Then he was released. But instead of heading home or heading for retirement in Tucson, Bonanno faded from sight, not to reappear for 19 months. During that time, according to rumors, he was in Haiti, deeply involved in the burgeoning gambling business and working closely with the Duvalier dictatorship.

But Bonanno was doing more than that. He was gathering strength and preparing to challenge and overturn the council's dictum, to launch

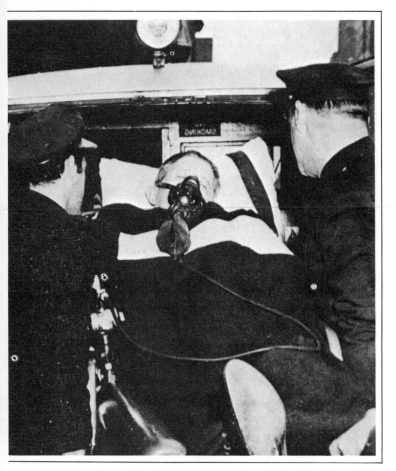

Carlo Gambino collapsed during a deportation hearing.

what would become known as the Banana War. That conflict erupted even before Bonanno's dramatic reappearance. The council's imposition of DiGregorio had not gone down well with the loyalists in the Bonanno family. If they couldn't have Joe himself, they were determined to be led by his son, Bill, until Joe showed up again to reassume control. The family split sharply, both sides arming and preparing for battle. It appeared that unless something radical was done, the Organization might be shattered

beyond repair.

That radical step was taken in January 1966. Emissaries from Di-Gregorio approached Bill with a request for a peace conference. Bonanno agreed and the meeting was set for late in the evening of January 28 at the home of one of Bill's relatives on Troutman Street in Brooklyn. As Bill and several of his men approached the house, shotguns and rifles opened up on them. They returned the fire and for several minutes, until both sides withdrew, a battle raged, though in the dark, marksmanship was poor and there were no casualties.

Bill's escape from the trap meant that the war would continue, but the shooting set off police and grand-jury investigations that kept the war cold through the winter and into the spring. About the only casualty was DiGregorio. His failure to eliminate the loyalist Bonanno faction did not make Gambino or other council members happy. He was booted out of the leadership (two years later, he died of a heart attack) and was replaced by a tough leader, Paul Sciacca.

Then Joe Bonanno was back. On May 17, 1966, wearing the same clothes he had on the night he disappeared 19 months earlier, he walked into Federal Courthouse in Manhattan. "Your Honor," he said to Judge Marvin E. Frankel, "I am Joseph Bonanno. I understand that the government would like to talk to me."

The government did, indeed, want to talk to Bonanno. He was formally charged with obstruction of justice and freed on $150,000 bail while authorities prepared cases against him. He walked out of court and began his war to take back control of his family. The leader of the ambush on Bill was the first victim, ambushed himself; he escaped death but was seriously wounded. Soon thereafter, a Bonanno killer walked into the Cypress Gardens Restaurant in Queens, pulled a submachine gun from under his black raincoat and, in full view of more than 20 diners, blasted away at three DiGregorio-Sciacca henchmen sitting at the table in the middle of the room. The gunman killed all three and then disappeared through the kitchen and out the back door.

The casualties mounted. Soldiers on both sides were taken for rides, gunned down as they walked the streets of New York or otherwise disposed of. Rumors spread that the war was about to reach a climax, that both Joe and Bill Bonanno would soon be hit. Twice the council had granted Joe his life—at the time of his kidnapping and again in September 1966, at La Stella Restaurant in Queens, where a gathering of Gambino, Trafficante, Colombo, Eboli, Miranda, Carlos Marcello, and seven other major underworld leaders was interrupted by police, who called it the Little Apalachin meeting. Now the council rescinded the clemency and ordered Bonanno's execution.

With the forces mounting against him, Bonanno removed himself from the scene of battle, flying off to his home in Tucson. There nature intervened. Early in 1968, he suffered a mild heart attack. It was enough to persuade him that perhaps the time had come really to retire, and he sent back that word to the council. But his peers had heard that story before, and this time they weren't so credulous. Bombs were planted in a garage and in cars at the home of Bonanno's neighbor and close friend in Tucson, Pete Licavoli, the Syndicate's Detroit leader; another bomb was exploded on the patio of Bonanno's home; another was delivered in a box to the house and failed to explode only because it had been poorly packaged. Evidence turned up later that the bombs had been planted by an overzealous FBI agent trying to foment an internal gang war; but Bonanno, in any case, had had enough. He really retired, though surrounded constantly by bodyguards determined to protect him from further attempts by the Organization. The rule of his family fell to Sciacca, and then, a little later, to an old friend of Genovese's and Gambino's, a man with a long narcotics history named Natale Evola.

It seemed that the last obstacles to Gambino's ascension had been eliminated. But the wars that marked the years since Genovese made his grab for leadership had brought Gambino into the open; now he was visible, a target of the authorities, of his enemies and of some he had considered his allies. Meanwhile, in those same years when attention had been riveted on the Italian underworld, Lansky had been carving out new empires.

OWER, AND THE COMPULSION TO acquire it, Robert Kennedy understood very well. Few families in American history had been more obsessed with power, had sought it with greater passion than his. But what counted with the Kennedys was how power, once won, was used. For them, it was a means of ordering events and changing them, to have some say over their own destiny and the nation's. Thus, Robert Kennedy could never quite understand, and had no sympathy for those who sought power only as a means of enriching and aggrandizing themselves.

Perhaps as much as anything else, it was his moral outrage at the misuse and corruption of power that made him instrumental in the war against organized crime during the last decade of his life. He was in unique positions to fight the Mob, first as chief counsel to the Senate Select Committee on Improper Activities in the Labor or Management Field, chaired by Senator John McClellan of Arkansas, and then as U.S. attorney general, under his brother, President John F. Kennedy.

It was as counsel to the McClellan Committee in the late Fifties that Robert Kennedy got his first close look at the entangled relationships between supposedly reputable labor leaders and the underworld. The committee's charter gave it wide latitude to investigate labor racketeering and the uses and abuses of unions' pension and welfare funds. In that endeavor, the committee called to testify a motley crew of labor leaders who had arrogantly abused the power and money entrusted to them by their followers, who had entrenched themselves in office by packing union hierarchies and local offices with men whose criminal activities and associations filled pages in police records. There were outcries from some that the committee, especially its chief counsel, was antilabor, that the purpose of the investigation was to destroy the labor movement, but it soon became evident that if anyone had been antilabor, it had been the leaders who had so loudly proclaimed their devotion to unionism.

Under the guidance of Kennedy and his staff of lawyers and investigators, the McClellan Committee presented the nation with a portrait of unions held captive by venal leaders who, often in alliance with underworld powers, gorged themselves on the funds entrusted to their safekeeping. As union official after union official sat at the witness table and listened to the seamy history of his misdeeds, a distressing picture began to take shape. Labor's early idealism had vanished and in too many unions, contract negotiations seemed designed only to benefit the leaders.

The looting of the unions for personal enrichment was exemplified by James Cross in the Bakery and Confectionery Workers International Union, by Maurice Hutchenson and his friends in the United Brotherhood of Carpenters and Joiners, by a string of officials in the International Union

Robert Kennedy was the chief counsel of the McClellan Committee. His understanding of power helped him in his fight against its misuse.

of Operating Engineers, the Sheet Metal Workers International Association, the United Textile Workers of America and others.

There was the Chicago Restaurant Association, whose corruption and underworld ties nobody seemed even to bother hiding. One of its prime locals was controlled by Joseph Aiuppa, a member of the Chicago mob's ruling council with a criminal record going back to the days of Al Capone. The union's counsel had been Abraham Teitelbaum; he told a committee investigator that as far as he was concerned, Capone was "a fine gentleman." And the ruler of the entire association was Louis Romano. His record: close and continuing association with Chicago mob leaders Tony "Big Tuna" Accardo and Sam Giancana, frequent arrests for everything up to and including homicide. When questioned about a number of murders, he snarled, "Why don't you go and dig up all the dead ones out in the graveyard and ask me if I shot them, you Chinaman?"

But the main thrust of the McClellan Committee was directed at the International Brotherhood of Teamsters, Chauffeurs, Warehousemen and Helpers, the nation's largest trade union, with more than 1,600,000 members at that time. What concerned the committee most was hoodlum control of locals all over the country and the activities of the Teamsters' two most powerful officers, President Dave Beck and James Riddle Hoffa. As chairman of the Central States Conference, Hoffa was the man who really ruled the union and who would soon become its president.

Dave Beck was an almost pathetic figure. Once he had been a respected and aggressive labor leader; he had founded the Western Conference of Teamsters and had been a tough and effective bargainer, negotiating contracts that set the standards for the other conferences around the coun-

Dave Beck (left) and James Hoffa (right) controlled the Teamsters Union.

try. But the acquisition of great power corrupted Beck almost beyond reason. With his ascension to the presidency of the international union in 1952, he turned into little more than a cheap crook; the union treasury became a source of easy loans he never had to repay; the union itself bought his house at a vastly inflated price and then gave it back to him for his lifetime personal use; his union office permitted him to hold up companies such as Fruehauf Trailer for huge loans. He went before the committee declaring, "I have nothing to fear. My record is an open book." Then he took refuge in the Fifth Amendment more than 200 times. When he walked out the door, he was a broken man and soon an imprisoned one.

"The fall of Dave Beck," the committee said, "from a position of eminence in the labor-union movement is not without sadness. When named to head this rich and powerful union, he was given an opportunity to do much good for a great segment of American working men and women. But when temptation faced Dave Beck, he could not turn his back. His thievery in the final analysis became so petty that the committee must wonder at the penuriousness of the man. What would cause a man in such circumstances to succumb to the temptation of using union funds to pay for six pairs of knee drawers for $27.54, or a bow tie for $3.50? In Beck's case, the committee must conclude that he was motivated by an uncontrollable greed."

It was not so easy to dismiss or sum up Jimmy Hoffa. He was, and is, a strange and complex man, whose compulsion to power probably matched the Kennedys', though he used it in a profoundly different manner. Born poor, he left school at 16 to take a laboring job—unloading boxcars in Detroit for 17 cents an hour. Within two years he had led a successful strike and been granted a charter to form a Teamster-affiliated local in Detroit. The world in which he lived and flourished was a violent one and he luxuriated in it. "I was in a lot of fights," he boasted, "got my head broke, got banged around. My brother got shot. We had a business agent killed by a strikebreaker. . . . Our cars were bombed out. . . . There was only one way to survive—fight back." And fight he did, clawing and gouging his way to so much power in the Teamsters that when Beck was president, Hoffa could snort, "Dave Beck? Hell, I was running it while he was playing big shot. He never knew the score."

In some ways, Hoffa was the equal of the United Auto Workers' Walter Reuther, proving himself one of the ablest leaders to arise out of the labor movement. Smart, tough, clear-eyed and totally dedicated to his own ultimate ends (he didn't smoke, drink or chase women; his only passion other than the union and his own position was physical fitness), he was a master of collective bargaining. Under his leadership, Teamster members scored huge economic advances, won fringe benefits that became a model for labor in general. He

Hoffa won the presidency of the Teamsters Union but had been, in fact, ruling it for some time.

Some members of the union were not happy with the leadership.

was a supreme organizer whose skills brought thousands in totally disparate fields into the Teamster empire; and he consolidated and concentrated union power in his own hands.

But what Hoffa lacked, and what brought him the deep and abiding scorn of Kennedy and of labor leaders such as Reuther, was principles. If Reuther or the Kennedys set certain moral limits, however ill defined, on the means to achieve power and on the uses of that power, Hoffa set none. He plowed Teamster money, in the form of rarely repaid loans, into grandiose but ill-conceived land-development projects in Florida, into gambling casinos and other enterprises sponsored by his racketeer friends in Nevada. He invested Teamster funds in companies employing Teamsters and he invested his own and his family's money to take control of companies whose workers were members of his union. "I find nothing wrong with a labor leader having a business or his family having a business that may be in the same industry that that particular union has organized," he blandly replied to a question from Kennedy. And he apparently saw nothing wrong, either, with borrowing money from other Teamster officials whose tenure depended on his good will, or from companies whose prosperity and continuing labor peace depended on his whim.

To consolidate his control over the union and to expand his power, Hoffa turned to the hoodlums who had infested the union, who had been granted charters to organize and run Teamster locals. The committee came up with a list of 47 "gangsters and racketeers about whom there is testimony regarding association with Teamster officials." Hoffa, it charged, "runs a hoodlum empire, the members of which are steeped in iniquity and dedicated to the proposition that no thug need starve if there is a Teamster payroll handy. . . . Hoffa does not now have nor has he ever had any intention of moving against his racketeer friends . . . he has never moved to exercise his powers even after convicted union officials have gone to jail and even though they continue to hold office and draw salaries and even Christmas bonuses while they languish in jail."

Scoffed Hoffa in reply: "I would take each man on his own. The mere fact that he happened to know somebody would not necessarily stop me from hiring him even though the people he knew were so-called alleged gangsters. . . . I've saw too many alleged gangsters who, when you checked on the actual persons alleged to be gangsters, had no more to do with being a gangster than you are a gangster. . . . I don't even know a Syndicate exists, and I don't believe you do, either."

Who, then, were some of these "alleged gangsters" hired by Hoffa? The roster reads almost like a rogues' gallery. The business manager of Teamster Local 102 in New York, for instance, was John "Johnny Dio" Dioguardi. His ties to the Syndicate went back as far as his strong-arm days for Louis Lepke; he had been arrested and convicted of labor shakedowns, extortion, tax evasion and bankruptcy fraud; he was accused of having ordered the acid blinding of crusading labor columnist Victor Reisel in 1956. "It cannot be said, using the widest possible latitude," the committee noted, "that John Dioguardi was ever interested in bettering the lot of the workingman."

The president of Teamster Local 560 in Hoboken, New Jersey, was a man named Anthony "Tony Pro" Provenzano. Among his closest friends were Carmine "Mr. Gribbs" Tramunti, Tony Bender and Antonio "Tony Ducks" Corallo. Corallo him-

Racketeer Tony "Ducks" Corallo (left) and local union Teamster Sam Goldstein (right) denied they knew each other.

self was a Teamster official in good standing, vice-president of one local in New York and the absolute if unofficial ruler of at least four others. Did Corallo's long arrest record, his earlier narcotics conviction or the fact that his puppets held union office concern Hoffa? The New York police taped a conversation between Corallo and another union official, who said of Hoffa, "The guy told me straight out, and I ain't making, like, my own words, I'm saying his words . . . 'You want to steal, you want to rob, go ahead,' he says, 'don't get caught.' . . . The guy is, you know, fine. I mean, he don't care one way."

It was not just that Hoffa didn't care. In Los Angeles, the secretary-treasurer of Teamster Local 396, with jurisdiction over private garbage collections, was a hoodlum named Frank Matula. When Matula was convicted of perjury before a California state-assembly committee, Hoffa responded by appointing him to the Teamster board of trustees, traditionally known as the "conscience of the union," and later even persuaded prison authorities to grant Matula a furlough so that he could help audit the books of the international union.

"Malodorous as the Los Angeles garbage situation has been," the Mc-

Clellan Committee noted, "it seemed sweet-scented by comparison with conditions in the New York sector of the industry." In that city, the boss was Vincent Squillante, reputed narcotics peddler and executioner for hire to others in the underworld. But despite that reputation and union office, he was still able to pull down $10,000 a year on the side as labor-relations counsel to the Greater New York Cartmens Association. Soon, he was the dominant figure in both labor and management in the garbage business. And to edit the industry's trade paper, *The Hired Broom* (slogan: "Out of garbage there grows a rose"), Squillante hired an ex-convict turned scholar named C. Don Modica. Modica also was private tutor to the children of Joe Adonis, Willie Moretti and Albert Anastasia and he became something of a watchdog for the Anastasia interests. When Albert was murdered, Modica found it expedient to throw up his job in garbage and retire to his New Jersey home in order, he explained, to write a treatise on such American perils as progressive education, delinquency and communism.

Then there was the situation in

The confrontation between Robert F. Kennedy and James Hoffa was tense and bitter.

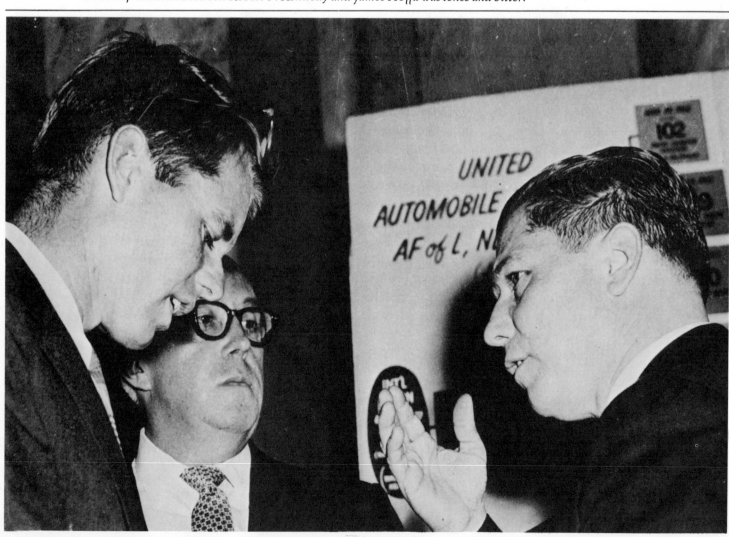

Yonkers, the Westchester County city abutting the Bronx. When the city' fathers decided to dump municipal garbage collection in favor of private cartage, they handed the contract to the Westchester Carting Company. Its president was Alfred "Nick" Ratteni, a convicted burglar and narcotics suspect. Though Teamster Local 456 had jurisdiction in Yonkers, Ratteni signed a labor contract with New York City Local 17, whose secretary-treasurer was Joseph Parisi. Parisi had a record of 11 arrests ranging from disorderly conduct to rape and homicide and his Mob ties went back to his working with Lepke and Lucky Luciano in labor extortion. The Ratteni-Parisi agreement might have gone off without a hitch had not Local 456's president, John Acropolis, objected to the encroachment into his local's preserve. When Acropolis refused to give in to threats, he was informed by one local Teamster official, "You are not that tough. Tougher guys than you have been taken care of." And Acropolis was taken care of. A few weeks later, he was gunned down as he stepped out of his home. There were no further complaints.

Gangster influence and infiltration of the Teamsters existed not just at the local levels. It permeated the central chain of command as well. The credentials of Robert "Barney" Baker that had brought favorable notice from Hoffa and other Teamster leaders included a stint as a professional boxer, a longshoreman's job and a term in prison for stink-bombing a

New York theater. He had been a close friend and working partner of John "Cockeye" Dunn, a New York waterfront hoodlum who wound up in the electric chair, and he had worked as a bouncer in a casino for Adonis, Meyer Lansky, Frank Costello and Vincent "Jimmy Blue Eyes" Aloi. Like so many other thugs, he found shelter in the house of the Teamsters, hiring on at one point as a driver in Washington, D.C., a job that led to his elevation to union office in Local 730. But Teamster leaders had bigger things in mind for Baker, and so he quit that post and moved to the Midwest, where he became an organizer for Hoffa's Central States Conference. When Kennedy questioned Hoffa about Baker's background, asking, "Does that not disturb you at all?" the Teamster boss replied, "It doesn't disturb me one iota."

Nor, apparently, did the fact that among Baker's close friends and fellow Teamster leaders was John Vitale, ruler of Local 110 in St. Louis, who was widely regarded as the Mob boss in that city.

As the evidence about hoodlum infiltration of the Teamsters and Hoffa's alliance with the Mob piled up, a determination grew in Kennedy. So morally repellent did he find Hoffa that he became obsessed with the desire to see him in prison. And that obsession grew as Hoffa seemed to live a charmed life, successfully defeating indictments growing out of charges that he had wire-tapped the phones of union officials and that he had illegally received documents be-

Hoffa had Frank Fitzsimmons elected to the newly created post of general vice-president to insure an automatic succession.

longing to the McClellan Committee.

Once Kennedy became attorney general in January 1961, the drive against Hoffa—which some saw as little more than a personal vendetta, in which illegal means were used to attain what few would deny was a just end—accelerated. Scores of grand juries were impaneled to investigate Hoffa's multifarious activities. A special unit in the Justice Department was set up, with the sole aim of getting the goods on Hoffa. That work finally paid off. In 1962, Hoffa went on trial for demanding and receiving improper payments from a company employing Teamsters. That trial ended in a hung jury, but then Hoffa was tried for attempting to bribe one of the jurors. On that charge he was convicted and sentenced to eight years in prison. In 1964, he was convicted once again, this time for improperly obtaining $20,000,000 in loans from Teamster pension funds and diverting $1,700,000 to his own use. When all the appeals on both convictions had been disposed of, Hoffa faced 13 years in prison. In March 1967, he entered the gates of Lewisburg Federal Penitentiary in Pennsylvania to begin his time.

THE "GET HOFFA" CAMPAIGN was only one of Kennedy's obsessions as attorney general. Another was organized crime as the country's political and social cancer, about which he had begun to learn so much while counsel to the McClellan Com-

mittee. Getting Hoffa was the simpler job. Organized crime had thrived during the Eisenhower Administration, partly because the enforcement arm of the Justice Department, the FBI, was led by J. Edgar Hoover, who had long insisted there was no such thing.

Kennedy, then, had two jobs. One was to get the Justice Department involved, and this he did by setting up an aggressive Organized Crime and Anti-Racketeering Section staffed by young and ambitious lawyers. The other was to somehow persuade Hoover that the Syndicate did, indeed, exist. Into his hands fell the tool that led to Hoover's grudging conversion, if not to his immediate involvement.

All his life, Joe Valachi had been a punk. From the time he was 11 and hit a teacher with a rock, for which he wound up in reform school, he had labored with no great success in the vineyards of the underworld, a common worker whose major claim to stature was his marriage to Mildred Reina, daughter of one of the early Mafia leaders slain in the Thirties during the Castellammarese War. By June 1962, Valachi's fortunes had reached their nadir. He was serving a term for narcotics in federal prison in Atlanta; there were rumors that he had turned stool pigeon; his cellmate and long-time boss, Vito Genovese, believing those rumors, had given him the kiss of death; he had narrowly escaped three attempts on his life and was certain a fourth would not be long in coming. Valachi was in a panic, and he was certain he knew to whom Genovese had given the contract for the next try at him. In the exercise yard one day, he thought he saw that would-be assassin; picking up an iron pipe, he raced across the yard and beat the man to death. Valachi had picked the wrong man. His victim was only a small-time forger with no Syndicate connections; he just happened to look like somebody else.

That mistake, Robert Kennedy would say later, provided the "biggest single intelligence breakthrough yet in combating organized crime and racketeering in the United States." For, in the weeks that followed, in peril from all sides—the government had a murder indictment against him, his underworld friends had a murder contract out on him—Valachi became what the rumors, until then untrue, had said he was, an informer. And he was probably the most important public canary since the days of Abe Reles and his revelations about Lepke, Anastasia and others in Murder, Inc., 20 years earlier.

Blessed with instant recall of almost every event in his life, and seething with hatred of Genovese and a determination to wreak revenge, Valachi spun out all he knew about organized crime for the Bureau of Narcotics and Dangerous Drugs, the FBI, the Justice Department and, in the fall of 1962, for the public before Senator McClellan's Permanent Subcommittee on Investigations.

What he provided was not a view from the top but the worm's view. It was, however, a view that spanned the decades, from the time before the Castellammarese War through the consolidations and modernizations of Luciano to the intrigues of Genovese and on and on. He might never have been present when the leaders made decisions and formulated policies, he might not have known firsthand of the rivalries and enmities among Syndicate rulers, he might have been unaware of the deep influence and high position of non-Italians. But, like a soldier in the field, which he was, Valachi helped turn the established policy into reality; he had heard all the rumors and secondhand stories, had heard the versions favored by those he served; had speculated on all the nuances and the reasons for changes in direction, on the rise or fall from grace of various superiors. Now he spun out this blend of rumor, speculation and personal knowledge. He could recite a *Who's Who* of the underworld, reveal the existence of five major crime families in New York and others around the country, tell who had killed whom and why (or at least the reasons he had been told), explain how policy had been implemented and, in the process, clear up many long-standing mysteries.

The tales that Valachi recited came as a shocking revelation to much of the country and to the senators on the McClellan Subcommittee. But for Kennedy and his anticrime unit, the tales were neither new nor particularly startling. In the Justice Department's files rested the voluminous history recited by a self-exiled *mafioso* named Nicola Gentile. Unlike Va-

Joseph Valachi told all he knew—and he knew quite a bit—about organized crime.

lachi, he had been high in the Syndicate councils during the Twenties and Thirties and so had direct knowledge and insight into the tangled events Valachi had witnessed from a much lower level. During the Eisenhower Administration, Gentile in his Sicilian exile had rambled on about his life and times to a special unit of the Justice Department. But nothing had been done with his story. When Kennedy took office, the Gentile

memoirs were resurrected, both as a check against Valachi and for an even more important purpose. And it was in this area that Valachi provided his really important breakthrough.

By rights, the war on organized crime should have been directed by Hoover. But he had no more enthusiasm for that struggle, nor any more belief in it, than he did for investigating civil rights violations or for protecting the lives of civil rights demonstrators south of the Mason-Dixon line. But when a soldier of the underworld got up in front of the television cameras and proceeded to draw Organization charts, recite names, places and events in excruciating detail, Hoover was, however reluctantly, forced to change his mind. That change was made a little easier when wiretaps and other listening devices provided the Justice Department with a new name by which to "discover" organized crime. In their conversations, mobsters had at times talked of "our thing" or, when speaking in Italian, of *cosa nostra*. Of course, it would not do to call the Organization "Our Thing"—that sounded more humorous than menacing. But to call it Cosa Nostra or, better yet La Cosa Nostra, or simply L.C.N., gave it a ring of sinister authenticity in an English-speaking world.

Acting as though he had suddenly come upon the much-rumored but consistently disbelieved mother lode, Hoover was galvanized into action—or, at least, inspired to make stentorian public pronouncements. "La Cosa Nostra," he was soon intoning, "is the largest organization of the criminal underworld in this country, very closely organized and strictly disciplined. . . . It operates on a nationwide basis, with international implications." To combat and defeat it, he would say repeatedly, would take all the forces at his command (not to mention a larger budget) and he was sending armies of FBI agents to war against L.C.N. with the kind of intense and total dedication that had

long marked his fight against domestic Communists. (This new war on organized crime, marching side by side with Hoover's continuing war on domestic Reds and other radicals, also gave him an easy alibi when the bureau was criticized for ignoring the civil rights struggle in the South. Hoover merely explained that he didn't have the funds or the agents to divert from these other, major battlegrounds. A few years later, though, when the peace movement gave rise to demonstrations against the war in Vietnam, he somehow found plenty of agents to throw into the fight against peaceniks and other social rebels.)

At first, Hoover's efforts in the organized-crime war were mainly confined to sending out publicity releases. Instead of FBI shock troops, spurred by an aroused director, using their wiretaps and bugs (legal and illegal), their informers, computers, files and all the rest of the crime-fighting arsenal developed by the bureau and turning the evidence over to the prosecutors, the G men balked and their director sulked. As former Attorney General Ramsey Clark noted, once Robert Kennedy took the lead, the FBI stayed on the sidelines until he had left the Department of Justice. "The conflict between Attorney General Kennedy and the FBI arose from the unwillingness of the bureau to participate on an equal basis with other crime-control agencies. The FBI has so coveted personal credit that it will sacrifice even effective crime control before it will share the glory of its exploits. This has been a petty and costly characteristic caused by the excessive domination of a single person, J. Edgar Hoover, and his self-centered concern for his reputation and that of the FBI."

But even Hoover's foot dragging, though it hurt, did not stop the Justice Department from opening the war. There was Attorney General Kennedy lobbying strenuously and effectively to get through Congress a host of strong new legal weapons. There was the anticrime division striking out in sudden and massive campaigns against specific targets in the underworld—illegal gambling centers in Florida, Kentucky, Arkansas and elsewhere were closed up tight and some of the operators, though not the real rulers like Lansky, were sent to jail; gangster-dominated union locals were harassed and broken and their rulers sent into courts and prisons.

The years that Robert Kennedy ran the Justice Department were years of frantic and often effective activity, and his hit-and-run tactics seemed to keep the Syndicate constantly off balance and in confusion. By the time he left office in 1964 to run for the Senate from New York, the number of federal indictments for organized criminal activity had climbed from 19 in 1960 to 687. But with his departure, the Justice Department's efforts again slacked off; the interests of the new attorney general, Nicholas B. Katzenbach, seemed directed toward advising President Lyndon Johnson more on the war in Vietnam than on the war

J. Edgar Hoover in the Sixties.

against crime. Then in 1967, the battle was stepped up once more, with the arrival of Clark as attorney general, who brought with him a dedication to defeat organized crime equal to Kennedy's and a new weapon with which to attack it—federal strike forces, set up on a semipermanent basis in a number of major cities.

"A strike force," Clark explained, "gathers and analyzes all available police intelligence about organized crime—its leaders, subordinates and activities—in a target city. By collecting relevant data possessed by all law-enforcement agencies operating in an area, an immediate and substantial reservoir of information is available for designing a plan of attack."

By the time Clark left office and Attorney General John Mitchell moved in, the work of the strike forces was resulting in more than 1000 indictments annually against members of the Syndicate, though lumped with that figure was a helter-skelter assortment ranging from street-corner narcotics pushers all the way to Carlo Gambino. Further, during the Kennedy-Clark era, massive files were accumulated on more than 300,000 Syndicate-connected businesses and businessmen. Fortunately, there were some very able prosecutors, such as Robert M. Morgenthau, the United States attorney for the Southern District of New York, who knew what to do with the evidence. Fortunately, too, the strike forces were under the control of essentially nonpolitical career officials in the Justice Department, such as Henry Petersen, head of the organized-crime section. These were men who stayed on from one administration to the next, and so even after Nixon and Mitchell assumed power in 1969 (and denounced Clark as being soft on the criminals), the work of the strike forces went on relatively unimpeded and some of the fruits of six years of labor began to ripen and fall.

And by then, even the FBI was deeply involved, though that involvement was concentrated along a narrow trail. Kennedy, Clark and their people at Justice had developed considerable sophistication. They were aware of the vastness and complexities of organized crime—spreading across ethnic lines and encompassing violent as well as victimless crimes, pandering to the illegal appetites of the public and infiltrating and controlling unions and businesses, controlling nickel-and-dime policy and international gambling, putting money onto the streets from loan sharks and legitimate lending institutions. Hoover was more simplistic. The song of Valachi had apparently convinced him that behind every crime was an Italian or a Sicilian, all wrapped in the cloak of La Cosa Nostra. And the Italian underworld initially did nothing to dissuade Hoover of this certainty. The Gallo-Profaci war and the other violent struggles of power in the Italian underworld during the Sixties made him certain that his view was the correct one.

So the main thrust of the attack was directed against the Italian-dominated branch of the Syndicate. But even with such a clear target, it was no easy thing to win victories over men who had spent their lives covering their tracks, erecting shelters of respectability and cultivating friends in high places, including Congress. It took years of hard and often frustrating work, accumulating evidence bit by bit, before a case could be made. There were some victories, of course. One of the weapons Kennedy had won from Congress was an immunity statute whereby a hoodlum, if granted immunity from prosecution, could not refuse to testify before a grand jury on grounds of self-incrimination. That law was used effectively against the Lucchese family in the years when Tommy Lucchese was in failing health and then immediately after his death. Vincent John Rao, a top Lucchese lieutenant, went to prison for five years for perjury when he decided to lie before the grand jury when granted immunity. Lower-ranking members of the Lucchese family gave in and talked, and the evidence they provided resulted in convictions of Johnny Dio for bankruptcy fraud, James "Jimmy Doyle" Plumeri for tax evasion and Tramunti

The new attorney general, Nicholas B. Katzenbach (insert) was succeeded by Ramsey Clark (bottom left) who brought a new vitality to the war against crime. He is seen here with Detective Frank Serpico.

for contempt. When Tramunti got out of prison, he moved to the leadership of the Lucchese family, with the blessings of the ruler of the Italian underworld, Carlo Gambino.

And, of course, there was Corallo, Teamster racketeer, strong-arm man and fixer extraordinary. One of Corallo's fortes was corrupting public officials, and that ability led to the messiest scandal in the administration of New York's then-Republican reform mayor, John V. Lindsay, in 1967. Even before then, Corallo had spent some time behind bars for practicing that vocation; in 1961, he had bribed a New York supreme-court judge, J. Vincent Keogh, and a former chief assistant United States attorney for Brooklyn, Elliott Kahaner. All three went to federal prison. No sooner was Corallo back on the streets than he found a new pigeon, this one named James Marcus, the water commissioner in the newly elected Lindsay Administration.

On the surface, Marcus seemed anything but a likely target for a bribe. He appeared the impeccable public servant, devoted to selfless service and already tagged to head a new superagency dealing with all of New York's environmental problems. According to the propaganda emerging from the Marcus offices, the new water commissioner had had a sparkling career in investments, had headed a major subsidiary of Interpublic, Inc., the huge public-relations firm, and was a brilliant administrator. His social connections, too, were exemplary. He was married to Lily Lodge, the actress daughter of John Davis Lodge, former governor of Connecticut and ambassador to Spain; her uncle was the estimable Henry Cabot Lodge of the Massachusetts Lodges; and Mayor Lindsay himself was the godfather of one of the Marcus children.

But behind this sterling image was the real Marcus, a man whose career was marked by one failure after another, from flunking out of college to disastrous business dealings; and a man who was weak, greedy and displayed little moral fiber. By the time he took over the water department in 1966, he was deeply in debt, heavily into the stock market on margin and seeing his investments turn sour, while his interest to his brokers was climbing to more than $1600 a month.

By then, though, Marcus had a friend. His name was Herbert Itkin, a self-proclaimed labor lawyer (whom no other New York labor lawyer had ever met). Itkin's labor law was of a special kind. He served as middleman in the passage of bribe money from hard-up businessmen to corrupt union officials, money paid to obtain large, and rarely repaid, mortgage loans from union treasuries. It was a calling that Itkin had been led to by a sometime friend, *mafioso* Jimmy Plumeri, who was then anxious to make a killing on some Teamster treasury money under his control. But on the side, Itkin was something else again. He was, he claimed, an undercover agent and informant for both the CIA and the FBI, though his information always seemed to be passed along after the fact, and after he had made his pile in the deals he informed about.

Marcus and Itkin had come together during the Lindsay campaign, when Marcus was seeking union endorsements for the Republican mayoral candidate, no easy undertaking in Democratic New York. Itkin had just the contacts Marcus needed, turning him on to Daniel Motto, president of a Queens local of the Bakery, Confectionary and Food International Union (a local that had been thrown out of respectable labor's house because it was under the control of Motto and other hoodlums). Motto obliged, setting up something called Labor's Nonpartisan League, which threw its support to Lindsay. He did even more. At Itkin's urgings, he lent the desperate Marcus enough money to gain him a little time.

Thus, when the moment came for a little financial finagling—which would line Motto's and Itkin's pockets and might also solve Marcus's pressing troubles—Marcus was easily persuaded to cooperate. The Jerome Park reservoir in the Bronx urgently needed cleaning, a job that might cost the city $1,000,000 (it actually cost $800,000-plus). Because of the urgency, it was also the kind of job that could be let, despite its size, without formal bidding, just by the water commissioner's assigning a so-called emergency contract to a qualified company.

The potential for graft in such an undertaking did not escape Marcus or Itkin or Motto. Nor did Motto and his close friend Corallo fail to appreciate the control that a little graft would give them over a rising politician like Marcus in the event Lindsay ended up in the White House (where it was evident his ambitions were directed) and took Marcus to Washington with him. The reservoir would be the tie that bound and would lead to bigger and better opportunities for graft.

A job the size of the reservoir, though, was a little out of Motto's league. It called for somebody with a lot more clout, somebody like Tony Ducks, who obligingly announced that he would do all the arranging. The graft would come to 5 percent of the contract—eventually, $42,000. Marcus could get $16,000 (just enough to take care of some of his most pressing needs but not enough to get him clear), while Motto, Corallo and Itkin would divide up the rest. That graft would come from Henry Fried and his S. T. Grand Company, which, as it happened, was actually qualified to handle the reservoir-cleaning job—in fact, had been recommended for the job by one of the water department's engineers.

The reservoir payoff was the start. As Marcus's needs kept spiraling, Itkin kept coming to the rescue. He found some friendly loan sharks willing to advance Marcus some costly cash. Thus, when the potential for the biggest killing of all presented itself, Marcus needed no urging. Consolidated Edison Company of New York was trying to get permission to rebuild some transmission lines into

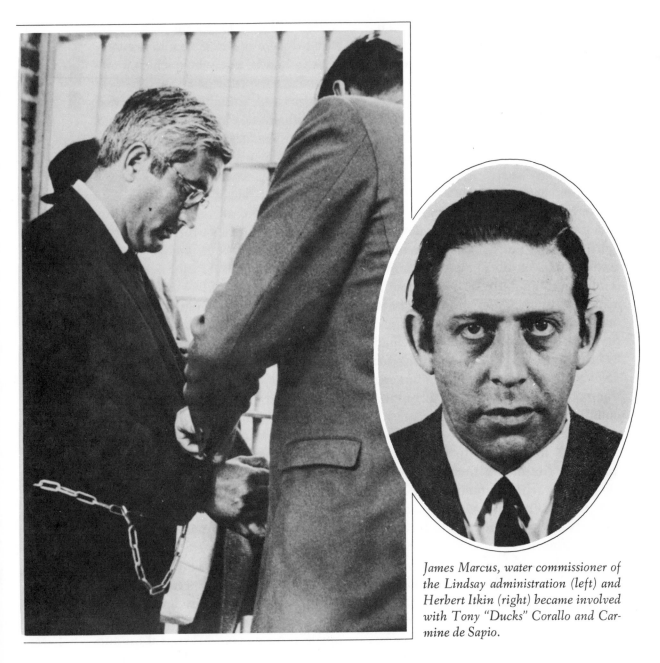

James Marcus, water commissioner of the Lindsay administration (left) and Herbert Itkin (right) became involved with Tony "Ducks" Corallo and Carmine de Sapio.

the city, and Water Commissioner Marcus was the man to grant that permission. The cost of the work was going to run well up into the millions, and the possibilities of diverting some of that cash into a few private pockets were not lost on Marcus, Itkin or Coral-lo, nor on Fried, either, who saw in the power of the Marcus pen some opportunities for himself. The figuring went that if Marcus delayed signing the authorization long enough, Con Ed would become desperate, would be willing to pay whatever graft was demanded, would be willing, even, to give Corallo a profitable contract to haul used copper from its plants and give Fried a lot more business than the $5,000,000 to $10,000,000 he was then doing for the utility.

But to approach Con Ed it would take somebody of considerably greater stature than Corallo. Such a man was Carmine DeSapio, once the all-powerful leader of Tammany Hall and still a politician to be reckoned with. DeSapio might be a Democrat and Marcus an officeholder in a Republican administration, but when it came to things like money and graft, nobody cared much about politics. Besides, the spoils in New York had been split along nonpartisan lines for decades, the only real friction among the political bosses arising during the months preceding an election.

In his discreet way, DeSapio made the approaches to Con Ed, to persuade the utility that the way to do business with Commissioner Marcus was to line his pockets and the pockets of his friends, including DeSapio himself. As one witness later described a luncheon meeting at the fashionable L'Aiglon restaurant on Manhattan's East Side, "Mr. DeSapio said he knew the Department of Water Supply and Con Ed were two vital organizations in supplying the lifeblood of the city and he was concerned—he had heard their relationships were not particularly good. . . . He felt he might be of some assistance to Con Ed . . . to act as some sort of referee."

In this oblique manner, the nego-

tiations for a major payoff dragged on. But before any money could actually change hands, the whole scheme collapsed. An investor in a company that Marcus and Itkin had established complained to Manhattan District Attorney Frank Hogan about the way his money was being handled. Hogan, and soon United States Attorney Morgenthau, began looking into the tangled affairs of Marcus and his friends, and the more they looked, the more they found. Suddenly it was time to cut and run, and every man ran for himself. Itkin rushed to his FBI contacts and belatedly spilled the story of the whole conspiracy (keeping the money that had been his share of the payoffs and turning in, as evidence, only the bank wrappers the money had come in). Trapped and facing a long prison sentence, Marcus suddenly resigned his job as water commissioner, to the shock and dismay of his patron, the mayor. He then took himself to Hogan and to Morganthau, telling his side of the plot, agreeing to be a witness against his fellow conspirators in the hope of leniency.

Then the trials began. Marcus, Corallo, Motto and Fried were convicted for their roles in the reservoir payoffs. Because of his repentant and cooperative attitude, Marcus got off with 15 months in prison; Fried and Motto each got two years and Corallo, three. With Marcus and Itkin the chief witnesses, Corallo and DeSapio were convicted in the Con Ed conspiracy, with DeSapio going to jail for two years and Corallo for another four and a half on top of the earlier sentence. As for Itkin, though indicted, he was never brought to trial. His FBI benefactors protected him. But that protection took the form of residence under guard at a military base, for Itkin was convinced, he said, that should he wander the streets again, he would be a target for a bullet from one of Corallo's friends in the Mob.

To some, it must often have seemed that the government's war against organized crime was not only directed solely against Italians but was being fought only in the streets and courtrooms of New York. Certainly, New York was the focus of a major drive and it was the struggle there against the principal crime families and their leaders—Gambino, Lucchese, Joseph Profaci, Joseph Bonanno and the rest—that got the biggest headlines. But there were plenty of mobsters elsewhere around the country who were not being ignored. Chicago boss Giancana realized this all too well.

Giancana had worked his way up from the bottom in the Capone manner and in the Chicago style—before he was 20, he had been arrested three times for murder and by the time he took command of the Chicago Mob in 1957, his record listed 60 arrests. But as he matured in the ways of the Organization, Giancana learned to forego muscle, cultivate the right people and put good friends in the right places. By the early Sixties, he had his son-in-law, Anthony Tisci, in-

stalled as the $900-a-month secretary to Chicago Congressman Roland Libonati, a member of the House Judiciary Committee who seemed to go out of his way to sponsor bills that helped Giancana and his friends avoid government surveillance.

An even closer friend was Frank Sinatra. Giancana hoped that cultivating Sinatra's friendship would help him resolve some of his legal troubles. In the end, though, it helped Giancana not at all and did considerable damage to the singer. Sinatra had thrown all his energies into the presidential campaign of John F. Kennedy in 1960 and hoped that with Kennedy's election he would be welcomed at the White House; he further expected that his own estate in Palm Springs would become a vacation spot for the new President and even built an addition with this in mind. But Robert Kennedy killed Sinatra's hopes of forming a close relationship with the president. His Justice Department agents kept stumbling across Sinatra's name as they delved into the dealings of the Fischettis, New England Mob boss Raymond Patriarca and others in the underworld hierarchy. Particularly disturbing were the reports of Sinatra's relationship with Giancana. In the early Sixties, Sinatra had acquired a controlling interest in the Cal-Neva Lodge, a luxurious hotel-casino on the California-Nevada border overlooking Lake Tahoe. Obviously, the singer wasn't going to run it himself. But the man he installed as manager was Paul D'Amato, a New Jersey mobster of

Giancana (right) was a good friend of singer Phyllis McGuire (top left) and an old friend of Frank Sinatra.

long standing. According to the stories that reached Kennedy, D'Amato's real purpose at Cal-Neva was to take care of the Giancana interests; the Chicago leader had boasted that through Sinatra he owned a piece of the lodge.

If such reports were true, Sinatra was in deep trouble with the Nevada Gaming Board. Giancana was on the board's black list, one of 11 top mobsters barred from owning or even visiting a casino in the state on pain of the casino's losing its license. Then, in 1963, Giancana actually showed up at the lodge with his constant companion, Phyllis McGuire of the singing McGuire Sisters. Sinatra turned up about the same time and the two were seen in close company. The gaming board demanded an explanation. Sinatra said he hadn't invited Giancana to the lodge; and he promised that thenceforth he would avoid contacts with him in Nevada; but then he added that Sam Mooney was an old friend and it was his business if he wanted to see him outside the state. With all its past troubles over mobster control of casinos and skimming operations, the last thing the gaming board needed was a big casino owner who openly and blatantly paraded his friendship with a top gangster. The board initiated formal proceedings to strip Sinatra of his gambling license at Cal-Neva. Some powerful friends tried to come to Sinatra's aid. Governor Grant Sawyer was told how unfair it was to persecute the singer and how he might be the beneficiary of large campaign contributions. When

this subtle approach failed, Sinatra voluntarily sold his interest in the lodge.

There was little doubt that Sinatra blamed many of his problems on Robert Kennedy. Through the succeeding years, his enmity toward the Kennedys and anyone associated with them increased (his once-close friend Peter Lawford, a Kennedy in-law, was even banished from the Sinatra circle). By 1968, all his energies were devoted to beating back Robert Kennedy's bid for the Democratic presidential nomination. And after Kennedy's murder, Sinatra turned up with some new and lasting friends, Richard Nixon and Spiro Agnew—and the Palm Springs quarters that had been designed for John Kennedy became a second home to Agnew, the new vice-president.

As for Giancana, it's possible that he began to have second thoughts about how valuable a friend Sinatra actually was. For he became a primary target for Kennedy's anticrime unit and the immunity law that had been passed at the attorney general's urging was used to nail him. Soon after his 1963 visit to Cal-Neva, he was summoned before a grand jury, granted immunity and then grilled about the Mob and his role in it. Giancana decided that his best course was silence, which earned him a year in jail. When he was released, it was obvious that the government's interest in him had not diminished. And it was obvious, too, that his much-publicized flings had earned him the displeasure of his Chicago associates.

So he took himself off to Mexico, Argentina and other southern regions, leaving the rule in Chicago to the two old Capone mobsters, Accardo and Paul "The Waiter" Ricca, the same men he had displaced nearly a decade before.

IF THE MOUNTING TROUBLES OF Italian mobsters worried the Gambinos, Accardos and the rest, they didn't bother Meyer Lansky. As a Jew, he was, according to Hoover and the FBI, only an associate member of La Cosa Nostra and so of less importance. This mistaken assessment suited Lansky perfectly. All during the late Fifties and through much of the Sixties, as the heat on the Italians increased, Lansky was off building a bigger and more lucrative gambling empire.

At first, this empire appeared shaky. In late 1958, Fidel Castro and his 26th of July revolutionaries came down from their Sierra Maestra stronghold and by New Year's Day 1959 had taken control of Cuba. Batista had fled with millions looted from the Cuban treasury and close behind him were Lansky and his Syndicate partners. The few who remained, hoping that Castro would become another Batista, keeping the casinos going and taking a cut for himself, were first jailed and then unceremoniously thrown out of the country. Celebrating the end of the Batista regime, the Cubans went on an orgy of slot-machine smashing. The casino era in Havana was over.

And it was not long, either, be-fore the illegal casino business in the United States was suffering under the onslaught of Kennedy's anticrime forces.

A farsighted man, Lansky had already planned for such exigencies. It was not far from Cuba, or Miami, to the warm sands of the Bahamas. American tourists had been streaming there for years and, with the closing of the Cuban playground, the tourist boom would surely be staggering. So one day in 1960, Lansky got off a plane in Nassau and taxied to the offices of Sir Stafford Sands, the islands' 300-pound, glass-eyed minister of finance and taxation and effective leader of the Bay Street Boys, the white power structure that ruled the Bahamas. Lansky had a proposition to make—one that would enrich Sands and guarantee a tourist invasion (and that might, if Sands and his fellow white politicians so desired, provide some employment and considerable economic benefits to the black majority, thereby keeping it docile). According to Sands, Lansky offered him $2,000,000 (others have put the offer at a mere $1,000,000), to be deposited for his personal use in one of those handy numbered Swiss accounts, if he would get legislation enacted to permit gambling.

Sands said he turned Lansky down, but the evidence indicates otherwise, for soon Lansky's ideas became reality with the help of Sands and two dubious characters. One was Wallace Groves, an American financial manipulator who had immigrated to the Bahamas after serving a prison term for mail fraud. He struck up a close friendship with Sands, who, in 1955, drew up and signed into law the Hawksbill Creek Act, which gave Groves vast tracts of land on Grand Bahama Island at $2.80 an acre. The only proviso was that Groves agree to develop the area and dredge a deepwater port, which would become Freeport, at the mouth of Hawksbill Creek. The other was Canadian-born Louis A. Chesler, close friend of Lansky (they had cooperated in some shady Canadian mining schemes), a successful Florida real-estate promoter with a firm called General Development Company and partner of Lansky ally, John Pullman.

With Sands as their attorney (and with Lansky, as usual, playing Svengali), Groves and Chesler formed Bahamas Amusements, Ltd., and proceeded with plans to turn Grand Bahama Island into a tourist attraction, complete with the 250-room Lucayan Beach Hotel. It was not long before the real purpose of that hotel was apparent. There was a law in the Bahamas banning gambling; but there was another statute, enacted in 1939 at the urging of Sands, permitting himself, as the minister of finance and taxation, to grant certificates of exemption from the law. In 1963, the attorney for Bahamas Amusements negotiated just such a certificate of exemption for the Lucayan Beach Hotel; and as his legal fee for handling this negotiation with himself, Sands received $1,800,000.

So gambling went to Grand Bahama, with most of the equipment obtained from the closed illegal casinos in the United States. With the gambling went all the old familiar faces from Lansky-run casinos in the States and in Havana—Max Courtney, Charles Brudner, Dino Cellini and others. And with these old familiar faces went the high rollers, on Syndicate-organized junkets from every major city in the United States. So successful was the Lucayan Beach that Groves began selling off some of the land he bought at $2.80 an acre. The going price for some of it was as high as $2000 a front foot. Some of it even went to competitors, such as the King's Inn Casino. But there was plenty of room for another casino and, besides, King's Inn had been built by Daniel K. Ludwig, a billionaire recluse who had dredged the Freeport harbor for Groves and who just happened to lease the King's Inn to two of Lansky's old friends, Morris Landsburgh, proprietor of Miami Beach's Eden Roc Hotel, and Sam Cohen (in 1969, both would be indicted with Lansky for Las Vegas skimming operations).

Still, Grand Bahama was only an out island. The real wealth lay in Nassau, tempting Lansky and other men of means. One was millionaire Huntington Hartford. Years before, he had bought Hog Island in Nassau Bay, renamed it Paradise Island and lobbied strenuously but unsuccessfully for a bridge to Nassau and a certificate of exemption. Suddenly, in 1965, Minister Sands had a change of heart. Not toward Hartford but with regard to gambling on Paradise Island. He

Meyer Lansky was briefly out of business because of the Cuban revolution...

announced that he had been hired as attorney by a partnership of Mrs. Wallace Groves (most of Groves's holdings were in his wife's name) and a Tampa corporation called Mary Carter Paint Company (by then, promoter Chesler had been frozen out). In the name of that partnership, Sands applied to himself and easily obtained a certificate of exemption to permit Paradise Island gambling. At the same time, he announced the imminent construction of a toll bridge to the island. As for Hartford, he, too, was frozen out, though permitted to retain a minority interest in the island itself.

At first nothing seemed strange about the deal—at least no stranger than usual. Groves, after all, had made a success of the Grand Bahama operation. And Mary Carter now had a financial interest in the Bahamas, having bought 1300 acres on Grand Bahama and turned them into a subdivision. Besides, a major stockholder in Mary Carter was one Thomas E. Dewey, former racket buster, former governor of New York, former Republican candidate for president, now senior partner in a prestigious Wall Street law firm and close friend and advisor to another prominent Wall Street lawyer, Richard Nixon.

Before this new Bahamian venture got fully under way, however, the lid blew off. Reporters for *The Wall Street Journal* did some digging and what they uncovered won them a Pulitzer Prize. They turned up a seamy story of massive payoffs to the white rulers of the islands, from the prime minister on down, to gain gambling concessions. The ensuing outcry led to a general election, and black voters turned out in a massive wave. When the votes were counted, the Bahamas, for the first time, came under the rule of blacks, with the Progressive Liberal Party in control and a black prime minister named Lynden O. Pindling.

But Lansky and his friends had, in fact, hedged their bets on the Bay Street Boys. Support, some clandestine, some open, had also gone to Pindling—including the use of a helicopter for him to tour the islands

…but found new fertile fields to plow in Grand Bahama Island and Freeport.

courtesy of a Lansky associate, Mike McLaney. Lansky knew that if Pindling tried even partially to live up to his promises of bettering the lives of blacks, he would need the gamblers; they would be the most important source of revenue.

But first, as prime minister, Pindling felt the need to shatter his opposition, to totally discredit the former white rulers. This he did by setting up a Royal Commission of Inquiry. It revealed the whole story of payoffs and corruption, the venality of Sands, the dealings of Groves and Chesler, even the manipulations and control of Lansky. Some of the peripheral testimony, though, made even the commissioners a little uneasy. Courtney, for instance, talked at length about his prodigious bookmaking activities in the States. His customers, he said, included some of the country's most important men. Such as whom? he was asked. Such as one-time Vice-President Nixon, he answered. (The allegation has never been denied.)

Then Pindling moved to assure Lansky and the gambling fraternity that he was, at heart, their true friend. When Sands announced that Groves was withdrawing from the Paradise Island enterprise, Mary Carter was given the go-ahead. Within a year, it had not one but two casinos— the Nassau Bay Club and the Paradise Island Casino. Of course, the American underworld was no longer involved. Well, only to the extent that the manager of one of the clubs was Lansky's man Eddie Cellini (brother

of Dino) and behind the tables were a lot of familiar faces from the Lansky circle. But that didn't deter the world's elite from jetting into Nassau to a gala celebration that opened gambling's new mecca in the Caribbean. And it didn't deter Wall Street Attorney Nixon from taking time out from his incipient presidential campaign to attend as an honored guest.

But then Mary Carter—or Resorts International, as it called itself after selling off its paint division— had an especial fondness for Nixon as well as Nixon's closest friend, Charles "Bebe" Rebozo, the one-time Florida filling-station operator who made his first millions selling recapped tires during World War II and then graduated to real estate, banking and other enterprises. During the 1968 Republican Convention in Miami Beach, the company offered Nixon free use of its yacht to rest and relax from the campaign rigors and bade him visit Paradise Island often after he reached the White House (the Secret Service said no to that, not when the casino catered to so many shady characters). And Nixon returned some of the favors. One of his Secret Service guards at the time of his vice-presidency, later the security director of the Nixon campaign headquarters in Miami Beach and later yet security director for the inauguration, was James Golden. When his work for Nixon was done, he moved on to Resorts International, as deputy director of security.

As for Rebozo, when 900 shares of IBM stock turned up at his Key

Biscayne Bank in 1968 as collateral for a loan—stock that turned out to have been stolen—one of the men Rebozo called to check on the stock and the loan was James Crosby, "the chairman of the board of Resorts International and an old friend of mine."

Through the Sixties, then, the money poured across the tables on Grand Bahama and Paradise Island. And Lansky's gambling empire expanded through much of the rest of the Caribbean, including Haiti, and even across the Atlantic to England. As fast as it flowed into the casinos' coffers, much of it flowed out again. For the venerable Lansky technique of the skim was working well and by then, Lansky and his associates had ready places for that cash to rest. A good part went into the Bank of Miami Beach and the Miami National Bank, which the government would later charge served as major depositories for skimmed funds.

Who ran them? It was no secret anywhere that the Bank of Miami Beach was Lansky's bank in the United States. The Miami National Bank was under the control of the Teamsters Central, Southwest and Southeast Pension Fund between 1959 and 1964. Then it passed into the hands of Lansky's close friend Cohen. But neither bank was the final resting place for the skim from Las Vegas or the Caribbean. From there it moved across the Atlantic to Swiss banks, one being the Mob-controlled Exchange and Investment Bank of Switzerland (among its officers, Lansky aides Ben Siegelbaum and Ed Levinson).

From Switzerland, the money went to a thousand different places: back to the United States in the form of loans to and investments in legitimate businesses as the wedge for Syndicate takeover and into dozens of Syndicate operations. Later it was rumored that much of the money also wended its way into investments in Bernard Cornfeld's grandiose Investors Overseas Service.

By the end of the Sixties, the tentacles of the Lansky octopus stretched in every direction, but its appearance was becoming deceptive. Lansky was growing old and he was beginning to attract some of the attention that traditionally had focused almost entirely on the Italian Mob. The world was changing and the face of organized crime was changing with it.

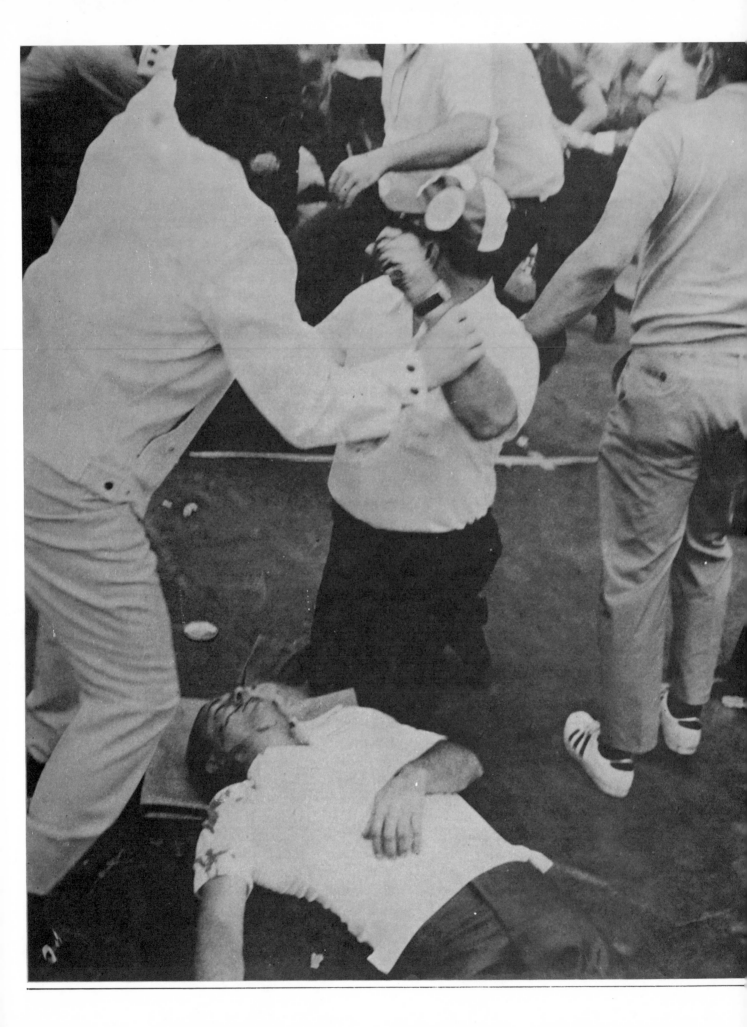

12
THE AMERICAN NIGHTMARE

WITH CONSIDERABLE JUS-tification, Italian-Americans by the beginning of the 1970s were seething. In the previous 20 years—since the Kefauver hearings and on through the McClellan investigation and disclosures of Joe Valachi—Italians and gangsters had become almost synonymous. The American public was devouring Mario Puzo's *The Godfather*, first as a book and then as a movie, and it was generally agreed that this must be the real inside story of the strange world inhabited by the sons of Italy, that everyone must be either a Don Vito Corleone, his son Michael or someone owing allegiance to them. These suspicions were only reinforced by Gay Talese's *Honor Thy Father*, the story of the family of Joe Bonanno and his son Bill.

It seemed that everyone was talking about the Mafia and La Cosa Nostra, and it seemed to Italian-Americans that everyone with an Italian name was suspected of membership in the underworld. Forget about Arturo Toscanini and Gian-Carlo Menotti, about painter Joseph Stella and architect Pietro Belluschi, about John Volpe and Joseph Alioto, about Joe DiMaggio and all the rest. Remember only Lucky Luciano and Vito Genovese, Joe Profaci and Carlo Gambino, Al Capone and Albert Anastasia.

It was a sore point, and not only with the mass of honest Italian-Americans. The Mob, too, was distressed, for the public preoccupation with hoods whose names ended in a vowel seemed to stir the authorities to greater efforts against them. No member of the underworld was angrier than Joseph Colombo. He might have been the youngest ruler in the councils of organized crime, head of a major family since 1963 when he was only 40; he might have a voice in Syndicate policy decisions and power over hundreds of hoodlums; he might have riches from gambling in Brooklyn and Queens, loan-sharking in Manhattan, thievery at the airports around New York, cigarette smuggling from the South and a dozen other rackets—wealth enough to own a home in Brooklyn and a country estate, replete with tennis court, swimming pool and horse track for the stable he had lately acquired (all on the salary of a real-estate salesman). But he deeply resented being legally harassed and socially snubbed as a wop mobster, for Colombo was, in every way, upwardly mobile.

As the 1970s began, everywhere Colombo turned he found his ambitions blocked. His underworld peers considered him only a puppet of Carlo Gambino, the man who had put him on the throne of the old Joe Profaci family and who had emerged as the first real and virtually unchallenged boss of bosses in the Italian Syndicate since the days of Lucky Luciano. And the law also had him marked after he was picked up in 1967 in company with Gambino and Philadelphia boss Angelo Bruno at the House of Chan restaurant in Man-

Joe Colombo fought for a minority: the mobsters.

hattan. He could hardly take a step without stumbling over a New York City cop, an agent of the FBI or a Justice Department attorney.

These were, of course, the perils and tribulations that most underworld leaders had long since learned to live with. But most of those leaders were, by then, aging men who had matured during the great underworld wars of Prohibition days, and their stoic acceptance had been bred by necessity. Colombo was a new kind of leader—young, American-born, impatient and easily frustrated.

In the spring of 1970, Colombo's

son, Joseph, Jr., was arrested by federal authorities. The charge: that he had melted down coins into silver ingots, whose value was greater than the face value of the dimes, quarters and half-dollars. Colombo was certain the arrest was only part of the government's constant badgering of him, that it was a frame (which was not unlikely in view of the fact that the charges were dismissed when the government's chief witness admitted in open court that he had lied in accusing young Colombo).

But Colombo sensed something else. The arrest could provide him with the opportunity to break free of Gambino, to challenge the decades-old cautions and dictates of the Syndicate, to become a man of stature not just in the shadowy world of crime but in the larger world of respectable society. With calculation born of frustration, he decided to parlay the arrest of his son into a major cause, to use it to play upon the legitimate grievances of all Italian-Americans over their universal Mafia image, and to seize the mantle of leadership in that cause.

Colombo, of course, was not the first Mob leader to sense that bitterness nor the first to exploit it. But in the past, the Mob had acted in its typically discreet and hidden way, as in the campaign against one of America's favorite television shows of the Sixties, *The Untouchables*, wherein Eliot Ness battled the Chicago Mob in the days of Capone, and every hero was Anglo-Saxon and every villain Italian. With the covert backing of the

Syndicate, an organization called the Federation of Italian-American Democratic Organizations was established under the leadership of Alfred Santangelo, a New York City congressman; the Mob's hand was nowhere to be seen, on the surface. The organization united the Italian-American community in a boycott of Chesterfield cigarettes, the program's sponsor; and in March 1961 Chesterfield bowed to the pressure and withdrew its backing of the show. *The Untouchables* died soon after, and so did the organization. In 1967, another attempt was made to foster a better Italian-American image, this time with the formation of the American-Italian Anti-Defamation League whose president was Frank Sinatra. But that project was aborted by the violent objections of the Anti-Defamation League of B'nai B'rith over the use of a name so similar and by disclosures of Sinatra's underworld associations.

There was a general feeling among many that the Italian-American community was just too disparate, dispirited and lethargic to be galvanized into any kind of concerted, long-term effort. But Joe Colombo thought otherwise. During the previous decade, the country had been swept by demonstrations—peaceful and violent—spreading from the civil rights drives in the South to the ghettos of the cities, moving outward and encompassing the nation's youth in opposition to the Vietnam War and domestic social ills. The Italian community, basically conserva-

tive, had stood to one side, giving vent only to a kind of hard-hat opposition to radicalism. But Colombo had the feeling that the techniques and successes of the young rebels had not been lost on the Italians and that if they could be made to believe their own self-image and social position were at stake, they could be mobilized and led into the streets.

The cause would be the blanket portrait of all Italians as gangsters, and the harassment and prejudice of the authorities. And there was a most conspicuous target—the FBI. Under

Colombo thought the arrest of his son, Joseph Jr. (bottom), was pure and simple harassment.

J. Edgar Hoover, the bureau had belatedly "discovered" the Mob and had been pouring out a flood of publicity about La Cosa Nostra and Italian thugs. Within days of his son's arrest, Colombo and a small group of his friends, mainly members of his underworld family, showed up outside FBI headquarters on Manhattan's Upper East Side, picketing and chanting slogans. Pressure was put on Italian merchants and others to join the campaign, and soon nearly 5000 demonstrators were parading outside the FBI office almost every night, chanting, "Hi-dee-ho, the FBI has got to go." In a van was Colombo, stridently directing the chorus and giving loud orations to anyone who approached.

It was as though he had released a tightly coiled spring. Smiles greeted him as he walked through the Italian neighborhoods, unsolicited offers of help poured in. When the government indicted Colombo for tax evasion, for perjury in lying about his criminal past when applying for a real-estate license, for contempt in refusing to answer questions under a grant of immunity before a grand jury, these actions seemed only to confirm his charges. Public support grew, and Gambino and the other Mob leaders, watching from the sidelines with some consternation, decided to give Colombo at least partial support.

Late in the spring, Colombo announced the formation of the Italian-American Civil Rights League to rally Italian-Americans: They could be proud of their heritage, and in unity they would have the strength to fight the authorities, to combat the Italian-gangster stereotype. The league, Colombo said, would demonstrate its strength and the strength of the community at an Italian-American Unity Day rally on June 29, 1970, at New York's Columbus Circle.

The strength was there. On the day of the demonstration, Italian-owned stores and businesses all over New York closed—not just a few because of the suggestions of soldiers in the Colombo family who had dropped by during preceding weeks. More than 50,000 people mobbed Columbus Circle, waving small red, black and white Italian flags and roaring approval of Colombo as he stood on a flag-decked platform and shouted, "I say there is a conspiracy against me, against all Italian-Americans. . . . But you and Joe Colombo are together today under God's eye . . . and those who get in our way will feel his sting." For the politicians, it was an educating and unnerving experience. Italian-Americans were finally comporting themselves as an organized pressure group to be reckoned with and Colombo was emerging as a leader who could direct that pressure. Nearly every major politician in the city and the state sat, a little nervously, on the platform with him and spoke a few words of support. Within weeks, even Governor Nelson Rockefeller accepted honorary membership in the league. About the only politician of note to offer criticism was John Marchi, a conservative Staten Island Republican, himself of

Italian descent. He was sure a Mob-backed betterment society was about the last thing needed, especially when it was offering the "preposterous theory that we can exorcise devils by reading them out of the English language. . . . I have only the feeling that the Italian-Americans as well as the larger community have been had."

Few paid much attention to Marchi's cautions, or the cautions of *The New York Times* and other newspapers. Colombo had become a hero. He had emerged from the shadows and was glorying in adulation. Suddenly he was everywhere, giving interviews to reporters (though not to those with a background of investigating the organization), appearing on television talk shows, attending public events. He was named Man of the Year by the *Tri-Boro Post*, a weekly newspaper; was guest of honor at a $125-a-plate dinner attended by 1450 people. The league flourished—Colombo claiming more than 150,000 members who anted up an average of $10 in dues each. New York's Felt Forum was the scene of a huge, star-studded benefit, with entertainment provided by Frank Sinatra, Sammy Davis, Jr., and others, for such unlikely guests as liberals Paul O'Dwyer, Allard Lowenstein and Richard Aurelio. The league reaped $500,000 from that affair, supposedly earmarked for such charities as a hospital and clinic.

The league and Colombo began to pick targets and apply pressure. It paid off. Television commercials plugging products with Italian-accented actors crying, "Momma mia, datsa somma spicy meatball," vanished. Movie producer Al Ruddy agreed to eliminate all references to Mafia or Cosa Nostra from his adaption of *The Godfather* and to donate the proceeds from opening night to a league-sponsored charity—an agreement that won him sharp criticism from *The New York Times* and from Marchi, but that won him, as well, the benevolent cooperation of a covey of hoodlums in the making of the movie.

Colombo could, perhaps, take his greatest satisfaction in the way he made the federal government crawl. Attorney General John N. Mitchell announced that the Justice Department would no longer talk about the Mafia or La Cosa Nostra but would use only the bland, though perhaps more accurate, terms like Syndicate, and a number of state governors made the same announcements. Even the FBI caved in; it, too, would drop the old appelations, and its approved television series, *The FBI* would no longer have underworld characters with Italian names.

All was high adventure and success for Colombo. But as time passed, there was no such corresponding euphoria within the underworld hierarchy. For more than half a century, the guiding principle had been secrecy; success was predicated on anonymity. But there was Colombo, luxuriating in the sunshine, and the reflected rays were striking the other bosses.

Initially, Gambino had been loathe to intervene. Colombo was his

Joe Colombo, three days before the shooting, points out the site for the second Italian-American Unity Day.

protégé, and if his league's efforts could take some of the heat off gangsters, so much the better. But while the league ended the official use of the terms Mafia and Cosa Nostra, it seemed to antagonize the government into greater efforts against the Mob. Just as distressing to the other leaders were the rumors that Colombo was pocketing a goodly share of the league's income and not splitting with them. By early 1971, disenchantment was widespread.

Almost at this moment, Crazy Joe Gallo walked out of prison and moved to pick up the reins of his shattered faction of the Colombo family. Within weeks, Gallo was complaining loudly and bitterly that all the promises he had made to end the Gallo-Profaci

War of the early Sixties had been forgotten and that the fortunes of his people were no better off under Colombo than they had been under Profaci, against whom he'd rebelled. He demanded reparations, specifically $100,000 in damages and a fair split of the rackets. Colombo rejected the demands. Gallo began to mutter threats, and those threats found him some sympathetic allies. One was Carmine "The Snake" Persico, a major Colombo lieutenant who had been fretfully watching the declining fortunes of the family as Colombo spent more and more time on league business. He would not be averse to using Gallo to unseat Colombo before dispensing with the unreliable killer.

Another sympathetic listener was Gambino. As the date for Unity Day, June 28, 1971, approached, signs were mounting that it would not be the happy event of the year before. Gambino's men began to withdraw from offices in the league, and so did the men of the other leaders. Tony Scotto, son-in-law of Albert Anastasia and himself now a major power on the waterfront, said he had no intention of showing up on the platform as he had in 1970 and, further, this year he was not going to give dockworkers the day off with pay. There were troubles in the Italian neighborhoods, too. Colombo soldiers telling shopkeepers to close up for the day and post signs announcing the rally, were followed by Gallo forces and those of other leaders warning the merchants to stay open and take the posters down. A number of Colombo canvassers were even beaten and chased out of the neighborhoods.

If Colombo was worried, he did not show it. On the morning of June 28, he turned up early with a crew of bodyguards and well-wishers, wandered through the noisy crowd—noticeably smaller than a year earlier—shaking hands and talking animatedly. Suddenly, a black man, Jerome A. Johnson, posing as a newspaper photographer, approached. A step away from Colombo he stopped, pulled out a pistol and fired three shots directly into Colombo's head. The stunned bodyguards reacted after only a moment, firing directly at Johnson.

In the pools of blood where Johnson lay dead and Colombo critically wounded (he did not die, though his brain was so severely damaged that he became little more than a vegetable), Unity Day and the Italian-American Civil Rights League were shattered beyond repair.

Behind the attack on Colombo, both his friends and authorities were sure, was Gallo, using the friendships he had cultivated with black convicts while in prison to recruit an assassin who would not be connected to him. Gallo was picked up, questioned and then released. For the next months, he stayed inside his house in Brooklyn, refusing to show himself and so become a target.

But, early in 1972, Gallo's life took a sudden turn. He divorced his wife and within months married a young hairdresser with a daughter of her own. And he began to cultivate a

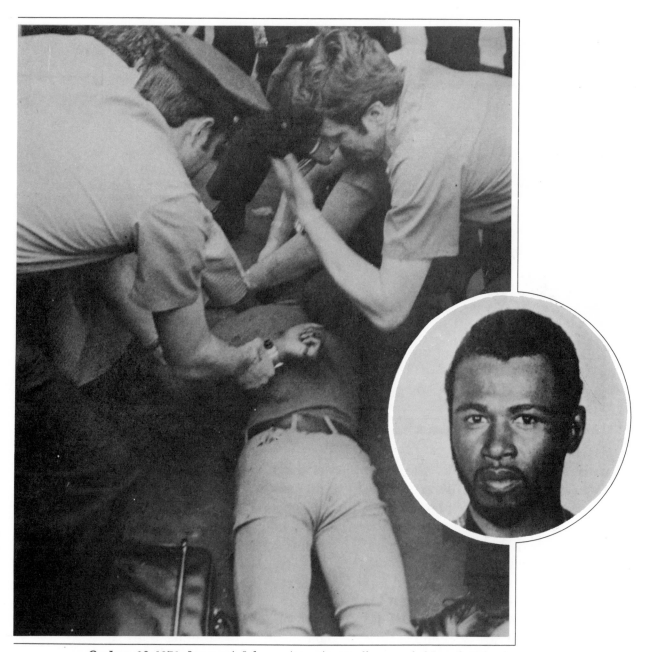

On June 28, 1972, Jerome A. Johnson (insert) critically wounded Joseph Colombo and was himself shot.

new circle of friends totally alien to the underworld, show-business celebrities like Jerry and Marta Ohrbach (with whom he was considering collaboration on an autobiography), Neil Simon, producer-director Hal Prince, actress Joan Hackett and others. He spent much of his time at the Ohrbachs' home in Greenwich Village, went to Broadway shows

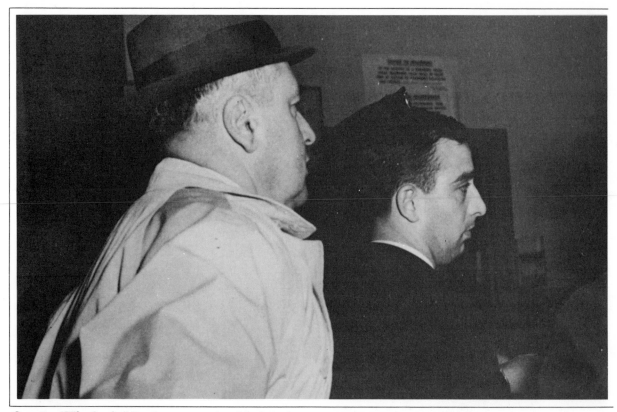

Carmine "The Snake" Persico was convicted for hijacking.

with them, to Elaine's, the "in" watering hole of the literary establishment, to Sardi's. He played chess, talked about Camus, reflected on life. He provided, said one of his new friends, "refreshing insight and intelligence in a world of clichés."

Though Gallo protested to his new friends that he had left the old world behind, there were indications to the contrary. According to underworld rumors, while he was frequenting the intellectual salons, he was also trying to muscle his way into some of the rackets controlled by Persico now that Carmine the Snake had been sent away to Atlanta on a 14-year stretch for hijacking. In the un-

derworld, and particularly in the remnants of the Colombo mob, it was open season on Crazy Joe. But all efforts to trap him or lure him into an ambush failed—until April 7, 1972. Only three weeks remarried, Gallo decided to celebrate; he took his new bride, her ten-year-old daughter, his sister and a bodyguard named Peter Diapoulas on the rounds, touring the Copacabana and other night spots and winding up, about four in the morning, at Umbertos Clam House on Mulberry Street in Little Italy. Suddenly, the door burst open and four men entered with drawn pistols. Gallo looked up, snarled, "You son of a bitch," and received two slugs in reply. He stumbled out of his seat and into the street. Another slug hit him and he collapsed, dead.

At his funeral three days later, his sister stood over the coffin and vowed, "The streets are going to run red with blood, Joey!" They did. In the next weeks, a dozen bodies were found scattered around New York, victims of Gallo revenge and Colombo justice. Among them were two innocent victims. One gunman walked into a Manhattan restaurant, the Neapolitan Noodle, with a contract on aides of Persico; but moments earlier

Joey "Crazy Joe" Gallo changed his reading habits but not the other ones. In that restaurant on Mulberry Street, New York, he paid his dues.

the targets had left their table and when the killer fired his victims were two merchants, Sheldon Epstein and Max Teklech, who had dropped by for dinner with their wives.

To some observers, the murder of the innocents, the murder even of Gallo, were signs of just how far and into what a sorry state the Italian Syndicate had fallen. That it was still resorting to violence was bad enough; that innocents were victims was worse, and worse still was the whole bungle of the Gallo affair. Within two weeks, Joseph Luparelli, a sometimes bodyguard and chauffeur to Joseph Yacovelli—along with Vincent Aloi, who had taken control of the Colombo family after the shooting of Colombo and the jailing of Persico—turned himself in to FBI agents in California and told the whole story.

It seems that he happened to be lounging outside Umbertos when Gallo drove up. Immediately he hurried to another restaurant up the street, a hangout of Colombo soldiers. There he found Carmine Di Biase, Philip Gambino (a nephew of Carlo), Alphonse Indelicato, Dominic Trichera and Joseph Gorgone and told them of his discovery.

"What's he doing there?" Di Biase asked.

"I don't know," Luparelli replied. "They're starting to eat."

Di Biase made some calls and got a go-ahead from Yacovelli and Aloi. In the good old days, at that moment Luparelli would have been told to go home, turn on the television and otherwise occupy himself innocently.

After all, he had fingered Gallo and he might have been spotted; and if he were sent home he would have no useful knowledge of the events that later transpired. But Di Biase and his friends took Luparelli along with them, and they apparently realized their mistake almost as soon as they saw Gallo dead in his own blood. They drove Luparelli to a hideout in Nyack, New York, to wait until the heat blew over, and, during the next few days, to confer several times with Aloi. It gradually began to dawn on Luparelli that maybe his friends didn't trust him anymore, especially when his food began to taste funny, like arsenic, and he became violently ill. (The question, of course, is why the subtlety, why he wasn't simply disposed of in the traditional fashion.) Luparelli decided not to eat more dinners in Nyack. He slipped away, fled to California, turned himself in and told the whole story. The result: a grand-jury investigation, the indictment of some of the killers, the jailing of Aloi for refusing to talk to the grand jury, and the disappearance of Yacovelli. It also resulted in the shattering of the Colombo family.

BUT THERE WERE MORE SERIOUS consequences to the shootings that began with the attempt on Colombo's life. Violence inevitably causes trouble; informers surface, talking to protect their own lives; front page headlines and stories and editorials demand police action; in-

Angelo "Gyp" DeCarlo was granted executive clemency by President Nixon.

vestigations are stepped up. All conspire to interfere with the orderly conduct of business. Thus, the result of the war between Gallo and Colombo was a marked increase in pressure on the Mob, and that, in combination with the natural inroads of age, began to decimate the leadership. A major vacuum was being created at the top of the Syndicate, one that would be hard to fill. The prison cells of the federal penitentiaries were filling up with *mafiosi*, young and old, as the

result of federal efforts that had begun nearly a decade before under Attorney General Robert Kennedy. Those mobsters not incarcerated were deluged in a paper flood of indictments and subpoenas, were hounded by constant surveillance, wiretaps and bugs, to an extent that many were afraid to even whisper anywhere but in the middle of a vacant lot. Still others discovered that their riches, power and influence were no shield against the ills of advancing age.

New Jersey mobsters like Angelo "Gyp" DeCarlo, once boss of the state's loan-sharking and gambling, went up for 12 years (only to be freed after 33 months when President Nixon granted him executive clemency, one of only five such grants made out of the hundreds of applications that year; DeCarlo returned home on a stretcher, for a time picked up the rule and then, ten months later, died of cancer). He was followed by such other Garden State mobsters as Sam "The Plumber" DeCavalcante, Phil Rastelli and Bayonne Joe Zicarelli. Boston's Raymond Patriarca went to jail for a time, and so did Philadelphia's Angelo Bruno.

The Chicago Organization, second only to the combined forces in New York, was in disarray. In the mid-1960s, Sam Giancana had retired to Acapulco. The leadership passed to such old-timers as Anthony "Big Tuna" Accardo, Paul "The Waiter" Ricca and Felix "Milwaukee Phil" Alderisio, to such Giancana friends as Sam "Teetz" Battaglia, Fiore "Fifi"

Buccieri and Jackie Cerone, to such now-aging one-time young Turks as Joseph "Doves" Aiuppa, Charlie "Chuck" Nicoletti, Gus "Slim" Alex and Sam Stefano, the king of Chicago "juice" (loan-shark) men and a special pet of Ricca.

Except for Accardo, who seems impervious to all efforts to nail him and who has remained at or near the top in Chicago since the days of Capone, the other leaders and would-be leaders have all suffered since Giancana's departure. Battaglia went to prison in 1967 on a 15-year extortion rap; in 1973, he was granted clemency, but only because he was dying of cancer. By 1970, it looked as though Cerone was about to emerge as the city's strong man; that year, he went to federal prison on a five-year gambling conviction. A year later, Alderisio was dead, and in another year, so was Ricca of a heart attack at 74. "I lost the best friend a man could have," mourned Accardo.

Indeed, Big Tuna's good friends seemed to be falling all around him. Buccieri went from lung cancer in the summer of 1973. Stefano went, too, only not from natural causes. For his imperious and violent ways (among the several murders credited to him was that of his brother; it was Sam's way of helping him kick a narcotics habit) had earned him some unforgiving enemies, especially among those close to Giancana. When Stefano was indicted for murder and the rumor spread that he might write his memoirs, his time had come. One morning in April 1973, he was cleaning his

garage when somebody walked in with a shotgun.

Even those who remained showed little stomach for the hard times that seemed to lie ahead. Aiuppa, ruler of the Cicero rackets, began telling everyone that he was past 65 and wanted only to retire. Alex began spending more and more time in Florida, insisting that he, too, was retiring. But, in light of all the troubles, he has been forced to pick up at least some of the reins in Chicago. Only the younger Nicoletti seems, in 1974, anxious to succeed to the rule when Accardo, now nearing 70, goes, but he is only in his forties and his elders consider him a little young for the top spot.

The pains of the Chicago Mob, however, pale beside those suffered in New York. None of the five major crime families has escaped serious trouble and some have been shattered beyond repair, to the point where there have been serious internal discussions about merging all into one or, at most, two families.

Should that occur, three families are almost certain to disappear—those led in the glory days by Profaci, Bonanno and Tommy Lucchese—and a fourth, once the most powerful under Lucky Luciano, Frank Costello and Vito Genovese, all now dead, may not survive much longer.

With Colombo incapacitated and such potential successors as Persico, Yacovelli and Aloi either in prison or vanished, the fortunes of that family are in sorry shape. As Dennis Dillon, head of the Federal Strike Force in

New York put it, "The Colombo family has not been put out of operation, but we see the end in sight."

The old Bonanno family is little better off. When Bonanno finally retired to Tucson, Gambino assigned a one-time Lucchese lieutenant to restore order. Natale Evola had notable success, for a time. He reconciled the warring factions and expanded the family's control in the New York garment center, both through the capture of more once-legitimate concerns and by organizing the Garment Truckers Association. But in the summer of 1972, the 66-year-old Evola died of cancer. No one else has merited the same respect that he earned, and every time Gambino seemed about to tap somebody, such as Rastelli or Zicarelli, his potential nominee somehow wound up in prison.

In even more desperate condition is the old Lucchese outfit. On October 16, 1972, a beaming Brooklyn District Attorney Eugene Gold called in the press and announced, "We have pierced the veil of organized crime, stripping away the insulation that has hidden and protected many of the most important people in organized crime." Well, that was stretching things a little, but Gold had certainly done something. At the moment he was boasting, more than 1000 New York cops were sweeping through the city, handing out 677 subpoenas, to such mobsters as Gambino, Evola, Carmine "Mr. Gribbs" Trumanti and Paul Vario, to more than 100 cops on the Mob's payroll and to a host of

politicians. It was the result of one of the most successful clandestine operations in the war on crime.

Almost a year earlier, Gold's office, in cooperation with police, had begun surveillance on a Mob hangout in Brooklyn, with police disguised as Christmas-tree salesmen setting up shop across the street (and making a tidy profit, too). That surveillance led to the discovery of a Mob command post, in a trailer parked in the center of Bargain Auto Parts junkyard. That gray and blue trailer, ringed by a 14 foot chain fence topped by barbed wire and guarded by watchmen and two attack dogs, was headquarters for Vario, *consiglieri* in the old Lucchese outfit now run by Tramunti, himself one of Gambino's oldest and closest friends. In the ceiling of the trailer, Gold's experts installed a sophisticated miniature listening device. They also tapped the three phones and from a building across the street undercover agents trained motion-picture and still cameras on the trailer. During the next 11 months, they amassed 1,622,600 feet of tape, including 21,600 feet from court-ordered wiretaps and took 36,000 feet of color film and 54,000 telephoto pictures. On that tape and film were the photos and voices of most of the important mobsters in the East, a number of policemen and detectives, and a string of politicians and judges.

"We have learned," Gold declared, "of deals involving the sale of narcotics, extortion and loan-sharking, corruption, coercion, bookmaking, policy, assault and robbery, burglaries, counterfeiting, hijacking, receiving stolen property, forgery, possession and sale of weapons, labor racketeering, stolen auto rings, untaxed cigarettes, insurance frauds, arson of businesses, the cutting up of autos and boats, prostitution and violation of alcoholic-beverage control laws." He had also discovered, he said, more than 200 previously legitimate businesses, running "the gamut of business activity in this city," into which the Mob had moved.

What Gold intended to do with all this was quickly apparent. A grand jury was empaneled to hear those subpoenaed.

There, under grants of immunity, they were asked to tell about the underworld. Gold, of course, expected few to talk. But under New York's stiff immunity law, if they didn't testify they would go to jail. One way or another, Gold was going to send a lot of top hoods to prison. Which is just what he did. Tramunti went up for three years for contempt, to which was soon added another term for perjury growing out of a stock-fraud trial. Vario found himself buried under six different indictments ranging from income-tax evasion to hijacking. And the old Lucchese family found itself virtually leaderless, more and more taking its orders from Gambino.

Then there was the old Luciano-Genovese outfit, once the most powerful. From the time Genovese went to prison, where he died, the outfit's fortunes and power steadily declined under the joint rule of Gerado "Ger-ry" Catena and Tommy "Tommy Ry-an" Eboli. For a time there were indications of a renaissance as Anthony DiLorenzo seemed to be moving toward the top. He was one of the new breed of mobsters, though in the beginning it looked as though he would never be much more than a thug (he had served one term in prison for assault with a baseball bat). But while behind bars, DiLorenzo devoted himself to books and emerged as a man with a cultivated manner and considerable sophistication; he had even learned to speak acceptable English. During the Sixties, he amassed power and riches as the ruler of the Metropolitan Import Truckmen's Association, which had a near monopoly on hauling air freight, gasoline and food to Kennedy Airport. By 1969, he was making motions to spread that monopoly across the country, and he might have done just that in concert with his friends in the Teamsters Union. But DiLorenzo soon found himself in a lot of trouble. He was deeply enmeshed in one of the Syndicate's newer and most important rackets: stolen securities. The government was able to tie him into a deal involving more than $1,000,000 worth of purloined IBM stock and thereby send him away for ten years. In 1972, DiLorenzo was given permission by prison authorities to visit an outside dentist, without any guards along. He never returned and there has been no word of him since, though there have been plenty of rumors: that he was killed by rivals; that he has remained underground, helping guide the Mob in its deeper penetration of the securities markets and other rackets; that he has skipped to Europe.

With DiLorenzo gone, there were no immediate rivals to Catena and Eboli. Early in 1970, however, Catena was summoned before a New Jersey investigations committee, granted immunity and ordered to tell all he knew about the Organization. He refused, and wound up in prison for contempt. In the fall of 1973, the United States Court of Appeals ordered him freed. But, at nearly 70 and in failing health, the chances for Catena to resume a major role appear slim.

Catena's imprisonment left the hot-tempered Eboli in command. It also made him the subject of intense scrutiny by half a dozen agencies, though by pleading a serious heart ailment, he was able to avoid testifying. But worse for him was the fact that he was falling into disfavor both with his own lieutenants and with Gambino. Though his own personal rackets—nightclubs, Greenwich Village bars catering to homosexuals, music and records, juke boxes and vending machines—all prospered, he had shown little inclination to share the profits or lead his troops with any vigor. The grumbling in the ranks grew louder and by the winter of 1972, the family's captains were just about ready to turn to Gambino for help, to seek the ouster of Eboli by one means or another and his replacement by Francesco "Funzi" Tieri, close friend to Gambino and himself a long-time power on the waterfront and in the garment center.

Gambino favored deposing Eboli. With Tieri as head of the outfit, Gambino's influence would be vastly increased; the leaders of all the families in New York would be men who were his close friends, men who owed their positions and so their allegiance to him. At that moment, only Eboli remained independent of Gambino, and Eboli was sometimes heard talking loudly that, as heir to Luciano and Genovese, the right of command was his by inheritance.

But there were other reasons to topple Eboli. According to some federal investigators, Eboli had cost Gambino and other leaders close to $4,000,000 in a botched narcotics deal.

At least since the mid-1960s, narcotics had played a diminishing role in the Mob's activities. Common sense had led to a decision to heed the advice of men like Costello that the profits from junk were not worth the risks. The entrapment and imprisonment of Genovese, Big John Ormento, Carmine Galante, even Natale Evola and a number of other high-ranking mobsters had driven that lesson home. Moreover, the base for sale of narcotics lay in the central cities, and by the mid-Sixties that territory had become the bastion of minority group hoodlums who thought they ought to control whatever rackets fed on their people. White narcotics distributors and pushers were regularly beaten, robbed and thrown out; white numbers runners and even the smaller policy banks were subjected to the same indignities. There were some in the Syndicate who wanted a war to put down the obstreperous minorities, but wiser men like Gambino realized that this was a war that could

James A. Scott, a Maryland legislator (insert) indicted for trafficking heroin, was gunned down before he could talk. Frank Matthews (left) was the narcotics kingpin who allegedly employed him as a courier.

not be won. Where possible, the minority racketeers were taken into partnership, or were sold the business, or, when it was the only recourse, ceded it outright. These new racketeers quickly entrenched themselves, making their own connections for narcotics in Europe and in Latin America, setting up their own pipelines and dealerships, and giving rise to what became known as the "Cuban Mafia." Of course, they followed the same route in the numbers racket.

By late 1973, though there were rumors that the Mob had decided to move back in, the minorities were pretty solidly in control. On the lists of major narcotics dealers compiled by police departments, the number of Italian or Syndicate names declined and more and more blacks, Cubans and other minority independents appeared. They were men such as Maryland's Frank Matthews who surfaced when he ordered the killing of one of his couriers; a black Maryland legislator named James A. "Turn" Scott, then under indictment for transporting $10,000,000 worth of raw heroin and rumored to be talking; Thomas "Fats" Burnside, a major cocaine distributor in Harlem; Charles Ashley, who ran a major cutting factory on Manhattan's West Side, and Leonides Suarez, one of the top junk men in Chicago. In numbers, the big names increasingly were those of men like "Spanish Raymond" Marquez in Harlem.

But for the Syndicate, retreat from the day-to-day narcotics business did not mean total withdrawal;

the Mob continued to bankroll major narcotics shipments which were then turned over to the new distributors. It was just this kind of deal that Eboli brought to Gambino and the other leaders in the summer of 1971. One of his friends, and a sometimes ally of the old Lucchese family, was a Bronx bagel baker named Louis Cirillo. As it happened, according to federal authorities, Cirillo was also the largest narcotics wholesaler in the United States, the American representative of an international syndicate that had poured heroin with a street value of more than $300,000,000 into the States from France. In need of cash to pay for one massive shipment, Cirillo turned to Eboli for financing. The cash he needed amounted to about $4,000,000, too much for Eboli to swing on his own, so he cut Gambino and the other leaders in on the deal. All went well until one of the smugglers, a Paris interior decorator named Roger Preiss, turned federal informant. His testimony earned Cirillo a 25-year prison term and cost the Mob its entire investment. Narcotics agents found more than $1,000,000 cached around Cirillo's home and there were rumors that millions more had been buried for safekeeping. Gambino and the other leaders blamed Eboli for their loss and asked him to make good. He refused.

Eboli, early in the summer of 1972, seemed unaware that he had fallen from grace. But that fact was driven home with finality in the early morning hours of July 16. His bodyguard-chauffeur, Joseph Sternfeld, drove him from his newly purchased $150,000 mansion in Fort Lee, New Jersey, to spend the evening in Brooklyn with one of several mistresses. As Eboli emerged from her home at one in the morning, somebody was waiting in a red and yellow van. That somebody put five slugs in Eboli's face and neck from a distance of five feet. Sternfeld insisted that although he was there, opening the Cadillac's rear door for Eboli, he hit the pavement at the sound of the first shot and never saw who was doing the shooting. That tale was greeted with considerable skepticism and a perjury indictment.

With Eboli dead, Gambino's friend, Funzi Tieri, was in command. "He's a real class guy," one federal agent said, "a real moneymaker, one of the classiest gangsters in the New York City area." Maybe. But the move to the top put Tieri out in the open, and within a year grand juries had twice indicted him—for extortion and loan-sharking conspiracy.

All of which left Gambino securely on the throne of the Italian Syndicate, at least in New York, but Gambino and his family had not escaped the official heat. In 1970, a New York grand jury indicted his chief aide, underboss and rumored successor, Aniello Dellacroce, for refusing to testify about gangster infiltration into businesses. He got a year for that, and before the sentence was up, five more years were tacked on for income-tax evasion. With Dellacroce away, it looked for a time as though Joe Manfredi might be moving up, but in 1972

federal agents got him for heroin conspiracy and put him away for 30 years.

As for Gambino himself, the aging ruler, now past 70, might still give the orders and make the plans, but probably not for long. He has been stripped of his citizenship and ordered deported back to his native Sicily. It is unlikely that the order will ever be carried out; Gambino has been in and out of the hospital with a deteriorating heart condition which, doctors say, leaves him very little time. Most of his days now are spent in bed in the safety of his tightly guarded home on Long Island.

So, much of the old leadership of the Italian-dominated section of the Syndicate is at the moment of its last hurrah. The same is true elsewhere. Meyer Lansky, so long the shadowy puppeteer of organized crime, has not escaped the ravages of age or avoided discovery. After years of intensifying probes of the Syndicate, federal authorities finally realized that the Organization was not a private club open only to Italians. Wherever they turned, they stumbled across Lansky, not as a hanger-on or mere associate but as the man whose fertile brain generated the most imaginative ideas and through whom was channeled much of the Mob's cash flow. This was especially true with gambling, the base for all the Organization's rackets. Gambling provided $20 billion to $30 billion a year, perhaps half the gross income, and much of this was funneled through Lansky to other rackets, into legitimate business for takeovers and out of the country into Swiss bank accounts, where the Mob's fortune is estimated to exceed $300,000,000.

So pervasive was Lansky's influence that by 1970 the Justice Department had set up a special 70-man strike force, Number 18, concerned only with him; as one agent put it, to "learn where his money is and who his successors will be." Initially, Lansky showed little concern with this sudden attention. He and his wife settled into a luxurious apartment on Collins Avenue in Miami Beach and he took long walks nightly with his little dog, certain that his own men and friendly police would protect him from any dangers. Clandestinely, he guided efforts to legalize gambling in the resort city—an effort that looked as though it would succeed until his role was revealed and a voter rebellion defeated the proposition.

In February 1970, Lansky suddenly disappeared from the beach, turning up a few days later in Acapulco, in room 993 at the Acapulco Hilton, next door to Moses Polakoff, for decades the legal adviser to Lansky, Luciano and other top leaders. In town was a host of other American and Canadian racketeers. They had come, they explained, to bask in the warm Mexican sun and play a little golf. It was merely a coincidence that they were there at the same time, just as it was only a coincidence that a few years earlier many of the same men had turned up simultaneously at La Costa Country Club outside San Diego, the resort community that is

home and headquarters of gambling giant Moe Dalitz.

In Acapulco, the mobsters did more than enjoy the climate. They also enjoyed the hospitality of Leo Berkovitch, an old racketeer who had settled in the Mexican resort some years before. And who should drop by the Berkovitch home on occasion but Chicago's Giancana, another recently arrived resident. According to reports, they talked about expansion of gambling in Latin America, in Europe, especially Yugoslavia where Marshal Tito was being urged to turn the resort coast into another Monaco, and about mounting campaigns to legalize gambling throughout Canada and the United States.

When the meetings ended early in March, Lansky flew back to Miami. His absence had been noted; authorities were waiting for him, and in his luggage they found a bottle of phenobarbital for which he had no prescription. The pills, he explained, were medication for his ulcers. While no federal law had been violated, a Florida law had been and Lansky was arrested and tried for illegal possession. The trial was a farce and he was acquitted.

But the mere fact of the trial, combined with major efforts to nail him on other charges, had an effect on Lansky. Within weeks of his acquittal, he and his wife Thelma boarded a plane for Israel and settled into the Dan Hotel in Tel Aviv. He then announced that he was claiming Israeli citizenship under the Law of Return, which grants citizenship to anyone

Meyer Lansky, sick and old, could not buy his stay in Israel.

born of a Jewish mother. Through the years, Lansky had tried to insure his welcome with massive donations to Israel, to hospitals, the university and other institutions there, and with investments in a number of industries. Now he offered to plow millions more into the state. He did not, however, abandon his old interests in the United States; a regular courier run was set up, with messengers arriving with money and reports and departing with orders.

Lansky, however, was an embarrassment to Israel, especially as his troubles in the United States mounted. In March 1971, a federal grand jury in Miami subpoenaed him. He ignored the summons and a warrant for his arrest was issued. Two weeks later, the grand jury indicted him and his friends, Mossir Landsburgh and Sam Cohen, owners of Eden Roc and other Miami Beach hotels, for skimming $14,000,000 from the Flamingo in Las Vegas (the amount was eventually raised to $36,000,000). A year later, in June 1972, he was indicted once more, this time along with his gambling associate Dino Cellini, for income-tax evasion. On the basis of evidence supplied by Mafia-informant Vincent "Fat Vinnie" Teresa, the government charged that Lansky and Cellini were really the men behind Colony Sports Club in London, ostensibly run by one-time movie star George Raft. The government also claimed they had established Travern and Resorts Enterprises, Inc., in Miami, to organize gambling junkets to the Colony and other foreign casinos.

Lansky was not about to return to face the multiplying indictments. He stayed in Israel, seemingly relaxed, talking on occasion with visiting reporters and cultivating acquaintances in the American colony. Said one, "It seems that he is an avid buff of American history and, while he was not able to enter the American Cultural Center of the U.S. Embassy for fear of arrest, he asked me to take out books for him. That relationship had led me to speak with the man on several different occasions at great length. During one of our discussions, one of the facts that emerged was his desire to engage in acts of homosexuality even though he was married."

American authorities began press-ing Israel for Lansky's expulsion and in 1973 the Israelis agreed to toss him out. But Lansky, citing the Law of Return, appealed all the way to the Israeli Supreme Court and his position won considerable backing from people who were determined that the Law of Return should remain inviolate. But the tide began to turn against him. Lansky offered $10,000,000 to Israel if he were permitted to remain; the offer was rejected, the supreme court denied his appeal and he was ordered to leave.

On November 5, 1972, he began his long voyage home, hoping that somewhere along the way some country would accept his offer of a multimillion dollar contribution and grant him sanctuary. But after two days of jet travel that carried him from Jerusalem to Geneva to Buenos Aires and through South America, Lansky was back in Miami. There he was met and arrested by a small army of FBI agents, Treasury men and local police, and later released on $650,000 bail.

The Lansky who returned was not the Lansky who had departed more than two years before. Now he was an old and tired man, past 70. He was also a very sick man, with a serious heart condition. Almost as soon as he was released, he checked into a hospital. In March 1973, his condition was critical enough to require open heart surgery and the Lansky who emerged was, physically at least, only a shadow of what he once had been.

And, there were the charges

pending against him. In June 1973, he was convicted and sentenced to a year and a day for refusing to answer the call of the grand jury. A month later, he had a victory; a jury in Miami acquitted him of the income-tax evasion charges. Ahead, however, still lies the often-postponed trial in Las Vegas for skimming, and when that is through, the government promises to tie Lansky in legal knots for the rest of his life.

No MATTER THE ULTIMATE DIS-position of the legal tangles of Lansky, Gambino and other top mobsters, one thing is clear. They are old men and sick men, and they have little time left. But when they finally die they will leave behind an organization or a group of cooperating organizations, that, despite the severe pressures and successful inroads of the law, are still flourishing and, indeed, moving into new and even more lucrative businesses.

A natural target for Mob invasion has been pornography. In the early days, it promised more hassles than profits. It was a tiny business, mainly one of selling a few books and photographs under the counters of sleezy stores and peddling a few stag films for college fraternity and social club smokers. Unlike liquor, where even Prohibition could not kill public taste or demand, dirty books and films had never had more than a subterranean market. But several ambiguous Supreme Court decisions of the 1960s

left local officials bewildered over just what, if anything, constituted pornography and what might have "redeeming social value." This meant that a long suppressed commodity now had the combined virtues of being a forbidden fruit, technically illegal but difficult to prosecute, and in New York, Chicago, Los Angeles and other major cities, porno bookshops, peep shows and hard-core movies soon began to flourish on the edges of the law. The mobsters quickly saw the gold in paper and celluloid and moved in, and a lot of familiar names were soon bankrolling the burgeoning porn industry. In the background, and sometimes even close to the front, were John Franzese, a captain in the Colombo family, Michael Zaffarano of the Evola family, Ettore Zappi, a next-door neighbor and close associate of Gambino, and his son, Anthony Zappi, secretary-treasurer of a Long Island local of the Teamsters.

The racket was one that suited the Mob's needs. The business was high profit, quick turnover and strictly cash. A film might cost only $100 or so to make but could be sold by the thousands for $30 a reel; a deck of playing cards or a stack of photographs cost only a quarter or so to turn out, but could be sold for $5; a publication costing less than 50 cents a copy to produce might sell for $10. And this racket provided a means of hiding the income from other rackets merely by inflating the proceeds from the movie theaters and bookstores and the rest.

Only slightly less profitable has been cigarette bootlegging. It seemed a good idea back in 1964, when the U.S. surgeon general started warning people to give up cigarettes, to kill smoking by putting heavy taxes on the butts; and if the smokers persisted, at least the states would have a new and vast source of revenue. That, at least, was the reasoning, particularly in the Northeast, where New York and other states began doubling the taxes. By 1974, taxes in New York City, for instance, had reached 26 cents a pack. Which meant that the price of a pack was 60 cents or more, or over $5 a carton.

But in North Carolina, the producing center, there were no state taxes. It was a situation made to order for the Mob: buy the cigarettes by the truckload in North Carolina at $2 or less a carton, haul them to New York by the back roads, stock them in Mob-controlled warehouses, add counterfeit tax stamps and then peddle them cut-rate through such Mob-controlled outlets as Eboli's Trayan, Inc. With the average price of a carton at $3.99 from the Mob, there were plenty of customers.

Despite stepped-up efforts by police, leading to dozens of arrests and the seizure of millions of untaxed

Pornography and its quick cash returns became a target for Mob invasion.

bootleg butts, the business still rolls along. New York officials now estimate that as many as 400,000,000 packs of cigarettes, between a third and a half of all the cigarettes sold in the New York metropolitan area, are bootlegged. The cost to the city and the state is $85,000,000 annually in lost taxes. The greatest danger for the bootleggers, it's turned out, is the same that was faced by Prohibition rum runners—hijacking by rival mobs. But even that danger has receded since the Organization entrenched itself in the business and forced out most of the independents. And, as states across the country have followed the Eastern example in boosting cigarette taxes, the butt bootleggers have only expanded their operations nationwide.

In the main, though, pornography, cigarette bootlegging, even the infiltration of the entertainment business (through payola and control of nightclubs, music publishing and bookings) are variations on the old-time rackets, using the same techniques and even some of the same personnel.

There are, however, other and more modern rackets which have tended to elude the old-time mobsters with their limited knowledge and sophistication. That violent breed is dying off and a new kind of gangster is now moving into power. Some, but not all, are the sons and relatives of the old leaders; others have names that now mean nothing to law-enforcement agencies or the public. Some, like Tony DiLorenzo, have

gone to jail, but many have never held a gun, knocked over a store, committed a violent crime, or ever seen the inside of a cell. Almost all, like Puzo's fictionalized Michael Corleone, are American-born, raised in the middle class, often college educated and versed in modern business techniques. In speech, manner and outward appearance, they are indistinguishable from the sons of the respectable; they could be, and sometimes are, young lawyers, bankers, stockbrokers and junior executives climbing the ladder of corporate success. They leave a suburban home in the morning and commute to the office of a legitimate business. But that office is a front behind which they engage in highly sophisticated crime. Without them, it is doubtful that the plundering of the country's and the world's financial and investment markets over the last decade could have been contemplated or carried out so successfully.

Wall Street money has always appealed to the underworld. But Wall Street has always been the stronghold of the very rich who might buy bootleg Scotch and visit casinos on vacation, but, the mobsters were certain, would never do real business with racketeers. Except for a few bucket-shop operations designed to bilk gullible investors, Wall Street remained virgin territory. It took the new, young and sophisticated racketeers to deflower it. By the mid-Sixties, they had taught the entrenched rulers of the Organization that Wall Street cash was of little immediate importance. The real treasure was those pieces of parchment with the fancy engraved lettering—stock certificates, bonds, letters of credit, certificates of deposit and all the rest.

Securities, after all, could be used as collateral for large bank loans, thereby providing legitimate and tax-deductible funds for corporate takeovers or for countless other purposes. Thus the $195,000 loan obtained by one Charles L. Lewis of Atlanta from Charles "Bebe" Rebozo's Key Biscayne Bank in 1968, using 900 shares of IBM stock as collateral. When Rebozo went to sell the stock, it turned out to be stolen. Indicted later for theft were two Lansky gambling associates, Gilbert "the Brain" Beckley and Anthony "Fat Tony" Salerno, a New York hood, strong-arm man and major loan shark.

Securities, of course, can also provide the perfect cover for laundering cash deposited in the Swiss banks, serving as collateral for obtaining that money on paper in the form of loans. Or, by lending the securities to a financially desperate company which can use them to inflate its balance sheet and so lure new investment capital, the mobsters opened new doors to the executive suite.

As for acquiring securities, this was fairly simple. One way was to counterfeit them, and the Mob had plenty of engravers, sources of good paper and expert printers, some of whom got their experience turning out ration stamps during World War II. Another, and perhaps easier way, was simply to steal them. It was not

necessary to hold up a stock messenger. The denizens of Wall Street were just as corruptible as businessmen and politicians uptown, and by late in the Sixties, loan sharks—not the venomous kind that infest the waterfront but an outwardly more genteel crew—were swarming through the financial district, getting brokerage house clerks into their debt and their clutches. Given the option of a beating, financial or physical, or a little certificate looting, most chose the latter, and under the tutelage of the new mobsters the recruited clerks learned how to steal with considerable sophistication.

The clerks were taught not only how to purloin stock certificates but how to destroy the microfilm records of such stocks and bonds in their brokerage houses. Gerald Martin Zelmanowitz, a Mob courier and front man in the stock racket who later turned FBI informant, declared that at one point Mob-controlled clerks made away with more than $1,000,000 worth of securities from Merrill Lynch, Pierce, Fenner and Smith, the nation's largest brokerage firm, and simultaneously destroyed the microfilms. Even when Merrill Lynch discovered that stock was missing, it couldn't determine which stock.

The lowly paid clerks were not the only ones to fall into the Organization's web. In order to put stolen securities to use, to move them from the United States to Europe, it is necessary to fill out Internal-Revenue forms showing prior ownership, the date the stock was sold and to whom, and the price paid. If the transfer is made from an American owner to a foreigner, a tax of 18 percent is assessed. Circumventing all this was no problem. "I have," Zelmanowitz told a Senate subcommittee, "at various times received as much as 3000 such certificates under probably 20 different names and have received the signature guarantees from commercial banks or blank certificates with no amount of securities, no purchase price, no date of purchase entered upon them."

Wherever he turned, Zelmanowitz—and others working the same field—found willing collaborators. On his payroll, he said, at $1000 a week, were agents of the Internal Revenue Service who falsified documents for him. He had allies at First National City Bank and Chase Manhattan Bank, the country's second and third largest banks (after California's Bank of America), and all it cost him was an occasional $50 or $100 bill to "induce a bank vice-president to guarantee in blank any name you so desire to place on these certificates." The brokerage houses, too, assisted the Mob with the necessary forms, even helped trade the securities on the markets. Executives at Hayden, Stone, Bache and Co., at Eastman, Dillon and many others, according to Zelmanowitz, "close their eyes to the fact that we would engage in a criminal activity. The inducement of great commissions being paid to them seems to have been the only motivating factor."

The vast bulk of the stolen and counterfeit securities eventually find their way across the Atlantic, where they form one of the bases for laundering funds from other rackets for return to America. "Banks in Basel, Geneva and Lausanne as well as brokerage firms and banks in Belgium were necessary for our manipulations."

No one is certain just how much loot the Mob has stolen from the securities market. By the early 1970s, known thefts were running to more than $45,000,000 annually, but the judgment of the experts is that this is a fraction of the total. A confidential report by investigators to Senator John McClellan and his committee estimates that there may be more than $25 billion in stolen and counterfeit securities floating around the country and the world today. That amount would have the potential to shake the financial stability of more than a few countries.

THE NEW BRAINS IN THE SYNDIcate are, as shown by the invasion of the securities market, experts in the use of the most vital of modern business tools, the computer. One area of computer readouts that has been studied with great diligence is demographics. The American middle class continues to shift west and south, from cities to suburbs, settling more and more in areas combining residence with leisure activities like golf, swimming, boating, tennis and other recreation.

Where the population has flowed,

the Mob has been right alongside, and often in the front, paving the way. Tipped off by hirelings on the public payrolls, the Mob has often bought land early and cheaply and then either developed it itself or sold it to other developers at vastly inflated prices. It was Mob money, usually well concealed, that bought the land and financed the hotels along the Miami Beach Gold Coast and in Las Vegas, that financed the welter of condominiums that have sprung up in the Florida Everglades, the deserts of the Southwest, in Palm Springs and all across Southern California. It was the Mob, anticipating the future long before most Americans, that plowed its money into a land-buying spree in Valdez, Alaska. As it happens, that land at the water's edge is the site where the terminal of the Trans-Alaska pipeline will eventually be built.

On the face of it much Mob investment seems legitimate. But soon zoning regulations are changed through bribes, scarce materials become available at cut prices, cheap and often nonunion labor is put to work. Even when the results are up to standard, the profit advantage far exceeds anything legitimate contractors can expect to make. And the underworld, if it so desires, can get away with shoddy workmanship that paid-off inspectors will pass and that buyers won't notice until long after they've moved in.

Big deals in real estate and building, of course, take a lot of money up front, and that is one thing the Syndi-cate does not lack. It has almost un-limited funds, from its own clandestine accounts and from the accounts of its old and traditional labor union partners, especially the Teamsters. It was Teamster money guided by the Syndicate that financed Miami Beach hotels and Las Vegas casinos, condominiums in the Everglades and Palm Springs, and numerous shopping centers and industrial parks in the Southwest. The money to purchase the swank Savannah Inn and Country Club in Savannah, Georgia, and the $6,000,000 that went into its improvement, came from the $1.4 billion Teamsters Central States, Southeast and Southwest Areas Pension Fund, a fund into which Teamster members were feeding $14 a week. Once the Teamsters had control of the club, the man chosen to administer it was Louis Rosanova. He was listed by Senate investigators as one of the top Chicago mobsters and has been indicted for mail fraud. For a time he ran the Riverwoods Country Club outside Chicago which he turned into the Midwest's favorite golf course for gangsters. Under Rosanova's direction, then, both Riverwoods and the Savannah Inn became favorite Mob resorts, which may not be exactly what reputable pension advisers would consider safe places to invest retirement and welfare funds.

But, then, gangster haunts have long been pet investments for the Teamsters. The union's pension fund has plowed more than $40,000,000 into Southern California real estate, and among its choicer stakes has been

Dave Beck (right), out of prison, was given a moratorium on the payment of his debt to the government. Frank E. Fitzsimmons (left) had good friends in high places.

Dalitz's La Costa. According to federal investigators, La Costa has become the major rest and recuperation center for top mobsters all across the country, the center for major meetings and the stopping off place for hoods on the run. Others, too, have enjoyed the comfort and privacy of La Costa, including high officials in the Nixon Administration who gathered there during the planning stages of the 1972 presidential campaign.

Ralph Salerno, a former New York City detective and Mob specialist, once said, "Organized crime will put a man in the White House someday and he won't even know it until they hand him the bill." That time may not yet have arrived, but the alliance between the Syndicate and the Teamsters also involves some ties to the Oval Office. Whatever their record, the Teamsters are still the nation's largest and perhaps most powerful union. With their passionate hatred of the Kennedys, who toppled Teamster presidents Dave Beck and Jimmy Hoffa, the Teamster bosses were the natural font of labor support for Richard Nixon. Nor was Nixon chary about cultivating that support.

By the middle of 1971, aside from some of the hard-hat construction workers, Nixon had no firmer friends in the union movement than the Teamsters and their new president, Frank Fitzsimmons. That June, Nixon turned up at a Teamster executive board meeting at the Playboy Plaza Hotel in Miami Beach, sat down next to Fitzsimmons and then, behind closed doors, wooed and was wooed by the labor leaders. Afterward Nixon, enthused, "My door is always open to president Fitzsimmons and that is the only way it should be." Fitzsimmons was just as enthusiastic about his new friend.

Just how wide open Nixon's door was, and the price he paid for Teamster support, became apparent. For instance: Dave Beck was out of prison, but he owed the government $1,-300,000 in back taxes, and a court order gave the Treasury Department the right to seize all Beck's assets to satisfy that debt. But then Nixon's Secretary of the Treasury, John B. Connally, approved a plan to grant Beck a moratorium on payment of that debt.

For instance: Teamster racketeer Daniel F. Gagliardi, a long and close associate of most of New York's major hoods, was under investigation by the Justice Department for extortion, and his indictment was reported to be

imminent. Gagliardi appealed directly to the White House for help so that he could be "gotten off the hook." The matter came before White House special counsel Charles W. Colson, who sent a reply to one of his aides, "Watch for this. Do *all* possible," with "all" underlined. Within weeks, the Justice Department dropped its investigation of Gagliardi, though the prosecutors denied that they had been subjected to any White House pressure.

For instance: By the fall of 1970, Hoffa had served three years of his 13 year prison sentence. He had already applied for parole and that application had been rejected by the United States Parole Board, which would also reject two further such applications. But in the White House there was Nixon confidante and close adviser, John D. Ehrlichman, who was talking with aides about the possibility of executive clemency for Hoffa. And two other high administration voices soon were being raised in support of freedom for Hoffa— those of Attorney General Mitchell and Colson (when Colson resigned from his White House post to join a Washington law firm, Fitzsimmons handed Teamster legal affairs to that firm). Just before Christmas 1971, six months after his love fest with Fitzsimmons, a few months after Hoffa's third parole bid had been denied, and just as the 1972 presidential campaign was about to begin, Nixon announced that he was freeing Hoffa with a presidential order of commutation.

Then Attorney General John N. Mitchell favored executive clemency for James Hoffa.

Hoffa was justly grateful: "I would say, President Nixon is the best qualified man at the present time for the presidency of the United States." Fitzsimmons and other Teamster officials shared Hoffa's view. Indeed, so enthusiastic was Fitzsimmons that when all the other labor union members of the President's Wage and Price Board quit in protest against the administration's anti-inflation economic policies, Fitzsimmons alone remained. During the campaign, he served as vice-chairman of Democrats for Nixon, threw the union's support solidly behind the president—the first time the Teamsters had ever backed a Republican presidential candidate—and told all Teamster leaders to contribute generously to that campaign. There are estimates that more than $250,000 was raised this way.

As Nixon's second term began, there was no sign that the love affair had cooled off. The Justice Department decided not to prosecute Fitzsimmons's son Richard, a Detroit Teamster official, on charges growing out of alleged illegal use of a union credit card. Said one federal attorney, "I wouldn't blame the press or the public for being skeptical about why the Justice Department decided not to prosecute."

Nixon and Fitzsimmons remained in frequent communication. In February 1973, the Teamster boss was out West, ostensibly to play a little golf in the Bob Hope Desert Classic. When the tournament ended, he drove to El Toro Marine Air Station to meet the president, who had been vacationing at San Clemente. The two men boarded Air Force One for a flight together back to Washington.

Watching Fitzsimmons and Nixon that morning, a California investigator shook his head in dismay. "I can stand crooks," he said, "but it bothers the hell out of me when a guy meets with mobsters and then with the president." For in the days prior to the flight, in addition to playing golf, Fitzsimmons had attended a number of interesting meetings. At the Mission Hills Country Club and the Ambassador Hotel in Palm Springs, and then at La Costa, he had

been joined in long and secret conversation by a host of California mobsters, including Sam Sciortino, Peter Milano, Joe Lamandri, and Lloyd Pitzer, and a crew from Chicago that included Accardo, Carfano, Charles Greller and Lou Rosanova. At Fitzsimmons's side during all these meetings was Allen M. Dorfman, the union's pension fund adviser, himself then under indictment (for which he was later convicted and sentenced to a year in prison) for obtaining a $55,000 kickback on a pension fund loan to a North Carolina textile manufacturer.

According to informants, the main subject of discussion at Palm Springs and La Costa was Teamster health, dental and legal plans under which union members would be provided services by specialists with the pension fund picking up the tab. The participation of Syndicate leaders in those meetings made federal investigators suspect that another raid was in progress, and wiretaps and informers began to confirm this. Just how it would be accomplished was simple. The specialists given contracts to service union members would pay a ten percent "commission," or kickback. According to a federal informant, the details of that kickback arrangement were discussed at length and a plan was approved to funnel the payments through a Mob-controlled Los Angeles firm called People's Industrial Consultants.

As the role of that company became clear, court-ordered wiretaps were placed on its phones. Then the

FBI Director L. Patrick Gray III was briefly the head of a demoralized bureau.

Charles "Bebe" Rebozo found stolen stock in his Key Biscayne bank in 1968.

investigation came to a sudden halt. The Justice Department rejected a request to continue the wiretaps after the court-approved 40-day period had expired. According to reports, that request was denied after then-acting FBI Director L. Patrick Gray III wrote a memo saying that the in-

formation emerging was potentially damaging and certainly embarassing to the Teamsters and Fitzsimmons.

"The whole thing of the Teamsters and the Mob and the White House," said one FBI agent involved in the investigation, "is one of the scariest things I've ever seen. It has demoralized the Bureau. We don't know what to expect out of the Justice Department.''

ORGANIZED CRIME HAS traveled a long way from the sleazy beginnings in the ghetto and back alleys of the nation's cities a century ago. It may be strong-er today and more pernicious than ever, its influence reaching into every corner of the country, and beyond its borders.

Wars against the Syndicate, mounted regularly and with increasing vigor, have had only partial success. In recent years they may have helped to decimate the top command, but, then, much of that command was aging anyway and would soon have

Then Vice-President Agnew, with a well-known friend, is greeted by Mrs. Tricia Nixon Cox at a Baltimore fund-raising party in 1972.

departed in any event. Some of the campaigns have paid dividends. The Mob, for instance, has backed away from narcotics, though that racket is being taken over by newer and newly organized minority gangs.

Far less successful has been the drive on the major sources of Syndicate wealth—gambling and loan-sharking. It is no easy task to persuade most people that the dollar or two bet with a neighborhood bookie or policy runner, the chips tossed across the casino table, the dimes and quarters dropped into the slot machines or even the usurious interest charged by shylocks mount up into billions that flow into the Syndicate coffers—and that this cash provides the leverage for infiltrating industries, and that such takeovers are inevitably followed by higher prices for goods and services. Even such efforts to circumvent the underworld by legal off-track betting, state-operated lotteries and (as New York's Governor Malcolm Wilson proposed in January 1974) policy games can have only limited success. The Mob still gives credit, after all, and still operates on every block; and it is not easy to persuade people to stop doing business at the old stand with the old faces, especially since those old faces don't keep records of winners for the Internal Revenue Service.

It is no longer enough to say, as the experts have for so long, that organized crime will continue to grow and prosper until the people are informed, aroused and demand its elimination. The people are, or certainly

should be by now, informed. Despite all that information, and except in sporadic and isolated instances, there are few indications that the people are aroused. Maybe it's just a deep sense of frustration, and inability to see where or how to launch an attack that will end in victory. The underworld, that distorted mirror image of the corporate overworld, has become so complex, sophisticated and vast, stretching across the whole of society, that to many it seems impossible to do anything but chip away at the edges.

Perhaps the one necessary ingredient in any successful campaign against the underworld is the existence of a moral climate that will no longer tolerate corruption. But the moral tone of a society is set by its leaders, in politics, business and labor. The corporate society today is ruled by men like those at ITT or the oil companies who see nothing wrong in fomenting revolutions against foreign governments of which they disapprove, who think it good business to buy and sell politicians like used stock cars. The union movement, too, has as leaders men like Hoffa and Fitzsimmons, dedicated to increasing their own power at any cost to the country and their followers.

And then there's the political establishment. The brunt of the battle against organized crime must necessarily be born by the armies of the Justice Department and the FBI. From the heady and euphoric days of Robert Kennedy's rule, when ambitious young idealists were striking out, often recklessly and prematurely but with a moral certainty in their cause, there has been a steady erosion of integrity to the point where, today, the climate for the success of the Syndicate has unquestionably improved. The forces of law and order have been demoralized and enfeebled by the scandals surrounding John Mitchell and Pat Gray, by the slaughter of Elliot Richardson and Archibald Cox.

At the White House itself, the moral climate has been epitomized by Watergate and the wheelings and dealings, the manipulations and de-ceptions, the arrogance and amorality of the Ehrlichmans, Haldemans, Colsons, Deans, Liddys and Hunts. And of the vice-president, Spiro T. Agnew, forced from office and branded a felon for payoffs and boodling that were so blatant they might have shamed even a Boss Tweed or a Jimmy Hines.

And the president himself. Someone once said that above all else, the one thing a president has to offer a nation is moral leadership. But the moral leadership and the moral tone set by Richard Nixon were such that he found himself compelled to tell his nation, "I am not a crook."

PHOTO CREDITS

COLOR ILLUSTRATIONS

INDEX

ABOUT THE AUTHOR

Richard Hammer was born in Hartford, Connecticut, attended Syracuse University, Trinity College and Columbia University. He worked for *The New York Times* as a staff member in "The Week in Review" section and has written extensively on civil rights in the North and South, crime, law, Vietnam and politics.

He is the author of several books including *Between Life and Death, One Morning in the War* and *The Court Martial of Lieutenant Calley* which was nominated for a National Book Award and is the coauthor of *The Luciano Testament*.